Association of Research Libraries
Association of American University Presses

In Collaboration With:

The University of Virginia Library
The Johns Hopkins University Press
The American Physical Society

Filling the Pipeline and Paying the Piper

Proceedings of the Fourth Symposium

Ann Okerson, Editor

November 5-7, 1994
The Washington Vista Hotel
Washington, DC

Association of Research Libraries
Office of Scientific & Academic Publishing
Washington, DC January 1995

ISBN: 0-918006-25-2

Copyright Notice

Credits

The image on the cover is reproduced from a photograph supplied by the University of Pennsylvania. It is the title page of the first edition of the *De Humani Corporis Fabrica* of Andreas Vesalius of Brussels, first published in Basel in 1543. The original woodblocks themselves were cut in Venice, perhaps in the studio of Titian, and passed by legacy and purchase through the hands of many early printing families. After loss and rediscovery, they were entrusted to the Bavarian anatomist H. P. Leveling of Ingolstadt who issued editions (with altered title page) in 1781 and 1783 at Ingolstadt -- where, says Mary Shelley, Victor Frankenstein was trained. The blocks remained in Germany until they were destroyed by Allied bombing in World War II. The impression reproduced here derives from restrikes made for a 1934 Munich edition of Vesalius entitled *Icones Anatomicae*. This image was used in Michael Eleey's presentation at the Fourth Symposium.

Association of Research Libraries
Office of Scientific and Academic Publishing
21 Dupont Circle, Suite 800
Washington, DC 20036

This book is printed on acid-free paper and the cover is printed on ph-neutral stock

Table of Contents
Scholarly Publishing on the Electronic Networks
Proceedings of the Fourth Symposium

FOREWORD

Man's mind stretched to a new idea never goes back
to its original dimensions

--Oliver Wendell Holmes

The organizers of the fourth ARL/AAUP Electronic Publishing Symposium have dedicated this event to the memory and creative spirit of Dr. Bill Readings of the Universite de Montreal. Bill was a brilliant, witty teacher and friend, a productive scholar, and a professor of comparative literature. He authored an important book, *Introducing Lyotard*, and most recently, was editor of a series of essays called *Postmodernism Across the Ages*.

Bill Readings was killed in the American Eagle airplane crash over Indiana the week before the Symposium and those of us who worked with him or benefitted from his creativity miss him greatly. He is survived by Dianne Elam, his wife; his sister; and his parents.

Particularly relevant to our Symposium audience is Bill's Co-Editorship of the electronic Internet journal *Surfaces*. He and Co-Editor Jean-Claude (a speaker at our meeting) have been pioneers in high quality scholarly publishing in this exciting new medium since 1991, which puts *Surfaces* in the class of the so-called "traditional" e-journals.

Surfaces is an interdisciplinary electronic journal and an open international forum oriented towards reorganization of knowledge in the humanities. According to the editors, the growth of inter-disciplinary study in the humanities and the emergence of new ideas of inquiry has reached a point that calls into question both traditional thematic comparisons and the pretensions of any one theoretical approach to delimit and dominate a field of study. *Surfaces* is published currently in English and French with further languages added as need warrants. It offers immediate publication upon acceptance of an article; opportunity for subsequent revision of articles; continuous availability of issues; letters, comments and polemics. In short, it combines the best features of the newest electronic technologies with strong scholarship.

The planning committee worked hard to assemble this event and we are delighted with the information, synergy, and collegiality that flowed in the three days that 160 symposiasts gathered, again, in Washington, DC. The papers represent the thinking and projects of some of the clearest and most creative minds in the not-for-profit scholarly publishing sector today and expand our ideas of what it is possible to accomplish and how we may freshly conceptualize the trickiest problems that electronic publishing poses to us. The papers on cost recovery and on fair use cannot fail to offer readers new and important insights, while the project descriptions move to a maturity and sophistication most would not have dreamed possible at the beginning of the Presses' and Research Libraries' dialogues together.

Once again, special acknowledgments to:

- Duane Webster, Executive Director of the ARL and Peter Grenquist, Executive Director of the AAUP, for their encouragement and support in our series and our evolving partnerships.

- Lisa Freeman, Director of the University of Minnesota Press, a leader in the academic publishing community, and Co-Chair of this series

- Beth King and Dru Mogge of the ARL offices for their tremendous support in assuring the success of the Symposium

- Karen Marshall, Alderman Library, University of Virginia, for organizing the Second "Day in the Electronic Village," the sellout post-meeting tour in Charlottesville

- Sue Lewis, the Johns Hopkins University Press, for masterminding the new post-meeting tour, "Day at the Press"

- Our speakers, for their ideas, words, and images

- Our 160 registrants.

On behalf of all of us, we send wishes for your continuing success and we hope to see you at our next Symposium.

Ann Okerson
Association of Research Libraries

Scholarly Publishing on the Electronic Networks
The Fourth Symposium Filling the Pipeline and Paying the Piper
(A Synopsis of the Conference)

Jinnie Davis
North Carolina State University

The Fourth Symposium ...

Each fall, university press publishers, librarians, and other academics interested in electronic publishing turn to the annual symposium on Scholarly Publishing on the Electronic Networks for a stimulating and information-packed venue. The 160 symposiasts attending the fourth such symposium, held in Washington, DC, from November 5 - 7, 1994, continued the tradition of trenchant information exchange established by its founders, the Association of American University Presses (AAUP) and the Association of Research Libraries (ARL). With the collaboration of the University of Virginia Library, the Johns Hopkins University Press, and the American Physical Society, the associations focused this year on the areas of cost recovery in an electronic environment and electronic fair use.

Symposium co-chairs were Ann Okerson (Office of Scientific and Academic Publishing, ARL) and Lisa Freeman (University of Minnesota Press). Susan Lewis (The Johns Hopkins University Press) chaired the Baltimore session held on November 8th, and Karen Marshall (University of Virginia Library) organized the Charlottesville session on the same day.

Last year, librarians and publishers stressed the importance of working together to resolve common problems. This year, the emphasis shifted to the creation of order out of the information chaos through experimentation with new models of cost recovery that allow profitability and fair use while fully exploiting the potential of electronic publishing to increase accessibility and utility. Presenters of the latest research and development from the not-for-profit sector demonstrated a willingness to plunge into new multimedia projects with diverse collaborators, even without solutions to the economic conundrums.

School's Out?

The keynote speaker was Lewis Perelman, author of *School's Out*, copies of which were sent to symposium attendees beforehand. Perelman's views of how education is changing and ***must*** change are provocative and have been widely discussed. The author commented that, since its publication in 1992, he has been surprised at how cautious and modest his vision was. Things have moved faster than he expected, and the learning revolution by and large is taking place not in schools and colleges, but in the workplace. Perelman also admitted that he now finds inexplicable how little he had to say about the role of libraries, possibly because their role is so obvious. He welcomes comments to him about the book via Internet at: pearl@media.mit.edu.

When asked what he thought the typical school would be like in the future, Perelman explained that he intentionally omitted such as description from his book. Not considering himself a futurist, he did not want, by making predictions that turned out to be inaccurate, to lead people to reject his entire work. Rather, he said, the future will be "what you want it to be." He does believe, however, that as a harbinger of how things will happen, major corporations will rapidly get rid of traditional education training programs and replace them with "hyper-learning." The drive is towards "just-in-time, just-enough" learning. Challenged on his characterization of technology as the driving force behind economic change, Perelman stressed the power of technology and observed that often those closest to an invention process cannot see the forest for the trees. Asked if he foresaw a market-based economy for education-based projections, Perelman said that the school would go the way of the post office (i.e., towards obsolescence) in traditional concept and design. As for retaining the values of the institution, Perelman re-stated his great faith in the power of the marketplace to create convivial, if not perfect, solutions. The traditional laws of economics do not apply to information, and we must learn new laws. Market demand for the experience of a place like the traditional college will continue to dwindle, so colleges must change to meet the new demand or purify their existence in traditional form.

Frankenstein Redux

Michael Eleey (Associate Vice Provost, University of Pennsylvania) offered a multimedia presentation of his institution's electronic publishing project. The Committee on Electronic Publishing and Interactive Technologies which organized the project is composed of representatives university-wide: faculty, library, university press, computing, university relations, business, and museum staff. Assigned the mission of exploring, proposing, developing, and supporting initiatives in electronic publishing, the group stresses communications in the form of upreach, inreach, and outreach. Another campus initiative, the Freshman Reading Project, offers students across four University of Pennsylvania schools a shared intellectual experience through reading and discussing a common text. In a happy confluence of these two projects, the text selected for discussion in 1993--Mary Wollstonecraft Shelley's *Frankenstein*--provided an exciting opportunity for electronic publishing with faculty and student involvement. Not only does *Frankenstein's* thematic breadth open up a rich array of materials, but the committee was able to take advantage of the presence of a foremost Shelley scholar at Penn, Professor Stuart Curran.

With the help of Curran and the University of Pennsylvania Press, the committee developed the project's scope, obtained seed funding and initial technical consultation, and pursued partnership opportunities with industry. Under Curran's guidance, the project began to collect massive writings on Mary Shelley for implementation in HTML (hypertext mark-up language) as Web documents. Curran conceived of electronic products that will appear as a trade edition, an educational edition, and a scholarly edition, for users at varying levels of skill and interest. The hypertext capability makes possible links and annotations cross-referenced from the text of *Frankenstein* to supplementary texts or to textual variants. Curran stated as key points of the project the expanse of materials immediately available, its profoundly democratic nature (i.e., no one "owns" it), and the way in which it facilitates the process of scholarship as much as being a product of scholarship. Eleey demonstrated links made to multimedia including photographs, woodcuts, and video with sound. He noted the experimental nature of this project, but paraphrasing Doctorow, he likened it to driving a car at night: you never see further than the headlights, but you can make a whole trip that way. In a time of rapid evolution of cultural forms, accelerated by technological change, we can use what's new or we can remain mute. The Frankenstein project has chosen the former route, which Eleey sees as the hope for individual intellectual empowerment.

One-Stop Shopping for Medieval Publications

Martin Irvine and Deborah Everhart (Georgetown University) presented a multimedia demonstration of *The Labyrinth*, a project that makes medieval resources available to scholars over the Web. Noting the chaotic growth of Internet resources, the speakers stressed the need to offer scholars an organized approach to this interdisciplinary area of study. By taking advantage of WWW (World Wide Web) and hypertext technologies, the developers of *Labyrinth* offer knowledge in nonlinear form, with infinitely expandable links between words in texts to images, sound, and video, thus breaking out of traditional linear and one-dimensional academic discourse. *Labyrinth* also allows readers to establish their own meanings and their own organization of information into knowledge. Use of client/server software offers advantages such as one-time storage costs and the ability to deliver specific packages of information that can be integrated with others. Irvine speculated that CD-ROMs, lacking this capability, are "docu-islands" that will soon be unused. *Labyrinth* is also intended as a model for collaboration among scholars, university presses, librarians, and WWW developers. Planned products include texts that will be encoded in TEI-SGML (Text Encoding Initiative-Standard Generalized Mark-up Language).

Irvine proposed ways in which the Web can be used for cost recovery, offering scenarios for merging the goals of wide access and profitability. Why, he posed, could university presses not continue--through the Web--their mission of producing high-quality works? Before obtaining a desired document from the Web, the user could fill in a form for billing purposes. As for journals, users could be asked to enter a password to get a subscriber's page, as *HotWired* now offers (experimentally without charge). Publishers could offer tiered subscriptions for access to a certain number of articles per year. Irvine believes that academics would use such a system if the charge levied is reasonable. For books, university presses could include abstracts in their online publishers' catalogs. On the basis of that information, users would select desired books, obtain billing information, and the press would deliver the text via the Web to the user's computer. To assure the security of credit card transactions, an intermediary could assign an account number to a credit card, so the number is not sent across the Internet.

Irvine believes that current copyright laws will not need much modification to cover electronic publication. Internet billing may prevent, rather than promote, pirating, which is done now only to ensure the availability of materials when and where it is needed. If publishers can ensure availability, profits would go to them and not to photocopiers. In answer to questions from the audience, Irvine confirmed that the driving force behind the project was its focus on the scholarly, intellectual concept and not on merely what resources were available on the Internet. Try the *Labyrinth* at URL: http://www.georgetown.edu/labyrinth/labyrinth-home.html.

Cost Recovery in an Electronic Publishing Environment: Issues and Perspectives

A panel of five speakers offered unique perspectives on cost recovery in electronic publishing. Sandra Braman (Institute of Communications Research, University of Illinois) delivered a brief introduction to the emerging field of the economics of information. Since the convergence of the computer with communications technology in the 1960s, economists have been struggling with new modes of thought to deal with the problems of: creation (in an environment where many products are not market driven), time (because the value of a product differs depending on when the user gets it), and space (in the distributed electronic environment, it is difficult to locate the point at which a transaction takes place). Braman offered three ways to conceptualize the situation: the dominant view sees the economy working as it always has, with all statistics based on existing categories of physical goods or products manufactured. But how does one distinguish the value of information, an intangible product whose value may be embedded in relations? A second view is of the economy expanded through "commodification" of the forms of information, public and private. Again, this approach assumes the economy works as before but reveals contradictions in that approach, which results in inequities. The third view of network economics recognizes that the nature of the economy has changed qualitatively. The market is replaced not by industry, but by humanized information flows and projects, which become the new unit of analysis. The emphasis turns from individual transactions to relationships and evolving forms of organization. In a network economy, the Internet is a resource, a commodity, a perception of pattern, and, most importantly, a constitutive force in society.

Braman predicts more competition among academics; academic publishers will still be gatekeepers, fulfilling their primary roles as certifiers of knowledge. After a period of turbulence, there will be far fewer academic scholars, fewer producers, and fewer people to give copyright to publishers. Braman recommends unbundling and re-thinking our commitment to the stages of the Internet production chain: creation of new thought, followed by the generation, collection, and processing of information. For example, much of the publication of new books is driven by tenure requirements. It would be useful for academics to talk with their institutions about changing tenure requirements in the new information environment.

While there are problems with copyright, it is necessary to distinguish authorial rights from copyrights; scholars want the former and are less interested in copyright and in profit. With intellectual property, many rights are more valuable when shared. Academic publishers, she continued, should support the Internet for information processing activities. For example, they could be publishing far fewer books and allowing ephemeral works to move into working paper format for short-term storage in electronic media only, while more enduring works would be printed in hardcopy on acid-free paper. Assuming a smaller audience in the future because more scholars will enter the private sector, Braman urged scholarly publishers to find ways to offer new products such as software serving new functions on the Net. Publishers need not maximize profits for every transaction but should look toward long-term relationships. She exhorted the audience to think about its role in society and to retain space for academic work in electronic publishing. Members of the audience questioned several of Braman's points. One objected that ephemeral materials should not be dumped on the Net--we must instead raise the quality of works on the Internet. Another challenged her position because, especially in the sciences, important solutions are not necessarily recognized as such initially.

Colin Day (University of Michigan Press) addressed the difficult problems of the pricing of electronic publications "in a context of remarkable unclarity." Cost recovery is usually seen as a minimum requirement for pricing. Cost recovery assumes, however, that costs are well defined, agreed on, and auditable. In the electronic context, this standard is questionable because the product is manufactured at one time, delivered at another, and paid for at yet another. Price level also influences surpluses, which provide both the means and incentives for innovation, growth, resource shortage and produce enhancement. Lowering prices, however, is not necessarily an improvement. The buyers added as costs are cut are those who place a lower value on the good. According to Day, when one thinks more precisely about the cost that sets the floor on price, it is not the average price (or cost recovery), but the cost of making the last example of a good (or the incremental cost). The fundamental problem lies in the need to reconcile the two conflicting objectives of making products available at a price that provides incentives for all who buy it at a value above the cost of production, and ensuring enough income to the producer to provide incentives to cover first-copy costs and to make publication possible. A conventional approach charges a two-part tariff, a high price for the first few copies and less for others. However, for this approach to work, each customer must buy multiple copies and be identifiable to publishers. This price discrimination separates high-valuation from low-valuation customers but would need to be justified. A possible alternative route to explore is product bundling--bundling a good with another good or service (e.g., additional software with help menus)--to recover add-on costs and first-copy costs.

Day sees the library as another customer,

generally a high-valuation customer because it serves many users and places a premium on durability. Or, the library can be seen as an intermediary that pays a high price to allow publishers to recover first-copy costs. As examples of pricing schemes for electronic journals, Day cited those of the Johns Hopkins University Press, the MIT Press, and *Mathematical Reviews*. All three show the merit of simplicity, with *Mathematical Reviews* the best example of differentiation between first-copy costs (a data access fee of $3,595) and incremental costs for differing delivery modes. Day noted the need to have incentives for both the supply side (to encourage innovation and investment) and the demand side (to make materials available to all who need them).

Asked about archiving costs, Day questioned whether publishers are durable enough entities to bear the responsibility, compared to libraries, which have shown a stability over the centuries. Day also finds ironic the presumption that the future will be driven by subsidy and he questions the source of such subsidies. When asked if university presses are making plans against the day that academic tenure is no longer a strong factor in publication, Day suggested that university presses may back away from more specialized academic monographs and publish more academic works that appeal to a wider audience.

Andrea Keyhani (Electronic Publishing, OCLC) offered a corporate perspective in the electronic journal arena. For OCLC, an electronic journal must offer at least the same features as print and even go beyond to be considered a viable alternative to traditional print on paper publications. Publishers can either join the first wave (and possibly find themselves unable to pay for it), or they can wait until prices drop but risk losing subscriptions of those who demand information in the new-technology formats..

Keyhani compared the relative advantages and costs of using various production techniques. The infinite expandability of use offered by SGML make it the most attractive goal; it will become easier and cheaper for publishers to consider encoding in SGML themselves. HTML, a more limited subset of SGML, has a market limited to those with Internet access. Scanning and page images (as in the TULIP project) is a more affordable alternative. It is not necessarily more desirable, however, because of the disadvantages of OCR imperfections and the lack of precision searching of the huge databases formed. OCLC has developed a retrieval system for Virginia Polytechnic State University and can offer SGML and scanned pages with similar searchability.

Keyhani described the new STEPS (start to finish electronic publishing) system that will help publishers streamline their work by integrating commercially available products that can be plugged in to allow SGML capture and conversion. Whether or not printing is eliminated, according to Keyhani, depends on the response of users and the nature of the publication. She noted that, while subscription models are not necessarily the most appropriate for electronic customers, publishers could offer combined print and electronic subscription packages to make their offerings maximally attractive. She anticipates a natural progression towards site licensing, although the situation is complicated by libraries joining together to share resources.

Publishers can create new products by recombining clusters of journals (e.g., by extracting all reviews from existing journals to construct a review journal). Keyhani noted that publishers and librarians are in a position to know what appeals most to users. She sees new opportunities in the sales (and online billing) of individual articles. With centralized systems, the user can create new pathways to information, be connected to bibliographic databases, and receive instant delivery. OCLC is trying to combine *FirstSearch* with online journals in a system that offers interdisciplinary browsing with links to bibliographic databases. Value-added features include raw data files and images. Keyhani sees these areas as the greatest opportunity for cost recovery. Who will buy these new products? Recent studies show that most Internet users are young males "with more time than money." Advertising on the Internet will need to be more "infomercials" than commercials, conveying substantial information about the product as well as offering instant gratification in the form of online ordering and information requests. The situation requires new modes of thinking; it is a great opportunity to create dynamic pathways of the greatest benefit to users.

Asked who would perform SGML encoding, Keyhani stated that she thought publishers would jump at it, but she did not know how many libraries would be willing to do it. She predicted price reductions because typesetters would see SGML as a way to get the edge over their competitors.

Jean-Claude Guedon (Department of Comparative Literature, Universite de Montreal), noting the specifically American context of the discussions so far, stated that his paper would take a global perspective of the economics of learned journals. The economic model of traditional print journals is well known, and the trend toward imminent collapse is clear. To fashion a new model, it is critical to focus on correct objectives and to raise hard economic questions. During the chaotic emergence of electronic journals, the emphasis has been on personal inventiveness and on technical design, to the neglect of Internet economics. Indeed, information that is free to the community seems appealing.

Guedon interjected a realistic dimension into this vision, questioning the treatment of research articles as commodities. Published research occurs mostly in universities or government labs that are financed by taxpayers, so the results should be available for free or at cost. They are noncommercial because scientific or scholarly value does not correlate with sales. The idea of collectively buying research articles and making them available would not even occur if they were only commodities.

Social relationships are also affected; technical change never works through straight substitutions. With scholarly publishing of electronic journals, savings may reach 25 to 30 percent as the costs of printing and mailing disappear. Guedon suggested separating individual monies from collective, institutional monies: sales to individuals constitute about 25 to 30 percent of profits, so in the electronic publishing environment, savings would equal revenues from individuals, and library subscriptions could balance accounts. By adding subsidies to library subscriptions, one can make them available universally. Scientific research would become a truly worldwide enterprise, with more opportunity for participation by Third World countries.

Admittedly, this vision must answer many questions such as, what is physical ownership, if a digitized document can reside anywhere? Guedon doubted that libraries could trade print ownership for electronic access and find a level of payment similar to print. UnCover, for example, sells articles piecemeal, and libraries could cancel their subscriptions to a journal and rely on the Uncover service to provide free access for their user community instead. This situation signals a new collaboration between journals and libraries, a new joint system of production and distribution of scholarly knowledge not as a commodity, but as an essential part of the search process. Libraries are a valued interface with the end user and a major player in the structure. The nature of scholarly publishing depends on what librarians decide to do with digitized scholarly documents. Guedon suggested that this convergence between publishing tasks and traditional librarianship can develop if academic journals become viable in electronic format. Libraries can provide good print versions with good typographical style and master new skills found only in publishing before. He believes that libraries will give up some physical ownership to get access to all resources.

Hal Varian (Department of Economics, University of Michigan) referred the audience to the Web address http://gopher.econ.lsa.umich.edu for materials on economics and the Internet and for FAQs (Frequently Asked Questions) about Internet pricing. According to Varian, the benefits of usage pricing are more efficient use of bandwidth and capacity, revenue generation for growth and expansion, and more effective support of new applications. He calculated costs based on NSF's $12 million/year for the NSFNet backbone. Social costs include loss of speed and packet dropping with increased congestion, a particular problem in the late 1980s. Varian sees the current period as a golden age, where previously bad congestion has been eliminated (although applications such as Mosaic do impose a heavy demand). The backbone capacity is good, with only about 5 percent use on average. The peak, however, is a worrisome five to ten times the average, causing some packet loss.

What will the effects of multimedia be? With the large file sizes required, Varian foresees a dramatic increase in gopher and Web traffic, with demand out of sync with bandwidth growth. Because different services tolerate delay differently (e.g., delay is more tolerable with electronic mail than with real-time video), users will have to declare a priority for usage but need an incentive to do so. Fixed costs would cause usage prices to recover only the fixed costs of network capacity; capacity-based connection fees would be a better approach. Varian suggested a two-part tariff of a subscription fee and a congestion fee. He calculated current ASCII text costs at an average of $1.20/year, given current traffic, going up to as much as $100/month, if everyone moves to use of video. The point of usage-based pricing is not to cover current costs through connect fees, but to match use to capacity. Pricing could be based on time of day or priority of use; with "smart markets" in which the highest bids for immediate access are admitted while others are buffered or dropped.

He referenced other interesting proposals including privatization, congestion quotas, and "ATM pricing" or connection-oriented pricing used in banking. Prices should be up to the market (as long as the market remains competitive), and standardization is necessary to pass the packets among different networks. Accounting costs must distinguish between incremental costs (for additional use) and average costs (based on total costs), depending on busy and slack periods. Internet use, however, is connection-less and thus not the same as telephone use. Varian also raised the question of whether the client or the server should be billed for Internet use. As for accounting, instead of establishing centralized accounts (as with phone companies), another approach is to practice distributed accounting (as with post offices, with users attaching a valid "stamp" to their packets). Varian stressed the need to think about ways to address Internet pricing before the crunch comes, and not after.

A Plea for Joy and Wonder

Pamela Samuelson (Faculty of Law, University of Pittsburgh) noted two reactions in the face of the electronic future: some view it with positive energy, wonder, excitement and joy, while others approach it with fear, loathing, dread and anxiety. Copyright issues in particular evoke dread (which is the predominant tone in the NII's Intellectual Property Task Force report as well, she believes). If publishing digital publications means the first sale is the last one, how do publishers recoup costs, asks the Task Force's Green Paper? The group's suggestion is that information producers may encrypt everything and have users pay for what they need. Samuelson urged the audience to think about copyright policy in a more joyful way: we all want information disseminated, knowledge produced, and made available on reasonable terms, with a balance between the publisher and user communities.

Samuelson mentioned that the NII report predicts no need for fair use because everything can be licensed. She believes, however, that fair use is needed even more in the digital environment than in the print world. She urged innovative thinking toward a new economic model. Asked about the abolition of the First Sale doctrine (whereby, in print, a transaction occurs when one gets a copy and gives it to another), Samuelson replied that it is unnecessary to abolish this right to prevent abuses of reproduction; the doctrine can still apply in the electronic environment.

Fair use allows a balancing mechanism, and Samuelson hopes that agreements can be reached without going to the courts or to Congress. Queried on the AAP statement on fair use and electronic reserves, Samuelson noted that opinions differ in the law community also, and most people have not asked the fundamental question of what is the right thing to do. Asked about the NII report, Samuelson referred to a critique that she has posted on the Net. She does not think the NII Green Paper was a consensus report, and the Registrar of Copyrights has also submitted a report questioning some of its recommendations. Samuelson believes that a number of its provisions would simply be bad law. She hopes that a coalition of those with doubts can slow down the process before legislation is passed--a CONTU type of commission, for example, would be a better approach. Samuelson stressed the need to begin by asking what we are trying to achieve and not making fair use into an act of civil disobedience.

Mini-Sessions

Concurrent sessions offered participants a chance to sample diverse aspects of recent or ongoing R & D projects.

Session 1: Using Technical Standards to Accomplish Projects

"The Combined AAUP Online Catalog/Bookstore Project" by Chuck Creesy (Princeton University Press) and Bruce Barton (University of Chicago Press). This project plans to offer a "one-stop shopping" site for the monographic and serial publications of over 100 university presses. So far, forty participating presses' titles are expected to be up by the end of the year. A centralized server will make available bibliographic information and abstracts for books and subscription information for journals. Creesy and Barton described the system architecture and design, implementation goals for the server, software used, and browsing and searching features. Users will view order forms online for items in print, as well as URL pointers to related works (e.g., reviews on other servers). Individual presses will be responsible for maintaining the data in their own files.

"Campus Publishing with TEI and HTML" by David Seaman (University of Virginia Library). Seaman described the works offered by Virginia's Electronic Text Center. While the bulk of the materials are commercial, the center is also building its own full-text databases. A staff of graduate students uses TEI to tag, mark up, and parse texts, and then change it automatically to HTML format. The center also offers a self-tutorial for training TEI users. Seaman outlined advantages and restrictions in TEI and HTML use; ideally, texts should be encoded in SGML and converted to HTML through use of a Perl filter.

Session 2: Publishing Your Entire Journals List Electronically

"Project Muse: Tackling 42 Journals" by Susan Lewis (Johns Hopkins University Press) and Todd Kelley (Eisenhower Library, JHU). This joint project of the JHU university press, library, and computing center will enable online access at reasonable prices to the press's journals while developing an organizational and procedural prototype for handling electronic journals. Four journals have been loaded so far, using a program that translates PostScript files to HTML files, including the insertion of footnotes and links. Libraries will be permitted to make copies for users, as well as archival copies for their institutions. An innovative pricing policy charges less for electronic subscriptions than for paper, and even lower prices for subscriptions to both formats or to the entire database. Try http://muse.mse.jhu .edu to view Project Muse.

"Publishing E-prints, Preprints, and Journals in the Sciences" by Robert Kelly (American Physical Society). The APS is committed to seeking new modes of disseminating its journals and other publications, providing choices in storage, distribution and usage of both paper and electronic formats. Working with librarians and physicists, the Society is developing access methodologies and experimenting with making available preprints and electronic prints in the stage before peer review. He urged dialogue on the subject and invited communication to him at rakelly@aps.org.

Session 3: In the Scholarly Pipeline

"Riding the Aftershocks: The Galileo Project" by Elizabeth Burr (Rice University). Burr emphasized the new role of the librarian in helping to create curricular materials in the Galileo Project. Instigated by a foremost Galileo scholar in Florence, the project is based on the digitization of a Galileo manuscript. The librarian, working with a staff of students, acts as an editor who develops navigational and linking tools (e.g., to the library catalog, to graphic images) that offer users as-yet-unknown ways of learning via the Web. Burr described the possibilities as endless, as collaboration with educators lead to new research and teaching projects.

"Towards an Electronic Middle English Dictionary" by Henk Aertsen (Free University, The Netherlands). The Free University makes use of Mosaic to make its Middle English dictionary available on the Web. He pointed out that insignificant differences in print versions can cause critical differences in electronic text. Aertsen also discussed problems in harmonizing different editions.

Session 4: Collaborations That Work--and How They Do It

"Scholarly Communications Project: Publishers and Librarians" by Gail McMillan (Virginia Polytechnic Institute and State University). The goals of this project are firmly based in the desire to pioneer in electronic communication of scholarly materials. By involving librarians, faculty editors, and publishers from various institutions in experimentation, the project strives to provide free and open access to seven journals and other electronic publications in several formats, including ASCII and HTML (available at http://scholar.lib.vt.edu/). VPI considers it the individual institution's responsibility to archive its own publications. The library at VPI maintains the electronic files because of its tradition of service, its commitment to the availability of materials, the ability of its staff to respond to user access and information-seeking problems, the expertise of its subject specialists, and its ability to make equipment available for patrons.

"Five Societies: One Journal Project" by Keith Seitter (American Meteorological Society). The American Geophysical Union, American Meteorological Society, Ecological Society of America, Association of American Geographers, and The Oceanographic Society have agreed to collaborate on the joint publication of the interdisciplinary electronic journal *Earth Interactions*. Seitter described the journal's basic philosophies, technical issues, and levels of collaboration. It plans to generate revenue through author charges and user subscription fees (flat fees, to encourage browsing). Subscriptions for a volume year will allow continued access to that year even if the subscription is canceled later. To build up an initial subscription base, the journal will issue subscription "coupons" that can be redeemed for a year's subscription. It will be a peer-reviewed journal, geared toward high-end users, with standards that equal the societies' best print journals and with a level of copy and technical editing consistent with an archive journal.

Session 5: Finding and Navigating Networked Scholarly Works

"Naming the Namable: Document and Version Identity" by David Levy (Xerox PARC). Levy discussed the nature of documents and the immense efforts undertaken to name, categorize, and catalog them, producing secondary artifacts such as libraries, catalogs, and finding aids. The rhythm of their production and consumption is now being questioned in the electronic environment. He urged changes in regulations to improve support of current collaborative efforts. For more precise identification of a document, use of a Uniform Resource Identifier will help trace it even if its Web location changes. Currently, however, there is no way to identify a particular version of a document.

"The Berkeley Finding Aid Project: Standards in Navigation" by Daniel Pitti (University of California, Berkeley). This collaborative project tests the feasibility and desirability of developing an encoding standard for finding aids. Finding aids are documents that describe, control, and provide access to collections of related materials. They serve as an intermediate step between bibliographic records and primary source materials. The Berkeley project incorporates the design of a prototype SGML encoding standard for finding aids and the construction of a prototype database of finding aids. The project uses various software programs to convert existing print aids into electronic versions that can be published on the Net.

Session 6: Reporting Out

"Research into the Reward System of Scholarship; Where Does Scholarly Electronic Publishing Get You?" by Julene Butler (School of Communication, Information and Library Studies, Rutgers University). Butler's study investigates whether contributors to electronic journals receive the rewards and recognitions that accrue to those who publish in traditional print journals. Preliminary survey results from 199 authors, editors, and members of editorial boards of ten electronic journals show that 71 percent believe the most important benefits of electronic publication is "speed," while 55 percent selected "ability to reach appropriate audience." However, 63 percent were concerned that electronic publication is not considered "real" publication, and 54 percent think that the electronic journal is less prestigious than print journals. Nevertheless, only 1 percent of the respondents thought that those who evaluate their performance considered electronic publication more important than print journals. About 14 percent said that their electronic publication had been formally questioned as a viable publication. Butler concluded that there is very little negative response towards electronic publications among academics. The primary barriers to their full acceptance appear to be not technical ones, but sociological factors of individuals' fears and perceptions.

"A Scientific Scholarly Publishing Proposal" by David Rodgers (University of Michigan). Characterizing the present time as "gold rush days," Rodgers stressed the timeliness of his proposal to create a general-purpose system for the distribution of scientific scholarly information. Based on his experience with Michigan's Digital Library Project and the readiness of large providers (e.g., Adobe, MCC) to work towards viable solutions for delivering scientific information in freely accessible components, Rodgers suggested scenarios and strategies for accomplishing the benchmark study. The upcoming NSF journals-publishing workshop can be used to identify the capabilities and features that must be implemented, to estimate costs for their cooperative development, to interview potential strategic partners, and to develop a funding proposal with 20 percent cost-sharing by prospects. Asked for their reactions, the audience commended Rodgers' conceptual design and urged him to widen the project to an international scope.

Like Trying to Patent Sunlight

In "Creating Multimedia: Intersections Between Teaching, Scholarship, and the Copyright Law," Fred T. Hofstetter (University of Delaware) used examples from his own PODIUM hypermedia application generator to demonstrate the ease with which text and media can be linked. He delighted the audience by taking a picture of audience members, digitizing it, and immediately inserting it in his multimedia presentation. Hofstetter noted, however, that under current guidelines of fair use, his actions in linking text with graphics and editing them would often be considered illegal. The problem is that publishers need a way to earn income, and some have gone to extremes, as in the attempts by Optical Data and Compton to "patent sunlight" in their recent patent claim cases. Hofstetter urged publishers to increase profits by investing in new technologies instead.

He pointed out four provisos in the some fair use and institutional guidelines that prevent fair use in the classroom. He referenced a new medium proviso that prohibits changing the medium of a work without permission and thus prevents, for example, improving upon a slide by digitizing it. A frequency of use proviso allows tapes of television shows to be kept for forty-five days and to be shown twice, which is a disservice to those students who need more time to learn material. The electronic editing proviso forbids electronic altering or combining of programs, but this type of editing is a basic right and need of faculty in an instructional setting. Finally, the transmission of audiovisual works proviso allows only the cable transmission of non-dramatic copyrighted works, which prevents faculty from placing literacy works in image banks for access over the networks by disabled or lifelong learners. Hofstetter generally has no problems with the copyright law, only with the certain multimedia guidelines and the conservative ways in which institutions of higher learning feel they must interpret such guidelines. He proclaimed it a great tragedy if we create new guidelines that will continue to make these types of uses unfair.

A Conversation With John McChesney

McChesney, Technology Correspondent for National Public Radio, noted the recent emergence of reporting on technology and the difficulty of finding a common language with the radio audience. It is also difficult to separate hype from reality, especially with the National Information Highway, "that great broad-band fantasy in the sky." McChesney thinks that, in the future, publishers will make more money on smaller incremental costs. If there are problems with fair use, they will be made equitable by subsidizing users and not providers. He believes that the function of librarians in this information chaos is to help users find what is available on the networks. He posed some questions for the audience: is anyone archiving all the computer-mediated communication now taking place? While mostly cybertrash, such communication sometimes contains a high level of writing and may be of value to historians of this period. What are people using as a storage medium? Paper is a good medium; electromagnetic materials are not. Finally, how will the digital library make sure that it stays around?

McChesney noted that NPR has not yet confronted the implications of these questions; it lacks the funds to digitize backfiles now on magnetic tapes. In addition, while he sees clear advantages to moving towards online technologies, the bandwidth is not yet available to do so, nor is there demand from NPR's member stations. McChesney lamented NPR's insufficient coverage of the information revolution, which he finds overwhelming, especially in its social ramifications.

Perspectives on Electronic Fair Use

Four panelists with long experience in this field offered their perspectives on fair use in the electronic environment. Terri Southwick (U.S. Patent and Trademark Office and staff to the NII Task Force on Intellectual Property) described the process whereby the NII task force solicited responses from the public before writing its Green Paper. At hearings last November (1993), the members collected oral and written comments on the adequacy of the copyright laws and licensing mechanisms. Deciding that they were not yet ready to issue a final report, they wrote the Green Paper instead as a preliminary draft to set out the state of the law, the amendments needed, and current problems. So far, the Task Force has received about 150 lengthy comments, which members are reviewing before producing a White Paper by the first of the year. The Task Force is also analyzing the international implications of copyright limitations and infringements.

In the area of fair use for librarians and educators, their principal legal conclusion is that the current copyright law is viable and can be modified to account for technological advances. Southwick cautioned that the widely distributed executive summary in the Green Paper is not comprehensive. The report intended to make the point that section 107 is fine and does not require modification. It expresses concern, however, over specific limitations in sections 108 and 110 regarding library and educational use. Recommendations on these sections are lacking because the Task Force is still gathering information to make its decisions. Southwick welcomed comments from the audience on any matters of concern. She noted that a conference on fair use and a conference on intellectual property education are planned to solicit more information and to educate users about the copyright law. Southwick did not think that another CONTU-type process is needed because of the time it would take for Congress to establish it and for the president to appoint members.

Patrice Lyons (Law Offices of Patrice Lyons) suggested a different approach to copyright issues by setting the framework for legislation "at the envelope level rather than the content." Lyons noted how little attention has been paid to the role and implications of communications law, where a different set of constructs may be relevant for fair use. Just as communications law provides for viewers to pay a set monthly fee for broadcasting and cable TV without regard for fair use of performances, it might offer a more appropriate way to frame the issue of public access to the National Information Infrastructure. Without a clear framework, the conflicting rights of information service providers and users may overlap and delay the implementation of the National Information Highway.

According to Lyons, a useful model is to consider information providers to be like banks which provide services but have limited liability, or like broadcasters who assume certain limited responsibilities in terms of content. Lyons urged separating the need for copyright clearance from the task of delivering packaged objects, independent of their contents. She believes that communications law can provide comfortably for elements that must be regulated while allowing information providers to create new products. Lyons thinks librarians have a major role as information service providers and must articulate that role.

John Lawrence (H-Net and Morningside College) brought the perspective of fair use administrators, who are "also prepared to squabble our way into the future." H-Net is a history network composed of fifty-two moderated discussion lists served by host computers at the University of Illinois at Chicago and at Michigan State University. Following the corporate model, H-Net has executive officers, a board of directors, and uniform policies for several lists. As list editor, Lawrence chairs the Copyright Policy Committee.

H-Net has a dual stake in fair use. It is the virtual publisher of more than one million messages per month, yet from the copyright owner's standpoint, it wants publishers to be fair with list contributors to whom everything offered is considered "free." Lawrence cited examples both of cases in which listowners had to scale back their idea of what it was fair to reproduce and disseminate electronically, and of instances in which the listowners prohibited others from connecting to their lists via gopher, without acknowledgement. To aid in clarifying the situation, H-Net has produced a working document on copyright and fair use, which is used for orientation of list members and moderators.

Lawrence also described the economics of scholarly list-owning: it requires reliance on funding sources such as grants, stipends, and capital donated by sponsoring universities, but it eliminates the costs of mailing and printing. Professional associations may be another potential source of income, while advertising is a cloudy area which may violate the spirit of the Internet.

Georgia Harper (Office of the Counsel, University of Texas System) represents a major university that is drafting a comprehensive copyright policy. As Harper began to investigate the issue, she grew alarmed over developments such as the upholding of the Texaco court decision which, she believes, threatens the academic community's idea of fair use and over the blanket licensing initiative of the Copyright Clearance Center. She thinks that the Green Paper of the NII Intellectual Property Task Force assumes that fair use is unnecessary in the electronic environment.

Harper explored the impact of the electronic environment on fair use and evaluated its benefits. She believes that the scope of fair use applies to research copying, which frees the user from the requirement to seek permission and from payment of fees. Many disagree on whether fair use is a constitutionally mandated, inherent part of copyright law or just a function of market failure. In the electronic environment, if transaction costs come down, fair use will be unnecessary. Harper believes that fair use means free access to the ideas of others as the building blocks of knowledge, and it should protect users from price escalations.

Alternatives in the new environment include market options that many at this conference suggested, as well as paying attention to the recommendations in the report of the Association of American Universities' Task Force on Intellectual Property Rights in an Electronic Environment. Legal options are also available in the form of case law development and legislation, but they are long and expensive processes. Contracting among the parties involved is another option. Harper characterized the players in this issue as being "assembled for a land grab" and urged all parties to shift their focus away from fair use to access at a fair price. Publishers and users need not be adversaries, and no one should expect one side to unilaterally give up its right to be unreasonable. Harper urged both sides to work out a mutual compromise. If the same benefits can be achieved without fair use, we will no longer need it, she maintained.

Lagniappes

Throughout the conference, attendees were treated to additional presentations of electronic projects by their colleagues. This year, Sandra Whisler (University of California Press) described Project SCAN, which is creating an electronic prototype of the print journal *Nineteenth-Century Literature*. The files can be reached by the following gopher path: at the prompt, use gopher to connect to infolib.lib.berkeley.edu (make sure your settings indicate port 70 and gopher+ [Gopher Plus] server). Once you have reached infolib through gopherspace, select menu items: Electronic Journals, Books, Indexes and Other Sources; Journals; Nineteenth-Century Literature. David Koch (Southern Illinois University) described his institution's CNI/AAUP initiative to make available on the Internet a three-volume annotated bibliography, *Freedom of the Press*. The online version will link items in the bibliography with holdings in the university's Freedom of the Press Collection. A demonstration is available through: http://reliant.c-cwis.siu.edu:8001/library/freepress/homepage.html (this is a temporary development server). Robert McHenry (*Encyclopaedia Britannica*) gave an update on *Britannica Online* (a canned demonstration is available at: http://www.ed.com). He urged users to think of *EB* not as an end in itself, but as the beginning of a search for information, exploiting the linking capabilities of the Web to point to resources from other sources, such as the *Labyrinth* Project. Dick Kaas (Universiteit Utrecht) described several electronic initiatives undertaken cooperatively by the university library and the academic computing center, including electronic publishing of full text of student essays and images from a large slide collection. Working with Elsevier, Kluwer, and Pica, they also plan to offer abstracts and full-text of electronic science journals based on collections of rare materials. Sian Meikle and Ian Lancashire (University of Toronto) demonstrated Toronto's *English Library* (available via the UT home page).

The project will mount scholarly texts in English literature but is intended for the ordinary reader as well, as seen in delightful examples from poets such as William Blake and Thomas Gray.

Ann Okerson concluded the symposium by affirming that we are in a period of enormous creativity, in part propelled by user discovery of the Web. In spite of our worries and agonies over issues such as copyright, we are also eager to face the challenges of building good content to fill the pipeline, creating new economic models based on partnerships and collaboration, and participating in the open arenas for national discussion now occurring. She urged attendees to seek further information from ARL, reminding them that "the law we create is ours and we get what we create."

Dr. Jinnie Y. Davis
Asst. Director for Planning & Research
North Carolina State University Libraries
Campus Box 7111
Raleigh, NC 27695-7111
E-mail: jinnie_davis@ncsu.edu
Phone: 919-515-2843

Is School Out? Is Academic Publishing Out?

Lewis J. Perelman
A Symposium Opening Conversation

Lewis J. Perelman Introduction

LISA FREEMAN (*Lisa Freeman is the Director of the University of Minnesota Press and Co-Chair of the Symposium series planning committee*): On my way to this Symposium, I was in the airport lounge -- at Burger King, in fact -- thinking about how to introduce our keynoter of the evening. I was on my way back from the Board meeting of a significant publishing firm that has been among us for decades. Sitting on the Board of Directors has been a significant opportunity for me to learn about the publishing industry outside the university press community. I had spent two days with a group of very smart, thoughtful, committed individuals discussing the various things that such boards discuss, including the future of the company. Like many organizations represented here, this company is struggling with the rapid pace of technology and with the simple fact that its future is not necessarily clear. The Board and management are confronted with trying to define a role for an organization which, until recently, used to believe and perceive itself as having a clearly defined function to an equally clearly defined audience.

I don't want to go too far into the specifics of their dilemma, but I do want to point out that all primary publishers, librarians, and researchers are struggling to redefine their roles in the emerging information-rich networked environment. I was struck in those two days that we all have been conducting our discussions in largely reactive and defensive modes. So, having this not terribly original insight, I picked up where I had previously left off reading Dr. Perelman's *School's Out* and came across the following quote: "Henry David Thoreau, no fan of the Industrial Revolution, made the mordant observation that 'Men do not ride railroads; the railroads ride the men.'"

As Dr. Perelman goes on to assert:

> Both things were true then, and remain true now. Technology is the defining characteristic of humanity; the creation, use and improvement of technology are the unique features that set humans apart from all species. Whether technology was a Promethean gift or a Faustian bargain, the deal is as irrevocable as it is ancient. The only choice remaining is whether we ride our technology or it rides us.

I think this observation is as relevant for us as it is for the K-12 educators for whom Dr. Perelman is large concerned in *School's Out*. For those who have not had an opportunity to read the book, I encourage you to do so. Although I must note there is much in it I disagree with, it is certainly clear from reading it that Dr. Perelman has a very rare ability to think outside the common paradigms within which we tend to view the options that confront us. This is a skill we should all cultivate, and I hope his remarks help us to do that.

As an independent consultant since 1983, Lewis J. Perelman has provided strategic advice to public and private policymakers concerned with economic developmental issues. His private consulting clients have included IBM, National Computer Systems, Hay Group, Ashton-Tate, L.F. Rothschld, National Education Corporation, the Edison Electronic Institute, and several energy utility companies.

He is the author of several books, most recently *School's Out*. The book is based in part on his work as a Senior Research

Fellow at the Hudson Institute and the Director of *Project Learning 2001*, a study of restructuring education and training sponsored by twelve U.S. corporations and foundations. Dr. Perelman is also the person who coined the phrase "The Learning Enterprise" to describe the total universe of education and training in a report with that title published by the Council of State Planning Agencies in 1985.

Currently he is an Adjunct Fellow of the Discovery Institute. He has had significant experience in corporate planning and as a senior scientist in national labs such as Cal Tech's Jet Propulsion Laboratory. He earned his doctorate in administration, planning, and social policy at the Harvard Graduate School of Education and he resides in Washington, DC. It is my pleasure to introduce to you Lewis J. Perelman.

MR. PERELMAN: I should warn you, I don't have anything very formal or structured to say. I suggested we have a conversation and I guess I should start by asking, how many of you have already read my book?

(Audience show of hands)

MR. PERELMAN: So you probably are all ready to have dialogue. In that case, I don't know if I need to say a great deal in the way of an introduction. For those of you who are interested, I would like to mention what has happened in the two years since the book was published and then we can continue from there. Two things come to mind.

One is that I have been mostly surprised at how relatively cautious or modest my vision has turned out to be. Things have moved along more swiftly and more dramatically than things I anticipated in the book. Secondly, most of the work I have done since then has focused increasingly on the modern workplace and the application of the technology (which I dubbed hyper-learning) to modern business practice and work. As I tried to emphasize in the book, that is really where the action takes place, and will continue to take place.

And as I also stressed in the book, the learning revolution is not taking place in colleges and universities by and large. Certainly there are some very exciting examples of people doing innovative things but institutionally and as an industry, education is pretty far behind the curve. Even as academia makes progress, it makes progress at a rate of change which is far less than the rate of change of everything going on outside its walls. Thus, there is a growing gap between the world of the classroom and world of everything else. I've focused primarily on trying to pay attention to the rest of the world.

And for those of you who don't know, I've had two more recent publications in *Forbes ASAP* in the last year, which describe in more detail, based on real experiences of real leading edge corporations, how this technology is rapidly being applied and changed.

It continuously surprises me when I look back in the book and see how little I had to say in the book about libraries. I can't tell you why there is so little discussion in the book about what I always felt very acutely is the very crucial role of libraries, except to the extent it seems so obvious to me it didn't bear a lot of discussion, which was wrong. On the other hand, as I told some of my colleagues here, two dozen or so people read drafts of the book and nobody said, "you need a chapter on libraries." Maybe when we think about cyberspace or information highways or Internet or whatever the appropriate metaphor of this new world is -- and it seems so much of it is a library or library of libraries -- that we just take it for granted that that is what we are talking about. Yet, I wish I hadn't taken it for granted.

Part of the reason school is out is that libraries are out. School as an institution is based on an architectural design or technology rooted in buildings and grounds and campuses, because knowledge was obtained in libraries; and therefore you had to put boxes close to the big box of the libraries so people could sit around and have access. Now, much of what this symposium is dealing with is the recognition that that is drastically changing. All libraries are rapidly becoming electronically in touch with all the other libraries. Location and physical structure are no longer important.

For instance, Columbia Law School has rapidly been pushing to convert its library to all digital form. In an article in the *Wall Street Journal*, the Law School's chief librarian raised the perfect question: What does the word 'library' mean any more? If all the information in the library is available on the Net to anyone who wants to have access to it, what does the concept of 'Columbia Law School Library' mean today?

That kind of statement will come up over and over and again. The answers to this and other questions are being addressed by people like you. And so I'm just as much interested in hearing what you have to say and observe as well as any questions you have. I invite you to comment, criticize, object, query.

MR. KELLEY: Todd Kelley, Johns Hopkins University Library. I feel a bit like Ed McMahon but I'm going to bite. You put it out there twice: Just how cautious were you in your predictions?

MR. PERELMAN: Well, I don't know how to scale that exactly. As a rough estimate (I don't remember if I said it explicitly in the book), the kind of drastic overturn of academia I foresaw would be some time ten to fifteen years in the future. Now, more lately I've said five to ten years. With each passing month we are closer to five than ten. I have spent a lot of time hanging out and conversing with my buddy and colleague George Gilder in the last couple of years and I have read a lot of George's writing. He is a very smart person, which is not to say he knows everything about everything, but I have learned a lot from George and he has tended to persuade me that things are happening more dramatically than I had expected.

Just in the last year or so, we've seen Bell Atlantic and other companies going on a feeding frenzy all of a sudden to stake out a new world Gilder calls the Telecosm. They said, "Wow, this is really important. We have to do something important about it in the way of a massive investment: multi-billion dollars of investment chasing something, chasing opportunities." Yet, a lot of the things these corporations are chasing are ill-conceived, misconceived and over-hyped. Inevitably beside the sort of things that get the spotlight are other things being missed all together.

I had a fascinating conversation in August at a conference in Atlanta, sponsored by the Progress and Freedom Foundation. It was called a "Magna Carta for the Knowledge Age," part of which was groping to deal with circumstances and issues we are dealing with: How do we protect intellectual property? What are basic rights? The night I got there I became part of a dinner conversation with Newt Gingrich, Alvin Toffler, George Gilder and George Keyworth. It was a really interesting conversation. It was fun -- Gingrich is a very interesting character who has real intellectual vision, one of the few politicians I have spent time with in over a dozen years in Washington who actually reads books. He said, "I may be Speaker of the House next year. Whenever I want to, I can appear on TV and speak to 90 million people. Tell me what to say." That is, he wanted to know how to translate the vision of the Third Wave into legislation -- an interesting request for dinner conversation. And there were some smart people offering him suggestions. And he said, "No, no, no, that won't work." The pragmatic politician said that our 'visionary' proposals were too far away from the public's knowledge.

During that conversation, I mentioned to Gingrich a review that I read earlier this year of a book called *Today Then*," a collection of 74 essays that were commissioned for the Great Colombian Expedition in 1883, which was a world fair intended to celebrate the coming 20th century. The organizers asked

74 great thinkers in America at that time to write what we would call scenarios about the world in 1993 and what it would look like. The thing that struck me was that most of these great thinkers were impressed with electricity and had visions of electric this and electric that, trains, planes, boats -- which was not totally wrong. In fact, electricity has been a major technology. But every single one of them completely missed the automobile and the internal combustion engine. They had no vision of that at all. Even as the "Great Minds" were writing their scenarios, people like Henry Ford and Orville Wright were in their sheds on their way to developing a revolution in transportation.

I commented to Gingrich that we are supposedly today's intellectuals. So the answer to the question on what you should do may be: "We really do not know. But that doesn't mean the answers are not being created by people out there who are just not famous yet."

Those of you who read my book will see a very close analogy between the early days of the automobile and what we are doing now. Part of the analogy is that in the 1890s very few people, even well-informed people, even people in the fledging automobile industry, could envision the drastic change in the economy and society and culture that that technology was about to unleash. It is a roughly similar situation now. Hyper-learning technology is doing to knowledge even more than what the internal combustion engine did to transportation. It is overturning another deeply rooted, highly established popular institution. In that case it was the horse-based transportation system; in this case it is the library-based educational system. That is the metaphorical comparison. It did happen. We all know it. It is ancient history to us.

Looking forward from the 1890s (let's say we were here talking about transportation), in twenty, twenty-five years the horse was gone. The whole industry was gone. And as I pointed out in *School's Out*, in the 1890s approximately half of the jobs in America depended on the horse.

It was a vastly bigger industry than academia today. Roughly five million jobs are educator jobs today (professors, teachers, administrators) out of a work force of one hundred and ten to one hundred fifteen million workers. Anything that has happened can possibly happen again.

So it is in that context I answer your question. I thought ten, fifteen years was reasonable; and now I have a sense, based on the events of the last year or so, that the rate of change has accelerated more quickly, and especially as I look at the workplace I see an intense, almost obsessive, determination to implement new technology as quickly as possible.

MR. McFADDEN: Tom McFadden from Northern University Arizona. I have read your book, by the way. I just have a comment and a question.

It just so happens the last book I read was *Amusing Ourselves to Death.* I experienced cognitive dissonance as a result. The other thing, though, is that I felt there was a chapter missing from your book and that was the chapter that was going to explain what the typical learning day would be for 14-year-old Johnny and 14-year-old Mary. That seemed like the next thing I wanted to know about and wasn't there.

MR. PERELMAN: Good question. One answer to your question is, it was intentional on my part not to write that scenario. Many people demand it of me. In many of the presentations I do people will ask: tell us how this is going to unfold. And I may be wrong about about not answering the question, but it is an intentional choice on my part. At one time in my youth, I used to hang around with the World Future Society. The work of *School's Out* and the work I do and have done, is not futurism. I'm not interested in saying, "this is what the future is going to be."

That would be an impertinent or an arrogant act. I don't really know what the future is going to be, even though in most of my work a certain amount of forecasting is involved. One corollary in this thesis I'm unfolding for you is that it is much easier to predict death than birth. That is an outgrowth of the Second Law of Thermodynamics. I can be fairly confident that in one hundred years from now all of us in this room are going to be dead. That is not absolutely guaranteed. We don't know what medical breakthroughs might occur, freezing people, et cetera. There is a non-trivial possibility that some of us will still be around, but there is a great likelihood that the people including me in this room are going to be dead. That is a pretty good prediction.

On the other hand, it is very hard to say what your grandchildren are going to be doing for a living or how many you are going to have or what color their hair is going to be, although it is very likely or possible that you here are going to have grandchildren. Who they are, how they are going to be living their lives, we don't know. There is an asymmetry in the nature of the future. That is part of the reason I didn't do the scenario you asked for. It is very likely I could be wrong, and if I was wrong, people could say "he was wrong about that and therefore we can ignore the message." I didn't want it to be that easy for people to ignore the message.

Another answer is: The future will be like what you want it to be. My argument in the book is that we *can and must* have a market-based learning system as an essential feature of the 21st century economy. Education is the last great socialist economy left on earth. In almost every country education is controlled, regulated or subsidized by the government. In America and Japan, it somewhat less but in most countries education is 100% run by government.

That will collapse. It will collapse in the same manner that the Soviet Union collapsed and basically for the same reason the Soviet Union collapsed: because of the fundamental rigidity of bureaucracy which is not viable in the Third Wave world. It will not happen incrementally, through step-by-step reform policies, but very much like the Soviet system: here today and gone tomorrow.

Predicting how things will be rearranged after that is nearly impossible, even in cases like the Soviet community, where there are some models because they look to us as a model. The countries of the Former Soviet Union say they want to be like the West in some ways but in some ways they don't want to be like the West. In a lot of ways, things are being invented from scratch. They will create a society and economic and cultural system that is theirs. It may be better or worse than ours in some ways but they will not become clones of the United States - that is for sure.

But the Former Soviet Union countries have existing models to look at. We are all participating in inventing the new learning economy. The market system by its very nature is diverse and responds to a whole spectrum of niches and communal demands. It is as impossible for me to predict what the product or the shape of this future hyper-industry will look like as it would be to say what the product of the American agricultural industry will taste like. It is irrelevant in that sense. It makes no sense because there is such a diversity of possibilities. In any case, those are some of the equivocal reasons I have avoided giving a scenario of the future learning environment.

Having said that, let me give a final answer to that question. In the last six months or so I have developed the scenario of how it is going to happen -- not how it is going to result, but how it is going to unfold from now on. Here is what I foresee. I see major corporations and other employers rapidly eliminating education and training and replacing them with a system I call hyper-learning, though they don't use that terminology. Nonetheless, they talk a lot about performance, support, virtual reality and simulation. These are part of the jargon around the environment of work. Leading organizations have discovered that the new learning technology precludes the traditional model of education training in the classroom teaching setting.

Hewlett Packard is a case study in the *Forbes ASAP* article I mentioned earlier. In a couple of years they eliminated 90 percent of in-classroom training for their work force and replaced it with just-in-time learning support systems. They have a combination of distance learning with interactive support from TVs, CD-ROMS, multimedia, libraries, etc., but the fundamental goal is to move as much as possible to just-in-time, just-enough learning: what you need to know *right now* in order to do what you need to do. So HP is doing it.

Apple began to move to the same strategy a year ago. I talked to their training director in January. The previous August she had said to Apple's top management, "This is crazy. We are selling twenty-first century technology to our customers and yet our own employees are put into 18th-century classrooms. It doesn't make sense." They abolished the training division. When I talked to her less than six months later, they had eliminated 75% of Apple's classroom training and replaced it with hyper-multimedia performance support systems.

As step one, I see leading employers all of a sudden changing the rules for tens of thousands of employees. "We don't care about that stuff anymore; this is the real program, get with it if you want to have a career." Then, users find out the new hyper-learning is user friendly, much easier, much more fun, more adaptable and adapted to them than being lectured to in classrooms.

Step two, employees take their learning home. Last year AT&T mandated that 80 percent of their salespeople have to establish home offices. Stop coming in to work -- take this technology home with you.

Next, parents discover that their children are better at using new technologies than they are. The younger generation knows what's going on. We grownups are the ones who are handicapped. The kids don't know anything else, so they become the tutors to mom and dad. At the same time, many parents begin to see that the current schooling system is badly flawed. I get notes, email, and faxes from readers regularly on today's educational system. Here's a typical one from a man in New Jersey: "The school said that our 9-year-old son is learning-disabled. But he works with me at home on the Macintosh and he is better on it than I am. My kid is really smart and they don't get it. So we are doing home schooling."

The interviews I did with various executives for the *ASAP* articles often produced the same message. Many of the corporate executives in charge of just-in-time learning are former teachers. They left the teaching world and entered corporate training and later segued into becoming systems analysts at places like Toshiba, Intel, Hewlett Packard. I would ask them, well, do you have kids? "Oh, yes, we have kids." Well, knowing what you know, doing what you are doing at work, what are you doing about your kids?

Almost every one of them was home schooling or planning to home school. There were one or two exceptions who found wildly alternative schools, in places such as Palo Alto, California the heart of Silicon Valley, that satisfied their criteria of what a good learning environment would be. One of the executives I wrote about and her husband were both former high school teachers. She said, "We don't want our daughter to be educated - we want her to learn how to learn." These anecdotes are small in number, they are not scientific research, but I think they are prophetic.

The signals these stories tell me is that this transformation of the work environment is rapidly leading to changes in perception among parents and families about what does and doesn't work. Once there is get a critical mass in a particular community, we will start seeing taxpayers and voters revolt. We will have major employers in a town where they hire 30 or 40 percent of the work force. And within six months or a year people will start saying, "Wait a minute - why are we paying taxes for the same old stuff for our kids?" Ultimately that will trickle up to the state level.

At some point we will have whole states completely changing the rules of the game. Somebody will say, what state, Perelman? I would say probably Utah for a variety of reasons. In fact, I was in Utah and I got a chance to talk with the governor for an hour -- he thought that could be true too.

That is the scenario to answer your question. What happens as a result of thousands of such things being offered in the marketplace? We saw one example demonstrated here this evening by some people from the University of Pennsylvania. Multiply that by a million times.

MR. LEVY: David Levy from Xerox PARC, one of the institutions that you probably know about. PARC is the institution that spawned the Institute for Research on Learning, which you credit in your book. I think you do a very nice job of explicating some of their basic findings and so on.

Let me start by saying I didn't get a chance to read your book very carefully. I scanned it on the plane. And my blood pressure did not go up and that's because I am from California and I have been meditating for about ten years. My sense is that there are two centers to your story -- you might have to correct me because I didn't read the whole thing -- one is the conclusion about socialism versus a capitalist market economy and education, which really seems to be where you are driving. The main motor for that seems to be what you say about technology and technology changes.

I can't say anything about the first. I'm not schooled in that area, but as a researcher, a long time researcher at one of the main institutions that has actually produced technology that is changing our lives as well as one of the very innovative research centers whose results you are quoting, I believe you are making a very big mistake in the way you argue from technological cause to social effect.

One of the things that a certain group of us at PARC and also at IRL (including the people you cite) have been learning and we have come to understand more clearly is the extent to which technical determinism is not the case at all. Indeed, technology provides ranges of possibilities that then network with ongoing social and political research concerns.

We are undergoing big changes. None of us really knows what the future is. We all care about it. We all want to have jobs. We want to know what kind of world our children are being born into. But a view that says this is a necessary, an inevitable future, is a perversion of technological research. To say that technology, whether it is the printing press or the telephone or whatever, inevitably is going to lead to certain results.

I suggest your comments are irresponsible and possibly even immoral, in the following sense:

First, they give to the technologists and people who are associated with them, a great deal of power -- everyone has to get on the train and it is going ***this*** way. ***We*** are the ones that are taking the train forward. Your comments basically dis-empower the people who are not on that train because they believe there is nothing they can do about anything; things are inevitably going to be a certain way.

You may be right. But if you are right, it is not going to be because of technological inevitability; it is going to be because of a whole range of political and social things. In fact your book is an argument for a particular position. I happen to disagree with it, but the biggest concern I have as a technologist is that we have the responsibility to understand the role that technology plays. Many of us understand technology so poorly that we are likely to believe things that other people tell us about it.

Almost everyone in this room has probably had dealings with people in computering who say, things have to be a certain, technologically-determined way. Well, it doesn't have to be that way. What happens in the future is up to us collectively. That is the only part of your book I can really comment on. I think the conclusions that you draw and the argument you make are actually at odds with the very research and researchers whose ideas form the chapters.

MR. PERELMAN: Those are good points. Let me say a couple of things about them. First of all, you should read the whole book. In Lisa Freeman's introduction of me this evening, you heard major part of my answer to your comments, in my reference to Thoreau. I tried very hard to make that exact point you were trying to make. In part, it goes back to my answer to our earlier questioner here, that I'm very cautious about predicting the future.

I have limited my scope to a couple of things I thought were highly probable. I do not think of the world in terms of technological determinism. I may very well be guilty of acts that might be described as 'economic determinism.' I believe technology is a driving force of human history and human development, but in the context of its role in economic processes, not in the sense that you were describing. Just because something is invented, it is not necessarily the way things are going to be.

I started out as a physicist. I feel I'm sensitive to the issues you've raised. And there was something else I wanted to add, which to some extent overlaps my earlier anecdote about the 1890s and the Great Colombian Exposition. I have myself worked at JPL and other labs. My understanding from reviewing our history is that often those of us who are very close to the invention process, do not see the forest for the trees. Often people doing high-tech work are not particularly capable of seeing the consequences of the very work they are doing, and they often tend to underestimate the impact. There are a lot of social, cultural, institutional, and sociological reasons why that is, so we could talk about it a lot.

But if you are a real scientist, you face a lot of peer pressure and communal pressure not to get too far ahead of the curve publicly, because you get slammed by people, as you said. It doesn't mean you are wrong.

Other people who have been more audacious in their visions have often turned out to be right. To me that is not the conclusive issue. Whether polling the scientists doing the work and seeing what they expect to happen is going to necessarily tell us, I don't know. I'm a fan of James Burke. I don't know if he qualifies as being a historian, but he certainly has a marvelous intelligence. There are many anecdotes in his work about people who did things with little appreciation of how drastically it changed the world.

One that comes to mind is Burke's story about the man who was working on finding a way to distill better scotch whiskey and wound up writing down the laws which turned out to be crucial for the steam engine. The whole industrial revolution started with somebody in Scotland who wanted to make better booze. And many, many stories like that illustrate my point: When you are doing the work, it doesn't necessarily mean you can see where it is leading. It doesn't mean I am qualified either, so we both may be wrong.

Xerox PARC in the last year added to my vision of what in the book I called the "smart environment" with the work you have been doing in "UBICOMP" or "ubiquitous computing." I was really impressed t how far down the curve you and other centers have been pushing this. One important point I want to return to is children - what are our children going to do? You mean our children are going to be sitting in a corner glued to the computer screen? That is not what the computer is. The computer is like an invisible medium that we live inside, or that we carry around with us.

I tried to have scenarios in the book to get the feeling across. It is not an anti-socializing but, as I see it, a pro-socializing technology. Again, getting back to your question, it is that if we are smart enough, human enough, to use technology in the right way. And I have no doubt some people stupidly are going to do it the wrong way and some people will do the right thing.

MR. LEVY: I don't want to monopolize this. Just a couple of things, if I can remember them. First, it is certainly true that inventors can't see the full scope of their inventions, but I don't think anybody can blame Xerox PARC or other companies. It wasn't inventors that I was speaking of, but the people who are at IRL and other anthropologists and other social scientists in my own group at PARC. What we have collectively been learning for a decade is the extent to which social relations are really the primary issues.

The question is, how is technology going to be used? I know it will be used for many things radically; there is no doubt about that. But if you say well, we don't need schools any more, we don't need buildings, that is the similar argument made about the virtual library; we are not going to need the physical building anymore. But I remember very distinctly a conversation with Kitty Gordon She said one of the things we are learning about the use of video at a distance is it doesn't take the place of group interaction. So whatever form the library is going to take in the future, whatever form schools are going to take in the future, there is going to have to be real face-to-face contact as well as the use of other technology.

MR. PERELMAN: I don't necessarily disagree with you on that. It is important for understanding my arguments to make a distinction between school facilities as gathering places, as custodial caring places, and learning as a process. Kids in many cases are still in need of daycare; in fact, daycare is a growing need. If the child is six years old and goes to a facility, we call it a school. If she is three years old, we call it a daycare center. But we also demand that the daycare center provide learning opportunities. These are independent variables in my mind. The popular perception that I believe is drastically erroneous is that school classrooms are the place for learning to occur. That has not been true for a long time. That belief is an obstacle for us in taking full advantage of the opportunities that current and future technology could potentially offer us. That is part of my argument, but let's get somebody else in on it.

MR. O'DONNELL: Jim O'Donnell from the University of Pennsylvania. I would like to ask you not to predict the future but describe what you see. Here is a room full of people who by and large spurn large profits and who exist to preserve particular communities that don't make themselves out to be traditionalist in a capitalistic sort of way. One of the reasons we are who and what we are, is that we see a social good for people who cannot afford to pay a market price for it. Sometimes we provide information to those who are not there yet.

Let's say we want to publish the papers of Andrew Johnson fifty or one hundred years from now. Do you see a all our transactions moving to a market-based economy for information production, that educational publishing isn't going to sustain itself on its merits, isn't going to recover its costs? If that is so, what will prevent education from becoming marginalized? The Postal Service marginalizes competition. It is the question of whether we keep the values of these institutions as we move to some kind of market.

MR. PERELMAN: The short answer to your question is, no. The point of the book is exactly what you are saying. The school is going the way of the Post Office in its traditional concept and design. You brought into question the values these institutions have. Let's put that on the table for the moment. I am an ardent capitalist and I have faith in the power of the marketplace to meet individual demands. It is not perfect, but it is more perfect than what the market forces of the political market place usually wind up creating. At this time, that is my point of view.

I said in my book there is a new economy and we don't understand the rules of it, but one of the features of it is that information is a different type of thing that the traditional laws of economics don't apply to. We have to learn a lot about how these things are going to work. Peter Drucker said the same thing in much greater detail in his latest book, and others have been making the same observations. Drucker made the argument that we need to do serious research and development of the economic theory of what we call the information age or the Third Wave -- whatever it is.

This is a very new world. It is a much newer world than the Western Hemisphere was five hundred years ago. All of us here in the room are participating in the social invention process, so I don't have all the answers by any means. However I think the marketplace is the best place those answers can be generated. I do believe that by and large most of these academic, centralized, architecturally rooted, campus-based institutions will prove to be obsolete, but not all.

Getting back to your point, I had a conversation like this a couple of weeks ago at Gonzaga University in Spokane, a very traditional Jesuit institution. The marketing director was the person who brought me there. She's a big fan of my book. "Tell us what are we going to do to continue the process of what we are here for, our mission if you will, in this new environment that you have described."

And I will share the answer I gave. On the one hand you can take Gonzaga or Georgetown into cyberspace and drastically redefine the medium, which will happen. Inevitably a lot of that will happen. But I was there wearing my business management consultant hat. As a consultant, I felt obliged to say to them, that is only one possible solution.

Our colleague from Xerox might be surprised, but I said that there will continue to be some market demand for the experience of a place like a Gonzaga, and some people are going to want that for a long time. But probably fewer than do now -- not nearly as many as in the past. Therefore, the number of such institutions that will be economically viable is going to dwindle, but they not necessarily disappear. One option for them could be to try to preserve that experience, that institution, that campus that whole goal, keep it viable for people who can afford to come and be able to buy it. You have to have income.

So I said to them, the alternative is to do nothing at all of the sort I have described in my book. Purify the Gonzaga experience and become as true as possible to that mission, and preserve it as absolutely as possible. Do not contaminate it with all the modern stuff because some people will want the traditional, not the new. It is like the 'Colonial Williamsburg' scenario -- people will want to go there and have the experience.

I talked metaphorically earlier about the horse industry collapse, but we still have ten million horses in America. There still are some number of people in this country who make their living, whose lifestyle and work rotate around and doing things with horses. It hasn't vanished. But the scale of that compared to the mainstream of activities of most people has dwindled to a mere sideshow and that in a sense is part of my answer.

I saw a piece in the paper last week that Bennington College has gone through a drastic re-invention, even though they made a lot of people angry, because they just were not economically viable. You simply cannot continue to do things the way you did them before.

For those of you who don't know about it, Bennington has abolished tenure, abolished departments and fired faculty and they are working hard to cut their exorbitant tuition costs by ten or fifteen percent to stay in business. Somehow to exist, you have to stay in business. And that is true of many of the enterprises and businesses of people in the room.

I acknowledge there is going to be some segment of the market that is going to continue to demand leather-bound journals on paper. There is going to be a demand for that, but not as big as it used to be. A lot of people in that business today are not going to be in business five to ten years from now, and they face individual choices. Do you want to try to be one of those few survivors? Should you still be doing that or something else? I think that is what that comes down to. Did I answer that adequately?

MS. FREEMAN: Thank you very much.

Frankenstein Redux: Organization and Cultivation of Electronic Scholarship

Michael Eleey
University of Pennsylvania

Introduction

From computers that recognize speech and handwriting, to the global information superhighway and the world of virtual reality, the digital revolution is transforming how we live, work, and relate to each other. Communications technology can interconnect us through real-time transmission of still and moving images, sound and data. Information storage technology provides us the ability to locate and access large amounts of information anywhere, anytime. Powerful computation makes possible realistic simulations and human-like interaction with machines.

Without a doubt, the digital age gives scholars powerful new tools for serving society and making research and education more effective, accessible, and personal. But perhaps the greatest challenge technology presents to the University is that of integrating these tools into coherent educational and scholarly programs. If students and professors can be anywhere and interact almost as if they were present in the same room, what is the place of the classroom and the traditional lecture? If information can be accessed everywhere, and stored anywhere, what then is the role of the book, and of the university library as physical repository of information?

We may prefer that our organizations respond to this technological revolution in a deliberate, purposeful way. It is more likely, however, that universities will react in an evolutionary manner, perhaps partly guided by our plans, but nevertheless channeled by external forces. As in other evolutionary processes, we may expect these developments to be characterized by morphological change, in which new forms -- here, the forms of learning, and the social organization of learning -- take shape through progressive derivations and unanticipated genetic combinations. How can we organize for this evolution and nurture the cultivation of new forms of scholarship? Can we develop structures and plans to facilitate our progress in a reasoned way?

The Committee on Electronic Publishing and Interactive Technologies

At the University of Pennsylvania, such an organizing effort began two years ago with a campus-wide group, the Committee on Electronic Publishing and Interactive Technologies. In 1992, an *ad hoc* group of faculty and senior administrators gathered, initially to explore the market potential in electronic publishing. This top-down initiative was expanded in 1993, adding members in a bottom-up fashion, with faculty and staff (and more recently, students as well) active in electronic publishing and interactive technologies in education. The expanded group broadened its vision, to share ideas about the possible impact of information technology on education, and to develop an action agenda to realize the opportunities that were being identified.

While by no means has this Committee on Electronic Publishing and Interactive Technologies involved all of the people working on such issues at Penn, it has grown to include key constituencies across the campus. These include faculty from several departments; students; central and school-based computing organizations; the Vice Presidents for University Relations and Business Services; the Director of Corporate and Foundation Relations; the Vice Provost for Libraries; the Director of the University of Pennsylvania Press; the

Director of the College of General Studies (which operates the extension programs for non-traditional students); the Vice Dean of the Wharton School and Director of its Aresty Institute for Executive Education; and officials from the University Museum and other special collections. Membership is open: as other interested parties present themselves or are discovered, they are welcomed.

More than a forum for the articulation of ideas and possible directions for the development and integration of technology and education at the University, the Committee has come to provide a safe environment for considering and supporting measured risks. The Committee's mission, fittingly, has been *self*-defined -- to explore, propose, develop, and support initiatives in electronic publishing and interactive technologies in education. In its mission and work, the members find a mutuality of interests in the organizational implementation of these new technologies.

The Committee has undertaken several activities in pursuit of its mission. An important thrust has been the promotion of awareness about new educational technologies at Penn, through what the Committee terms "upreach," "inreach," and "outreach." These are communications targeted, respectively, to Penn's top leadership, to faculty and students, and to audiences beyond the campus. *Upreach* has proceeded through the involvement of senior administrators in the Committee itself, and through periodic briefings and programs for Trustees. In addition to articles in numerous campus publications, the major *inreach* effort has been the recent production of a sixteen-minute video distributed to every standing faculty member, which highlights several innovative educational applications of new technology by Penn faculty. Selective external distribution of this video, along with other written and personal communications, has also served to promote *outreach.*

A second area of Committee activity has been advocacy on key issues, such as intellectual property rights and other issues related to these technologies. A third program has been to identify and secure funding for important initiatives from internal and external sources. And a fourth major focus has been to undertake sponsorship of projects which offer opportunities for institutional learning, particularly across organizational boundaries such as academic departments, schools, libraries, the University of Pennsylvania Press, faculty, administrators, students and trustees.

Currently the Committee is sponsoring two such projects. One is a "textbook re-engineering" effort for a large undergraduate course in materials science offered in the School of Engineering and Applied Science. Using a case-study approach to this complex, information- and concept-rich course, the "text" focuses on two familiar products, the bicycle and the Walkman. Within this framework, the project is exploring the use of simulation, animation, hyperlinks to symbolic mathematics software (Waterloo's *Maple*) and other analytical tools, as well as automatic assessment techniques. At various stages, this project has involved faculty, students, the University of Pennsylvania Press, graphic designers, programmers and other resources. While a broad range of fertile experimentation may characterize the effort for some time, intermediate products are planned in the near future, including a mixed-mode workbook involving both print and electronic components.

The second major project sponsored by the Committee had its roots in the Penn Reading Project, which requires some preliminary background.

The Penn Reading Project

The approximately 9,000 undergraduates at the University of Pennsylvania may matriculate in either the School of Arts and Sciences, the School of Engineering and Applied Science, the School of Nursing, or the Wharton School. The four-year old Penn Reading Project was instituted to provide a shared intellectual experience across the four undergraduate schools, and to promote the experience of Penn as "one university." In the summer before they arrive, all incoming first-year undergraduate students receive a copy of a common text selected for that year. They are asked to read this during the summer and then, shortly after they arrive on campus, the students discuss the text during orientation week, in small groups led by faculty volunteers. The faculty discussion leaders come from all over the university, and as a group represent virtually every School and department. After the orientation week discussions of the text, there are follow-up activities which are appropriate to the text, for example, film screenings, lectures and other events. These carry on the theme of that particular reading throughout the remainder of the year.

In the Fall of 1991, the first year of the Program, entering students received *The Bacchae*. Among the follow-up activities, a student group produced that play during the year. The next year, the text was *The Narrative Life of Frederick Douglas*, followed in 1993 by Mary Shelley's *Frankenstein*. The most recent selection was *Einstein's Dreams*.

The Penn Reading Project has succeeded in breaking down inter-school barriers, among both faculty and students. Faculty have been enthusiastic participants. Students have begun to identify their class with that year's text: in the first years of the program, in fact, students in the younger classes began good-naturedly to taunt the older classes, because the latter had arrived at Penn before the inception of the Penn Reading Project and as a result had been deprived of a text with which their class could identify.

The Committee on Electronic Publishing and Interactive Technologies was struck that the Penn Reading Project provided interesting opportunities for advancing its objectives. First, the program was very visible, successful and recognized by many on campus, including trustees: it thus provided an excellent "upreach" opportunity. Second, it had broad faculty interest and universal student involvement, on which "inreach" efforts could be based to promote the idea of electronic publishing. And third, some product possibilities immediately came to mind -- work that was already being done on campus each year for the Penn Reading Project text could be further pulled together into electronic products that could be useful for schools and other colleges and perhaps the general public, thereby serving "outreach" purposes and possibly generating revenue.

Mary Shelley's *Frankenstein* seemed particularly interesting to the Committee as it began considering what type of electronic Penn Reading Project initiative might be developed. For one thing, *Frankenstein* not only happened to be that year's (1993) text, but was thematically very broad, spanning issues in science, technology, history, and philosophy. Second, there is a rich array of materials which surround Frankenstein, including collateral texts and other literature, as well as cinematic treatments and other popular cultural artifacts. Third, Penn enjoyed the advantage of having on its English faculty Stuart Curran, a leading Mary Shelley scholar.

The Frankenstein Project

The Committee approached Professor Curran in the Spring of 1994. An electronic edition was a new idea to him, but in the course of discussions with the Committee, he quickly became enthusiastic. Because the Director of the University of Pennsylvania Press was a member of the Committee, the Press became involved in the project almost immediately. The Committee was further instrumental in helping Professor Curran develop the project's scope. And, based on his preliminary plan, the Committee was able to secure initial seed funding for the effort.

As the project gathered momentum, the Committee next arranged an intensive technical consultation, by convening a meeting of experienced multimedia and instructional software developers from around the campus, to collaborate with Professor Curran and help him select the approach and development tools that he would need to meet his requirements. In conjunction with the Press, the Committee also began pursuing external collaboration and partnership opportunities on behalf of the project, in anticipation of future full-scale development and various production and publication possibilities.[1]

The project itself was led by Professor Curran, but like many faculty members, he perhaps is especially effective when assisted by talented graduate students. In Professor Curran's case, we were extremely fortunate that he was able to recruit two advanced graduate students from his department, who not only were knowledgeable about the Romantic period and Mary Shelley, but came with significant prior work experience as professional programmers. In addition, two part-time undergraduate students were available to assist in collecting materials and providing general support for the effort.[2]

By Summer 1994, the project was in full swing, developing a working prototype in hypertext markup language (HTML). HTML was chosen for the prototype because, as the basis of the Internet's World Wide Web technology, it is very widely used and is likely to continue as a standard for a reasonable time. Furthermore, it is relatively easy to code; handles a range of text, image, sound and video material; can be accessed by public-domain and commercial viewers like Mosaic and Netscape, which also happen to support both Microsoft Windows and Macintosh -- the key user platforms Professor Curran had identified; and, the HTML files can be distributed either by CD-ROM or over a network. In the next phase of the project, the HTML prototype will be submitted to the Press's editorial review process, and subjected to early field testing in courses at Penn and elsewhere.

Today, Professor Curran's vision for the project is ultimately a new kind of edition, incorporating with the text a broad and deep range of resources that would facilitate individualized exploration. In his words,

> It [Mary Shelley's *Frankenstein*] is a work of enduring value. Students love it. Older people keep going back to it. The important thing about what we are trying to do is to make available a massive amount of information that has never been collected before.
>
> We can take the formative writings of Mary Shelley, of her father and mother, and we can embed scientific technology in terms of electricity. We can make a small library available along with this major text to support it and to allow people then to use it as a means of their own independent research.
>
> This is absolutely democratic. Nobody is going to be the keeper of this knowledge. The idea is for everybody to use it at whatever level of skill or interest those people have.[3]

It is interesting that eight months before these words, Professor Curran had not thought about electronic editions of *Frankenstein*. In his current thinking however, he sees three possible products from this project: a trade edition, an educational edition, and a scholarly edition.

The *trade* edition would be for a general audience interested in literature. It would incorporate some of the research options Professor Curran describes, but with significant emphasis on multimedia elements and popular culture components. Its base would consist of a selected, somewhat directive, view into the collected resources Professor Curran is now building as the digital foundation for the entire project. To this would be added an enhanced interface incorporating images, sounds and video. The University of Pennsylvania Press and the Committee on Electronic Publishing and Interactive Technologies are working with Professor Curran to explore the best approach to the trade market for such a product, which most likely would be distributed on CD-

ROM.

The *educational* edition, on the other hand, would be for later high school or early college studies. It would be more text-oriented than the trade edition, with a good amount of reference and other materials combined in a hypertext and hypermedia package to support study and analysis. This edition would be distributed by the University of Pennsylvania Press, which has the expertise in that particular market, and could be produced either as a CD-ROM, or perhaps as a networkable version that could be licensed to schools.

The *scholarly* edition would be for audiences of advanced scholars and researchers. It would probably have many of the characteristics of a variorum, incorporating all significant editions and textual variants, along with all important source materials, scholarly annotations, and major critical perspectives, as well as treatments of the work or its themes in other media. A large body of relevant non-text materials could also be included. With appropriate security and transaction support systems (now under development by a number of parties), it would be possible and appropriate for such an edition to be accessed over the network, probably the Internet. As such, it could also be subject to continuous updating at whatever rate ongoing scholarship might warrant. This edition, with its collaborative openness, and its integration of learning and research tools, raises perhaps some of the most interesting practical and theoretical questions of all. For example: What is the role in such a project of a university press? Of a university library? Is this a type of publication? Or is it a research center? In the end, is it a product, or a process? And how can it be supported on a continuing basis?

We do not have the answers, but these are questions we must investigate. In fact, we are perhaps here a bit like Victor Frankenstein himself -- such exploration is a main reason for undertaking such ambitious projects at this point in time.

Frankenstein Redux? Some Questions

Our experience in undertaking this sort of project is not unlike what E.L. Doctorow observed about the writing process: "It is like driving a car at night; you never see further than your headlights, but you can make the whole trip that way."

Of course, that presumes we know where we are going. But since at this stage, we don't yet have a good road map, we may perhaps find ourselves following Yogi Berra's rather confident advice --"When you come to a fork in the road, take it." We will encounter many forks, and should, in fact, be prepared to take them all, and retrace our steps as necessary.

We ask, What are we creating? So far, (again, shades of *Frankenstein*) it seems to be turning out somewhat different from what we thought when we started our project. Instead of one product, it may be several; instead of CD-ROM, it may be a network product; instead of a definitive final scholarly edition of the work, it may be a continually growing resource center for scholarship itself.[4]

As we look around us, it does seem that new cultural forms, at least these kinds of educational and publishing forms, are evolving rapidly. They are accelerated not only by technological changes, but also by the daily development and discovery of new ideas about learning and research.

When will we reach the first inflection point of the learning curve? We are spending a lot of time moving out along the flat zone, discovering new complexities indeed, but perhaps not yet learning much about how to proceed more systematically. But at some point we will be crossing over to the steep and productive part of the curve. Is it close?

And finally, we may ask, Why do this, now? Partly, our motivation is as the English novelist J.G. Ballard wrote in 1974, "Science and technology multiply around us. To an increasing extent they dictate the languages in which we speak and think. Either we use those languages, or we remain mute"? But from what we have seen so far from our small successes, it is more. The enthusiasm of the faculty, and the excitement of the students involved in these experiments suggests that Marshal McLuhan was correct thirty years ago when, in the final chapter of *Understanding Media,* he observed:

> Persons grouped around a fire or candle for warmth or light are less able to pursue independent thoughts, or even tasks, than people supplied with electric light. In the same way, the social and educational patterns latent in automation are those of self-employment and artistic autonomy.

. . . To which we might today append,

"and greater individual intellectual empowerment."

---

[1]There is a good reason for commercial entities to enter into such university partnerships, beyond the simple economic viability of a given project. Orson Welles once said,"Hollywood is the only industry, even taking in soup companies, which does not have laboratories for the purpose of experimentation." Publishing houses today are in much the same situation, and Universities would seem to be well suited to serve as research and development labs for those firms seriously interested in learning how to compete in this developing digital marketplace.

[2]Furthermore, in these and other projects, developers have found that the user perspectives provided by involving students throughout the project are invaluable.

[3]From *Educating in the Information Age,* a 16-minute video produced by the Committee on Electronic Publishing and Interactive Technologies, University of Pennsylvania, 1994 (available from Academic Computing Services, Suite 335B, 3401 Walnut Street, Philadelphia, PA 19104).

[4]Our textbook re-engineering effort also has shown similar tendencies to progress in several directions.

Michael Eleey
Associate Vice Provost, Info Systems and Computing
University of Pennsylvania
eleey@crc.upenn.edu

The Labyrinth: A World Wide Web Disciplinary Server for Medieval Studies

Deborah Everhart and Martin Irvine
Georgetown University

Part 1: Overview, Theory, and the Importance of Specialized Web Servers

The Labyrinth is a World Wide Web disciplinary server for medieval studies. This field has always been interdisciplinary, embracing research in the humanities and social sciences, and the Labyrinth, therefore, is the first major Web server for a large interdisciplinary area of study, providing access to an organized body of Internet resources. Our Web server receives over 500 file requests per day for Labyrinth files, and requests have come in from over 40 countries around the world. Most of our users are from universities and colleges in North America.

We began building the Labyrinth over a year ago, responding to a need to organize existing resources and to plan new initiatives for an electronic library and an image database. We found that the rapid development of electronic resources outpaced the means of organizing and coordinating them for ease of use and access. The Internet and World Wide Web have expanded in all directions, with no center, top, or organizational structure. Electronic resources scattered across the Internet are like books in an uncatalogued library; what cannot be found cannot be used. The useful search and indexing tools on the Net and Web do not produce an organized or interpreted body of information. Furthermore, scholars and teachers who use the Internet often lack the time to learn all the daunting telecommunications protocols to navigate through the vast sea of servers and files. But most scholars and teachers can now get to the Labyrinth through a Web client like Lynx or Mosaic, and all the connections to resources are made for them through hypertext links. The Labyrinth thus provides a simplified point of access, a structured but open configuration of Net and Web resources. Although the Labyrinth project will never be finished in the sense of finishing a building, our goal is to help organize and manage on-line resources into a meta-library with the multiple access points available through the Web.

The Labyrinth project also responds to parallel developments in technology and in the conceptualizing of knowledge in the humanities. Electronic text and images are presented in a form extraordinarily different from that of the printed book; rather than following the strict linear order of lines on a page and pages in a book, electronic information presents links among and within texts and other bits of information as they appear in different contexts or in other media. Hypertext, the technological method whereby context after context can expand out from a single word or phrase, provides us with a new way of conceptualizing and visualizing information. With hypermedia, word and text can be linked to even wider contexts of image, sound, and video.

Hypermedia may supplant the printed book and rewrite not only our understanding of textuality, but also our concepts of author and publisher.

The hypertext and hypermedia capability of the World Wide Web mirrors recent work on intertextuality, cultural studies, and history. Theories of intertextuality assume that any text or cultural expression is a subset of larger fields of discourse or systems of meaning. Cultural studies and new historical studies are methodologically interdisciplinary and emphasize the necessity of understanding culture as a large horizontal field of interconnections and contexts. Academic discourse has traditionally been concerned with making and representing knowledge, but regardless of its conceptual density or analytical precision, discourse is linear and one-dimensional. As a representational medium, discourse can attempt to describe language, culture, and history, but it cannot represent their intertextual and multidimensional foundations. Studies of intertextuality and the making of hypertext documents render textuality more granular: a text becomes a mosaic of references, cross-references, and pieces of meaning assembled from many cultural sources, some of which may be conflicting and contradictory. Rather than obscuring the constitutive features of texts and culture in an illusory sense of the independence and unity of individual texts, hypertext and hypermedia can both represent the web of interconnections and allow readers to intervene in the web and establish their own points of view, their own interpretive organization of information.

The Web, a global hypertext network, provides a technologically sophisticated way to represent this way of organizing information into knowledge. The Labyrinth facilitates new ways of using information in hypermedia form, allowing users to make their own connections relationally across many sources and to use this information immediately on their desktops.

Part 2: World Wide Web Technology and Hypertext Capability

Recent technological advances allow us to construct not only organizational structures for electronic resources, but also infinitely expandable webs of hypertext links among resources. The World Wide Web, one of the most sophisticated networking systems ever developed, is expanding with extraordinary speed on servers around the world. The Web networking technology was designed to be a fast and easy way for academic communities of researchers to share information and work collaboratively. From this origin, it has quickly grown to include a full range of data from diverse sources: educational and government organizations, non-profit groups, commercial entities, and private individuals. The potential for continued expansion of the Web is unbounded.

Web networking technology has many advantages that set it apart from other Internet protocols. The most distinctive of these advantages, and the characteristic that accounts for the Web's rapid expansion, is its hypertext capacity, its ability to link documents, databases, indices, and other forms of electronic media through keywords or tags. Hypertext links can provide connections within texts (for example, a reference to another section of the document can take the reader to that section), between texts (taking the reader to a relevant passage in another text), and even between different parts of the Web (taking the reader to another database or other remote source). Users can easily compile their own sets of preferred links in a "hotlist" or "bookmark" file so that they may quickly retrieve resources they wish to use again.

The Web, like previous Internet utilities, is based on client/server technology. There are thus two hardware and software components that make the Web work, one the server software running on an Internet system that responds to incoming file requests, and the client software running on the user's local system that sends out the requests to the server, receives the sent files, and then displays them on the screen with the proper formatting and hypermedia links. But the great advantage of the Web is its backward compatibility with prior Internet standards: Web clients like Lynx, NCSA Mosaic, and the new Netscape Mosaic can be used to access gopher and ftp files, and with a simple configuration on the user's home system the Web clients can also be used to run telnet sessions and access news group archives. In short, Web clients are a simplified front end for the whole Internet. The Web thus incorporates existing Internet efforts, and university press and library gophers can easily be incorporated into new Web projects and resources. University presses are just beginning to exploit the potential of the Web as a distribution system for electronic texts and journals.

What are the benefits of using the Web to market and deliver electronic publications? There are distinct advantages over CD ROM's and diskettes. First, there is only a one-time storage cost. Hard disk space for servers is getting cheaper all the time, now around $ .80 a megabyte. Second, the Web provides the ability to deliver specific packages of information in ways that can be integrated and connected to other information. CD ROM's, as Gregory Crane, editor in chief of the Perseus Project put it, are "'docu-islands,' standing in isolation from other products" as closed sets information requiring specific hardware and software ("At Cyberspace University Press, Paperless Publishing Looks Good," *New York Times Book Review*: Oct. 30, 1994, p. 53). Most electronic text developers recognize CD's as a transitional technology, useful now but with severe limitations. CD ROM's are really black box technology, useful for storing and retrieving a very finite amount of information, but information closed off from the larger universe of data. The earlier limitations of the Internet-- storage limits, slowness of connections, few access points -- are being reduced daily with Web technology, and CD ROM's may soon be stacked up unused on people's shelves.

Part 3: Collaboration

The practical implications of hypertext networks are manifold. The Web is already fostering unprecedented collaboration among scholars, allowing researchers to undertake joint ventures that would not have been possible before. We already see Internet technology being used to facilitate collaboration within the university press community: the Association of American University Presses Online Catalog/Bookstore provides a unified interface for the presses collectively, but it also includes pointers to each of the individual press's on-line resources, both Web home pages and Gopher main menus (URL: http://aaup.pupress.princeton.edu/). Many of these presses' home pages in turn provide pointers to the AAUP home page. MIT Press provides a good example, since they have a link to the AAUP Catalog/Bookstore in a prominent place on their Web home page (URL: http://www-mitpress.mit.edu/). This type of reciprocal connectivity is what Web technology does best, offering opportunities for collaborative ventures that were previously inconceivable. The web of university presses' on-line resources is the precursor of much broader collaborative connections among bookstores and book producers on commercial and scholarly servers.

Publishers can use not only their own servers to distribute information, but also disciplinary servers in appropriate scholarly fields as outlets for information, thereby gaining access to very wide audiences and/or the specific communities of readers they target. I n the Labyrinth, we are pleased to provide links to publishers' information, and, when available, full texts for sale online. We view this as yet another way of serving the scholarly community, providing information on and access to the texts that scholars write, purchase, and use in their research and courses. In our

"Professional Information" menu, we already provide links to the AAUP home page, the Johns Hopkins University Press Tables of Contents of academic journals, and the full text journals that Project Muse delivers online (URL: http://www.georgetown.edu/labyrinth/professional/professional.html).

Links to publishers' information is one of many ways that we collaborate with others to organize and distribute vital information in our field. The Labyrinth has quickly gained a reputation as the server providing "one-stop shopping" for medievalists, and we aim to maintain this reputation not only by providing well-organized, easy access to a wide range of resources, including high-quality resources that we have developed ourselves, but also by working closely with others who are building related servers. For example, the Medieval Academy of America, the premier scholarly organization in our field, is in the beginning stages of developing a Web server for Academy documents and news; the Academy server will provide a prominent link to the Labyrinth, and the Labyrinth will provide a link to the Medieval Academy server from the home page as well number of links to specific Academy resources from other relevant sections of the Labyrinth (e.g., the Labyrinth "Professional News" menu will provide a link to the Medieval Academy Newsletter). Not only will these links benefit the users of both servers, but they will also benefit the developers, as we work together to avoid duplication of efforts.

Since Web networking technology allows access to an unlimited selection of materials without necessitating that these materials be stored in one location, the amount of data available through the Labyrinth can be expanded ad infinitum. The Labyrinth already provides connections to text and image archives, on-line journals, bibliographies, discussion list archives, library catalogues, and many other resources on Web, Gopher, and ftp servers around the world. One of the great advantages of Web technology is that our connections to other resources do not intrude upon the autonomy of existing projects. For example, we provide a connection to the Dartmouth Dante Database, a public-access database including all of Dante's works and Dante criticism (URL: gopher://gopher.dartmouth.edu/1/AnonFTP/pub/Dante). The Labyrinth's connection to the DDD does not interfere with the DDD's independent operations. The Dante files remain on their server at Dartmouth, and users can access them directly rather than through the Labyrinth. One advantage of having the Dante project and others like it connected to the Labyrinth is that potential users need not know how to make their own connections to these remote databases; in fact, they might not know in advance that the databases exist. The Labyrinth, acting as a heuristic system, allows users to make new discoveries in previously unknown or inaccessible resources.

Whenever possible, we coordinate our efforts with the developers of other databases and on-line initiatives. For example, we are grateful to David Seaman, Director of the E-Text Center at the University of Virginia, for his work in marking up and making publicly available Middle English texts from the Oxford Text Archive (URL for the E-Text Center: http://www.lib.virginia.edu/etext/ETC.html). We now provide links to these texts in the Labyrinth Library and through the appropriate subject menus. We will follow in David's footsteps as we prepare more e-texts for the Labyrinth Library, picking up where he left off with OTA texts relevant to medieval studies; we will adopt his guidelines for analyzing and verifying texts, converting existing markup to Text Encoding Initiative markup, and providing full headers and cataloguing information. David has made an enormous contribution to the field of medieval studies, not only by marking up and delivering a substantial body of Middle English texts, but also by developing the tools that we need to build our e-text library.

Over the course of the next two-to-three years, we plan to mark up and add to the Labyrinth Library approximately 100 OTA titles from Old English, Middle English, Old French, Old Norse, Old High German, and Latin. The texts that we will be producing for the Labyrinth Library will include only minimal TEI markup, but by providing a large body of such texts, we hope to introduce a wide range of scholars to the advantages and possibilities afforded by TEI-encoding, thus fostering a community of academics who will not only use e-texts but also encode and publish them. To this end, we will also be working closely with the publishers and directors of text initiatives such as SEENET, the Society for Early English and Norse Electronic Texts, and OEOE, Old English On-line Editions. These initiatives, like ours, will be producing TEI-encoded versions of medieval studies texts, and we will coordinate our efforts to avoid duplication. In most cases, e-texts produced by academic presses will include more markup and auxiliary materials than the basic markup we will be providing for texts, and in many ways, the Labyrinth Library will serve as a starting point for scholars who would like to choose texts in their areas of expertise for further editing, markup, and publication. Basic e-texts in the Labyrinth Library will therefore not deter further publication, but could in fact promote further scholarly work and publication by university presses.

Part 4: Financial and Copyright Concerns, Cost Recovery

We would like to propose some ways that the Web could be used for cost recovery by publishers, suggesting some scenarios for the merging of wide access and profitability. Users now can go to the Labyrinth Library, click on a text title, and the text will be delivered to their screens. These texts have been produced either with volunteer labor or with institutional funding, completely by-passing the academic presses. But why shouldn't university presses continue their missions in producing high-quality journals and books in electronic form distributable through the Web? For example, on a disciplinary server like the Labyrinth, a link can be made to a press's server which sends out a file with a form to be filled in by the user for billing purposes. Some Web servers are already experimenting with this procedure.

There are at least two workable procedures already supported by the current state of Web technology. First, for journals: *Wired* magazine, the hyperhip vehicle for the overly computer literate, has just set up a subscription only service called *HotWired*, an on-line magazine supplement (URL: http://www.wired.com/). Using Mosaic, readers bring up the Home Page of the *HotWired* server, and if they are a current subscriber, they click on a link that brings up a username and password entry window, which when filled in takes them to the subscribers' Home Page. Non-subscribed readers are asked to fill in a form with various information, and as yet *Wired* is providing this service experimentally without charge. But there's no reason why this forms feature of the Web cannot be modified to include credit card or other billing devices. For a university press, a subscribed user could read and download current articles, or search through a database of archived articles for specific information. The press could decide to cost this out in various ways -- tiered subscriber levels, for example, some giving access to a set number of articles per year, to only the current issue, or to the whole archive. Very soon, most university teachers will have access to the Web, and I don't know any who wouldn't pay a realistic fee for getting exactly the articles they want when they want them.

Another workable scenario is available for books. A press's on-line catalogue could include an abstract and table of contents for each book. A reader could select a book, and a form for billing information could be sent to the Web client. The form would include the details of the request (whole book, single chapter, selected chapters) and the billing procedure. Another click would send the information to the press's server, which would deliver the requested e-texts through the Web to the customer's computer.

There are several Internet billing systems already in the works. We have read about

Digital Cash, a system where a intermediary assigns an ID linked to a credit card number so that the actual credit card account number is never sent across the Internet. There is also the Internet Billing Services Project at Carnegie Mellon, which has developed a program called "Netbill." The IRS is implementing an on-line banking system where taxpayers can pay electronically. Since the commercial potential of the Net and Web is eagerly being exploited by commercial users, it won't be long before a secure, reliable Web billing system will be available for use by university presses.

Publishers and librarians know much more about copyright issues than we do, but from our point of view, Internet distribution of electronic journals and books with on-line billing may actually prevent pirated copies rather than promote them. The appeal of wider and easier access to materials would far outweigh the impact of cost to the user and remove some of the motives behind the making of bootleg copies of journals and books. Through electronic storage, a book or journal issue can be kept in print forever, with none of the high costs of print and storage, and selected parts of the e-texts can be made easily and readily accessible from any scholar's or teacher's networked computer. If the fee for downloading exactly what you want when you want it is felt to be reasonable, most academics would jump at the opportunity to have those materials. Today, most academics and students make pirate copies in order to guarantee their access to the materials when they want them. If a journal article or book chapter were easily and permanently available on the Web, a publisher's copy could be accessed by a user with some profit going back to the publisher rather than to the copier company, the paper company, and the dry ink manufacturer.

We were very pleased to participate in the joint conference of the Association of Research Libraries and the Association of American University Presses, and we hope to continue the dialogues begun at the conference. Please contact us concerning your plans for on-line delivery of publications so that we may coordinate our project with your newest developments. You can contact us via e-mail (labyrinth@gusun.georgetown.edu), by phone (202-687-7091 or 202-687-7533), or surface mail (Academic Computer Center, 238 Reiss Hall, Georgetown University, Washington, DC 20057).

The URL for the Labyrinth is: http://www.georgetown.edu/labyrinth/labyrinth-home.html)

Deborah Everhart
Coordinator for the Labyrinth
Georgetown University
labyrinth@gusun.georgetown.edu

Martin Irvine
Associate Professor
English Departgment
Georgetown University
labyrinth@gusun.georgetown.edu

Scholarly Publishing in the Information Economy

Sandra Braman
Institute of Communications Research
University of Illinois

Looking at the Future of the Information Economy

Scholarly publishers need to reconsider their activities and their relationships to other organizations and to society as they determine their niche within the emergent information economy. The much-discussed problems in the treatment of information creation, processing, flows, and use from a neoclassical economic perspective (Babe, 1994; Braman, in press) manifest themselves regularly in the growing economic difficulties faced by publishing houses. What's happening to scholarly publishers is, of course, what's happening to everybody -- the nature of the economy has undergone a qualitative shift to what is now popularly known as an "information economy." There are several ways, however, in which just what that means can be -- has been -- conceptualized.

This paper introduces the three dominant conceptualizations of the information economy, argues that the most fruitful line of approach appears to be offered by an "enriched" version of network economics, and applies this approach to the analysis of scholarly publishing in this environment.

Underlying this approach is an understanding of information that responds to the definitional question by offering a four-fold typology of types of definitions of information as distinguished by the complexity of the social structure to which the definition applies, the range and breadth of the social processes explainable using this definitional approach, and the amount of power granted information per se within the social structure: information as a resource, as a commodity, as perception of pattern, and as a constitutive force in society. It is suggested that in decision-making situations, it is important to start and end with the focus on the effects of information creation, processing, flows, and use as constitutive forces in society; at intermediate stages of decision-making processes, however, it may be more appropriate to use one of the other definitions of information. Sometimes it is most useful to think of information as a commodity. To do so does not require abandoning the understanding of the role of information in constituting society (Braman, 1989).

Second, a heuristic that has proven useful in identifying the informational content/activities in various types of texts and social processes, articulates stages of an information production chain. Numerous models of an information production chain have been offered by this point; the model offered here was originally inspired by the work of Fritz Machlup and Kenneth Boulding; use of the heuristic in a variety of areas and continued exposure to the thoughts of by now many others has refined this model over time. The model of the information production chain used here includes: information creation (including creation de novo, generation, and collection [as in the scientific method]), processing (cognitive, algorithmic, and material), transportation, distribution, destruction, and seeking. To use this model neither requires nor implies that all types of information are treatable as commodities. Information policy can be, following Merton, latent or manifest (Braman, 1990).

Alternative Approaches to the Information Economy

Three different approaches to

conceptualizing the information economy are available in the literature: (1) those that say this is an information economy because the industries in the information sector of the economy are proportionately more important than before; (2) those that say this is an information economy because the economy has expanded by commodifying types of information and information flows not previously quantified; and (3) those that say this is an information economy because harmonized information flows have replaced the market as the key coordinating mechanism of the economy, or the network economics approach. While there is at least some truth in all three of these approaches, they differ in their relative validity and in their utility for decision-making. The approach of network economics, enriched with insights from others, seems the most fruitful path to pursue for deeper understanding of the particular qualities of the information economy.

These approaches have appeared in order chronologically, and may be understood as stages of a Kuhnian paradigm change, moving from interpretations in response to accumulation of troublesome data, to consideration of alternative explanations, to the particular alternative explanation that seems likely to become dominant.

The Information Economy as Growth of the Information Sector

The first approach, based on an evolutionary view of human economies that looks at development from hunting and gathering through agriculture and manufacturing to the information economy of today, was the first to appear chronologically, offered in Japan by Umesao (Ito, 1991?) and in the US by Daniel Bell (1976) and Fritz Machlup (1980). Being first chronologically helped this approach dominate the public imagination, though two other factors contributed. This approach speaks in entirely familiar terms; all of the discussion fits easily within current habits of discourse and conceptual frameworks, increasing the ease and speed of its diffusion. And this approach is easily operationalized using existing statistical and decision-making techniques, a factor that made it easy for the US Department of Commerce and other statistical organizations in the national and international environments, to use this approach as the basis of its accounting approach. As a result of the interactions of these three factors, this approach dominates US and international policy-making.

Those who take this approach deny that there are any ways in which the economic treatment of information creation, processing, flows, and use need differ from the economic treatment of the creation and distribution of material goods. The economy is understood to operate the way it always has, with the one difference that it is the information sector that is now dominant.

This approach may be understood as the first stage of a Kuhnian paradigm change, for it is responding to the accumulation of data that are problematic under dominant neoclassical modes of thinking, by a combination of tactics: denying there are any problems in general, but adding one category (of the information industries) into which all the problematic data can be put together, thus incorporating the difficult data into the model.

While at the global, national, industry, and firm levels this approach is increasingly problematic in use, as an approach it is likely to remain dominant as long as it is the only approach associated with known, easy to use analytical tools and decision-making techniques. Figures on the information economy, for example, will continue to be based on SIC codes that divide up the industrial world, despite the facts that categorization of many of these codes is arbitrary, and that because many informational products and services never reach material form at all increasingly large proportions of economic activity are not represented by these codes, and thus by our statistics, at all -- until an alternative that is as comprehensive, usable, easy to comprehend, and aligned with specific decision-making procedures is offered.

Thus there is an additional burden on those who represent other perspectives on the information economy to at the same time develop the decision-making tools that would be based upon and serve that perspective.

The Information Economy as an Expanded Economy

The second approach understands this economy to be an information economy because it has expanded through commodification of forms of information and types of information processing, flows, and use that had not previously been commodified. This approach is often -- but not only -- framed in Marxist terms, and is driven by concerns about the social, cultural, economic, and political effects on those whose information has become commoditized, and on society as a whole. Types of information that have become commodified over the past few decades include that which is most personal (what is in our thoughts, what is in our urine, details of our personal lives), that which is most public (government information becoming privatized), and that which is communal (ritual communications).

Adherents to this approach also believe that the economy is working the way it always has -- but that the problems we face in trying to treat information creation, processing, flows, and use with neoclassical economic concepts reveal contradictions that have always been there and that we now must face. Those who adhere to this perspective suggest radical restructuring of the economy, either as socialist (eg, Mosco, 1989; Schiller, 1976) or as a gift economy (Hyde, 1983).

Focusing on the increasing commodification of information creation, processing, flows, and use is valuable in understanding both the workings of the information economy and the effects of the use of new information technologies on various classes; and it has intuitive appeal. This approach is limited in what it has to offer operationally. While there are implications here for the crafting of any new typologies, identification of specific new industries (such as surveillance) that require attention, and the all-important reminder to retain our moral and political vision while considering economic matters, focusing on the commodification of information as we think about the information economy has yielded little in the way of usable decision-making tools.

Because of this, because those who present this perspective for a number of years have presented their arguments cast in moral terms, and because the changes that are suggested are radical, this approach has not gained much acceptance among active decision-makers. Its insights, however, remain important, useful, and available to those working from other perspectives as well. In terms of the history of a Kuhnian paradigm change, those who work from this perspective are those who argue for a shift to an alternative to the historically dominant paradigm.

Network Economics

A third approach to conceptualizing the information economy has emerged over the past few years based on decades of empirical work into the changing nature of transnational corporations. The position taken here is that the nature of the economy has qualitatively changed, and that harmonized information flows have today replaced the market as the key coordinating mechanism of the economy. In this environment, cooperation and coordination are as important as competition (Antonelli, 1992). Innovation, today's most important product, is understood to emerge more quickly and efficiently out of networked relations than by those who hold their intellectual property rights close to their chests in isolation (Swann, 1993). The network, or "embedded" (Grabher, 1993), firm is thus in this environment more successful than those that isolate themselves; the long-term project, rather than the firm or industry, turns out to be most useful for purposes of economic analysis.

(European analysts have for a while

referred to the entire network of corporations that exist largely in and through the net as well as the telecommunications network itself for policy purposes, terming this the "filiere electronique" [Mattelart & Cesta, 1985].) Economic success in the network economy comes not from maximizing profit with each transaction, but from building the long-term relationships that ultimately are profitable.

This approach reaches the far end of a Kuhnian paradigm change, substituting for the previous vision an alternative that is in many ways radically different. The network economics approach essentially applies the McLuhan (1964/1994) argument that the medium shapes the message to the network as a technology; as the written word is the content of television, so the economy is the content of the network.

It is appealing because it is based on a great deal of empirical data, appears to have greater validity than the other approaches, and is useful strategically. It also builds its thoughts in the terms of neoclassical economics, so that its impact is experienced as more incremental than it would if it were cast in less familiar language -- incremental, and therefore easier to adopt conceptually.

The network economics approach, however, is problematic because it requires the development of new research methods as well as new statistical categories. It requires organizations to think quite differently both strategically and tactically, and to change as organizations. Because this is a new economic environment, we are all still feeling our way along; there are few if any self-evident truths, nor do the same rules apply the same way to all. Success of any kind depends upon accurately identifying the specific niche of each organization within the global information economy. New approaches to decision-making and problem-solving may be required.

In Kuhnian terms, this approach is one that has turned entirely towards a particular alternative expected to become the dominant paradigm once the shift is completed.

"Enriched" Network Economics

The network economics approach to conceptualizing the information economy seems to provide the strongest basis for further research and theoretical development: it is based on empirical data, it offers descriptions that appear to be not only accurate but also useful predictively, it is cast in terms understandable to the general economics community while providing the conceptual grounds for further development of economic concepts and theories, and it provides some radical insights into the qualitative changes in our information and economic environments. As network economists continue to work forward, their efforts might usefully be enriched by ideas derivable from the other two approaches to conceptualizing the information economy, and from other theoretical work both within economics and elsewhere.

In the terms used statistically by governments, it is of course accurate to say that the industries in the information sector are now more important relative to other sectors in the economy. An important step in the process to transform decision-making procedures will be providing a translation calculus from those figures long in use to the new indicators -- once those indicators themselves are developed.

It is of course also true that the number of kinds of information and information processing that are being commoditized has expanded the domains of our lives that lie within the economy. This insight might also be usefully incorporated into the network economics approach as a reminder of the human values that must also be incorporated and incorporatable into any decision- making calculus. Specific details from studies of gift economies and other alternative approaches to economic organization might also be usefully taken up by network economists as metaphoric models worth exploring for their utility in understanding the network environment.

Of work outside the domain of economics, work in self-organizing systems might usefully be used to explore successes in the network environment since we now newly have the calculating tools (mathematical theories plus computing capability) to explore the complexities of the network environment and at least some of the non-linear processes that unfold in the network environment. Explorations in political science, sociology, and communication of the nature of community, the nation-state, citizenship, and the public sphere in this environment might also usefully expand the conceptual range of network economists.

Roberto Scazzieri (1992) is an economist who theoretically explores the phenomena and processes that others talk about based on empirical works. Scazzieri envisions a productive environment comprised of virtual and actual materials, and of virtual and actual processes (virtual in this sense referring to imaginable but not yet existing). Production chains are comprised of networks of elementary production processes that may lie within one organization or be distributed among a number of networked organizations. "Scale" refers not to size of an organization or the number of multiples of its products manufactured, but to the number of elementary production processes involved. Innovation is spurred by efforts of different elements of an organization or network of organizations to bring elementary production processes in line with each other.

Scazzieri's insights provide a useful way of using the model of an information production chain to map the information and communication elements of the network economy. This approach should prove useful to those who seek to organize information systems for an organization or organizations, to those whose job it is to analyze the economy, and to those organizations seeking to understand their own particular niche within the global information economy as a basis for further strategic planning.

Unbundling Scholarly Publishing

Scholarly publishing has historically bound together several stages of the information production chain with an identification shaped by its material form -- the book, the journal. With the central role of scholarly publishing in the sociology and history of knowledge, relationships of the community with information processes and materials are particularly important. With the notion of the information production chain, however, we can unbundle scholarly publishing into processes of information creation, processing (both cognitive and material), distribution, use, and seeking. With Scazzieri's insights into the nature of scale, we can see that technological change has shifted the scale of organizations successful in information processing. For publishing that may mean organizing the scale of efforts at each stage of the chain differently as appropriate.

Scholarly publishers are involved in information creation at the macro- social level, in two ways at the communal level, and at the individual level. At the most macro level, scholarly publishers play a significant role in shaping the intellectual climate and manifesting its shifts. The general intellectual climate plays a role in shaping both of the communities in which scholarly publishers are involved -- the scholarly communities organized around research specialties and dispersed across space and institutions, and the university communities with which many are institutionally involved.

Scholarly publishers provide a significant venue for discussion within the scholarly community, often providing first publication of significant research results as well. For universities, scholarly publishers provide among their most important public faces, as universities become identified with the books and authors published by their publishing houses as well as with those on their own faculties. At the individual level, scholarly publishers encourage the creation of information by individual scholars through the currying and encouragement of particular authors and lines of work.

While the first role of scholarly publishers regarding information creation at the macro-social level remains, to some degree, the general credence and importance of the content of work published by scholarly publishing houses appears to be declining relative to other voices increasingly dominant in the public sphere, largely those provided by the mass media and popular culture. As we move further away from print culture and into a situation in which an ever-larger percentage of people will have spent significant portions of their socialization period being shaped cognitively by broadcast rather than print -- and we know that people cognitively process information differently depending on which is their primary medium for information acquisition. Increasingly, the value of information published by scholarly publishing houses may be their utility in decision-making of some kind.

Another cognitive shift is to be expected in those whose primary information source is the net, which increasingly provides additional competitors to scholarly publishers for dominance in shaping the cultural milieu. The relative lack of gate-keepers -- once one is on the net -- is going far in offering alternative voices channels for their own information flow to the public. One of the more popular types of conversations, for example, is e-mail with people undergoing attack in time of war (eg, the Gulf War, the wars in the former Yugoslavia, etc.), surely a voice not heard during a war in the past. Credible individual or institutional presences in the net stimulate in their audiences the sense not that these were voices that were previously often largely unheard, but that the net had permitted boundary- spanning that had resulted in acquaintance with new but important people and institutions. The general problem of verifying identity and the accuracy and reliability of information received through the net may increasingly affect the relative credibility of net voices as the curve of sophistication move across the population and time passes (so that experience accrues).

From the perspective of an "enriched" network economics, the scholarly publishing industry can be unbundled into several different types of information creation, processing, and distribution processes. Historically we have thought about scholarly publishing as resulting in the making of books, and journal activities as the print venue for the scholarly conversation that leads to books. The different types of activities involved in the ultimate production of books and journals, however, can be distinguished for separate treatment as scholarly publishers reposition themselves within the network economy.

Information Creation

Scholarly publishers are involved with the creation of information in several ways. In their relationship with universities, scholarly publishers provide the print voice and therefore support for institutions devoted to the creation of information through research. The publication of research journals sustains the conversation through which information is shared that stimulates further information creation and provides the venue through which new information is often first introduced. Individual editors encourage the development of specific information through their currying of potential authors and the encouragement of a particular line of work through the mechanism of the book contract.

Intellectual property rights had been held largely by publishers, but in relationships in which ties between both publishers and universities and scholars and universities were more secure than they are now. On the publishing side, most universities have been abandoning the economic support that had been provided to assist the scholarly presses, now asked to be economically self-sufficient. On the scholars' side, too, it had historically been acceptable to yield copyright to the presses as one part of the exchange for the security provided by tenure. As tenure goes, scholars, too, will have greater reason to struggle to retain their own copyrights as part of their general marketability and as sources of revenue.

One factor that is contributing to the rise, therefore, of intellectual property rights in salience on the policy agenda is the multiplication and intensification of battles over ownership of rights of intellectual property that is group produced in any way. Scholarly presses are urged to be participants in the debate over intellectual property rights, defending in particular the range of types of authorial processes and entities which need to be treated differentially, and the need of society to encourage the production of academic work as a public good. We need to remember the distinction between authorial rights and property rights (for often it is the former and not the latter that is the matter of true concern), what network economics tells us is increasingly the gain in value of intellectual property rights when shared, and the difference between receiving sufficient recompense and receiving all of it.

Cognitive Processing

Scholarly publishers are involved in information processing both at its cognitive levels, as information is shared among researchers within a field (through the public discussion space of scholarly journals and book lists), and physically (as that conversation is produced in the physical medium of a periodical and ultimately in book form).

Scholarly journals continue to provide venues for scholarly discussion that are distinguished from others by being linked in terms of their authority to universities. The number of scholarly journals, however, is exploding, accurately reflecting the loss of a consensually dominant perspective in many fields, the birth of new fields, and the particular yields of interdisciplinary work.

It was the scholarly authority of universities that enabled them to produce and reproduce communities through journals, conferences, mail and phone communications, and travel; it is even easier logistically and economically to participate in these communal activities through the net. Both books and journals are being published in electronic as well as print form today; increasingly, some are being published only electronically.

We can see either of these moves -- the multiplication of journals and their move to electronic form -- as reducing the economic value of journal activity. This kind of trend might be projected from the history of the impact of the photocopy on electronic journals; far more journal articles are now read in photocopy form than in the original. These publications retain their economic value when one looks to long-run effects and externalities, however. Ownership and protection of intellectual property will continue to play a role here.

Material Processing

Numerous new journals are being launched through the net. Net distribution of course saves print production and distribution costs. It has the disadvantage of not being able to control the aesthetics of the ultimate product, dependent on the receivers' screens and print equipment and choices. The problem of how to receive payment safely for all involved is not yet solved, though a number of institutional solutions providing varying degrees of privacy are under development. In the net, however, the ability of receivers to further distribute a text without further recompense to the publisher is easier than in any other medium. Thus if a publisher is attempting to recoup the costs of producing the journal -- and under a peer- reviewed system these are still considerable -- sales to readers in cyberspace will most likely be neither reliable nor sufficient.

If one shifts focus, however, to the providing of a public venue for attended scholarly discussion and away from specific journal article products of that discussion, one can understand journal production as a fundamental way of building long-term dependent relationships upon the publishing institution as an information source as well as a venue. In these terms, publishing scholarly journals through the net might move from being considered a potential profit center and towards more long-term investment, including but going beyond public relations and advertising functions for the publishing institution.

Some information is "transient," only passing in interest but necessary in its detail, while other information is more permanent in its interest or importance. In many fields scholarly journals provide the place for conversation along the way that brings work to an enrichment and maturity that it finally reaches book publication form. For those fields, distributing journals electronically may be more appropriate than asking for the increasingly large expenditure of resources required for everyone to access the material in printed form. The problem with this move, however, may also be one with socio-economic consequences, for there are those who will not have access electronically to those scholarly journals and may therefore be excluded from certain disciplines.

Scholarly publishers may want to produce fewer books. This may require distinguishing between their functions as participants in the personnel process of universities via the centrality of scholarly publishing for tenure and promotion from their functions as book publishers. It may be that service as a book review editor has jaded this author's perspective, but generally each theoretical or conceptual argument is put forward at least half a dozen times with varying degrees of originality, timeliness, intellectual aggressiveness, and utility. Publishing fewer books in each area would help the sales of each while causing the most damage in the domain of tenure and promotion -- here again scholarly publishers may want to address this type of question in joint conversation with universities. This would have the simultaneous effect of encouraging scholars to take on the role of public intellectual, since success in speaking intelligently and usefully to audiences larger than those of academia will increase sales and the appeal of such authors to publishing houses.

Information Distribution

The net is of course increasingly providing competition in the delivery of text. Because the replication and distribution costs are almost nil once sending and receiving organizations are linked into the net, this offers quite a challenge to scholarly publishers who must continue to charge for their information products. It is suggested that scholarly publishers use the net to their economic advantage in the distribution of journals, and for its advertising advantage with books (some publishers are putting up first chapters on the net to entice readers....).

Information Storage

In their roles as information storage media, the aesthetics and print qualities of the book are not yet being touched by the net. For this reason, too, scholarly publishers may want to continue to attend to the quality of the books they publish as books, as material objects with beauty capable of being treasured.

Verification of the reliability of a text to be accurately what it claims to be and error-free will become an ever-increasingly important element of the net as a storage environment, however, as text are both deliberately corrupted or altered and decay materially over time (electronic media decay far more quickly than does even poor paper).

Information Use

It is one of the advantages of the products of scholarly publishing that they are often consumed in the course of being socialized into what to read. Undergraduate and graduate students significant readerships. Thom McCain of Ohio State has suggested that universities could make provision of course materials to students over the net an additional profit center, with cost savings on the production and distribution end, and the ability to charge for the materials along with fee collection for class credits.

The indexing materials discussed below are also significant in preparing readers to approach information in certain ways. There is concern among the arts community, for example, that search tools will be monovocal in their approach and thus curtail our exposure to alternative modes of thinking. This concern gets expressed as a desire that "a thousand flowers bloom" in the design of net search engines.

The nature of the audience for scholarly material is changing. We can expect the number of scholars within universities to go down as universities continue to down-size and to move teaching into electronic environments that require fewer professors. At the same time, ever-more significant realms of decision-making are moving from the public to the private sector, making corporate decision-making of great interest from a policy perspective. These two factors together suggest again the model of the public intellectual, the scholar who is speaking to the community at large rather than only to a few specialists.

Information Seeking

One of the most important functions filled by scholarly publishers is the assistance they provide in information seeking. Readers know that scholarly publishers publish work that has been peer reviewed and edited with varying degrees of care. They are to some degree ranked by intellectual status relative to the universities with which they are associated, editorial vision in particular areas of strength, sustained participation in the development of specific fields -- and/or, as MIT Press and others are finding out -- the beauty of the books as books. As specific lines of books become of interest, their domain of references too becomes a certified path of intellectual exploration.

This function continues to be of importance in the net environment -- perhaps more than ever, as search engines of varying degrees of intelligence have already become the most sought-after product in cyberspace, and it is already said that if you don't know where you're going with Mosaic, you're not likely to get there. Scholarly publishers may want to distinguish this particular function and enhance their role in this domain in the network economy. This might mean developing software divisions that publish search programs specific to particular fields or annotated bibliographies or indexes as well as the more easily achieved and familiar advertising through the net. Recently a decades-old shoestring small press publisher's home page was listed on the Netscape "what's new" home page, with the possibility of completely changing this publisher's economic conditions. Small bookstores were early among the small businesses to find themselves becoming more competitive commercially through net exposure.

It is important that the quality of scholarly work published remain high in order to support what we might call the certification element of the activities of scholarly publishers -- the trust they generate in the scholarly quality and importance of any work published under their name, including their responsibility for running a peer review process and various stages of editorial work.

Conclusions

If we understand the information economy through the perspective of "enriched" network economics -- an approach that starts on the far, rather than the near, side of a Kuhnian paradigm change regarding the way in which we understand our economic activity -- a particular niche for scholarly publishing stands out. The field might be characterized as specializing in four things:

- providing a venue for scholarly conversation

- providing certain types of search tools

- providing certification of the level and quality of information processing (a statement, in essence, of scale)

- providing accessible permanent storage for the best work created by scholars (the book)

Scale, then, may be the key to the niche of scholarly publishing houses, which publish only content that has been processed multiple times. In Scazzieri's terms, scholarly publishing is large-scale, meaning it involves a number of different elementary processes. Making the most out of this fact is what will provide the key to economic success in any of the several activities involved in scholarly publishing once unbundled in terms of the stages of the information production chains. In some cases that means providing superb search tools; in others, facilitating a conversation; and in yet others, publishing a beautiful as well as important book.

The insights of network economics into the value of coordination and of shared intellectual property rights also is useful as we consider the role of scholarly publishers within the public sphere, the centrality of such publishers to the production and reproduction of community. Precisely because long-term commitments to publishers and scholars, along with other supporting tissue, is being cut away, scholarly publishers need to be self-aware and proactive in thinking through the moral, cultural, social, and political obligations they face while simultaneously solving economic problems.

We need to remember that this is also a time of turbulence -- as scholarly publishers and others in the information industries dance to determine their niches, connections, and bounds in the emerging information economy, each of these activities and our conceptualizations of them themselves feed back into the policy process and environment. We know from self-organizing systems theory that being aware of being in such a period enhances the possibility of successfully surviving it; and this, too, I commend to scholarly publishers. The self-reflexivity of the role should encourage us to aim high. Scholarly publishers should all be keenly aware of their pivotal roles within the sociology of knowledge, and the relationship between the sociology of knowledge and what happens in the rest of society. To guiding rules, then, might be to aim high, and to be willing to experiment.

References

Antonelli, C. (Ed.). (1992). *The Economics of Information Networks.* Amsterdam: North-Holland.

Babe, R. E. (Ed.). (1994). *Information and Communication in Economics.* Amsterdam: Kluwer Academic Publishers.

Bell, D. (1976). *The Coming of Post-Industrial Society: A Venture in Social Forecasting.* New York: Basic Books.

Braman, S. (In press). "Alternative Approaches to the Economics of Information," in I. Goddens (Ed.), *Advances in Librarianship*, 30.

Braman, S. (1993). "Harmonization of Systems: The Third Stage of the Information Society," *Journal of Communication*, 43(3), pp. 133-140.

Braman, S. (1990). "The Unique Characteristics of Information Policy and Their US Consequences," n V. Blake & R. Tjoumas (Eds.), *Information Literacies for the Twenty-First Century*, pp. 47-77. Boston: G. K. Hall.

Braman, S. (1989). "Defining Information: An Approach for Policy-Makers," *Telecommunications Policy*, 13(3), pp. 233-42.

Grabher, G. (Ed.). (1993). *The Embedded Firm: On the Socioeconomics of Industrial Networks.* New York: Routledge, Chapman and Hall.

Hyde, L. (1983). *The Gift: Imagination and the Erotic Life of Property.* New York: Vintage Books. Ito, Y. (1991)?.

Machlup, F. (1980). *Knowledge, its Creation, Distribution, and Economic Significance.* Princeton, NJ: Princeton University Press.

Mattelart, A. & Cesta, Y. S. (1985). *Technology, Culture and Communication: A Report to the French Minister of Research & Industry*, trans. D. Buxton. Amsterdam: North-Holland.

McLuhan, M. (1964/94). *Understanding Media: The Extensions of Man*. Cambridge, MA: MIT Press.

Mosco, V. (1989). *The Pay-Per Society: Computers and Communication in the Information Age*. Norwood, NJ: Ablex.

Porat, M. U. (1977). *The Information Economy*. Washington, DC: US Department of Commerce.

Scazzieri, R. (1993). *A Theory of Production*. Oxford: Clarendon.

Schiller, H. I. (1976). *Communication and Cultural Domination*. White Plains, NY: International Arts and Science Press.

Swann, P. (Ed.). (1993). *New Technologies and the Firm: Innovation and Competition*. New York: Routledge.

Sandra Braman
Institute of Communications Research
University of Illinois
braman@vmd.cso.uiuc.edu

Pricing Electronic Products

Colin Day
University of Michigan Press

The Role Prices Should Pay

In thinking about the pricing of electronic publications, we are facing very difficult questions in a context of remarkable unclarity. Even the product to be sold is not easily defined.

In this paper, I will consider the role that prices should play, then focus on the central reason why pricing electronic publications is difficult, look at some of the general strategies that are available in this kind of situation, and then review three examples of electronic publication pricing that demonstrate desirable features. I will also pay some attention to the role that libraries play in the solution of this pricing problem.

The first question then is what do we want the price of an electronic publication to do? Frequently the issue of pricing is discussed in the context of cost recovery. This is, in some ways, not a bad starting point as it certainly defines a minimum requirement -- without cost recovery from some source or another there are not going to be any electronic publications.

But should we be content with prices that recover costs? Indeed, is that even a meaningful standard?

Cost Recovery?

It does assume that costs are well-defined and easily agreed upon. It implies that some auditor could examine a publishing operation and easily determine exactly what each publication costs. The awkward fact is that there is no precise answer to that question. Every publisher, every information supplier, produces many products. At the same time, many of the expenses of those organizations are not directly related to any one product. Of an average publisher's costs something like 60% fall into this category. Those costs can only be ascribed to individual products according to some conventional but basically arbitrary rule.

Even if we somehow surmount that obstacle and all agree on a suitable allocation of costs to individual electronic products, we may still have disagreements about which costs are to be included in the total to be recovered.

In particular we need to think about the cost of capital. Running a business whether profit or non-profit requires capital. This is because products are manufactured at one time, delivered at another and paid for at yet another. Suppliers and staff have to be paid before customers pay their bills. That requires that someone lend money to bridge that financing gap. Publishers also buy equipment, much more now than they used to, and probably even more in the future, that needs to be paid for on purchase, but it lasts many years giving up its value and repaying the initial outlay over its life time. The publisher needs to borrow money to finance that investment.

Is the interest that publishers pay to the lenders a cost? Something that the moral auditors will allow to be recovered from our customers? Does a cost recovery price include that cost?

I am not trying to make a big point about the cost of capital, but I am trying to point out by that example that the principle that prices should be based on cost recovery is not simple, unambiguous, or necessarily uncontroversial.

Even with resolution of the definitional problems, is cost recovery an appropriate basis for setting prices? Although I work in a non-profit and very much believe in the non-profit approach, I worry about the lack of incentives that cost recovery implies, incentives to innovate, to grow and to improve products. Our society primarily allocates resources according to profitability. By excluding profits from the publishing of academic work, are we not risking slower innovation and slower growth and a persistent of shortage of resources? After all, would we have fast processors, and all the other technology which makes these discussions worth having, if Intel, for example, were operating on a cost recovery only basis? I am afraid the answer is very obvious. The organizations who make profits attract extra resources, money to invest and grow.

Just as the price plays a significant role in generating investment and thus supply, so more obviously it plays a role in determining demand. Of course a high price deters some buyers and a low price attracts more buyers. Is then a low price always better? There is a limit.

With each cut in the price, someone extra decides to buy the good. Who is the new buyer? It is someone who did not buy at the previous higher price because they did not think the good worth that price to them. Now their valuation of the good is higher than the new price and therefore the good is worth buying.

So as we reduce the price we bring in buyers who place a lower and lower value on the good. How far should we go in making the good attractive to them? It makes no sense to make it available to people who place a value on it which is less than the value of the labor and materials used in making the good. We could use the labor and materials in better ways making other products. In other words the price should not be reduced to below the cost of producing the good.

It sounds as though we are back to pricing for cost recovery. Not quite. Because when we think more precisely about the cost that sets a floor on the price, we see that it is not the average cost of making the good, but the cost of making the last example of the good. It rarely costs the same to make every example of a good, the cost sometimes increases as we make more and frequently decreases as we make more. When we are wondering whether to cut the price one more step and attract some more buyers, the question is whether those extra buyers will put a value on the good higher than the costs of making the examples of the good for them. I will refer to this cost as the incremental cost.

Principles and Conundrums

So we should lower price and expand output until the price is just equal to the incremental cost of making the last example.

This is a principle that we should strive towards as we think about the pricing of information goods. It is also a principle that immediately leads us into another conundrum. The nature of the costs of providing information goods means that such a price based on incremental costs will not provide the manufacturer with enough income to cover his total costs. By now this is a familiar result to most people so I will just sketch the argument.

Simply, there are substantial costs in making the first copy of a publication and very low costs in making subsequent copies. A price that is close to the incremental cost of making another copy will not make any contribution to the first copy costs that have been expended. We are therefore faced with a very interesting problem: how to combine two conflicting objectives. The first is to make the publication available at a price close to incremental cost and thus provide an incentive for everyone to buy it who places a value on it that is greater than the value of the resources used in making it. And the second is to ensure enough income to the manufacturer to give him or her the incentive to incur the first copy costs and make the publication possible.

While this has always been a challenge in the paper world, the challenge is dramatically enhanced in the digital world. First copy costs can be much higher as we embed audio and visual materials and build elaborate links within the document. While the cost of additional copies is lower or even zero given the ease of electronic copying.

The general form of this problem is a common one. A classic case much studied by economists is electricity supply where the power stations and distribution network involve an enormous expense but once the customer has received the first unit of electricity subsequent ones can be supplied at very low cost. A conventional approach to this problem -- known as a two-part tariff -- is to charge the customer a high price for the first few units and a decreasing charge per unit as he or she buys more. Decisions about discretionary uses are thus made on the basis of a price close to the low incremental production cost. For this solution to work, each consumer must buy multiple units of the product and each consumer must be identifiable to the supplier and maintain a relationship with the supplier.

Strategies

Thinking now about those two characteristics in the context of publishing, it would seem that the electronic book is not going to lend itself to two-part tariff pricing as customers usually buy only one copy of each book and there is no continuing relationship between publisher and customer. Likewise for the paper journal, the subscriber buys one subscription. But the journal in electronic form does perhaps permit such an approach. The subscriber would pay an access fee at the beginning of the year to cover the publisher's first copy costs and then a much lower charge for every article selected and delivered.

The approach I have just suggested is an example of what is also called country club pricing. You pay a substantial fee for membership, but then pay the incremental cost for each use of any of the facilities.

The other standard strategy to solve the general economic problem is known as price discrimination. You will recall in my explanation of the basic problem that I presumed some customers valued the good more highly than others. If the high valuation customers could be segmented from the low valuation customers, a higher price could be charged to the former than to the latter. The lower price would be close to incremental cost while the high price would permit first copy costs to be recovered.

An example of this in publishing is the delayed paperback. First, the high priced hardcover is published for those with a strong and urgent need for the book. Then when the high valuation customers have bought and the first copy costs have been recovered, the paperback is brought out with a price that is close to the incremental production cost.

While I am aware of no electronic publications overtly using timing to separate high valuation from lower valuation customers, I do notice that some of the magazines that claim to be also available on the Internet in fact seem to delay making the latter version available. Thus those who pay a non-zero price get the news and information earlier than those who seek it at zero price.

The essential element of such pricing schemes is a method for segmenting the customers into valuation groups -- there could be more than two. Selling the same product at more than one price is not going to work unless there is a way of determining which customers get to pay which price. This calls for creative thinking. By the way, under the Robinson-Patman Act there does have to be some cost justification for such price differentials and any especially ingenious scheme would need to be considered in the light of that act.

Another way to segment customers is to bundle the good with another good or service. If the added item is generally wanted by the high valuation customers but not by the low valuation customers, then the combined package can be priced so as to recover not only the cost of the bundled item but also some of the first copy costs of the basic item. A possibility here for a software manufacturer would be to sell the complete package with sophisticated help menus for one high price and the bare software for a lower price. The business user for whom time is money will want the help; the individual user may be more willing to seek a solution by trial and error Or one could envision selling a data resource of some kind and bundling with it access to an online service providing frequent updates. A document with hypertextual add-ons might be sold for one price with access to the add-ons and another lower price without. Bundling is definitely a route to explore in endeavoring to solve the problem of recovering first copy costs.

So far I have carefully eschewed discussion of the library in all this. We could think of the library as just another customer for a publication. Because they serve many users, they will in general be customers who place a higher valuation on a publication. So libraries are a distinguishable category of high valuation customer. Thus we see the logic for, and also the practicability of, the common practice of charging libraries a subscription price for a journal that contributes to first copy costs while the individual subscription rate is closer to incremental cost. We can also consider libraries as customers who put a premium on the durability of the objects they buy. Thus we see that bundling a durable binding with the book is another way of charging that category of higher valuation user a price that contributes to first copy cost recovery.

But libraries can be thought of in quite another way, not as straightforward customers but as intermediaries in the transaction between originator and final reader. To recover first copy costs, the publisher has in many circumstances to price far above incremental costs. The various devices I have been discussing will not always be applicable. So there will be cases where many potential users will find the price of the information good above their valuation of it. They will be deprived of its benefit even though their valuation is higher than the incremental cost of making the good for them. The library steps in. It pays the publisher's full cost recovery price and then makes the book or journal available at zero price. Thus solving, indeed over-solving, the pricing problem[1].

Some Pricing Examples

Although there is more to say about libraries on this topic, I want now to look at some examples of actual pricing schemes for electronic publications and then return to libraries and related topics at the end.

The first scheme I want to present is the Johns Hopkins University Press approach to pricing journals included in Project Muse. The admirable feature of their work is the clear analysis of costs. They have carefully distinguished between those costs that are common to both print and electronic forms, those specific to the paper form and those specific to the electronic form. This is an essential step on the way to any well-thought out pricing scheme for a product being published in more than one form. In the Project Muse case, taking the paper subscription as $100, it is estimated that $60 of that is for items that are medium independent and $40 are for costs specific to the paper edition. By contrast for the electronic edition, the specific costs are down by about one quarter to $30, so the electronic edition price is $90. Where a customer wishes to have both paper and electronic editions, the combined price includes the base price once, and the specific costs of each edition. The overall figure is $130. While this distinguishes between the common costs and the medium-specific costs in an attractively clear way, it does not fully distinguish between first copy and incremental costs and some first copy costs are in the medium-specific figures.

Although not presented as an explicit two-part tariff structure, the pricing for MIT Press' *Chicago Journal of Theoretical Computer Science* actually does fit this scheme. The journal is distributed electronically and so most of the costs are first copy costs. The basic price is an institutional one of $125 explicitly designed to cover the first copy costs. Within a subscribing institution, access and printing out individual articles is permitted without further charge. So for the individual user the price is equal to the incremental cost of zero for another electronic copy. There is also an individual subscription rate of $30. As any customer involves some overhead and transaction costs, a non-zero price is appropriate.

The third example is the new pricing structure for *Mathematical Reviews*. This is to my mind the best example as it makes very clear to the customer the difference between the first copy costs and the incremental costs. The subscribing institution pays a $3595 data access fee which pays for building and maintaining the database from which all *Mathematical Reviews* products are derived. (I quote from their publicity.) Then any subscriber pays a product delivery fee which is the incremental cost for the particular product, e.g. an annual $315 for the paper form or $520 for the CD version. This is, by the way, a huge journal. What I think distinguishes the *Mathematical Reviews* scheme is the very clear explanation of the underlying logic -- the distinction between first copy and incremental costs, and the distinction between incremental costs for different delivery modes. I incline to believing that as we launch electronic products such clarity in presenting the logic of what we are doing is very important.

A merit common to all three cases that I have described is simplicity. As we struggle with the pricing problem it will be tempting, at least to people like me, to construct complex structures. That temptation has to be resisted both to ensure the prices are just workable for seller and buyer, but also so that the customer can understand the logic and see that the schemes have integrity.

That principle of simplicity also bears on a much more fundamental problem. What is the product? I have carefully and deliberately skirted that awkward issue but it cannot be entirely avoided. Are we selling a file that is transferred to the customer, or are we selling access to that file? Is access charged by time or by the access? The more I try to resolve this type of question the more difficult it all seems to become. Despite it meeting none of the standards I have established in this paper, I find myself thinking that Ted Nelson's idea of a price label on every digital packet and a charge for every movement across the network may be the only practical solution.

Roles, Benefits, and Incentives

But I want to get back to the question of the library and its role as the agent who makes the publication available at zero price. This is possible because the library is subsidized rather than being expected to recover its costs from its users. In general, one possible route to a solution of the first copy cost problem is through subsidies. This is being argued vigorously for academic works by Steven Harnad in his "subversive proposal." For most of us who deal with university budgets regularly, the assumption that we should plan on extra subsidies seems rather hopeful. Of course if the actual publication's prices decline to or close to zero then perhaps the requisite subsidies could be liberated from library budgets.

Apart from all the obvious naivete of such a remark, there is actually a fundamental problem. Universities and communities support their libraries because the benefits are concentrated locally. But subsidies to a publisher bring benefits which are diffused widely at least nationally and often globally. So why, we can hear a Provost asking, should her university spend substantial amounts of scarce resources to make publications available at zero or low price throughout the world? This is not, I think a minor debating point, but a very serious problem for a rational reappraisal of the system and the funding of a new system for disseminating scholarly work.

The answer to the provost's doubts might well be based on the local benefits of providing for the publication needs of the local faculty. Then the funds that drive scholarly publishing are allocated according to the needs of the author. Is this desirable? I think not and that brings me back full circle to the incentive effect of the pricing system.

As we consider pricing in the electronic environment, I believe that we need to maintain some dependence by the producer on demand from the final user. At present in much of scholarly publishing, and in university presses in particular, we have a very healthy balance between the incentives of the market place -- choosing the publications that will sell, and the incentives of the academy -- choosing publications of intrinsic importance. A complete dependence on subsidies eliminates the influence of demand. And, if those subsidies are directed to support the publication of local authors, we will also see a rapid slackening of the standards of scholarly importance.

It all comes down to incentives. As we think about pricing particular products or as we think about the general shape of pricing structures for electronic products, the crucial issue is one of incentives. We need incentives that on the supply side encourage innovation and investment, and that encourage a balance of emphasis between intrinsic academic quality and the needs and interests of the readers. And on the demand side we need to create pricing systems that make the material being disseminated available to all who would find it valuable. While I think the examples I have cited are good and set patterns that could well be followed, I see considerable opportunities for the ingenious to devise new systems that work more effectively to meet both the demand and supply side objectives.

---

[1] I owe this insight to Scott Bennett.

Colin Day, Director
University of Michigan Press
colinday@umich.edu

Innovations in Cost Recovery

Andrea Keyhani
OCLC Electronic Publishing

Introduction

The cost of producing an online journal is not insignificant and can be prohibitive for publishers operating on a tight budget. At the same time, publishers, especially in the STM area, are feeling particularly threatened by forces outside of their control, such as informal preprint bulletin boards and start-up electronic journals, offered at little or no charge. The pressure to counteract this groundswell that threatens to eliminate traditional journal publishing is leading many publishers to investigate electronic publishing opportunities.

Analyses of electronic publishing, as described in the current literature, indicate that simply producing the journal in electronic form is not enough to guarantee success. Electronic versions that do not offer at least the same features as traditional paper, such as illustrations and equations, are doomed to failure in the long run. Indeed, successful electronic journals must go beyond the paper features before they are perceived as acceptable substitutes by the users. However, truly innovative electronic products that offer value-added features are not inexpensive.

Publishers have a choice of being in the first wave of innovators (and paying a substantial price) or waiting until the prices drop; the latter option puts the publishers at risk of losing their subscribers as new avenues for information distribution come into being. The reality is that many publishers continue to lose subscriptions and don't have the option of waiting. So how do they pay for the investment?

There are several areas that can be targeted, but all require a departure from the traditional ways of thinking and operating. The areas are:

Production
Pricing
New products
Advertising

I. **Production**

First copy costs -- costs for assembling and preparing the content -- account for anywhere between 50-80% of the total cost of producing a printed journal. Those costs will remain in place for an electronic journal, with some savings realized through computerized publications systems, as described below.

As publishers contemplate creating electronic versions of their print publications, they must understand that to fully realize savings in the long-term, the production process itself must be modified to incorporate the preparation of electronic texts. The degree to which a publisher foresees the use of the electronic medium will help guide that modification. To simply create a second production system whose sole use is the conversion of data from typeset copy to electronic format is both costly and labor intensive. The publication process can be streamlined so that the output derived from producing a journal can be used in a wide variety of ways (CD-ROM, electronic journals, paper, etc.). The initial expense incurred can thus be spread over a wide variety of potential new products and services, that should more than adequately offset the up front production changes.

SGML/HTML

To take greatest advantage of the new medium, the publisher should consider

SGML encoding, which enables elaborate full text retrieval and hypertext links, among other features. SGML requires some initial intellectual work in devising the Document Type Definition (DTD) that will accommodate the journal and the level of retrieval and hypertext linking, plus some changes in how documents are processed. However, with the introduction of the ISO 12083 standard DTD, that process should be streamlined considerably. As more and more publishers adopt the standard, the cost involved in tagging articles will also be reduced.

Who should do the SGML tagging (encoding)? As printers and typesetters look at a future where electronic publishing may someday surpass print publishing, they realize that it is to their advantage to offer SGML tagging to remain competitive. New tools are continually being created to automate that process to a large degree, reducing the tagging cost and also making it easier for publishers to consider doing the document creation and tagging themselves.

There are many advantages of SGML that help to justify the initial and ongoing expense. SGML establishes a standard means of identifying and tagging parts of an electronic manuscript, such as the title, author, and abstract (see Fig. 1). With the proper retrieval system, SGML enables users to search with precision for information in specific parts of the manuscript and to navigate easily through the manuscript to the exact information they are looking for. SGML provides a logical way to represent special characters, symbols, and tabular material, using only the ASCII character set. Since it is concerned with the content rather than the page layout, the information can be processed on any hardware or software system. Because it is device-independent, SGML can be used on multiple platforms (CD-ROM, online, Macintosh, IBM, etc.) and new technology yet to be developed. In short, SGML is insurance for the future.

HTML

With the emergence of the World Wide Web (WWW) and a multitude of browsers (such as Mosaic), many publishers have considered experimenting with HTML and the WWW before committing to SGML completely. HTML is a subset of SGML with a limited tagset, which allows users to learn the basics and produce very quickly. The disadvantages, however, are numerous:

(1) Having a limited tagset offers only a few ways to mark up data, and even fewer ways to search it;

(2) Since each browser displays HTML documents differently and many allow the end-user to manipulate fonts, publishers have very little control over the look and feel of their journals;

(3) Since the Internet is the only way to access WWW servers, readers without Internet connections cannot access those servers; and

(4) HTML has a limited number of characters and special symbols; those not handled within HTML must be rendered as images and manually typeset into HTML documents, a very time consuming process.

(Figure 1 shows SGML & HTML examples)

Scanned pages

While SGML can be considered the ultimate tool, it can be particularly costly for legacy material that is not in electronic form. If a publisher wishes to create an online version of the journal and feels it necessary to have several years of older material that is not in machine-readable form, scanning pages is a more affordable, though somewhat less desirable, option. The Elsevier TULIP project is an example of the use of scanned pages, coupled with ASCII files containing the text of those pages, produced using Optical Character Recognition. The user can search the ASCII text and view the retrieved article as scanned pages. There are several disadvantages for using such a system: first, the OCR system is not perfect and can create inaccurate translations of the data; second, the precision searching

Figure 1. SGML Document Tagging and Display Text

UK Amniotomy Group. Comparing routine versus delayed anmiotomy in spontaneous first labor at term: a multicenter randomized trial. Online J Curr Clin Trials [serial online] 1994 April 1;3 (Doc No 122):[4148 words; 40 paragraphs] 28 figures; 7 tables.

COMPARING ROUTINE VERSUS DELAYED AMNIOTOMY IN SPONTANEOUS FIRST LABOR AT TERM

A MULTICENTER RANDOMIZED TRIAL

UK Amniotomy Group

For the name of the reporting author, see paragraph number 40. For a listing of the members of the UK Amniotomy Group, see paragraph number 37.

Institute of Epidemiology and Health Service Research, University of Leeds, 34 Hyde Terrace, Leeds, LS2 9LN United Kingdom.

Document Classification: Parallel publication: The abridged version of this paper appeared as follows: UK amniotomy group. A multicentre randomised trial of amniotomy in spontaneous first labour at term. Br J Obstet Gynaecol 1994 Apr;101:307-9.

Keywords: amniotomy on nulliparae, pethidine, oxytocin, randomized trial, routine amniotomy effects

Date of Publication: 19940401

HTML Equivalent

File Edit Search Help

```
<article><front><cite>UK Amniotomy Group. Comparing routine versus delayed
anmiotomy in spontaneous first labor at term: a multicenter randomized
trial. Online J Curr Clin Trials [serial online] 1994 April 1;<voln>3</voln>
(Doc No <docn>122</docn>):[4148 words; 40 paragraphs] 28 figures; 7
tables.</cite>
<ti>COMPARING ROUTINE VERSUS DELAYED AMNIOTOMY IN SPONTANEOUS FIRST LABOR AT
TERM</ti>
<sbt>A MULTICENTER RANDOMIZED TRIAL</sbt>
<aublk><cau>UK Amniotomy Group</cau> <aff>For the name of the reporting
author, see paragraph number 40.  For a listing of the members of the UK
Amniotomy Group, see paragraph number 37.  Institute of Epidemiology and
Health Service Research, University of Leeds, 34 Hyde Terrace, Leeds, LS2
9LN United Kingdom.</aff> </aublk>
<class>Parallel publication: The abridged version of this paper appeared as
follows: UK amniotomy group. A multicentre randomised trial of amniotomy in
spontaneous first labour at term. Br J Obstet Gynaecol 1994
Apr;101:307-9.</class>
<keyword><phrase>amniotomy on nulliparae</phrase>,
<phrase>pethidine</phrase>, <phrase>oxytocin</phrase>, <phrase>randomized
trial</phrase>, <phrase>routine amniotomy
effects</phrase><dcode>RRE</dcode></keyword>
<pubdate>19940401</pubdate> </front>
<abstract> <st>ABSTRACT</st>
<p><pid>1</pid> <b>Objective:</b> To measure the effect of a policy of
routine amniotomy on nulliparous labor.</p>
```

described with SGML is not possible, unless SGML tags are added to the ASCII data; and third, even though compression is used, the 43 Material Sciences journals provided by Elsevier Scientific Publications produce over 10 gigabytes of data per year.[1] Retrieval systems would add to that amount as part of the indexing process.

At OCLC, we hedged our bets by expanding the graphical user interface we developed to accommodate scanned pages (see Figure 2). OCLC developed a retrieval system for Virginia Tech, one of the TULIP participants. This development now enables us to offer both SGML and scanned pages options to publishers who wish to use the OCLC Electronic Journals Online system. It is possible, for example, to produce scanned pages for backfile material, and then move forward with SGML data, using the same interface.

Electronic editing and production systems. As mentioned above, most first copy costs cannot be eliminated. However, new systems are being created to help publishers automate and streamline their production systems. The STEPS (System of Total Electronic Publishing Services) program, developed by OCLC and IDI for the Association for Computing Machinery, is an example of a state-of-the-art electronic publishing system. [2] ACM wanted a system that would allow them to build an electronic repository of their publications, while reducing the use of paper in the publishing process, beginning with the author's submission and ending with the presentation to the end-user. STEPS is a collection of commercially available products, integrated together through open systems architecture. This "plug and play" solution permits publishers to select the products they prefer for each phase of the publishing process. The core of the system is SGMLserver, an IDI product based on the BASISplus database engine. Integrated together as a unit, the products produce a system for SGML document capture and conversion, editing, composition, management, and electronic distribution.

Print elimination

A final area to explore in reducing production costs is the elimination of print production altogether. As users become more accustomed to the advantages of electronic journals, there could well be a significant shift in print vs. electronic subscriptions. The likelihood that a publisher will discontinue the print version will of course be dependent on the response of the users and will also be dependent on the nature of the publication. Frequently published journals with time-sensitive material are prime candidates for such a migration.

II. Pricing

Print/electronic subscriptions

How should publishers charge libraries who wish to try out the electronic versions of journals, yet maintain their print subscriptions? Charging an equal amount for the electronic version is frequently the publishers' knee-jerk reaction. However, the library response is usually one of outrage at the publisher's lack of sensitivity to the library's budgetary constraints. If publishers really want to get a good sense of the effectiveness of the online version, they will need to make the electronic pricing attractive by offering a combined print/electronic subscription. The American Institute of Physics has been aggressive in this area, offering combined subscriptions for about 15% more than paper alone. Elsevier Trends Journals have taken a different approach, giving away the electronic version of Immunology Today to current subscribers of the print for the 1995 subscription year.

Subscription model

The traditional subscription model currently used for most scholarly print journals may not be the most appropriate model for the electronic environment, though it is the one that most publishers are initially proposing for the electronic versions of their journals. However, the issue that concerns them is the

Figure 2. EJO incorporating scanned images from TULIP Project.

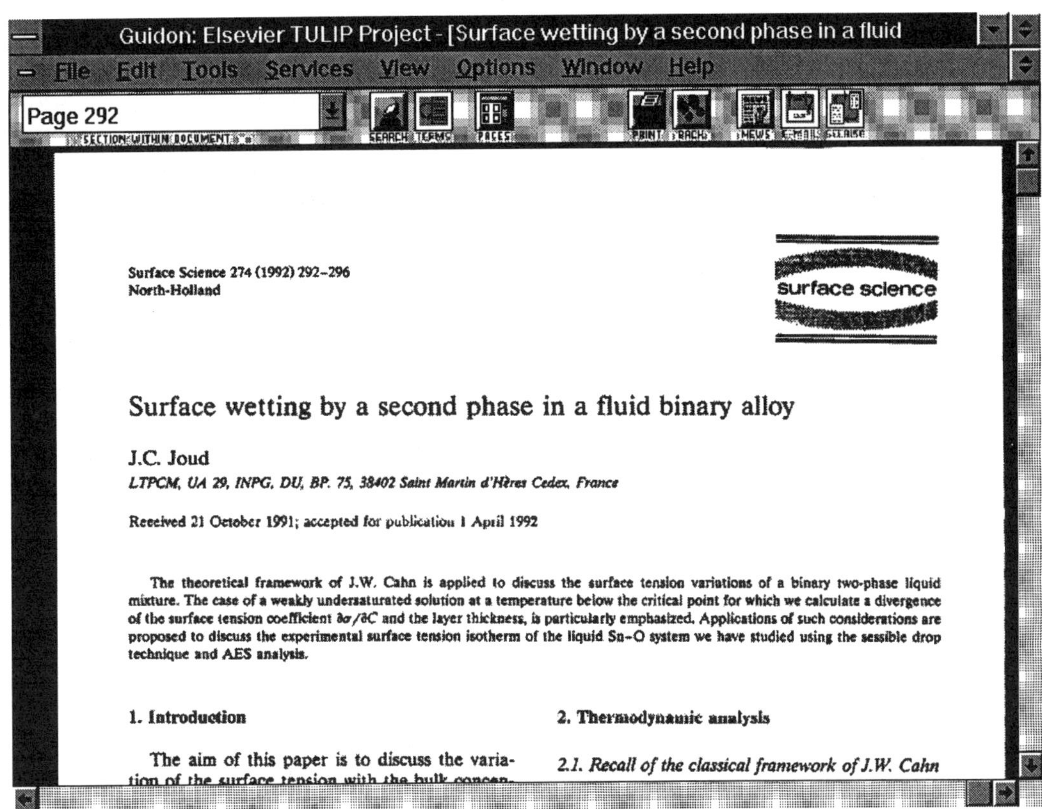

Surface Science 274 (1992) 292–296
North-Holland

surface science

Surface wetting by a second phase in a fluid binary alloy

J.C. Joud

LTPCM, UA 29, INPG, DU, BP. 75, 38402 Saint Martin d'Hères Cedex, France

Received 21 October 1991; accepted for publication 1 April 1992

The theoretical framework of J.W. Cahn is applied to discuss the surface tension variations of a binary two-phase liquid mixture. The case of a weakly undersaturated solution at a temperature below the critical point for which we calculate a divergence of the surface tension coefficient $\partial\sigma/\partial C$ and the layer thickness, is particularly emphasized. Applications of such considerations are proposed to discuss the experimental surface tension isotherm of the liquid Sn–O system we have studied using the sessible drop technique and AES analysis.

1. Introduction

The aim of this paper is to discuss the varia-

2. Thermodynamic analysis

2.1. Recall of the classical framework of J.W. Cahn

number of print subscriptions that will be dropped as a result. Will libraries assume that one electronic subscription can take the place of multiple print subscriptions? If that is the case, how should the electronic subscription be priced? How many users can technically access one electronic subscription? Moreover, how many should be allowed access via one subscription? One of the primary advantages of electronic journals is the ease with which users can access the journals whenever and wherever they wish. In a university that is "wired," multitudes of users could access a journal in a single day and could be accessing the journal from their offices, classrooms, laboratories, and dormitories 24 hours a day. A control mechanism is to limit the number of simultaneous users and to incorporate into the pricing model an additional charge for multiple simultaneous users. "Illegal" distribution of the access password to users outside of the subscribing institution is one of the greatest nightmares for publishers, given the level of electronic communication facilitated by the Internet. OCLC has addressed this problem by allowing users to change passwords at a moment's notice.

Site licensing

Given these circumstances, one can anticipate a natural progression towards site licensing for institutions. Site licensing is already heavily used by abstract and indexing services which produce electronic bibliographic databases. However, there are many varieties of site licenses, based on anything from the total population of the institution to the acquisitions budget of the library. The current popularity of consortia is another factor in institutional pricing that must be dealt with. The fact that libraries are joining together to share resources complicates the pricing structure and tests the creativity of the information provider.

III. New Products

The reality of electronic publishing is that, once a journal is in electronic form, it becomes a collection of data, which can be broken down into much smaller units than the traditional journal issue. Similarly, the units can be combined together to create larger units. This is both good news and bad news for the publisher. It is good news because it allows for new possibilities for creating new collections of information.

Clusters

Clusters of journals that naturally "fit" together can be created as a new product. As an example, OCLC is working with Current Science to create two new electronic "mega-journals" from the Current Opinions journal series. One set of six will focus on the biological sciences, while the other represents a group of 24 review journals in clinical medicine, each journal in the group specializing in a particular field. Taken together, they create a broad collection in which many crossovers can be instantly recognized, enabling specialists in one area to stay apprised of new developments in other specialties and to find useful applications that can be applied to their own fields. One search will span all of the journals in the collection. The recent announcement of two drugs, methotrexate for cancer treatment and misoprostol for ulcers, now being used successfully to produce abortions, is a cogent example of interesting crossovers that can be facilitated by such mega-journals.

Combining journals into clusters can also help keep some less frequently used journals off the library "hit list", benefitting both the library and the publisher. Clusters of journals can be produced economically if the publisher follows the same DTD and stylesheet for the whole collection. Publishers who offer clusters comprising a mixture of frequently and infrequently accessed (though important) journals at a substantial cost savings over single journal purchases help the library maintain access to a critical mass of information.

New journals

Just as whole journals can be appended together to form a cluster, similar pieces of multiple journals can be appended together to create a new journal. A simple example would be to extract all of the reviews from a group of journals in a particular subject area and construct a new review journal. Other examples include a journal of abstracts, or a "Best of..." journal. The new journal could be distributed as an electronic-only journal, bypassing the creation of a new print journal altogether. The technology is in place to create new clusters and new journals. Publishers and librarians are in the best position to determine which new formulations make sense and are of greatest appeal to the user community. The days are gone when librarians will simply buy whatever is published. The future of traditional publishing will depend on publishers responding to the needs and concerns of libraries and their users.

Individual article sales

Journals can also be broken down into smaller units; namely, the individual articles. This is the "bad news" for many publishers, who see sales of individual articles as the first step in the demise of the traditional subscription model. However, a broader view should be taken to see the new opportunities that this environment creates. Imagine a user reading a journal online and finding a reference to an article in another journal. In the traditional model, the user realizes that obtaining this second article will require considerable effort; namely, leaving the first journal and going in search of the second journal, which may or may not be easily accessible, and is almost certainly not within arm's reach. Depending on the level of effort and the importance of finding the second article, the user may or may not decide to pursue the endeavor, with the realization that there will inevitably be a delay factor.

Now imagine that same user in an electronic environment, where the user can access the second article AND find other articles by the same author OR other articles on the same topic, all obtained instantly with a few keystrokes, and of course some method of payment for the individual articles. This exciting new environment can be highly dynamic, compared to the static print. However, such systems will require cooperation among publishers as well as the establishment of trust. To quote Clifford Lynch,[3] "[there is] a need for a new sense of trust and community not just among users of scholarly information, but among scholarly societies, university presses, and other organizations that contribute to both the information base and the user community. Publishers of scholarly works and facilitators of scholarly communication must be confident that the user community recognizes the importance of their role and makes funding available to them to continue to fulfill it as they continue to be responsive to the needs of that user community."

There are opportunities to expand information access in many ways. Consider a scenario in which users can see and influence the evolution of research findings. The electronic dissemination of high-energy physics preprints is a prime example of research in the making. As findings are disseminated, researchers discuss these findings and provide their input. This process, in turn, affects other research in progress. Under such a scenario, there is no finite conclusion to the process.

Centralized system

In the same way, a centralized system that can create new pathways to information by offering a critical mass of primary and review material from various publishers, connecting that material with bibliographic databases, and providing for instant delivery of articles should be of great benefit to researchers worldwide. OCLC is attempting to create such a system by connecting its Electronic Journals Online system and its FirstSearch system, the latter consisting of 46 premier bibliographic databases. The success of this system will depend on publishers agreeing to make their online journals available on an individual article basis so that cross-connections can be made.

A recent article in Library Journal entitled "Serial Killers: Academic Libraries Respond to Soaring Costs"[4] describes the dilemma of a researcher in the Nutrition Science Department at University of California-Berkeley, who was accustomed to browsing journals outside of his field, such as water resources and environmental microbiology. Alas, 200 journals have been cancelled in the last year at the Biosciences Library, precluding him from browsing as he once did. He laments, "[Interdisciplinary browsing is] where the innovations and new developments are going to come from, but because of journal cancellations, the number of cross-connections and new ideas that we stumble onto has gone way down."

The article goes on to say that it is the junior faculty and graduate students who are hardest hit by the cancellations, because they are more dependent on the library for this information than are the senior faculty, who are better connected to the information through preprints, etc. Thus, a system that can offer opportunities for interdisciplinary browsing and searching, with connections to bibliographic databases should be of great interest to librarians and researchers alike.

Other new products

Other new products are possible in the electronic environment, including preprints and CD-ROM archival discs, which may be appropriate for sale in areas with poor telecommunications facilities. Moreover, there are great opportunities for expanding and enhancing the journal by adding such items as data files used in the original research, computer algorithms, images that can be rotated, sound, and video. As greater bandwidth becomes more broadly available, these value-added features make electronic journals even more attractive than paper.

IV. Advertising

An area of great interest is electronic advertising, particularly over the Internet.

Much publicity was given to the two Arizona lawyers who advertised their services over the 'Net and were subsequently "flamed" for it. A recent interview with the two states that business for them is booming, as a result. MecklerMedia Corporation announced the creation of MecklerWeb for dissemination of product information. For an annual fee of $25,000, companies could be included in the MecklerWeb electronic forum[5]. However, only two weeks after going live on the Internet, Meckler announced a change to a more conventional advertising vehicle. Meckler had apparently attracted only one company[6].

Several organizations, such as CompuServe and Open Market, have also announce services to help corporations build their own storefront on the Internet. But who is using the Internet and how likely are they to use this vehicle to buy goods and services? Two studies have been conducted by MIT and Georgia Tech, with interesting results. The MIT survey shows that the average Internet user's age is 30.7 years old, and that 86.5% of Internet users are male. The occupations of those users are primarily college students, faculty, and staff, a group characterized by the San Francisco Chronicle[7] as having more time than money. The Georgia Tech survey focuses on users of the World Wide Web, with similar results. The average Web user's age is somewhere between 21 and 30; 94% of those users are men. These statistics do not bode well for immediate revenues for advertisers.

There are ways to promote electronic advertising that should help publishers recover some of the costs incurred for electronic journals. However, it is necessary to understand that the nature of online advertising is different from print advertising, and to convey that difference to potential advertisers. Since an online journal is not browsed in the same way as a print journal, publishers cannot depend on the likelihood that users will see the advertisement nor that the graphic will have the same impact in an online environment.

Commercials to Infomercials

The shift in the electronic medium is to information. Most users of electronic products want to have information available at their convenience, not intruding in their "cyberspace". Advertisers in the electronic realm will need to convey substantive information about their products. Users will also want immediate gratification of their interest in a product; the ability to order the product directly from the advertisement is key.

Perhaps a better, more usable scenario is to create online advertising as product information that can be linked in a logical fashion to information that the user is looking at. For example, a user looking at articles on AIDS will be interested in seeing information on new drugs to treat AIDS, including their advantages as well as their side effects. Similarly, an article describing a new piece of equipment used in a study can have a link to specific information about that product, as well as to reviews and comparisons of such products. So long as the product information is clearly labeled as such and is not forced upon the user, the effect should be quite positive, and the information will be perceived as beneficial.

Several of the journals in the OCLC Electronic Journals Online system will be experimenting with product and company information, beginning in January, 1995. Such information will be presented to users in a variety of ways, including hypertext links. Mechanisms are in place to enable the user to obtain more information about a product directly from the producer via the online system. In addition to tracking the number of requests for more information (which publishers can demonstrate to advertisers), we will also monitor the frequency with which users access the product information. Such statistics will provide useful information in gauging the merits of online advertising.

Conclusion

The new electronic publishing environment

requires new economic models and new modes of thinking by publishers and their user communities. Great opportunities exist to create dynamic pathways to information of great benefit to the user community. Technological advancements that bring a new dimension to the ways people use information are here and evolving. The question to both libraries and publishers is not who will have the upper hand in the electronic revolution, but how we can work together to help each other and ultimately those who benefit from the information they provide. As Teilhard de Chardin wrote in the Future of Man: "No one can deny that a world network of economic and psychic affiliations is being woven at an ever-increasing speed which envelops and constantly penetrates more deeply within each of us. With every day that passes, it becomes a little more than impossible for us to act or think otherwise than collectively."[8]

---

[1] Willis, Katherine, Ken Alexander, William A. Gosling, Gregory R. Peters, Jr., Robert Schwarzwalder, and Beth Forrest Warner, "TULIP-The University Licensing Program: Experiences At The University Of Michigan," *Serials Review*, Fall 1994, 39-47.

[2]*OII Spectrum*, August 1994, Volume 1, No. 11.

[3]Lynch, Clifford, "Scholarly Communications in the Networked Environment: Reconsidering Economics and Organizational Missions," *Serials Review*, Fall 1994, 23-30.

[4]McCarthy, Paul. "Serial Killers: Academic Libraries Respond to Soaring Costs," *Library Journal*, June 15, 1994, 41-44.

[5]Hutheesing, Nikhil, "Internet Inc.," *Forbes*, October 24, 1994, 259-260.

[6]"Meckler Pulls Plug On Mecklerweb," October 24, 1994, *Newsbytes* [Online]. Available: Individual, Inc. Item: 655123.

[7]"Internet Advertising May Not Pay Study Finds Users Have More Time Than Money," October 26, 1994, *San Francisco Chronicle* [Online]. Available: Individual, Inc. Item: 755094.

[8]Chardin, Teilhard de., *Future of Man*. New York: Harper and Row, 1964.

Andrea Keyhani
Manager, Electronic Publishing
OCLC
Andrea_Keyhani@oclc.org

Electronic Journals, Libraries, and University Presses

Jean-Claude Guedon
Universite de Montreal

I. Some background remarks

The road leading from print journals[1] to their electronic counterparts increasingly reveals a well-known fact in the history of technology -- namely that no true substitution ever takes place. Rather, whole series of displacements, relocations and redefined functions are layered in a complex process of sedimentation where social, economic and psychological dimensions are intertwined in various, unexpected ways. Electronic journals are no exception to this rule. Even though they must fulfill the same roles as printed journals, they will do so with second-order effects that are quite different from those of print. More precisely, electronic journals, like their print counterparts, are expected to act as communication tools, to allow for archival functions and to provide a degree of legitimacy and authority to authors. However, they will achieve these goals in ways sufficiently different from the print journals to open entirely new possibilities for the research system.

As I have already delved on these points in a number of papers that will appear -- ironically enough -- in print form in the near future,[2] I will focus here on another facet of electronic publishing -- namely its economic foundation. The emergence of electronic scholarly publishing, because it constitutes a technical shift of great magnitude, is helping question some of the assumptions that underpin the present economic and institutional relationships that characterize our print system. But, at the same time, as it threatens (or promises) to modify the importance of the various kinds of players relatively to one another -- namely various kinds of publishers, librarians and research personnel -- it is greeted with great caution, not to mention worry.

We have one certainty: the economic model of print journals is well known, and the trends that go with it are eminently clear. They all point to the impending collapse of the whole system so that we have no other choice but to look for alternatives, presumably based on electronic and digitized documents. The point here is to invent, but to invent with our eyes steadfastly focused on the correct objects, and not on some mirages stemming either from too strong a nostalgia for the past or too great a fascination for technical hype.

Hitherto, that is to say in the last four or five years, we have essentially witnessed a flurry of experimental designs for scholarly electronic publishing. On the upside, these were the result of a good deal of volunteer work, patchwork financing, personal enthusiasm, sometimes laced with utopian thinking and a dash of impatience with the old ways, inventiveness and creativity. All in all, it often required an unlikely mixture of personal qualities and flaws. On the downside, this mildly chaotic emergence of a hundred plus electronic scholarly journals in the last five years has not lent itself easily to comparative analyses and syntheses. There may not be a one best way to design scholarly electronic journals, but with what we have at hand, it would even be difficult to select a few 'better ways'.

In terms of economic models, this burst of creative chaos has left us without good handles on the problem because the accent so far has been placed on technical design, on convincing authors to commit themselves to this new medium, on ensuring easy access for better readership, on solving difficulties for libraries, and so on. In other words, most individuals involved with electronic journals have been too busy with the design of the new tool to treat the economic context as anything more than what is required for successful prototyping. Bricolage has been the name of the game so far, but as bricolage, it stands like a kind of prehistory to a history that remains to be written. With luck, this conference may be writing the very first few lines of this impending history.

At the same time, this phase of bricolage is also shaping this history in the making because it has nurtured hopes and fostered forms of thinking that would not have emerged as easily otherwise. In particular, a good deal of the efforts expended to make electronic journals possible have taken place away and apart from market considerations. Many people who pioneered electronic publications did so out of a feeling of growing economic crisis coupled with a desire to improve the efficiency of the communication system of research communities. Present Internet economics have acted as a greenhouse in this regard and this somewhat unusual situation has fostered new hopes, particularly that of greater equity. We now know that the financing of electronic scholarly publications is not only different from that of print publications, but that it also brings into question its commercial underpinnings. In effect, the advent of electronic journals has allowed some of us to explore new possibilities, particularly that of making the results of research freely available to the whole research community, world wide. Economic models inspired by public libraries or the financing of public roads have thus started to look like appealing alternatives to the present system. With them also came the insight that the research communities might regain control over the communication of their research results. That too has appeared as a desirable goal.

To be sure, the vision of free research journals may appear so unrealistic, so unlike the prevailing ways of academic publishing, that it runs the risk of being greeted by skepticism at best and derision at worst. Yet, I would like to explore the sensible dimensions of this vision. However, before doing so, I should like to point out that we are presently living with a fiction that has worked so well and for such a long time that we mistake it for reality -- namely, treating research articles as vulgar commodities. This fiction, incidentally, was but a gleam in the eyes of a few publishers in the nineteenth century, but it has now taken hold to the point of becoming the dominant form of thinking nowadays. And if research-as-commodity looks real now, it is because it belongs to a dominant current of thought, not because it is intrinsically true.[3]

I will argue, therefore, against the fiction of published research as a commodity. For one thing, published research essentially takes place outside industrial or commercial laboratories. Despite the well-known exceptions of Bell laboratories, of some sectors of the pharmaceutical industry and of some high-technology companies where a fraction of the research is published to favor links between industrial and university researchers, most published research is carried out in universities or governmental laboratories. Even within private universities, most research is financed by taxpayers' money. From that perspective, therefore, one may wonder why the results of publicly-funded research should not be made freely available to the whole research community.

There is another angle to consider as well. Independently of its public source of support, research publishing is inherently non-commercial for a number of reasons that should be fairly obvious. For example, scientific or scholarly value does not correlate with sales for the simple reason that research processes generate their own kind of symbolic market and symbolic capital.[4] The way pre-prints, printed articles, proceedings of conferences, and various other informal means of communication relate to one another and contribute to build a workable communication system, demonstrates this point. Even estimates of readership and citations do not always provide reliable measures of scholarly merit because much time may be needed to build it up. For example, no one would question the value of Einstein's famous papers on relativity; yet the very complexity of his arguments and the arcane nature of the mathematics he used severely limited their readership at first. But they are still being regularly studied by historians of science, and even by physicists on occasion.

The very success of commercial presses shows how a fiction can be made socially real. Not only do they treat research products as if they were merchandise, but they reinforce this fiction by a second step: they relentlessly go after any prestigious publication, do everything to acquire it, and thus build a quasi-monopoly on prestige which they then claim to produce.[5] There is an interesting lesson in all of this: the fiction constructed by commercial presses is crass, without dreams; yet they have managed to make it appear real. Conversely, the vision of research products circulating freely is anything but fictitious, and it has the beauty of a dream. As such, it should stand an even better chance to exist. In the rest of this presentation, I will try to prove this. In other words, what is at stake is to make real dreams come true.

II. The economic realities of scholarly publishing

As a good starting point to this question, let us examine the question of savings induced by moving to electronic publishing. Debates over this question have been raging on the electronic networks. Some claim that enormous gains can be achieved, of the order of 70%,[6] if not only we abandon print, but print mentality as well; others, closer to the interests of publishers, argue that the gains to be achieved are minimal at best. My own evaluation eschews those two extremes. On the one hand, I would argue that to make electronic journals succeed, one has to pay a great deal of attention to the users, and, consequently, far from dispensing with the print mentality, we must in fact mimic it. Innovations always include a measure of healthy conservatism to succeed as such. Radical innovations are simply not accepted or not understood by the social system. On the other hand, it looks obvious that electronic publishing costs no more than preparing the first copy of a text in the print world. Printing and binding costs disappear and so do mailing costs. The weight of printing and access is placed on the shoulders of the user but both are low and she pays for what she needs and no more. All in all, a conservative figure that seems to recur regularly is that savings of the order of 25 to 30% are made possible in this way.[7]

In examining the economic context of print journals, the distinction between expenses and revenues obviously comes immediately to mind and it stems from the publisher's legitimate concern to balance books. However, this viewpoint also hides some interesting dimensions that merit being underscored. If, instead of looking at the best way to make and sell scholarly journals, one looks at the research process as a whole, and views the publishing of scholarly periodicals as just one particular phase within it, then money matters appear in a very different light. For one thing, most scholarly journals that are not in the hands of private presses, are subsidized in some fashion or another by some kind of public money. The same public money that contributes to bringing a scholarly journal to light, is still needed afterwards to buy it back in part. While the left hand subsidizes production, the right hand subsidizes a public library model of access.

Let us now examine the situation more closely. The revenues of any scholarly journal, once subsidies are taken out, stem from library and individual subscriptions. Sales of individual issues are generally not a significant factor in this context. If here we reapply the distinction between private money on the one hand, and collective money on the other hand, then a new interesting fact appears. The proportion of revenues originating from individual subscribers seems rarely to exceed 25 to 30% of all revenues (subsidies plus sales of all kinds).[8] The rest comes from library purchases and from subsidies or grants.

An intriguing perspective now begins to emerge if we remember that, earlier in this study, the savings stemming from going electronic were evaluated to be about 25 to 30% of total costs in the print world. In other words, moving from print to electronic publishing generates savings roughly equal to the revenues accruing from individuals. As a result, and on a global scale, the general economic sustainability of an electronic journal turns out to be largely independent of individual subscribers.

This reasoning leads to another important result. If individual buyers are no longer needed as part of the economic structure of electronic journals, it means they become again what they should have always been in the first place -- namely users or readers, and not consumers. Finally, if each scholarly electronic journal can live on nothing more than all the public money involved in its full life-cycle, from production to distribution and acquisition, this means that adding subsidies to library subscriptions is sufficient not only to support the scholarly system of publication, but to make it freely accessible to everybody, everywhere. The vision is somewhat dizzying in its implications as it removes one of the main obstacles on the way to transforming scientific research into a truly world-wide enterprise. Third world scholars would have at last a fighting chance of accessing the needed documentation for their research.

To be sure, the reasoning above remains theoretical. It is a global, macrovision, a dream. How we can hope to make it real will be the object of the next and last section of this presentation.

III. Toward a new scholarly publication world order

Admittedly, moving from the macro level just sketched out to the level of individual journals is difficult. There may be enough public money globally to support a world-wide system of electronic scholarly publication, and it is true that scholarly results often have an inherently international vocation. However, the funding of most academic journals remains a national or even a local concern. Consider, for example, journal X. While its production involves a combination of public funds all located within country Y, say Canada, it is sold to a number of foreign libraries. However much these foreign libraries may be supported by their own kind of public money, it is not Canadian public money. In other words, how could these various sources of public money originating from many countries be expected to converge toward journal X by a mechanism that does not involve a sale (a subscription)? Probably the most fundamental function of a market-driven economic model for scholarly journals is precisely to provide ways to focus widely scattered sources of money on a single title. This, incidentally, is probably the best argument in favour of the myth that research results are saleable commodities. The point, however, is to find other ways to coordinate the effects of variegated sources of public money, wherever they may be located and the goal is to make the world's communication system of research work more efficiently (and more equitably, particularly for third world countries that can ill afford the costs of journal subscriptions in hard currencies). Can some coordinated rationality be substituted to the workings of the invisible hand? Such in essence is the fundamental question!

For electronic scholarly journals, the question is all the more important that the dual presence of a digital medium and the presence of global networks do not agree easily with traditional subscription models. To be sure, passwords can always be used to control access, but, unlike print, duplication is fast, absolutely identical to the source, and can be transmitted easily to great numbers of people all over the place. Any ideologically-nourished challenge to the prevailing economic model of scholarly publications would find ample opportunity to achieve its objectives through. From the point of view of libraries, the emergence of electronic scholarly journals poses another problem that is hardly less daunting, for what is the meaning of physical ownership when everyone knows that digitized documents are essentially independent of location? They can be accessed from almost anywhere. What counts in this environment is not the importance of a collection, but the bandwidth (and pricing) of a connection, as well as the quality of the tools connected to it. On the global network, libraries can no longer act like mere knowledge vaults; instead, they become connecting nodes and local distribution centers for a kind of information that cannot and should not be constrained by boundaries smaller than the utmost reaches of humanity.

This said, what about the libraries' financial contributions to the communication system of the research communities? So far, the possibility of physical possession justifies the large outlays of money libraries expend each year to keep up with the current production of journals and it is true that showing stories upon stories of shelves filled with bound volumes is far less abstract, and therefore more easily comprehended than a form of permanent access to the world's scholarship. Besides, on many campuses, the size of the library is a factor in the ranking of a university's worth. If everyone has equal access to everything, what was the meaning of investing so much into Harvard's library, for example?

Questions like the ones just raised are very difficult to answer. In effect, the presently established division of labor between publishers and libraries creates like a mental block that we should try to overcome. But the Renaissance saw metallurgists and humanists learn to work together. By analogy, it is not surprising to see the present technical transformations contributing to a re-definition of various tasks. In particular, if publishing and accessing scholarly journals were to appear as a unified process in the total cycle of research, then chances of seeing resources pooled in a more fruitful way would certainly grow. As the main actors here are university presses and university libraries, the chances for cooperation are even greater. This said, processes presently at work also show that this new form of cooperation is growing out of the very forces reshaping the universe of academic publishing, and not out of some categorical imperative, or a voluntaristic urge to act according to an overarching cooperative principle. To demonstrate this point, I shall allude to a library initiative that raises a number of interesting questions while opening the door to possibilities that would have simply appeared impossible only a few years back. I am referring to UnCover, a bibliographic undertaking initiated by the Colorado Alliance of Research Libraries (CARL). UnCover is financed in an original fashion. Its designers creatively reasoned that some scholars always have an urgent need for some kind of information and they decided to use this particular market as leverage to support the whole bibliographic effort. In practice, they began offering the possibility of transmitting articles by fax for a price. Meanwhile, the world community can now freely search thousands of journal titles for articles.

UnCover's scheme harbors implications that reach well beyond its obvious functions. Libraries, for example, could calculate (as they probably should) how much they would save on less frequently used journals if they just cut out the corresponding subscriptions and relied on UnCover instead. They could even declare that some fraction of the savings would go into a fund allowing faculty and students to order articles from the cut journals directly from UnCover. The corresponding journals, on the other hand, would start losing a significant number of library subscriptions, a loss in revenue that certainly would not be entirely compensated by the royalties paid for the sale of some of its articles. This is due to the fact that the bundling of articles into the form of a journal issue was first invented to unload unwanted items along with desired texts.

A device such as UnCover, therefore, induces consequences that had probably not been anticipated in the original design. In particular, UnCover's presence is bound to increase the economic pressure on the more marginal journals, and, as a result, it intensifies the factors favoring a move away from print. As UnCover gains in popularity, prices of articles will tend to decrease, and more journals will be affected. In other words, a service offered by libraries to help retrieval and access may end up profoundly modifying the economic context of a significant number of journals. One should not deduce from all that has just been said that libraries are on the brink of playing a prejudicial role with regard to scholarly publications. On the contrary, it demonstrates the very central role they already play within the communication system of research. Not only are they the valued interface between the end user and the information, as most people are apt to see them, but they are also poised to become a major player in the whole structure of this important, yet fragile edifice. It also underscores that the future of scholarly publication depends as much on what librarians will collectively decide to do or not to do, as the future of research librarians depends on the form the scholarly will adopt once it is globally digitized.

In particular, and UnCover provides a hint that this is in the offing, libraries may find themselves in the position to become publishers on demand in a digitized world. They could do so for two reasons: first, as libraries tend to act more and more as information brokers, people will also tend to turn to them to obtain some useable form of the information they have helped track down; second, libraries might have tools that go beyond what individuals, in particular students, can afford. Other reasons could be added if we shift viewpoint. For example, if, as is likely, journals find that library subscriptions are fast decreasing without the revenues being made up by royalty payments, they could decide to go the electronic route and ask UnCover or an UnCover-like outfit to become, in effect, its publisher.[9] In this fashion, convergence between the publishing world and libraries could be sparked and lead to a redistribution of roles as momentous and significant as the invention of the modern publishing house after Gutenberg.

There are other ways in which libraries may take on publishing functions. For example, if a number of academic journals do manage to become viable in some digital format, libraries will be expected to provide access to them and, more importantly, to materialize them in the form that best suits the reading mode of the user. For example, if what is required is the close study of a text, the kind of study presently carried out most of the time with a pencil in hand, then libraries may well want to provide a good print version of the document requested. At this point the five or so centuries of publishing experience that have eased the task of reading through judicious page layout or the use of good typographic styles will certainly not be neglected, forgotten or abandoned. Instead, the library may find that it has to master some of the skills that used to be confined within printing shops and publishing houses.

At this junction, we might ask: but what about university presses? Let me first underscore again that I am talking here about scholarly journals exclusively. Monographs pose a different kind of problem that I do not try to solve here. In the context of scholarly journals, it is true that the vision displayed here appears to leave the leading role to libraries, and not to presses. But this is largely due to the fact that I tried to address the vexing question of moving from the macro to the micro level. In working through this difficulty, it appeared that a number of library initiatives that are already sprouting everywhere, will likely be determinant. However, occupying a leading role in a process of change does not necessarily translate into a commanding position in the outcome. Besides, university presses will always have important, in fact essential, functions to fulfill. For one thing, they will always be needed in the editing phases of texts that necessarily precede publication *per se*. They also know how to organize peer review. Libraries, on the other hand, have no experience or traditions in this regard and they will naturally tend to turn to university presses to take care of this task. In effect, university presses could become the interface between authors and the archived, legitimized and accessible document, while libraries would provide the interface between structured information and the user or reader. Asking whether libraries or presses will come to be dominant in this deep reconfiguration of the research communication system is a moot point as the ultimate outcome would then be an institution that is neither library nor press, but a true synthesis of both.

IV. Conclusion

Whether journals find themselves forced to look for ways of surviving in an ever more difficult economic environment or whether libraries find themselves placed in positions that invite them to develop new functions and services even as old ones start fading away, or whether again some initiative, for example of a bibliographic nature, leads to modifying the workings of the communication system of research, a constant refrain recurs and it tells the convergence between editing, publishing and librarianship. It is this trend toward convergence which, in my opinion, will facilitate the direct adding of subsidies to library subscriptions so that public money may at last work in a coordinated fashion rather than be focused on the same object through the artificial mobilization of market considerations applied to the wrong objects.

It has been the thesis of this paper that, at the macro level, the economic public support of scholarly journals is sufficient, but that the recourse to a commercial model of sales leads to distortions best noted in the following points:

- They induce the need for further funds from private hands;
- They allow some private presses to take undue advantage of a captive market by charging incredibly high prices;
- This induces a number of non-profit, professional organizations to be tempted into following a similar route;
- Poor countries are penalized and forms of elitism having little to do with excellence are encouraged.

It has also been the thesis of this paper that going the electronic route would allow to provide a free or, at least, a very cheap access to scholarly journals, provided that the present level of public support continues at about the same level as is gloablly the case presently. However, this thesis is good only if the funds allocated to libraries are somehow combined with the subsidies given to the publishers, and, to achieve this goal, this paper has argued that a new combined role, a new convergence must emerge between publishing houses and libraries. The best evidence in favor of this thesis is that the process has begun and is now becoming visible in some sectors, as other papers in this conference show.[10]

In the end, if the convergence works itself out fully, including at the international level, libraries and publishers will have undergone a somewhat paradoxical evolution: the former will gradually relegate physical ownership and conservation of materials in favor of access to, and structuring of, research information. At the same time, they will be far more involved with the material production of this scholarly information to the point of looking very much like publishers on demand. Publishers, for their part, will abandon their efforts to market scholarly journals; instead, they will capitalize on their irreplaceable ability to add value to texts. In the end, they will focus on being editors and instruments of legitimation. Such a redefined division of labor will ultimately characterize what may be known in the future as the 'Second Renaissance.

---

[1]The paper that follows deals exclusively with *scholarly journals*. I believe that the question of scholarly books, although related, is sufficiently different to warrant a kind of analysis different from the one presented here.

[2]"Bibliothèques universitaires, communication savante et nouvelles technologies,"

Communication scientifique, nouvelles technologies et rationalisation des ressources: un défi pour les bibliothèques universitaires. Actes du Colloque organisé à l'occasion du 25e anniversaire du sous-comité des bibliothèques, Conférence des recteurs et des principaux du Québec (Montréal, bibliothèque nationale du Québec, 1993). "Why are electronic publications difficult to classify?: the orthogonality of print and digital media" in the 4th *Directory of Electronic Journals, Newsletters and Academic Discussion Lists*, Ann Okerson, ed. (Washington, D. C., Association of Research Libraries, 1994), pp. 17-21. "Electronic publishing of academic journals and the structure of research results.": dans Teresa Harrison et Tim Stephen, eds, *Computer Networking and Scholarship in the 21st Century*. (SUNY Press,to appear in 1995). "Electronic Journals: Flexible Design for shifting Objectives," in *Proceedings of the 1993 International Conference on Refereed Electronic Journals*. Winnipeg, octobre 1993 (University of Manitoba, october 1994), pp. 3.1-3.14. "L'édition électronique savante et ses spécificités" to appear in 1995 in the *Proccedings* of "Les autoroutes électroniques: usages, droit et promesses", conference held in Montréal in May 1994. The French version will be published by Yvon Blais Inc. in Canada and the English version will be published by Kluwer (Holland) in its "Information Law Series". "Research Libraries and Electronic Scholarly Journals:Challenges or Opportunities?" to appear in *Serials Librarian* (August, 1995). "The Seminar, the Encyclopedia and the Eco-museum as Future Forms of Scholarly Electronic Publishing.," to appear in Robin Peek and Gregory B. Newby, eds., *Electronic Publishing Confronts Academia: Agenda for the year 2000* (Cambridge, Mass., MIT Press, 1995).

3 On this topic, see W. H. Brock, "The Development of Commercial Science Journals in Victorian Britain," in A. J. Meadows, ed., *Development of Science Publishing in Europe* (Amsterdam, Elsevier Science Publishers, 1980), pp. 95-122. The author takes a positive view of this development as he sees it as a move that essentially broke the monopoly learned societies held over scientific research, with related problems: no controversial or marginal topic, slow publication pace, etc.

4 These expressions belong to Pierre Bourdieu's vocabulary.

5 And of course, this allows them to impose incredible prices on these journals. The only limiting factor is "what the market can bear" , a rule that generally applies to luxury items, but hardly seems adequate to help the communication of research results. The real perversity of this system appears more fully when one notes that some disciplinary or professional associations, although non-profit, follow suit because they can finance other activities with the revenues accruing from such practices. At the same time, they vindicate the attitude of the private presses and contribute to creating an atmosphere of normalcy to a situation that is better viewed as quite scandalous. Needless to add, this ensures that most poor countries will either not gain access to this information, or will have but little choice but to transgress international copyright laws.

6 Stevan Harnad and others have recently debated such figures on the list VPIEJ-L list over the Internet.

7 Sandra Wolfrey, "The Economics of Journal Publishing and the Rhetoric for Moving to an Electronic Format," in *Proceedings of the 1993 International Conference on Refereed Electronic Journals*, op. cit. (note 1), p. 2.6, 2.9 and 2.10. The author mentions savings ranging from 24 to 36%.

8 This result needs to be verified and I hope to do so in the year to come. However, preliminary results obtained either through a few private enquiries to editors of scholarly journals, and through partial figures obtained from the Social Science and Research Council of Canada (SSHRC), and from the Fonds de formation des chercheurs et d'aide à la recherche (FCAR) in Québec seem to support this claim. Of course, the general practice of charging subscription rates that are higher for libraries than for individuals, is an important factor in this result.

---

[9] In a sense, the OCLC program to invite journals to go electronic while using their proprietary interface, Guidon, is another example of the ways in which organizations based on libraries are moving into this publishing role.

[10] Particularly telling is the story of how Johns Hopkins University Press and the library of the same university have collaborated to transfer a number of scholarly journals into an electronic form. See the paper by Susan Lewis and Todd Kelley in these Proceedings.

Jean-Claude Guedon
Professor, Dept. of Comparative Literature
University of Montreal
guedon@ere.umontreal.ca

Some FAQs about Usage-Based Pricing

Jeffrey K. MacKie-Mason
Hal R. Varian
University of Michigan

Acknowledgment: This research was supported by the National Science Foundation Grant SES-93-20481. The NSF is not responsible for the content of this document.

Abstract

This is a list of Frequently Asked Questions about usage-based pricing of the Internet. We argue that usage-based pricing is likely to come sooner or later and that some serious thought should be devoted to devising a sensible system of usage-based pricing.

Debunking some myths

• Is usage-based pricing a "threat" or a "menace"?

Neither, we hope. We think that some form of usage-based pricing for the Internet is likely (eventually) for reasons that we outline below. If some thought goes into designing a good pricing system, it should not cause problems for the vast majority of users. If a bad pricing system is adopted, it could cause a lot of problems. It is important to think carefully about how a reasonable pricing system might be designed far in advance of when one might be implemented.

• Why is usage-based pricing desirable?

A major role of prices is to present information to people about the true costs of their actions. If prices accurately reflect costs then individuals can compare the benefits of their actions to the costs of their actions and make informed decisions.

Usage-based prices can be used to prioritize usage of a congested resource like a WWW server so that those who value access the most get the highest priority. Prices can also be used to allocate service classes to different uses and to recover costs of providing services. A key aspect of pricing services efficiently is that the revenues raised by the prices can be used to guide investment decisions and expand capacity.

• Why is usage-based pricing undesirable?

The major objection to well-designed usage-based prices is the accounting and transactions cost. (We discuss these costs below.) Poorly-designed prices could have other costs such as impeding technical innovation and network usage. Usage-based prices may or may not be a good idea; it depends on how well they are designed, and whether the benefits they provide exceed the accounting and transactions costs.

• Isn't usage-based pricing just a way to raise provider profits?

No. If Internet transport is provided by competitive firms (as it is today) then profits are determined by the degree of competition, not by the pricing mechanism. Some people have raised concerns about the potential monopolization of Internet transport. We think that this is unlikely in the foreseeable future. But regardless of how monopolization of the industry is, it doesn't have much to do with usage-based pricing: high profits can be obtained with flat rates and subscription charges, too.

• Doesn't usage-based pricing necessarily raise users' total expenditures?

No. Again, if the industry is competitive or

effectively regulated, then revenues will approximately equal costs. Costs may increase because of the added cost of accounting and billing. On the other hand, costs may decrease because usage-based pricing increases the efficiency of the network's functioning. When faced with usage charges, frivolous and low-value uses are likely to decrease, lowering total costs. In any case, instead of all users paying their average share of costs (through a connection, or subscription charge), they will start to pay for something closer to their own incremental share of costs. This means that low-intensity users should see a reduction in their total payments; high-intensity users will pay more.

• Won't small users be hurt?

No. With flat-rate pricing, all costs are recovered through connection fees. These fees are based on average usage of a connection. That means that small (below-average) users are actually subsidizing the big users! With usage-based pricing, the heaviest users pay most of the costs. As we argue below, the heavy users are apt to be consumers of images and video; traditional text-based uses of the Internet will be tiny by comparison to multimedia.

Rationale for usage-based pricing

• Why start pricing the Internet at all?

Internet transport is already priced, though many users seem unaware of that. Pricing is on the basis of a fixed monthly subscription fee for a connection of a given bandwidth. In most cases in the U.S. the incremental usage of that bandwidth is priced at a flat rate of zero. The reasonable question is not whether the Internet should be priced at all, but what type of pricing should be used.

• How should prices be set?

One of the fundamental principles of economics is that prices should reflect costs. More specifically, the price of something should reflect it's incremental social cost, meaning the total cost to society of providing an additional unit of the good.

• What are the costs of providing the Internet?

The easiest data to gather is data on the NSFNET, since it must report financial figures to the NSF. In recent years the NSF paid Merit about $12 million per year to maintain the NSFNET backbone. In addition they paid about $7 million to subsidize regional networks, and helped to subsidize various universities who wanted to connect to the Internet. In round terms the NSF support amounted to about $20 million per year.

The costs of Internet provision are dominated by the fixed costs. About 80% of the budget for the NSFNET goes to pay for line rental and routers. About 7% of the budget goes for the Network Operations Center. The incremental operating costs to servicing additional traffic are negligible at least up to the capacity of the network.

• What about incremental social costs?

If a network resource is operating near capacity, other users who want to use the resource may be inconvenienced or delayed. If our file transfer delays your work by a minute, then the cost of our usage includes the value of that minute of your time. If our usage breaks up your interactive video conference, then our cost includes the value of your lost conference. Such congestion costs should be counted as part of the social costs of increasing network traffic.

• What is the history of congestion on the Internet?

Congestion was quite severe in 1987 when the NSFNET backbone was running at much slower transmission speeds (56 Kbps). Users running interactive remote terminal sessions were experiencing unacceptable delays. As a temporary fix, the NSFNET programmed the routers to give terminal sessions higher priority than file transfers. Subsequently, the NSFNET was upgraded to higher transmission speeds.

• What is the current level of congestion on the Internet?

More recently, many services on the Internet have experienced significant congestion problems. Large ftp archives, Web servers at the NCSA, the original Archie site at McGill University and many services have had serious problems with overuse. The Mosaic home page at NCSA receives 1.3 million accesses a week. See [Markoff 1993] for some anecdotes about "traffic jams on the Information superhighway." Afternoon delays in telnet sessions are observable every weekday in the Bay Area. As the use of multimedia increases, we expect to see significantly more congestion.

The average utilization of the NSFNET backbone is only about 5% of total capacity. But this is very misleading: IP traffic is very bursty and peak usage can be 10 times the average. With network traffic growing at 100% a year, we may easily face serious problems in the near future.

• How much bandwidth does multimedia use?

The difference between plain old ASCII and multimedia is dramatic. Ordinary ASCII text uses about 44 bits per word. Telephone-quality voice uses 21,000 bits per word, and stereo CD uses 466,000 bits per word. Network quality video without compression is about 100 megabits per second. With compression, it's about 45 Mbs-which is the entire capacity of the NSFNET backbone! (Figures taken from [Lucky 1989]. Some new compression schemes look like they will cut the bandwidth demands of video about in half.) Present-day video conferencing systems require about 400 Kbps.

In terms of file sizes, a 700 page book in ASCII is about 1 megabyte. On the other hand, a single non-compressed GIF image is about half a megabyte and a compressed JPG image is about a tenth of a megabyte. A 13 second compressed movie is over 4 megabytes.

• What about new users?

The NSFNET backbone carries about 56 billion packets a month. If there are (conservatively) 10 million users on the backbone, the average user is sending 11,200 packets, or about 1 megabyte per month. This is about 1 ASCII book a month, or around 25 pages of text a day. This may seem like a lot-but one megabyte per month is only 2-4 GIF images per month, or about 4 seconds of a compressed movie. Existing users shifting to more bandwidth-intensive applications will put serious pressure on Internet bandwidth.

It also appears that there will be many new users of the Internet in the near-term future. The next release of MS-Windows and OS-2 are said to be "Internet ready." New users are likely to be attracted by high-bandwidth applications, which could also contribute significantly to an Internet crunch.

• What might the future level of congestion look like?

If everyone just stuck to ASCII email congestion would not likely become a problem for many years, if ever. But even now, email only accounts for 15% of network usage; new ways to use the Internet are consuming ever increasing amounts of bandwidth. (NSFNET backbone usage has been increasing at 6-10% per month for the past 6 years, so total traffic has more than doubled each year.) The largest use of network bandwidth (37%) is ftp transfers. According to [Ewing et al. 1992], around 9% were of these files were images. (This estimate is based on the file name; this is certainly an underestimate since it does not count images that are compressed, tarred, or transferred using a non-standard naming convention.) WWW traffic, which makes heavy use of images, is one of the fastest growing components of network traffic. Hence, even today a significant component of network traffic is multimedia.

• Won't technological progress increase the supply of bandwidth?

It is true that the supply of bandwidth is

increasing, but so is the demand. The routers that handle network traffic are just computers. Improvements in the technology that increase their switch speed of the routers will also increase the speed of the computers that generate traffic on the net. Furthermore, the number of users with ever-faster computers connected to the Internet is exploding. There is no reason to think that bandwidth supply will fall in cost faster than demand increases. At some times there will be periods where the supply of bandwidth exceeds the demand. Between now and the time when every household on the planet is wired with a fiber optic connection (and every citizen has a broadband wireless device) we anticipate that congestion will be an increasingly serious problem.

• What is the relationship between pricing and type-of-service?

Different kinds of traffic requires different treatment from the network . E-mail can be delayed without much loss; real-time video needs very rapid service. In order to provide appropriate treatment for different kinds of service, the person who generates the data has to indicated what type of stream it is. But if some sorts of data get "better treatment" than others, and all data costs the same to send, what is to prevent users from misrepresenting the type of their data? (For example, some advocate identifying traffic types by TCP port number in a TCP/IP network. As www users are well aware, however, it is straightforward to configure applications to use different port numbers.)

In order for a pricing system to "incentive compatible" it is necessary that use of higher quality service incurs a higher cost to the user. We have stated this principle for "priority," but it also holds for any type of special handling. This argument is laid out in detail in [Shenker 1993].

• What about recovery of fixed costs?

We don't think that usage prices are a very good way to recover the cost of providing network capacity. Since the network costs are primarily the fixed cost of capacity, it makes more sense to charge users a fixed fee depending on the capacity of their connection to the net. This is essentially the scheme that is used now . In general you want to recover costs that aren't sensitive to usage with non-usage-sensitive prices, and costs that are sensitive to usage with usage-sensitive prices.

• How large would usage prices be for the current Internet?

The current NSFNET backbone costs about $10^6 per month and carries 60,000*10^6 packets per month. This implies a cost per packet of about 1/600 cents. If there are 10 million users of the NSFNET backbone then full cost recovery of the NSFNET subsidy would imply an average monthly bill of about 10 cents per person. If we accept the guesstimate that the total cost of the U.S. portion of the Internet is about 10 times the NSFNET subsidy, we come up with one dollar per person per month for full cost recovery. The revenue from congestion fees would presumably be significantly less than this amount, since if revenue from congestion fees exceeded the cost of the network, it would be profitable to expand the size of the network.

Different approaches to allocating network usage

• What are "smart" markets?

In [MacKie-Mason Varian 1994a] we proposed a way to price network usage that we called "smart markets." Much of the time the network is uncongested; at such times the price for usage should be zero. However, when the network is congested, packets are queued, delayed, and dropped. The current queuing scheme is FIFO. We propose instead that packets should be prioritized based on the value that the user puts on getting the packet through quickly. To do this, each user assigns her packets a bid measuring her willingness-to-pay for immediate servicing. At congested routers, packets are prioritized based on bids. In order to make the scheme incentive-compatible, users are not charged the price they bid, but rather are charged the bid of the highest priority packet that is not admitted to the network. It can be shown that this mechanism provides the right incentives for users to reveal their true priority.

• Why are smart markets incentive compatible?

The basic idea is that the price a user pays is not determined by the priority he sets, but by the bid of the first packet that is rejected from the network. This means that the user has no incentive to misrepresent his true valuation of his packets. This is a form of a "Vickrey auction" or "second-price auction," which economists have shown to be incentive compatible. See, for example, [Vickrey 1961].

• Why do smart markets send the right signals for capacity expansion?

The price for network usage set by the smart market is effectively the value of the packets that are not admitted to the network. If the total value of those packets exceeds the cost of expanding the network in order to handle them, then it is appropriate to expand capacity. Investing the revenues from congestion fees in capacity expansion is just the right rule to follow.

• What are other proposals?

[Bohn et al. 1993] have suggested using a mixture of altruism and quotas to implement priority-based routing. In their framework, users voluntarily declare a priority for their packets, and these priorities are subsequently charged against a usage quota. In their scheme, user quotas are charged for the requested priority whether or not the network is congested, unlike the smart market in which the price reflects the current state of congestion.

There are also several other interesting suggestions worth exploring. [Hardy-Tribble 1993] describe a low-cost, bilateral transfer arrangement for routing packets based on "trust" and repeated interaction. [Cocchi et al. 1992] provide motivation for pricing, describe a general framework for dealing with pricing issues and conduct some simulations. [Murphy 1994] describe some simulations with pricing ATM traffic.

• What about pricing multiple qualities of service?

Most studies to date have considered pricing for a single service dimension (priority in a first-come, first-served network, or call admission to an ATM network). However, with the growing demand for multimedia, we need to think about how to allocate multiple service qualities in an integrated network. For example, file transfers tolerate zero errors, but can tolerate substantial delay. Interactive video can tolerate some packet loss, but requires tight bounds on maximum delay and variation in delay. It is possible to use some generalizations of a smart market for pricing multiple qualities of service, but the computational burdens are significant. It may be that responsive pricing will be feasible in the near term only for reserving bandwidth and service qualities in advance.

• How would prices be set in a free market?

We are not advocating imposing usage prices on the Internet. However we suspect that usage pricing will emerge for the reasons that we've outlined above. One scenario might go like this. In 5 or 6 years there could be a half-a-dozen competing backbone providers in the U.S. who interconnect at NAPS, or something like NAPS. (NAPS [Network Access Points] are switching centers where several independent networks interconnect.) f high-volume users disrupt network traffic seriously, one or more of the backbone providers might institute usage-based fees of the sort we described above (e.g., on the order of a thousandth of a cent per packet). If this happens, the high-volume users would move off of the charging network and on to one of the non-charging networks, immediately congesting it. The non-charging networks would be forced to follow suit quickly to avoid being swamped with traffic.

[MacKie-Mason-Varian 1994b] sketch out an economic model of how a competitive market for network services might function.

• What is the role of standards setting?

We don't think that the private market alone can provide a complete solution to the pricing problem. Although we think some form of usage pricing is likely, the form it takes could improve or worsen the quality of the Internet. To implement good usage pricing there clearly must be coordination among different carriers about what forms of pricing they will implement: for example, they have to interpret header information that sets "bids" or "priorities" in the same way. Furthermore, they will likely have to make "settlements" to compensate each other for carrying large amounts of each other's traffic. If we want an effective and beneficial pricing system, we must think now about standards for the necessary infrastructure to support such a system.

Accounting Systems

• How much does it cost to keep accounts for telephone calls?

Lots of numbers are tossed around about accounting costs in the telephone system. It is important to distinguish two categories of cost: incremental cost, (also known as marginal cost) and average cost. Average cost is just total cost of providing some level of service, divided by the total amount of that service provided. Marginal cost is the cost of providing additional units of service, given that some level of service is already being provided. The difference between the two boils down to the fixed costs.

In the telecommunications industry, as with the Internet, almost all costs are fixed costs: once the lines and switching equipment has been provided, it costs very little to use it, up to its capacity. When capacity has been reached, you have to pay to increase capacity if you want to increase usage.

This means that the marginal cost of a phone call is essentially zero if it is made in an off-peak period. The question is, how much does it cost to make an additional phone call during a peak period? [Mitchell 1990] estimates that the the incremental capacity cost of a call during peak usage is about 0.5-1.0 cents per call.

How does this compare with billing costs? As of July 1990 he estimates:

incremental itemized billing cost = 0.7--1.2 cents per call incremental summary billing cost = 0.1--0.2 cents per call account maintenance and collection costs = 50--75 cents per month

Itemized billing costs are therefore more than 50% of the cost of an incremental call. But this is because the cost of an incremental call is so small, not because billing costs are so large. Since it costs almost nothing to make a call during non-peak periods, accounting costs are almost 100% of the incremental cost of a non-peak call!

It is also worth observing that summary billing costs are only about 10% of itemized billing costs: just counting message units is a lot cheaper than itemizing every call.

This gives us a picture of the marginal costs of billing; what do the total costs of billing look like? In 1984 AT&T paid the regional Bell operating companies to do their billing. The RBOCs charged them about 10 cents a transactions for billing, which was about 6% of their revenue from long-distance calls. (By way of comparison, [Hansell 1994] reports that transactions costs amount to 4% of banks' cash deposits.) When AT&T was regulated, its revenues were supposed to be about the same as its costs. This suggests that billing and accounting were probably no more than 10% of total costs.

The difference between the 100% and 10% figure is that they use a different denominator: accounting costs are a large fraction of incremental costs, but a small fraction of total costs. This is because total costs are dominated by fixed costs and incremental costs are almost zero.

• Are there differences between telephone and Internet accounting?

Unfortunately yes. Telephony is a connection-oriented service: each call has a setup phase, during which a connection is established. The connection is maintained for the length of the call. A single call generates only a single accounting record, no matter how long the connection lasts. The Internet, on the other hand, is a connectionless packet service. A given session is broken into many small packets, each of which traverses the network independently of the others. (The problem of accounting for a connectionless service arises for applications as well as for network transport. For example, www and gopher are connectionless: each client request is a separate session. Accounting for www server usage requires a separate record for every "hit," even if a single user makes 30 hits during what she perceives to be a single continuous session.) If telephone-style accounting were implemented, the equivalent of a one-minute local phone call would generate about 2500 accounting records, and a ten-minute call would require 25,000 records! If usage-based pricing is to be feasible in a connectionless network, it may be essential to devise more efficient methods of accounting.

Another problem for Internet accounting is the pervasiveness of client-server applications, like www, gopher, and anonymous ftp. With telephony, the person placing the call is billed. (There are well-known ways to take advantage of this. For example, people on the East Coast of the U.S. will generally place late evening calls to people on the West Coast, where it is still early evening and the rates are higher. Similarly, there are redialing services that re-establish international calls so that they seemingly originate in the U.S. because U.S. rates are much lower than those in many other countries.) With a client-server application, most of the traffic may be sent by the server, on behalf of the client. A one-packet user request to a www server may generate a few hundred thousand packets of return traffic to download a file. To the network it appears that the server originated most of the traffic, but naturally it is the client who should be charged.

• Are their other ways to do accounting?

Since organizations that use the Internet can be assumed to have ready access to computers, there may be ways to automate the billing process. One idea that we have been thinking about is distributed accounting. In this model, consumers purchase "digital stamps" -essentially numbers. These numbers are then sent along with the information that is being transferred. The routers can examine the numbers to make sure that they haven't been used already. If they are valid, the packet will be transported. T here are a variety of encryption techniques that can be used to ensure security in such a system.

This idea is closely related to [Chaum 1985]'s idea of digital cash and [Tribble 1993]'s "digital silk road." The advantage of such a system is that there is no centralized billing overhead. The burden of network accounting is distributed among the users, just like the burden of keeping track of postage is distributed among the customers of the Post Office.

• Have other countries tried usage-based pricing?

Chile and New Zealand both have several years of experience with usage-based pricing. [Baeza-Yates et al. 1993] describe the situation in Chile and [Brownlee 1994] describes the situation in New Zealand. According to these authors, the Chilean experience has not been very positive, but the New Zealand experience has been much more successful. The accounting software developed by the New Zealanders, NetTraMet, is available for anonymous ftp at ftp.funet.fi in /pub/networking/management/NeTraMet.

• How do we keep things the way they were?

We can't. The multimedia genie is out of the

bottle. The bad news is that this is going to mean that the Internet is going to have to find new ways to allocate bandwidth. The good news is that if the increases in capacity to handle multimedia are put in place, there should be plenty of room for plain old ASCII transactions.

Many people are forecasting movies-on-demand, real-time video conferencing and other bandwidth-consuming applications that require orders of magnitude more bandwidth than we use today. If people are going to use these new applications they will have be priced so they are affordable-but this means that traditional text-based uses of the Internet will end up being essentially free. The challenge facing the Internet will be how to make the transition to this new multimedia environment.

References

Baeza-Yates et al. 1993
Baeza-Yates, R., Piqnera, J. M., Poblete, P. V., "The Chilean internet connection or I never promised you a rose garden," in *Proc. INET '93*.

Bohn et al. 1993
Bohn, R., Braun, H.-W., Claffy, K., Wolff, S., *Mitigating the coming Internet crunch: Multiple service levels via precedence*, UCSD, San Diego Supercomputer Center, and NSF.

Brownlee 1994
Brownlee, J. N., *Kawaihiko charging workshop report*, Computer Centre, The University of Auckland, Auckland, New Zealand.

Chaum 1985
Chaum, D., "Security without identification: Transaction systems to make big brother obsolete," *Communications of the ACM*, 28(10), 1030-1044.

Cocchi et al. 1992
Cocchi, R., Estrin, D., Shenker, S., Zhang, L., *Pricing in computer networks: Motivation, formulation, and example*, University of Southern California.

Ewing et al. 1992
Ewing, D. J., Hall, R. S., Schwartz, M. F., "A measurement study of Internet file transfer traffic," Department of Computer Science, University of Colorado. ftp://ftp.cs.colorado.edu/pub/techreports/schwartz/FTP.Meas.ps.Z.

Hansell 1994
Hansell, S., "An end to the "nightmare" of cash?" *New York Times*, Tuesday, C1.

HardyTribble 1993
Hardy, N. Tribble, E. D., *The digital silk road*, Agorics, Inc.

Lucky 1989
Lucky, R. W., *Silicon Dreams: Information, Man and Machine*. St. Martin's Press, New York.

MacKie-Mason Varian 1994a
MacKie-Mason, J. K. Varian, H. R., "Economic FAQs about the internet," *Journal of Economic Perspectives*, 8(3).

MacKie-Mason, J. K. Varian, H. R., "Pricing congestible network resources," University of Michigan http://gopher.econ.lsa.umich.edu.

Markoff 1993
Markoff, J., "Traffic jams already on the information highway," *New York Times*, November 3, A1.

Mitchell 1990
Mitchell, B., "Incremental costs of telephone access and local use," R3909, RAND.

Murphy Murphy 1994
Murphy, J. Murphy, L., "Bandwidth allocation by pricing in ATM networks," EECS Department, University of California, Berkeley.

Shenker 1993
Shenker, S.,"Service models and pricing policies for an integrated services Internet," Palo Alto Research Center, Xerox Corporation.

Vickrey 1961
Vickrey, W., "Counterspeculation, auctions, and competitive sealed tenders," *Journal of*

Finance, 16, 8-37.

Addresses

Jeffrey K. MacKie-Mason, Hal R. Varian
Department of Economics
University of Michigan, Ann Arbor, MI 48109-1220
E-mail: jmm@umich.edu; Hal.Varian@umich.edu

Biographies

Jeffrey K. MacKie-Mason

Jeffrey K. MacKie-Mason is an Associate Professor of Economics and Public Policy at the University of Michigan, and a Research Associate at the National Bureau of Economic Research in Cambridge, MA. He works in a number of fields in economics, including utility pricing, industrial organization, taxation, and corporate finance. He received his Ph.D. from the Massachusetts Institute of Technology in 1986, and a Master's in Public Policy from the University of Michigan in 1982. He has been a National Fellow at the Hoover Institution (Stanford), and a Visiting Scholar at the University of California, Berkeley, and the University of Oslo, Norway.

Hal R. Varian

Hal R. Varian is the Reuben Kempf Professor of Economics and a Professor of Finance at the University of Michigan. He received his S.B. degree from MIT in 1969 and his MA (mathematics) and Ph.D. (economics) from the University of California at Berkeley in 1973. He has taught at MIT, Berkeley, Stanford, Oxford, and several other universities, and has been at the University of Michigan since 1977. Professor Varian was a Guggenheim Fellow in 1979-80 and was elected a Fellow of the Econometric Society in 1983. He has served as Co-Editor of the American Economic Review, and is currently on the editorial boards of several journals.

Professor Varian has published numerous papers in economic theory, industrial organization, public finance, and econometrics. He is the author of a graduate textbook, Microeconomic Analysis and an undergraduate textbook, Intermediate Microeconomics.

The Combined AAUP Online Catalog/Bookstore Project: Server Design

Bruce H. Barton
The University of Chicago Press

The American Association of University Presses' (AAUP) combined online catalog project is in the early phases of implementation. Our goal is to deliver via gopher and World Wide Web on the Internet a searchable catalog of the 100,000 books and journals available from our 113 member presses and associations. We hope that in time the catalog will prove to be effective both as a marketing tool and as a way of establishing the presence of university presses in the electronic world. This paper briefly describes our strategies for presenting a large collection of titles to customers in an intuitive and inviting way, and for building a server that will not become a maintenance nightmare down the road.

Organizing the store

While I cannot claim to have strong marketing credentials, a couple of points of organization are obvious, even to me. A bald listing of 100,000 titles will not induce customers to buy. Customers will not wade through so much information even if they have the patience and disk capacity to retrieve it. On the other hand, a single prompt commanding them to search the on-line catalog is not terribly inviting. It does not suggest the kinds of things customers may wish to search for.

To provide customers with a familiar point of entry, we have modeled our catalog on the academic bookstore. We segment the catalog using menus into broad subject areas like history, philosophy, and the biological sciences. We further segment each area into subdisciplines like US history, ethics, and evolutionary biology. We continue segmenting until the collection of titles available in each subdiscipline can be conveniently and effectively browsed. At this level, we present a menu listing author and title for each book available. Selecting an item from this menu yields a sub-menu containing a pointer to a document that describes the book, another pointer to an order form that can be mailed or faxed to the publisher, and possibly one or more pointers to additional information that resides elsewhere on the Internet. Excerpts, jacket images, and book reviews are examples of the things that may be available elsewhere.

The descriptive documents are the entries typically found in university press print catalogs. Each entry displays the standard bibliographic information and may also display selling copy, quotes from reviews (favorable), or a table of contents.

At the broad subject level, we offer full-text searches of these documents across all subdisciplines within the category. A successful search yields the same type of browse menu customers find when drilling down through subdisciplines. We may also implement key word searches across subdisciplines if we find that full-text searches do not yield reasonably small hit lists for some terms with the consequence that some titles are unlikely to be selected through a search. We also offer full-text searches by publisher.

Maintaining the server

Just as 100,000 documents is more than our customers can easily handle without the right access methods, so many documents be can unwieldy to maintain. Based on our experience at Chicago, I estimate that as many as 20% to 25% of the documents will change each year. Our members will continue to publish new books, publish paperbacks of backlist titles, put books out-of-print, and change prices occasionally. If each of these changes were to be made by hand, we would need to hire a full-time employee to keep up with the work. But our mission is to build the catalog on the cheap, not to add staff.

To meet this challenge, we have adopted a design that will make server maintenance nearly automatic. At the heart of the design is a Standard Generalized Markup Language (SGML) document type definition (DTD) and a collection of PERL[1] scripts. Documents coded using this DTD contain the information needed to determine in which base subdiscipline menus and in which search indices the title is to be included. The document also contains the information needed to build the title sub-menu described above including external references, and the information needed to construct an order form. Order forms, incidentally, are built on the fly by inserting title specific order information (ISBN, price, etc.) defined as an element in the SGML document into the order form template to which another element in the document points. Full-text indexes are built by indexing only the "catalog entry" element of the document. Building key word indexes is instance of the same technique.

Our PERL scripts parse the SGML document to serve "documents" to the customer, build search indexes, generate subdiscipline menus, and construct title sub-menus and order forms. Because execution of the scripts is triggered by either a customer request or a timer, very little needs to be done to maintain a document at the server other than to drop in the updated version.

This approach allows us to maintain off-line the information we serve, and to distribute the work among our members.

Because implementation is at an early stage, the URL for the server is subject to change. To obtain its current URL, send e-mail to: bbarton@press.uchicago.edu

In conclusion, let me note that we are using a gopher/http server for UNIX systems developed by John Franks of Northwestern University, and glimpse indexing software developed by Udi Manber of the University of Arizona. PERL was developed by Larry Wall.

---

[1]PERL is a scripting language optimized for text manipulation and is readily available for UNIX systems.

Bruce Barton
MIS Manager
University of Chicago Press
bbarton@press.uchicago.edu

The AAUP Online Catalog Project: A Progress Report

Chuck Creesy
Princeton University Press

At last year's symposium, I reported how a number of university presses had discovered Gopher as a means of putting their catalogs online, often relying on their campus information services to take care of the technical work. I recounted how Princeton had constructed the first comprehensive Gopher menu pointing to these online catalogs, providing a convenient locator (soon pointed to by many other Gophers) and giving university presses a presence on the Internet. I told how Chicago had constructed the first Jughead to enable unified searching of these resources and mentioned that we were starting work on a combined AAUP server. Now I'm back a year later to explain why it's taking so long.

One school of thought back then contended that we did not really need a centralized server. After all, one of the beauties of Gopher -- and the World Wide Web -- is that you can build these things in an entirely decentralized way, letting each part of the whole manage its own component. But there were practical problems with that approach, evidenced by the fact that even today very few presses have their catalogs organized in such a way that Jughead and Veronica can index their books by author and title. At most universities, presses turn their data over to the campus wide information service and thereafter have little control over how it is organized. And many presses don't even have the option of turning to a CWIS.

So the main impetus behind creating a combined AAUP server was to provide one-stop shopping for our customers, eliminating the need to search catalog by catalog, and to provide a place where presses that lacked facilities at their own sites could put their bibliographic data online. Besides offering a comprehensive catalog of university press books, we hoped to stand out in this increasingly crowded field by offering superior search tools as well as frequent updates and an easy ordering capability. In the first phase, ordering will be facilitated by letting the user download or printout a customized order form that can be e-mailed or faxed to the appropriate press; later, we will provide online ordering and the system will automatically forward the orders to the presses.

How to collect data from 100-plus separate entities with separate database systems (except for those that have no systems at all) and with vastly different levels and styles of computerization? In an effort to get the process started, Michael Jensen of Nebraska, the early champion of this project, worked out an arrangement with the Library Corporation -- a service provider for libraries -- whereby it would supply us with the Library of Congress MARC records for our books in exchange for whatever descriptive information (such as catalog blurbs or quotations from reviews) we might amass. We thought this would give us the basic bibliographic data we needed, including items few presses had digital records of -- such as LC control numbers, classification codes, and subject headings -- which would be helpful in constructing search aids.

Bruce Barton, Chicago's MIS Manager and a "C" programmer (which in this context is much more than average), wrote a "parser" to pull the data from the MARC records and load it into standard dBase DBF files. The idea was that once we had this information in a central database, it would be easy to combine with other data supplied by the presses. And once the MARC data had been corrected and augmented, we could run programmatic routines on the database to generate plain ASCII text files for Gopher, HTML-encoded files for the Web, menu and index files for display and searching, and control files for generating custom order forms on the fly.

Very early on, however, we discovered that the MARC records are somewhat incomplete when it comes to things like current prices, in/out-of-print status, even type of binding -- items that are critical to an online bookstore. S o at a bare minimum, we needed to get that information from the individual presses into our centralized system. In addition, we found that MARC often neglects to assign ISBN numbers to paperbacks when a cloth edition already exists and that it generally assigns just one control number to multi-volume collections. In the case of the 69 volumes of the Woodrow Wilson Papers, to take a Princeton example, we had to add 68 records, since we wanted a separate entry for each volume. Not only does MARC lack many ISBN numbers, a lot of the ones it has are wrong. There is a high incidence of cases where two titles and control numbers get assigned to the same ISBN. And when you scan the database for a single press's ISBNs, you can see dropped digits, obvious transpositions, and the like.

In short, for our purposes, the MARC data turned out to be pretty dirty. We had to provide a way for presses to clean it up as well as enter descriptive text. So Bruce Barton went back to work programming, this time using FoxPro's application development tools for Windows and Macintosh, and built editor packages for both platforms to make it easy for a press to inspect and correct its MARC data and also to add to it by cutting and pasting from word processor files or spreadsheet files or other database files. To use this most effectively, we needed to merge as much of the presses' own data as possible with the MARC records before packaging it with the editor.

Many university presses use an order fulfillment system called the Cat's Pajamas which creates a plain ASCII file named FILEBOOK.TXT that contains the critical items ISBN, price, print status, binding, and enough of the title to enable matching of cloth and paper editions. So we worked out a way to use FoxPro's low-level input/output functions to scan these files and merge those items into our database, even to create records for paperbacks absent from MARC, incorporating the appropriate data from the records for their cloth counterparts.

For presses that do not use Cat's Pajamas, we defined formats by which they could submit their data as ASCII-delimited or tagged files. Using similar techniques, in a couple of cases we were able to accommodate style-tagged export files from PageMaker. We also provided a detailed data dictionary for the benefit of presses that have highly developed bibliographic databases of their books and that might find it easier to supply us with fully structured DBF files. And we developed routines to run against the database to identify ISBN conflicts and generate "exception reports" to help presses fix incorrect ISBN numbers.

Cambridge University Press, which was among the first to submit its data, sent us the most complete submission we have received to date in terms of number of fields utilized and also the largest number of titles: 9,200. It was the first press to have its catalog mounted on our server after it moved from the "Potemkin Village" prototype stage to the "early phases of construction" stage. We will be adding other presses' catalogs as we receive their corrected data and hope in a few more months to have a critical mass assembled.

Meanwhile, we have converted the AAUP Journals Subscription Catalog -- which contains basic information about nearly 300 journals from 36 presses -- to digital form and mounted it on the central server. It is expected to grow over time to include most of the 800 journals published by AAUP member presses. Like the book catalog, it can be viewed via either Gopher or the Web. Like the printed version, entries for individual journals can be looked up by title or by a subject index. The online version also provides a Jughead search on title keywords and a WAIS search on the full text of each journal entry. In addition, it has links to the online journals catalogs of individual presses, some of which contain more detailed information, and to other online resources like Johns Hopkins Project Muse.

Chuck Creesy
Director of Computing & Publishing Technologies
Princeton University Press
creesy@pupress.princeton.edu

Campus Publishing in Standardized Electronic Formats -- HTML and TEI

David Seaman
University of Virginia Library

Introduction

In the past year, HyperText Markup Language (HTML) has done more to popularize the notion of Standard Generalized Markup Language than any single use of SGML that has preceded it. Used on the World Wide Web through a graphical client such as NCSA Mosaic, HTML documents and their associated image, sound, and digital video files result in sophisticated network publications and services. And even when viewed through the plain text (VT100) client Lynx, HTML files can still be exciting clusters of interlinked documents.

In common with Internet users all over the world, the University of Virginia Library now uses and produces HTML documents; unlike most other institutions, however, we came to HTML with practical experience in another, more sophisticated, form of SGML, that of the Text Encoding Initiative Guidelines. For two years the Electronic Text Center has been using the TEI Guidelines, through several drafts, to tag and distribute hundreds of electronic texts. The purpose of this paper is both to explain how we are using these various forms of SGML mark- up to publish a variety of documents, and to sound a cautionary note about the wholesale use of HTML as a primary authoring language.

HyperText Markup Language: HTML

HyperText Markup Language is exciting as an implementation of SGML not least because it is easy to use and to learn. It has a real pedagogical value as a form of SGML that makes clear to newcomers the concept of standardized markup. To the novice, the mass of information that constitutes the Text Encoding Initiative Guidelines, the premier tagging scheme for most humanities documents, is not easily grasped. In contrast, the concise guidelines to HTML that are available on-line (and usually as a "help" option from the menu of a Web client) are a good introduction to some of the basic SGML concepts. The combination of a small number of tags with a viewer such as Mosaic means that in the space of a single training session a user new to the concept of standardized markup can create a document from scratch and see it operate with images and hypertext links in place. In HTML we finally have a way to build functional hypertexts easily and cheaply and to publish the results in a networked manner that will never be an option with the proprietary hypertext software packages (ToolBook, HyperCard, MediaView, AuthorWare, and so on).

This ease of use is a mixed blessing. The current Web clients such as Mosaic and Netscape are very forgiving, requiring no real conformity to the HTML rules (the Document Type Definition, or DTD). This in turn leads to bad habits in all of us. HTML documents become in a practical sense defined as "texts that work when viewed through Mosaic," rather than files that conform to a specific set of rules governing tag names and their usage. Leaving aside the potential long-term problems that non-conforming HTML texts may cause, there is a more pressing problem: we need to be careful that the texts we mark up primarily in HTML are ones that do not suffer from the use of such a simple form of SGML.

In the other SGML tagsets with which I am familiar, the aim of the markup is to describe structurally and conceptually what an item is. For example, in a TEI text a chapter might appear thus:

```
<div type="chapter" n=1>
<head rend="italics">
Chapter Name
</head>
[TEXT OF CHAPTER]
</div>
```

In the example above, the structure as well as the typography of the text is explicitly named. In contrast, about all the HTML tagset allows one to do is to mark for line breaks and typographic features:

```
<br><i> Chapter Name </i>
<br>
[TEXT OF CHAPTER]
<br>
```

It does not necessarily take appreciably longer to mark up a text in a structurally specific manner than in a non-specific one. To indicate that a chapter starts and ends here, and that a phrase is an italicized chapter heading (the TEI way) is no more work than to indicate that this is a line break, and this is an italicized phrase of unspecified type (the possibilities given to us in HTML currently). However, the former is inherently more useful over a wider range of uses. In a collection of a thousand novels one may well want to search for items that appear only in opening chapters or for words only when they appear in chapter headings, and the former example provides the level of specificity to do exactly that.

There are practical and appropriate uses for HTML as a primary form of mark-up, rather than as a form to which another variety of SGML is converted. At the Electronic Text Center, and elsewhere in our Library and our University, HTML is being used to publish on-line guides and brochures for various projects, including the University Press of Virginia's Fall 1994 Catalog. In my on-line description of the Etext Center, I have color images and a web of hypertext links that are too expensive or impossible to duplicate in print.

The URL is:
http://www.lib.virginia.edu/etext/ETC.html

And HTML works very well for the various training handouts that accompany the humanities computing courses we teach. These documents are written and printed out for class in WordPerfect, and they change with great frequency. I use a WordPerfect-to-HTML converter to perform the conversions, and it is a quick and easy way of keeping the on-line documentation up to date. For training manuals such as the Electronic Text Center's *Guide to Optical Character Recognition*, there is much to be gained from using HTML to show digital images of a range of different typefaces linked hypertextually to the results generated by our OCR technology. HTML functions perfectly well for me when I am building such a helpsheet, and the ability with no extra work to make it available to others on the Internet is an added and welcome bonus. Little by little, our faculty too are seeing HTML as a useable pedagogical tool for constructing supplementary courseware items, "Kinkos Packets on-line," as they have been called.

For the moment, I have no real qualms about using HTML as the primary mark-up language for such items. What is clearly inappropriate and unnecessary is to undertake any large amount of text production and markup in HTML for the following items: finding aids, full texts, sets of journal titles, encyclopedia, and dictionaries. Such items are only really useful and navigable if their structure is clearly and explicitly delimited. And this is where tagging schemes such as the TEI come in.

The Text Encoding Initiative: TEI

I have become fond of saying that the TEI Guidelines are 1,600 pages long and the HTML guidelines are 16 tags long. This is an exaggeration, but it is not an outrageously distorting one. The TEI is a splendid if somewhat daunting undertaking; it provides us with a full set of tags, a methodology, and a set of Document Type Descriptions (DTDs) that allow the detailed (or not so detailed) description of the spatial, intellectual, structural, and typographic form of a work. For a library such as ours at the University of Virginia, which is busy buying and creating texts for use on-line through a single SGML-aware software package, TEI is just what we need. It means that each new work tagged by us can be added to an existing database of related work and can be searched and analyzed either as an individual entity or as a part of a larger context (to do this we use Pat, an SGML textual analysis and display tool from OpenText Corp.). Moreover, it is comforting to work within a large tagset so that a user in the future can add to the complexity of the mark-up and still conform to the same general tagging universe.

TEI-to-HTML Conversion

As we began at Virginia to create a set of public domain SGML texts (in addition to the commercial databases that we have on-line via license for University of Virginia users only) we ran into something of a problem, one for which the World Wide Web is a partial answer. We wanted to be able to share access to the public domain SGML materials, and we could do this by putting copies on an ftp site or by depositing them at another central repository such as the Oxford Text Archive. In both of these cases, a user retrieving a file would get a "raw" SGML text and, in all likelihood, would have no SGML-aware software thorough which to use the item. The advent of HTML and the World Wide Web meant that we could provide on-line access to HTML copies of these public domain materials. Because both the TEI tags and the HTML tags are predictable, it was no great undertaking to write a search-and-replace routine to turn the TEI tags into HTML tags automatically. Converting from a specific and precise form of SGML to a simpler form (TEI to HTML) presents little problem. Crucially, the access to the texts through the World Wide Web is achieved without the need for us to maintain two copies of every file: a TEI-encoded and an HTML-encoded version. Instead, the TEI-to-HTML conversion is performed by a Perl script on the Unix machine that houses all the electronic texts in the University of Virginia on-line archive. For most of the full texts available through our Web server, the conversion is set in motion by the action of choosing a particular text. The conversion is done "on the fly," and the freshly-generated HTML version is sent to whatever Web client one uses.

This, then, is a convenient and low maintenance means by which to mark up the data in a manner appropriate to the subject matter and also to get Web-browsable HTML copies with no real additional effort. As the HTML tagset grows, the filter can be enlarged to let more of the TEI tags through without the need to do anything to the texts.

The Problem of Unidentified Images

Almost as soon as we had this system of TEI-to-HTML conversions running, a problem dawned on us. A growing number of our electronic texts have book illustrations and other book-related images along with the tagged ASCII text. Our TEI-to-HTML filter takes the TEI manner of indicating the location of an image:

```
<figure entity="TarFlir1">
<head> "You Darling!" </head>
</figure>
```

and turns it into an in-line image with a hypertext link to an associated full-size version:

```
<A href="TarFlir1.jpg">
<img src="TarFlir1.gif"></A>
<br>
<h1> "You Darling!" </h1>
```

It is at this point that the problem arises -- if a user saves a book illustration from one of our works, there is often nothing on that image to identify what work it comes from, where the image was created, or by whom. A month after saving a book illustration such as the narcissistic frontispiece to Booth Tarkington's <i>The Flirt</i> *[see Figure 1]*, the user has in all likelihood forgotten where it came from or to what work it belongs. By strewing unlabelled images across the Net, we would be contributing to the problem of unattributed texts that we have been complaining about for two years. For many

Figure 1

"You Darling!": the frontispiece from Booth Tarkington's *The Flirt*, with the TEI-derived image header visible.

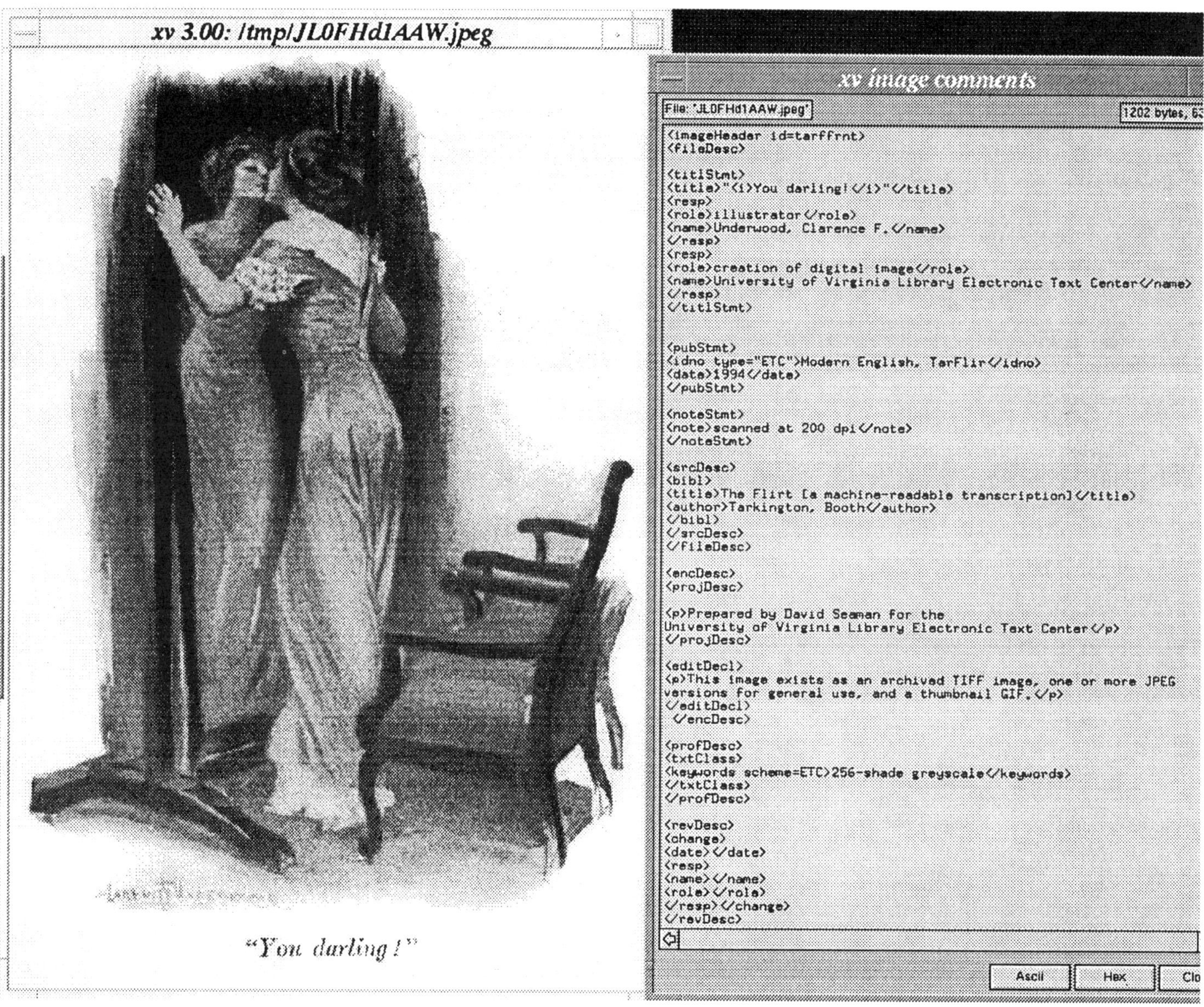

Figure 2

Rita Dove's "Lady Freedom among us." The image is of the second stanza, with the TEI-derived image header visible. Note here that the ASCII text buried in the code of the image contains the text found on the page, in addition to the bibliographical header.

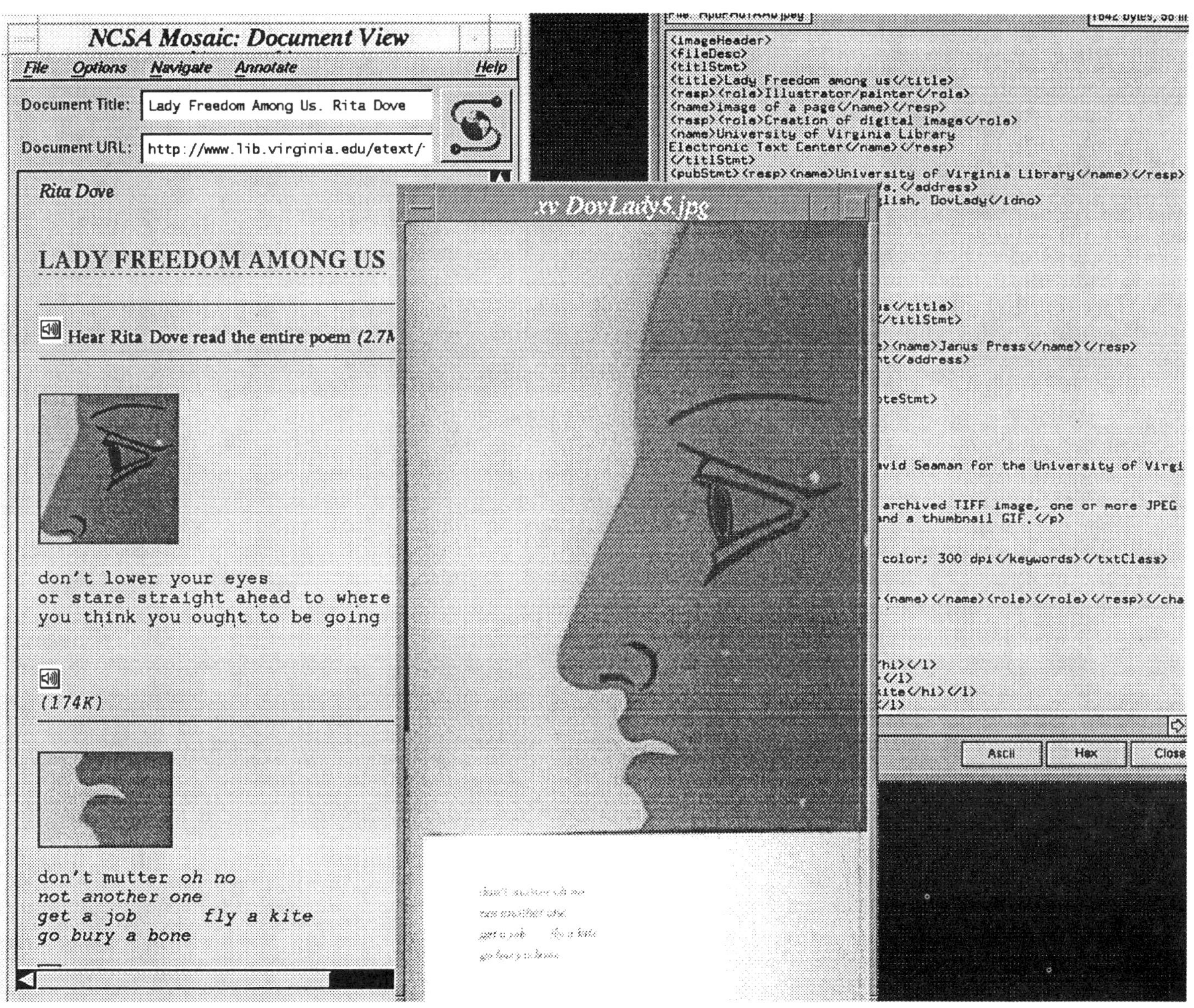

of the public domain texts we have taken off other network sites, we have had to spend a lot of time trying to identify the source texts. Without the print source in hand the checking and tagging is largely impossible; without knowledge of the print source, a user cannot safely make scholarly or pedagogical use of the material.

The solution to the problem of unlabelled book illustrations wandering free from their texts presented itself quite readily: the user who downloads an image file of a book illustration or manuscript page needs to have delivered along with it a copy of the bibliographical header that is at the top of every TEI text [see Appendix A for an example]. The TEI header is a catalog record, a finding aid, and a description of the production of the electronic text. A user saving a copy of the text gets the bibliographical information along with it, because the header is part of the TEI text file and is converted along with the rest of the text into HTML.

By the surprisingly simple expedient of taking a version of the TEI header out of the text and burying this image header into the binary code of the image itself, the user who saves an image from our server now gets, in Trojan Horse fashion and whether they know it or not, a tagged full-text record of the creation of that image as part of the single image file they save. [See Appendix B for an example of an image header from the Rita Dove work whose TEI header appears in Appendix A]. If a user has an image tool that permits the viewing of text comments in the image file (I use XV, the XWindows viewer with XMosaic) then both image and header can be seen simultaneously [*Figures 1 and 2* show what this looks like through XMosaic], but any program that lets you see the contents of a file is sufficient to read the text.

I am hoping that the practice of burying tagged ASCII data in the code of an image file will become much more widespread in the electronic data communities, and I am writing up the procedure we use to aid others who wish to do the same. The practice may even be extendable to sound files or digital video files in the future, although we have done no experiments with these file formats yet. The text that goes into the image file does not have to be SGML-tagged data, of course, but it does seem to be a logical extension of the purpose of the TEI header, and there are long-term advantages to making this "text in the image file" contain clearly delimited fields. When we have software that can search (rather than simply view) the text contained in image files then suddenly we will have the possibility of a database of images that is searchable by keyword. And when that happens, the text in those images will be much more useful over much larger collections if various fields are marked with SGML tags, so that the text is searchable within specific categories.

Anticipating such "text in image files" search capabilities, we have started very recently to add into the image file not only a bibliographical header but also any written text that occurs as part of an image. In the case of the example in *Figure 2*, for example, the TEI header in the image file is followed by a tagged text transcription of the words on the page:

```
<text>
<lg type="stanza">
<l n=4> don't mutter<hi>oh no</hi></l>
<l n=5><hi>not another one</hi></l>
<l n=6><hi>get a job   fly a kite</hi></l>
<l n=7><hi>go bury a bone</hi></l>
</lg>
</text>
```

At the point at which we have the ability to search this ASCII text then we suddenly have images of typescript (or manuscript) pages that are fully searchable, long before tools for matching the shapes of letters within an image give us searchable images in any form that requires pattern recognition. The addition of a series of key descriptive terms to the text in the image file would allow for images to be searched according to content.

Conclusion

New and significant electronic documents are being produced at a rapid pace, many of them driven by the excitement generated by the arrival of the World Wide Web. At the University of Virginia all sorts of guides, manuals, teaching documents, finding aids, and texts are appearing on Web servers, and the Electronic Text Center's short courses in HTML fill up repeatedly. In the Center itself, we are making heavy use of both HTML and TEI tagging as we create and/or convert full-text collections, and we are facing some of the issues involved in describing the texts and images we send out onto the Internet.

Despite the allure of the Web as a distribution medium it is increasingly important to choose the SGML tagging system that best allows one to describe with precision the material being created. For different texts this may be the TEI Guidelines; Dan Pitti's Finding Aids Project (showcased elsewhere at this conference); the AAP tagset; HTML; or something else entirely. The decision to use a form of SGML other than HTML does not deny one the use of the World Wide Web as a delivery mechanism for that document; it is not difficult to convert a specific set of SGML tags to a simpler, less descriptive form by employing a "search and replace" conversion routine that provides HTML output with little extra effort and no extra tagging. Crucially - - the central message of this paper -- the electronic document that one creates needs to receive the form of standardized description suitable to the nature of the document, and not one simply dictated by a desire to publish in HTML on the Web.

A hypertext versin of this article can be found at the following University of Virginia URL: http://www.lib.virginia.edu/etext/articles.html

David Seaman
Coordinator, Electronic Text Center
University of Virginia Library
etext@virginia.edu
http://www.lib.virginia.edu/etext/ETC.html

Appendix A: TEI Header for the recent Janus Press edition of Rita Dove's poem "Lady Freedom Among Us."

<header type=aacr2>
<fileDesc> <titlStmt> <title>Lady Freedom among us [a machine-readable transcription]</title>
<author>Dove, Rita</author>
<resp><role>Creation of machine-readable version:</role>
<name>David Seaman, University of Virginia Library Electronic Text Center</name></resp><resp><role> Conversion to TEI-conformant markup</role>
<name>University of Virginia Library Electronic Text Center</name></resp>
</titlStmt><extent>ca. 4 kilobytes</extent>
<pubStmt><resp><name>University of Virginia Library</name>
<role>Publisher</role></resp>
<address>Charlottesville, Va.</address>
<idno type="ETC">Modern English, DovLady</idno>
<avail> <p>Available for anonymous ftp at etext.lib.virginia.edu, and at the following URL: http://www.lib.virginia.edu/etext/fourmill.html</p> <p>Copies of this file are also available to UVa faculty, staff, and students; please contact the Electronic Text Center.</p> </avail>
<date>1994</date>
</pubStmt> <serStmt></serStmt>
<noteStmt> <note>Digital images of the pages from the Janus Press version created by David Seaman, Electronic Text Center. The HTML copy also includes sound files of Rita Dove reading the poem, and background information on the Janus Press and on the poet, provided by Rick Provine, Multimedia Resource Center. </note>
</noteStmt>
<srcDesc> <biblFull> <titlStmt> <title>Lady Freedom among us</title>
<author>Rita Dove</author></titlStmt> <extent></extent>
<pubStmt>
<resp><role>Publisher</role><name>Janus Press</name></resp> <address>West Burke, Vermont</address>
<date>[1994[, c1993</date> </pubStmt> <serStmt></serStmt>
<noteStmt><note>"Copy number one of this edition of one hundred was added to the collections of the University of Virginia Library on 8 November 1994 as its four-millionth volume and in honor of United States Poet Laureate Rita Dove, Commonwealth Professor of English at the University of Virginia."</note>
<note>"The text is Century Schoolbook printed on Mohawk Superfine at the Janus Press in West Burke Vermont in 1994; the handmade papers are Sky blue from MacGregor & Vinzani in Whiting Maine, Gelatin sisized white and Mica rose from Twinrocker in Brookston Indiana. The slipcases were made by Mary Richardson and Judy Conant in Guildhall Vermont. Images and design are by Claire Van Vliet with cutting executed by Audrey Holden. ... and edition of one hundred plus ten hors commerce copies ...."</note>
<note>"This poem was read at the occasion of the return of the statue Freedom to the dome of the Capitol on 23 October 1993."</note></noteStmt> </biblFull> </srcDesc> </fileDesc>
<encDesc> <projDesc> <p>Prepared for the University of Virginia Library Electronic Text Center</p></projDesc>
<editDecl> <p>Verification made against printed text.</p> <p id=ETC>Keywords in the header are a local Electronic Text Center scheme to aid in establishing analytical groupings.</p> </editDecl>
<refsDecl><p>ID elements are given for each page element and are composed of the text's unique cryptogram and the given page number, as in SpeFQue1 for page one of Spenser's Faerie Queene.</p></refsDecl> </encDesc>

<profDesc><creation><date>1994</date></creation><langUse><language>English</langua
ge></langUse>
<txtClass><keywords scheme=ETC>Fiction; poetry</keywords></txtClass></profDesc>
<revDesc> <change><date>November 7, 1994</date> <resp><name>Edward Gaynor,
University of Virginia Library,Cataloging Services Dept.</name><role>TEI header
completed</role></resp></change>
<change><date>October, 1994</date> <resp><name>David Seaman</name><role>TEI
tagging added, and parsed against uva.dtd. Images scanned, and HTML copy
generated.</role></resp></change> </revDesc>
</header>

Appendix B: Image header for the image of the first page from the recent Janus Press edition of Rita Dove's poem "Lady Freedom Among Us." The image header is derived from the TEI header in Appendix A.

```
<imageHeader>
<fileDesc>
<titlStmt>
<title>Lady Freedom among us</title>
<resp><role>Illustrator</role>
<name>Claire van Vliet</name></resp>
<resp><role>Creation of digital image</role>
<name>University of Virginia Library Electronic Text Center</name></resp>
</titlStmt>
<pubStmt><resp><name>University of Virginia Library</name></resp>
<address>Charlottesville, Va.</address>
<idno type="ETC">Modern English, DovLady</idno>
<date>1994</date>
</pubStmt>
<srcDesc>
<biblFull>
<titlStmt>
<title>Lady Freedom among us</title>
<author>Rita Dove</author></titlStmt>
<pubStmt>
<resp><role>Publisher</role>
<name>Claire Van Vliet. Janus Press</name>
</resp>
<address>West Burke, Vermont</address>
<date>[1994[, c1993</date>
</pubStmt>
<noteStmt><note></note></noteStmt>
</biblFull>
</srcDesc>
</fileDesc>
<encDesc>
<projDesc><p>Prepared by David Seaman for the University of Virginia Library Electronic
Text Center</p></projDesc>
<editDecl>
<p>This image exists as an archived TIFF image, one or more JPEG versions for general use, and
a thumbnail GIF.</p>
</editDecl</encDesc>
<profDesc> <txtClass>
<keywords>24-bit color; 300 dpi</keywords>
</txtClass>
</profDesc>
<revDesc>
<change><date></date><resp><name></name><role></role>
</resp>
</change>
</revDesc>
</imageHeader>
```

Project Muse: Tackling 40 Journals

Susan Lewis, Johns Hopkins University Press
Todd Kelley, Milton S. Eisenhower Library, Johns Hopkins University

Project Muse is a collaborative effort that expands traditional scholarly publishing and is a model for the future. The collaboration involves the university press, the library, and the computing center at the Johns Hopkins University in a large-scale effort that will eventually lead to the online publication of forty of the Press's journals in the humanities and social sciences.

The Prototype

The first result of our alliance is a prototype consisting of four journal issues, fully formatted text, a powerful search engine, full-screen illustrations, subject indexing, and many additional features. The prototype was released to the scholarly community in March 1994 for testing and comment. It is available on a server at Johns Hopkins University and can be accessed through the Internet with software such as Mosaic, Lynx, Cello, or any other World Wide Web browser. The prototype has been viewed by thousands of users from all over the world, and comments and reactions have been generally favorable. The homepage address or Uniform Resource Location for Project Muse is http://muse.mse.jhu.edu.

The homepage offers users the option of browsing through a particular journal, searching across journals, finding out about Project Muse, or leaving a comment or question. Users can select any of these options through hypertext links that make selection a matter of moving the cursor to the choice and clicking a mouse button or pressing the Enter key. A reproduction of the homepage can be seen in Figure 1.

Selecting the browse option on the homepage brings up a list of the journals that are available for browsing (see Figure 2). This list is presented graphically as well as textually so that users without graphics capability can make selections as well. Besides selecting a journal for browsing, users can retrieve subscription and editorial information.

Browsing a journal (see Figure 3) allows a user to view the tables of contents of the selected journal for all issues that are currently available online. The issues appear sequentially with the most recent issue listed first. Each article listing has full title, author, and subject information. The subject indexing is provided by librarians who use Library of Congress Subject Headings. This controlled vocabulary helps the users of the tables of contents by providing insight about the article beyond that found in the title. An article can be selected for reading by clicking anywhere on the title of the article (see Figure 4).

The other method of intellectual access to articles involves using a search engine (see Figure 5). This feature enables users to search all journals that are currently online. One option involves searching all the words in all the tables of contents. This means that the search is limited to words found in the article, titles, authors' names, or subject words. Users can also conduct a full-text search across all articles in all journals. In both instances, users can expand and limit the search via Boolean terms such as "or" and "and." The search *France and Russia* (see Figure 6) will pull up two articles if the full text of all articles are searched (see Figure 7). No articles are found using the tables of contents search.

Other features of the prototype include instant footnotes and lavish illustrations. The *MLN* article by Stephen Nichols, "Picture, Image, and Subjectivity in

Figure 1

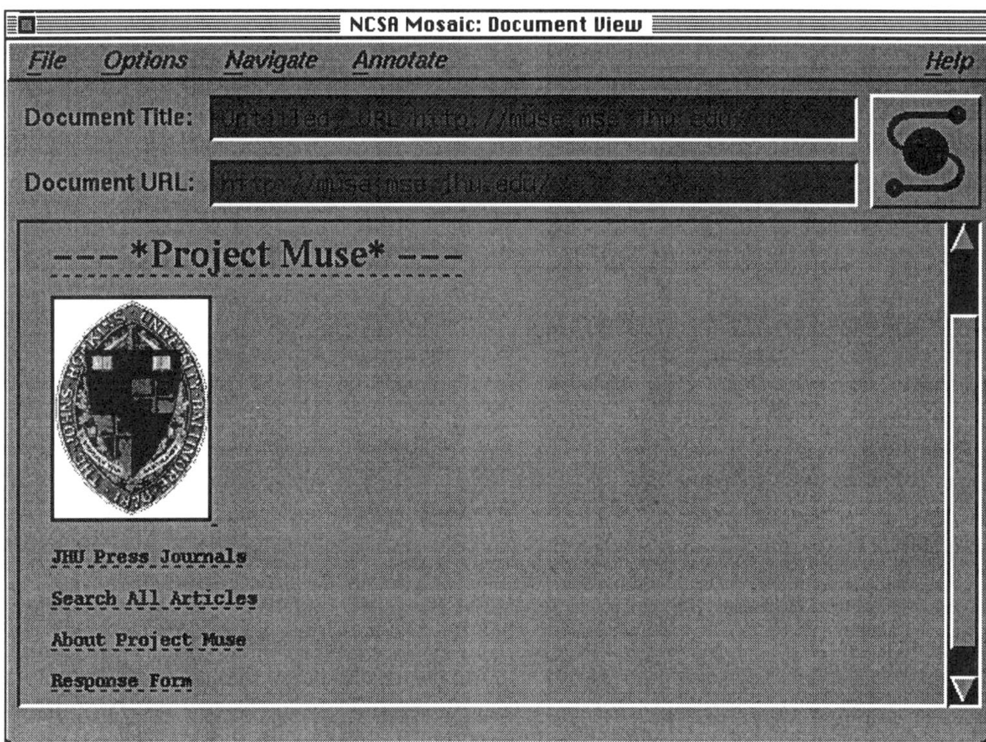

Figure 2

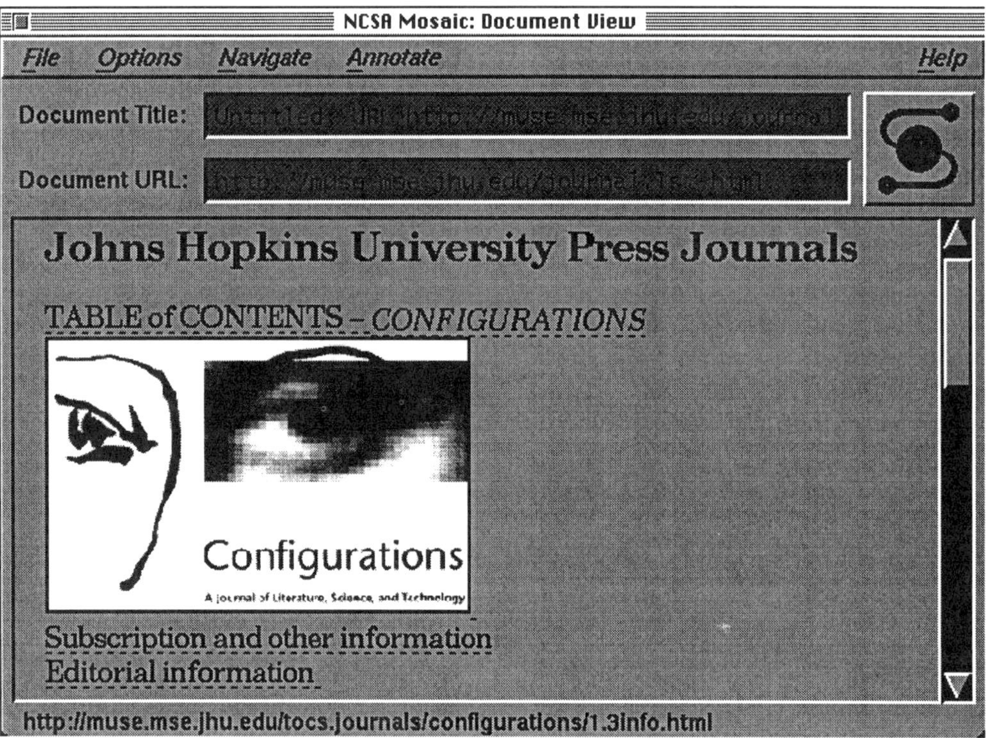

Figure 3

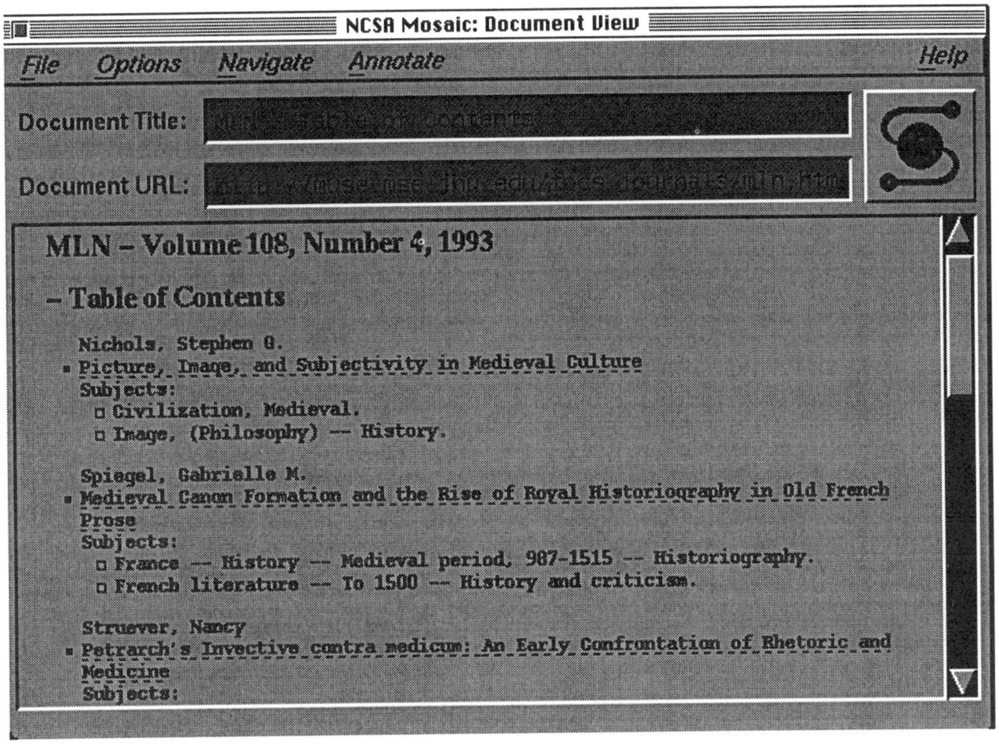

NCSA Mosaic: Document View

File Options Navigate Annotate Help

Document Title:

Document URL:

MLN – Volume 108, Number 4, 1993

– Table of Contents

Nichols, Stephen G.
- Picture, Image, and Subjectivity in Medieval Culture

Subjects:
- Civilization, Medieval.
- Image, (Philosophy) -- History.

Spiegel, Gabrielle M.
- Medieval Canon Formation and the Rise of Royal Historiography in Old French Prose

Subjects:
- France -- History -- Medieval period, 987-1515 -- Historiography.
- French literature -- To 1500 -- History and criticism.

Struever, Nancy
- Petrarch's Invective contra medicum: An Early Confrontation of Rhetoric and Medicine

Subjects:

Figure 4

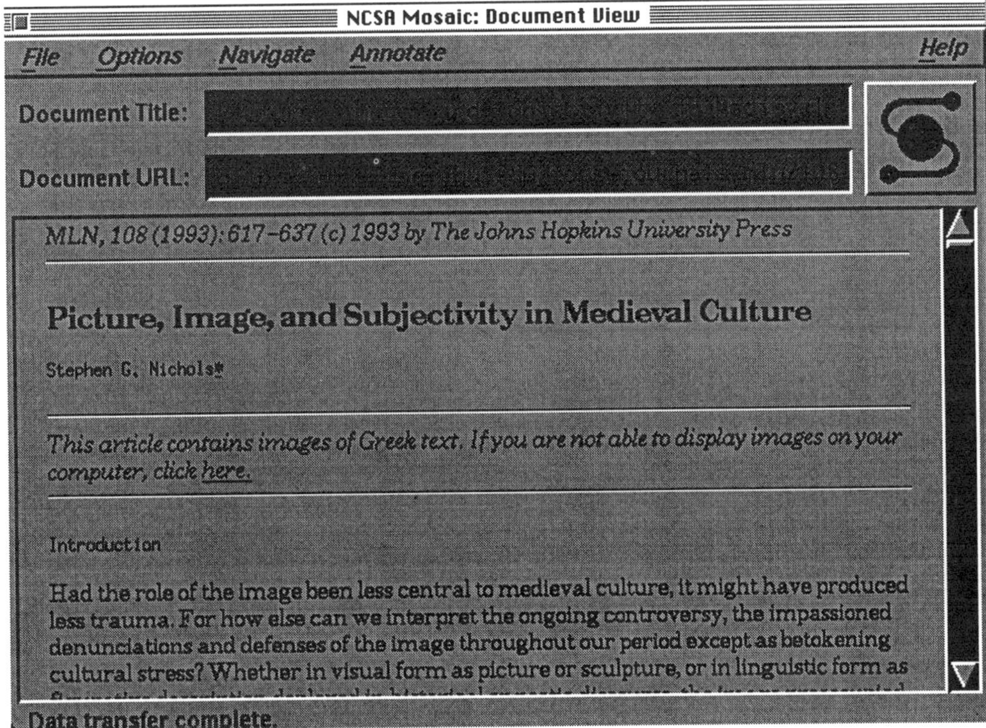
NCSA Mosaic: Document View

File Options Navigate Annotate Help

Document Title:

Document URL:

MLN, 108 (1993):617–637 (c) 1993 by The Johns Hopkins University Press

Picture, Image, and Subjectivity in Medieval Culture

Stephen G. Nichols*

This article contains images of Greek text. If you are not able to display images on your computer, click here.

Introduction

Had the role of the image been less central to medieval culture, it might have produced less trauma. For how else can we interpret the ongoing controversy, the impassioned denunciations and defenses of the image throughout our period except as betokening cultural stress? Whether in visual form as picture or sculpture, or in linguistic form as

Data transfer complete.

Figure 5

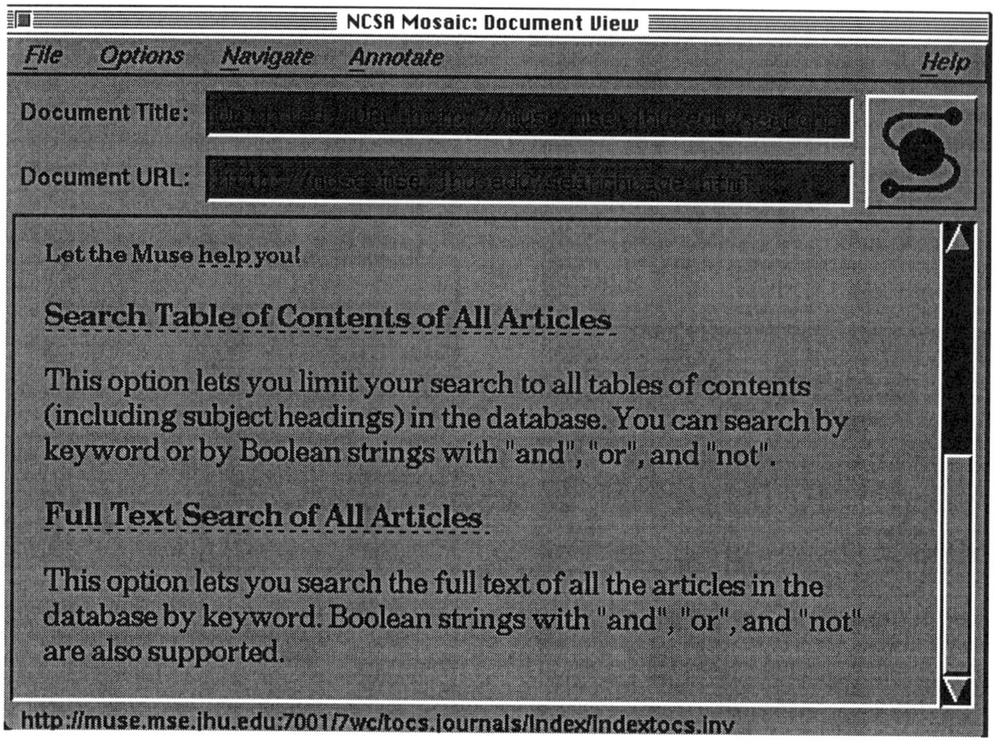

NCSA Mosaic: Document View

File Options Navigate Annotate Help

Document Title:

Document URL:

Let the Muse help you!

Search Table of Contents of All Articles

This option lets you limit your search to all tables of contents (including subject headings) in the database. You can search by keyword or by Boolean strings with "and", "or", and "not".

Full Text Search of All Articles

This option lets you search the full text of all the articles in the database by keyword. Boolean strings with "and", "or", and "not" are also supported.

http://muse.mse.jhu.edu:7001/7wc/tocs.journals/index/indextocs.inv

Figure 6

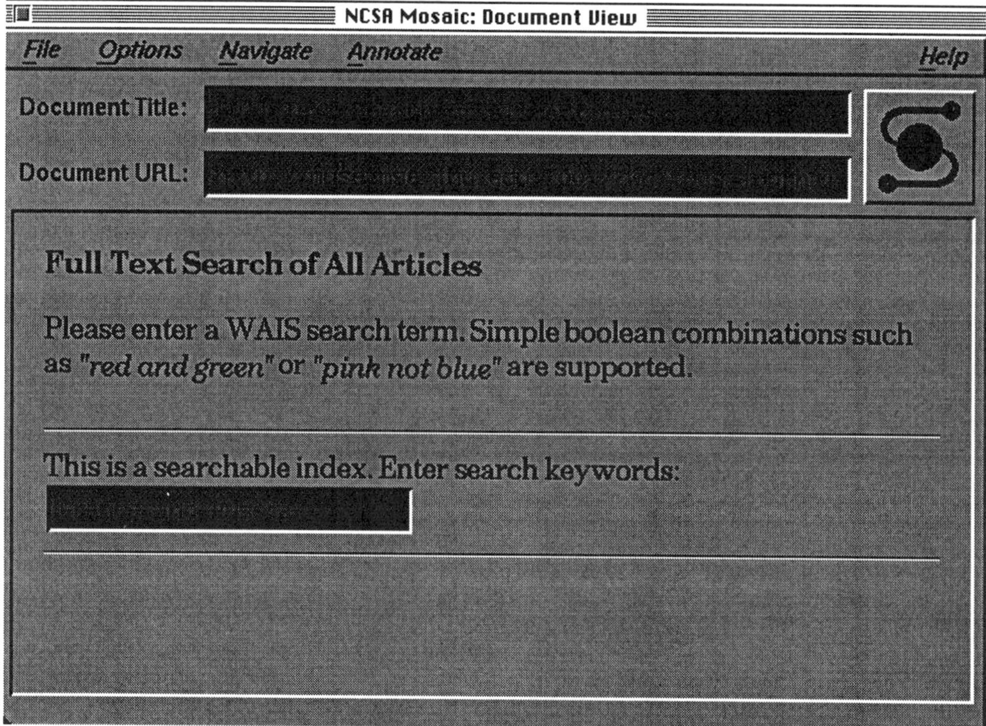

Medieval Culture", for example, has numerous footnotes. The footnotes appear at the end of the article but can be accessed instantly by clicking on the footnote number. Clicking on the corresponding number in the footnote returns users to their place in the text.

Embedding illustrations in the text of articles that have more than one illustration would make a noticeable difference in the time it takes the article to reach the user when requested. Thus multiple illustrations are available as links within the article or from an index of illustrations. All illustrations are available in two file sizes depending on the needs of the user.

One of the advantages of online publishing is that color and enlarged illustrations can be used more lavishly. Photos that are routinely cropped and rendered in black-and-white for reasons of cost in the printed journal are enlarged and available in color in the online prototype (see Figure 8).

Page numbers that correspond to the print journal are currently embedded in the text for consistency in citations. In the future, we hope to use a paragraph- or line-reference scheme that is more appropriate to the online environment.

Partnership of Interest

Beyond the value-added features described above, most notably a sophisticated search engine and enhanced illustrations, we believe that the electronic journals offered through Project Muse can be economically priced if certain criteria are met. Meeting them involves a new way of doing business for the university press and its library subscribers by engaging subscriber libraries in a "partnership of interest" that will enable us to deliver scholarly publications in a way that integrates library involvement and feedback so we can tailor the form of our publications to serve the actual needs of scholars and readers.

The Project Muse prototype and the partnership between the press and the library have enabled us to identify four areas that are key to the success of this larger process. These include marketing, rights and permissions, true costs, and product pricing. The effect of our approach to these issues will affect staffing and the traditional production process at the Press and has implications for the role of librarians.

Market Readiness and Marketing

Subscriptions to the electronic journals will initially be available to libraries rather than individuals. These subscriptions will entitle the network of users served by the library to access the journals. Access may be from networked computers on campus or from computers in the library. Current estimates indicate that only 50% of all faculty have computers in their offices and only 25% of all students have their own computers. This means that access within the library walls is still important for the vast majority of both groups. Working closely with subscribing libraries is therefore important since libraries must support their users both within the library and on the campus network.

Physical access to these journals requires building and managing the hardware, software, and network infrastructure. Libraries must provide both physical *and* intellectual access by creating records in the local catalog that indicate how the journals may be accessed. In some cases, links may be built that connect the user directly to the Project Muse journals from the library catalog record for the journal. In others, links will have to be created from local servers to Project Muse.

Libraries are already being called on to provide instruction and support to their users for the resources that the library provides. To do this effectively, they must feel confident about their ability to deliver a high-quality product that meets the needs of their user community. Designing, implementing, and maintaining systems of physical and intellectual access to Project Muse, as well as instructing and supporting

Figure 7

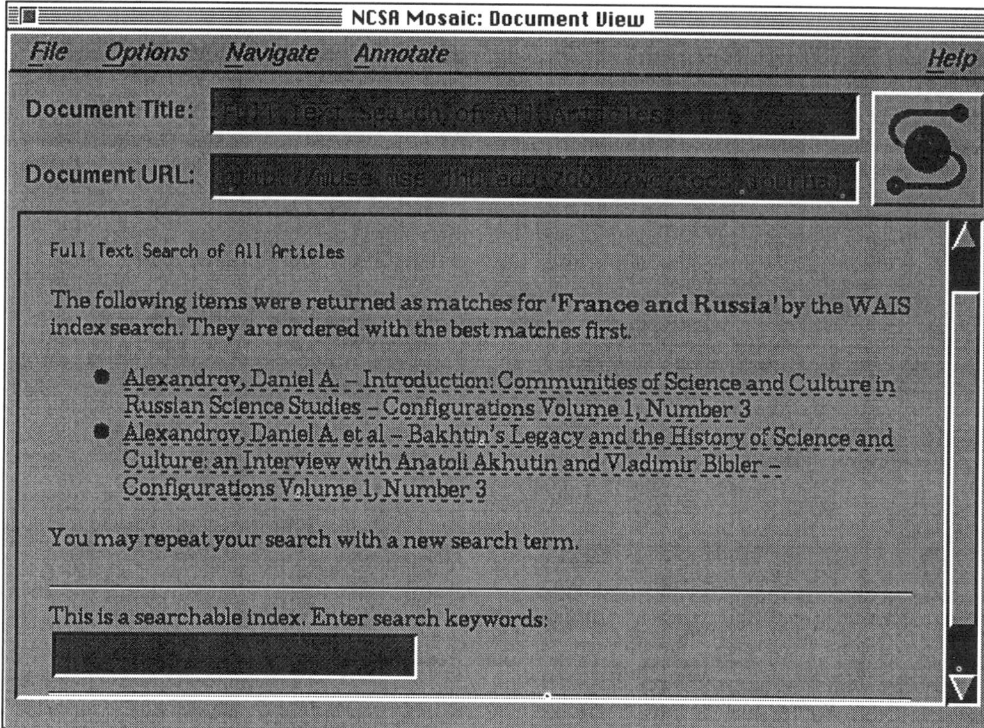

their users, requires careful attention. It is therefore an important goal of Project Muse to work with libraries in meeting these needs.

In the context of a partnership, rather than a relationship as suppliers and customers, *Marketing* becomes *Education*. This is a very different approach, designed to inform and gather feedback, rather than simply announce and persuade, as is done in traditional sales and advertising campaigns. By making education and technical assistance the focus of our marketing efforts, we can actually create a product and a market based on input from those who will use it. This approach is not just mutually beneficial to the partners, it is absolutely essential since libraries must have in place an electronic environment that benefits their readers before they can take full advantage of electronically delivered journals.

To facilitate the creation of this environment, our initiative will involve assessing library needs so we can provide the consultation and information most relevant to these needs. In other words, educating libraries about the advantages of our approach for their readers will involve working directly with libraries and "focus groups" of users to determine:

- library readiness and experience with full-text databases
- library hardware and network infrastructure, including "front end" software
- reader sophistication and usage patterns
- online access to reader training materials

Reader involvement is an important part of the educational process, and the end users of our electronic journals will be encouraged to respond via electronic forms and questionnaires, as they have in the simplified but very useful form developed for the prototype. One scenario might

Figure 8

include forwarding comments about the local electronic environment to the contact person at the local site; forwarding comments about the journal content to the appropriate editor; and remaining comments about the quality of the electronic product for use by the publisher to improve the product.

Rights and Permissions

Conversations between the press and library at Johns Hopkins revealed that the archiving of electronic publications is directly related to the issue of rights and permissions. This understanding came about in the process of identifying two possible disadvantages of electronic journals from the library's point of view: the library is left with no holdings if and when it stops subscribing to electronic resources, and the digitized materials could be lost forever if the publisher goes out of business.

Because of these concerns, the Press decided to make their electronic journals available as subscriptions rather than license agreements. This means that the subscribing library has archival rights to the journals and may make archival copies if it wishes. As permitted by fair use and other provisions of the 1976 copyright law, university libraries may also provide paper articles for interlibrary loan and may also send articles electronically for downloading and printing by another library on ILL but not for electronic storage at the borrowing library.

Full subscribers to the Press's electronic journals, in other words, will be able to make unlimited copies for internal use and up to six copies for interlibrary loan. For digitized text, we believe that conversion to media such as film or CD-ROM is entirely appropriate for the purpose of preservation, but not selling print copies or sending electronic copies to file servers located at other universities or other electronic networks, listservs, bulletin boards, etc.

Interestingly, networked document delivery from our database will very probably turn out to be more economical than interlibrary loan, and may be a profitable way to replace ILL to the mutual benefit of the Press and subscribing libraries. This is another area that we are examining closely, too.

Determining True Costs

The goal of our collaborative effort is not simply to offer electronic journals, but to price them in a way that is cost- effective for libraries, i.e., at lower rates than their paper counterparts. But cost-effective pricing is not possible unless electronic publishing is cost-effective as well.

To set pricing effectively, we have had to ascertain the economics of electronic publishing, including differences in first-copy and additional copy costs for paper and electronic formats. First-copy costs are those incurred to produce a single copy of the journal, including vetting, editing, and marketing. While these costs are constant, ideally, in either print or electronic format, certain elements may cause them to vary. The use of additional color illustrations in the electronic format, for instance, may raise first-copy costs. Authors' increasing use of word-processing programs for article preparation, on the other hand, may lower them. For our purposes, we assumed that first-copy costs are constant and that those areas where fluctuations occur do not represent a very large percentage of total costs.

Additional copy costs include manufacturing additional copies, distribution, and storage. Unlike first-copy costs, these costs are greatly affected by the final form of the journal.

Through data gathered from the Project Muse prototype, as well as our paper-based operation, we have ascertained that additional copy costs are about 10% lower for electronic journals than they are for paper journals. Excluding start-up costs for equipment and labor, we therefore believe we can sell electronic journals for 10% less than paper journals.

This projection is based on labor and cost estimates extrapolated from a small prototype and applied to a forty-journal program, and it assumes only a modest number of library subscribers in the first three years. As more subscribers come on board, and as we become more efficient in the electronic medium, we expect that greater cost reductions may be possible.

Pricing Strategy

While ongoing tasks and equipment for electronic publishing are less expensive than the manufacturing costs for paper journals, start-up costs are problematic. In our case, these will be covered by grants and special university funding; otherwise it is unlikely that in the first three years a paper-based publisher of humanities and social-science journals, even a Press with as large a program as the Johns Hopkins University Press, can move to electronic publishing in a way that results in lower prices for libraries.

This leads to a second concern. Exactly how can a publisher ascertain a means of licensing, set appropriate fees, and collect payments for the use of electronic materials that is practical? Expanding the Project Muse prototype so it includes all 40 of the Press's journals has required a long, hard look at paper pricing and distribution procedures and then comparing them with pricing and distribution for electronic media.

Of the two models we considered, site

licensing and subscription, we decided on the second. The first, site licensing, often involves pricing according to each university's Full-Time Enrollment (FTE) and is commonly used by software publishers to distribute a variety of packages on campus. Both librarians and computing-center professionals, however, report that while these arrangements seem very comprehensive in the beginning, they often end up escalating to an astronomical yearly fee designed to cover possible losses from unlimited access by the university community.

The second model, subscription, involves charging a flat rate for an electronic publication, regardless of a university's size, and works the same way paper subscriptions do. For publishers and libraries alike, this model is more convenient because it doesn't require a detailed contractual agreement, offers renewals on an annual rather than a multi-year basis, and is not based on the university's FTE, as site licensing is. The disadvantage here is either that the subscription rate must be set to absorb one-time costs and possible losses in the first five years, especially if the publisher is paper-based and must absorb the costs of moving to electronic media, or that a one-time fee must be charged in addition to the regular subscription fee.

In order to assure that Johns Hopkins electronic journals can be offered for less than paper journals, we developed a financial plan in which grants and special university funding cover one-time costs and revenue losses during the first three years. Over this period of time, the Press will move its paper journals to electronic form at a rate of about twelve journals per year, enabling us to offer a package that includes the following features:

- individual journals purchased in electronic form only will be priced lower than paper journals. Subscriptions to both print and electronic versions will be lower than the full price of each.

- subscribers to the entire database of electronic journals (which will move from twelve to forty over three years) will receive a discount off the combined single rates of all titles included in the database.

- charter subscribers will receive the first year's electronic-journal subscription free, as well as a guaranteed discount for a fixed number of years. There will be no extra charge for any new journal titles added during the current year, and free access reports will be available.

Staffing Concerns for the Press

It's not that the Press is changing what it does. Just the way it does it. For marketing, as detailed above, this means engaging in educational activities as well as promotional ones, and for rights and permissions, costing, and pricing it has meant reexamining the way we do business and crafting a model and financial plan that benefits both the publisher and its library partners.

The shift from paper to electronic media affects us at an even more basic level, however — adapting our existing staff to a new process and adding new positions with titles like "systems manager" and "technical support." It is in these areas where our partnership with libraries will help us the most, where developing a prototype involved not only looking to our library and academic computing center for advice but also for descriptions of staff positions essential to the success of an electronic venture.

Implications for Librarians

Most academic librarians work in close partnership with their faculty and students to provide the library research support that is required by their communities. Librarians have a great deal of experience in selecting materials for their constituencies. The new electronic environment for scholarly communication means that librarians must become just as adept at selecting electronic resources. As the universe of digital information expands at an ever increasing rate, librarians will need to use the same criteria of quality and relevance in selecting digital resources that they have used for print materials. They will also need to construct new systems for access to these resources and educate their users as to their use.

Participation in these activities follows from the traditional role of the academic librarian. What may be more interesting to consider is the role that librarians might play in the identification and creation of new electronic resources that can help meet the needs of their user communities. Librarians are in an ideal position to know what types of resources would be useful and how they should work for maximum effectiveness. On the other hand, they have very little experience with cost recovery and the bottom line of publishing. The Press has this expertise. The requirements of an electronic environment encourages partnering projects like Project Muse. Perhaps through these types of collaborative ventures the academic community will gain a new degree of control over the scholarly communication process.

Conclusion

University libraries and scholarly publishers need to adopt a new way of doing business — a partnership of interest that offers the opportunity to move from space — and resource-consuming paper products to networked, digital text that promises better access to more robust resources with a friendlier environmental impact. The Johns Hopkins experience is just the beginning of this metamorphosis and will certainly not accommodate every contingency at the start. We believe, however, that it will serve as a useful model for publishers and libraries to begin developing partnerships with the mutual goal of reinvigorating and redefining the scholarly communication process in the 21st century.

Tod Kelley
Co-Manager, Project Muse
The Johns Hopkins University Library
kelley@milton.mse.jhu.edu

Susan Lewis
Online Projects Manager
The Johns Hopkins University Press
suelewis@jhuvm.hcf.jhu.edu

Publishing E-prints, Preprints, and Journals in the Sciences

Bob Kelly
The American Physical Society

Introduction

The constitution of The American Physical Society states the aim of the Society as: "The object of the Society shall be to promote the advancement and diffusion of the knowledge of physics."

The American Physical Society has been actively supporting this objective since 1899. The process chosen to support this objective was the peer review process. The technology chosen was that used by the publishing industry at the time: ink on paper. The end result of the process is the archiving of journals in libraries, either individual or institutional. Funding is through subscription revenues from members, institutions, libraries and page charges to authors, that is, mainly from research/government sources.

Currently, in support of this objective, we publish the following journals:

- *Physical Review* A through E, the archival journals that publish important new results in the various subfields of physics.
- *Reviews of Modern Physics*, which publishes selected review articles in important subfields of physics.
- *Physical Review Letters (PRL)*, which publishes important and timely short articles judged to merit speedy production

The Society also publishes the *Bulletin of the American Physical Society* containing the abstracts of papers presented at meetings.

In 1893, the first year of *Physical Review*, 240 pages were published by Cornell University. In 1993, The American Physical Society published over 80,000 pages of *Physical Review*. In fact, over two-thirds of all of our pages ever published were published in the last twenty years.

The widespread acceptance of the Internet, computers and desktop publishing technologies has presented the APS with opportunities to find new ways to support our stated objective of "the advancement and diffusion of the knowledge of physics." Thus, in September 1993 we adopted the following vision:

In support of our objective, the American Physical Society will:

- Seek new modes of disseminating its journals and other publications providing both paper and electronic storage, distribution and usage choices
- Contribute to and take advantage of, advances in publishing and information technologies
- Be alert to financial implications of electronic publishing initiatives with the aim of protecting APS financial stability

Our technical strategy is to produce our journals in a way that provides choices to both the readers and to the authors. We are basing this strategy on the concept of Standard Generalized Markup Language (SGML). This approach, producing the content of a journal with structure but completely independent of any presentation format, will permit the widest variety of presentation choices. (See Figure 1). APS, along with several other societies, is migrating the production processes to SGML and is adopting the DTD specified in ISO12083 as a standard. Today we produce the *Physical Review Letters* using SGML. The other journals are produced using a combination of RevTeX and TROFF for production. We are developing plans to migrate the production of the rest of our journals into an SGML production process.

Figure 1

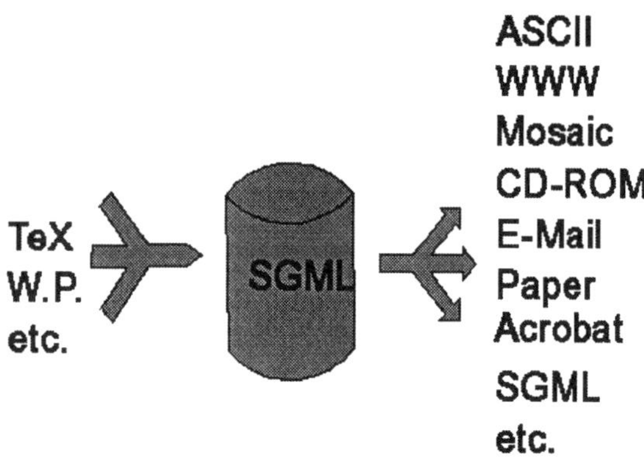

We accept manuscripts in one of two formats: on paper or in RevTex. A little over one third of the submissions come in electronically in RevTex. One of our goals is to expand the electronic submission of manuscripts to include popular word processors and other forms of representations such as full motion video, etc.

Technical Projects

From a usage point of view, having reusable information implies that there is a repository for that information. One use is the current printed journal and another is the delivery of an electronic version of the printed journal. (See Figure 2)

Figure 2

Technical Projects - APS Journal Archive

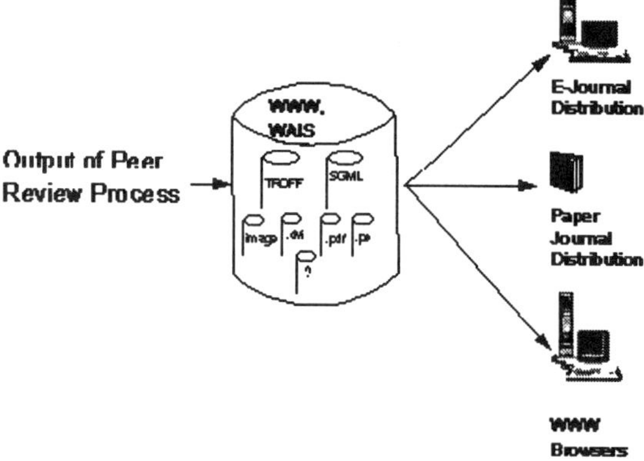

In September 1993 we placed an advertisement in the Sunday *New York Times* Business Section stating that APS was about to issue a Request For Proposal (RFP) seeking a vendor(s) to assist us in delivering *Physical Review Letters* on-line. By 15:00 that Sunday afternoon I had received 7 e-mail responses. The bidding ended in January 1994 with over 200 inquiries and a dozen firm bids. We are currently in contract negotiation with a vendor with a July 1995 target for start of service.

The evaluation team for the bids included representatives of many of the components of the process. There were authors, referees, editors, librarians, and readers on the team, as well as staff members and committees of the APS. Our approach was to involve as many users as possible in the evaluation and not just make a technical decision. As you may expect, agreement on a vendor was not unanimous. This led us to the idea that we should provide choices and that perhaps a 'one size fits all' delivery system is not the right approach. However, in this case, the market will decide.

As stated earlier, from a usage point of view, having reusable information implies that a repository for that information exists. We have embarked on several projects designed to test the capability of reusing APS articles. The idea is to create an archive from the SGML and other production files that would allow subsequent use. Included in the archive would be PostScript, Adobe Acrobat PDF, DVI, SGML and for older articles, images of the pages.

We have two projects underway to test the validity of providing an accessible archive. The first project, *Physical Review Archives (PROLA)* is being conducted with the laboratory at Los Alamos. For this project we are taking 8 years of the TROFF files from the composition of *Physical Review*, starting with December 1993 and going back in time. The TROFF files are being indexed using the Wide Area Information Server (WAIS). The archive will be available via the WWW http://www.c3.lanl.gov:8080/apswelcome; it will be available to all over the Internet. We are planning on scanning in

5 to 8 years of images and will present the image of an article after it has been found by searching or browsing. We are working with the Office of the Chief Librarian at the Naval Research Laboratory as well librarians at five U.S. and German universities to develop the techniques and processes that may be used to manage the access to this archive.

For the second project, Beacon Graphics has developed a WAIS-indexed SGML database using the production files from *Physical Review Letters*. Vis the World Wide Web, a user searches the WAIS index and is presented with a list of search hits. Selecting the abstract field for a title and author causes the system to do an SGML to HTML conversion and present a title, author(s), affiliation list, abstract and figure list with captions. The user can further click on and view the figures. To view the full article the user can select either an SGML file or a PDF file. We will test this with SoftQuad's Panorama when it is available.

One of the goals of this, the second project, was to prove the concept. We have proven that it is possible to take a pure SGML file and reuse it without modifying the file for different formats.

Consumer Involvement

The American Physical Society has always prided it self on listening to the consumer. In our case the consumers of our journals are authors (physicists), readers (physicists), and librarians (sometimes physicists). The Society has a hierarchy of committees (mostly physicists) involved in looking for electronic publishing opportunities and additionally has constantly sought the advice of librarians and physicists from all over the world. We also collaborate with other scholarly (physics and non-physics) societies as well as scientific publishers.

The process of scientific publishing is conceptually straightforward. It starts with an article from an author, moves through peer/review, then to an editorial process to production to the archive. (See Figure 3). Sub-processes such as proofreading, composition, etc. are part of this flow. Most of the people in the APS process are physicists. Reading has traditionally been done at the end of this process; however, with the introduction of new technologies and networks, the reading step can occur at any point.

Figure 3

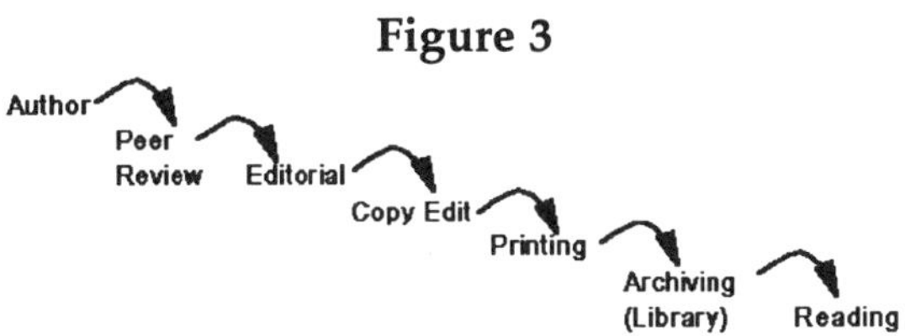

As mentioned earlier, we invited an evaluation team, of physicists and librarians, to us through the RFP process for *Physical Review Letters* on-line.

I have set up an alias (sgml@aps.org) for discussions about SGML and the rational for complying to a particular DTD. This alias will eventually become a list server discussion group using hyper mail on the home page of the American Institute of Physics http:.//aip.org. Access is open to all interested parties.

Many manuscripts published by APS and other physics publishers start their journeys as preprints. The e-print archives, pioneered by Paul Ginsparg at the Los Alamos National Laboratory have revolutionized the circulation of preprints and are making the dissemination of information quicker and more efficient, at least in some major subfields of physics. We imagine that this phenomenon will spread to subfields not thus far affected.

The American Physical Society has followed the e-print archive phenomenon with great interest. The APS may have an important role to play at this critical juncture. The Society has established a WWW page http.//aps.org/EPRINT/eprthome.html as a temporary archive for discussions, meeting bulletins, papers, etc. concerning e-print archives. This discussion is also open to all interested parties.

Figure 4

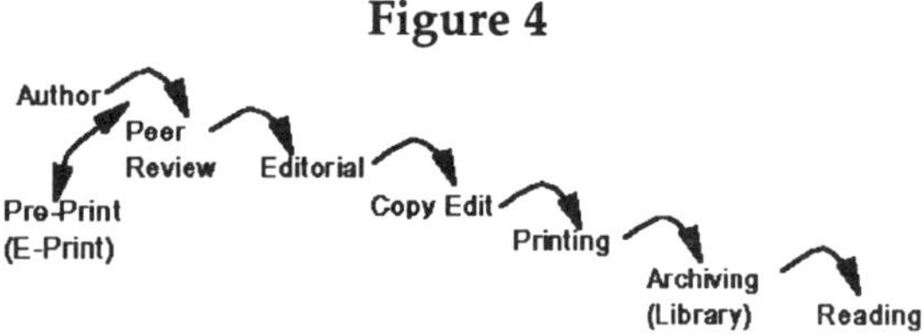

We conducted a workshop on the topic at Los Alamos on October 14 & 15, 1994. The workshop was attended by over 80 physicists, librarians and representatives of other physics societies from the USA and Europe. The proceedings of the workshop will be available at the above URL. The Report on the Workshop by the Editor-in-Chief of the American Physical Society can be found here.

The following ideas were key in the workshop (Figure 4):

1. The landscape of scientific publishing is changing rapidly.
2. We can use technology to not only accelerate the process but to improve it and add value.
3. A 'one size fits all' paper based policy is obsolete. We can craft a process that fits the different needs of many users.
4. Author tools and education are necessary.
5. There is a place for eprints in the current and probably future APS publishing policy.
6. The definition of future processes should be explored through a number of small experiments.
7. We should establish a collaborative effort with universities, libraries, and other societies; representatives from all of these were present at the workshop.

The American Physical Society will digest these ideas internally as well as externally and will continue to support and improve scholarly communication in physics.

Future Trends (opinion)

I conclude with a vision that several colleagues, librarians and physicists and I are developing. This vision of a new model for scientific publishing is not, as yet, embraced by the American Physical Society. I include it in this presentation to generate comments and discussion. My colleagues and I hope to post a paper on this vision on the e-Print Archive Forum in the near future with the intent of generating discussion and debate.

In the first two paragraphs of this paper I commented that the constitution of the American Physical Society states the aim of the Society as: "The object of the Society shall be to promote the advancement and diffusion of the knowledge of physics." The American Physical Society has been actively supporting this objective since 1899. The process chosen to support this objective was the peer review process. The technology chosen was that used by the publishing industry, at the time ink on paper. The end result of the process is the archiving of journals in libraries, either individual or institutional. Funding is through subscription revenues from members, institutions, libraries and research/government sources.

I believe that the objective and the use of peer review is still valid. To protect the aims and to encourage new thinking and the development of ideas, I believe that the peer review process should be private and not open to public viewing or executions. There maybe, however, benefit in allowing open comment on articles posted in e-print databases.

However, were the societies to start all over, I question that the technology, archiving and funding choices would be the ones we made in the past. Internet and e-publishing technologies provide a much more robust and timely deliverable than paper. For example, full motion video can be included in a electronic article. To include full motion video in a paper article, one would use a fan-fold stack of paper glued to the article page. The opportunities for hyper-linking, multimedia, etc. make the new technologies superior to paper.

The advent of the World Wide Web permits archives to be anywhere and linked together. In the Web world, the role of the librarian expands beyond the current boundaries and includes a major component of data processing skills. I have long thought that we will witness a convergence of the traditional librarian role with the traditional information systems role, in the future. That future is Now!

When I look at the funding process, it seems to me that we could design a better process then the current one.

1. Universities and the governments already underwrite research expenses and also underwrite journal acquisition expenses; the publisher adds value to the process through the management of peer review and editing of the manuscripts.
2. The cost of journal acquisitions is rising rapidly, threatening both the ability of scholars to have access to traditional materials and the well-being of the societies that publish the materials (the first is well documented the second is a logical conclusion based on recent journal acquisition trends).
3. Subsidies from the government to the Society may be one way to reduce overall research expenses (lower journal acquisition costs should result in lower research overhead rates) while offering greater access to published materials
4. The current process, of automatically printing and distributing all peer reviewed articles contributes to the enormous amounts of paper and expenses in the system.

Vision

One of the possible futures of scientific communications is based on an expansion of the e-print phenomenon. Societies and publishers providing a peer review role will continue to do so. However, the peer review process will end at the electronic archive. Papers will no longer be automatically be reproduced and distributed. Instead collections of articles will be packaged, reproduced and distributed based on the editors' perceived market value of the package. The scientific communication process will be served by the e-print and the peer reviewed archive. Societies and publishers will find additional revenue opportunities in the archive.

I believe that the use of e-prints will become common in scientific communications. Societies, universities, research institutions will set up e-print archives for their constituents. Copyright for the articles will remain with the author. These archives will be linked on the World Wide Web.

Papers, at the discretion of the author, will be available for public comment. At some point, the author will elect to submit the paper to a peer reviewing society or scientific publisher. When the paper is successfully passed through the peer review process, it will be placed in the archive of the society of the scientific publisher. Copyright will transfer to the society or scientific publisher. The act of placing the paper into the archive will have the same weight as publishing the article does today. (See Figure 5).

Figure 5

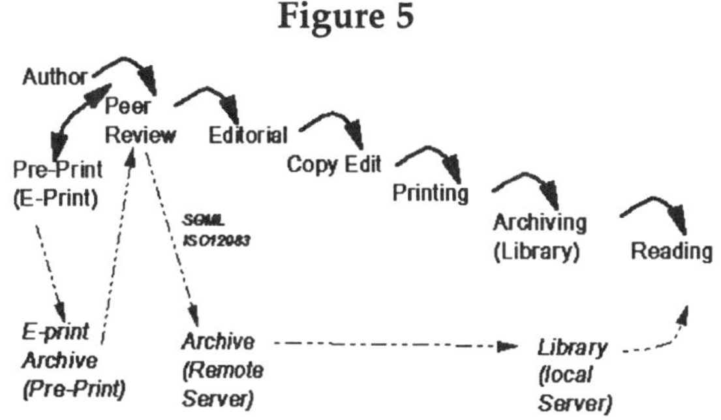

- Peer reviewing societies no longer publish everything that is peer reviewed.
- Archive everything
- Publish selected articles
- Archives available at a reasonable cost

The adoption of SGML standards for the archive will facilitate subsequent use integration at the local level. The prime archive will be at the society or publishing organization; however, libraries will have the opportunity to create local archives with the SGML files obtained from either publishers or societies.

The process from author to archive, currently supported by government-sponsored research funds should be directly funded. Societies or publishers will have the opportunity for additional revenue by adding value to and publishing portions of the their archive. This vision is very much work in progress. I am developing the vision with several colleagues who are physicists and librarians and am discussing it at this conference in the hope of raising questions and generating dialog.

Some questions are:

1. Physics is a international discipline. How can we manage the sharing of government support across national boundaries?
2. Does the UN have a role in this?We hope to eventually publish this vision, so one can consider this conference proceeding to be a preprint or abstract-length version of it.

Summary

The American Physical Society is actively preparing itself to take advantage of the opportunities afforded by technology. Our approach is to have broad visions yet take small technical steps. We have adopted a baseball strategy, one of wining through base hits. To continue the baseball analogy, our team is made of players who represent all steps in the process. Hopefully we will continue to contribute to scientific communication and ".. to promote the advancement and diffusion of the knowledge of physics."

Robert Kelly
American Physical Society
rakelly@aps.org

Riding the Aftershocks: The Galileo Project

Elizabeth S. Burr
Rice University

In 1993, the Fondren Library at Rice University received a grant from the Council on Library Resources to explore the role of librarians in the creation of online curricular resources. Rice has a strong commitment to educational computing: The campus network is the backbone of education in engineering: a computer lab with advanced modeling and graphics software had been installed in the school of architecture; courses in art history had used a networked software to make images available for study. Curriculum development projects are supported by the Electronic Studio -- an initiative to encourage faculty to use information technology and the campus network for new approaches to education.

The project chosen for the grant was a new history course. Dr. Albert Van Helden, a historian of science, had found his teaching becoming static, confined to lectures with minimal time for discussion. Independently, he had come to believe that an experiment in changing the method of information transfer in his course might provide him with the opportunity to "reinvent his teaching." His desire to experiment with the use of computers in a new history of science course coincided with the library's participation in the Electronic Studio. Dr. Van Helden's project was supported by the Fondren Library, with a professional librarian serving as the project manager.

After a year of development, the Galileo Project is a multimedia, hypertextual resource that has been created to be read using a World Wide Web browser. The project consists of nearly 50 short essays on topics related to the life and work of Galileo Galilei. It consists of over 200 images, ranging from portraits of 17th century scientists to NASA photographs of the solar system. The reader is presented with several entry ways in the web of texts, including a detailed timeline of Galileo's life, a set of maps which organize the information geographically, and a conceptual organization based on the visual metaphor of the villa where Galileo lived the last years of his life. Recently, two eminent historians of science from outside Rice have contributed to the project, expanding its scope and suggesting new avenues for development. The project includes a searchable bibliography, using Webbase, an enhancement to Mosaic developed at Rice. Most significantly, the project points outside the local Rice server, connecting through the World Wide Web to electronic resources such as the Vatican Library exhibit, the Museum of Astronomy at the University of Bologna, and the multitude of online resources for modern astronomy. The new course on Galileo will be taught the spring semester in 1995. No doubt, ideas for new enhancements to the project will emerge once students begin using it.

The development of the Galileo Project is closely linked with many of the issues raised by the seemingly seismic event alluded to in the title of this paper -- the

Galileo's Residence

(An image from the Project)

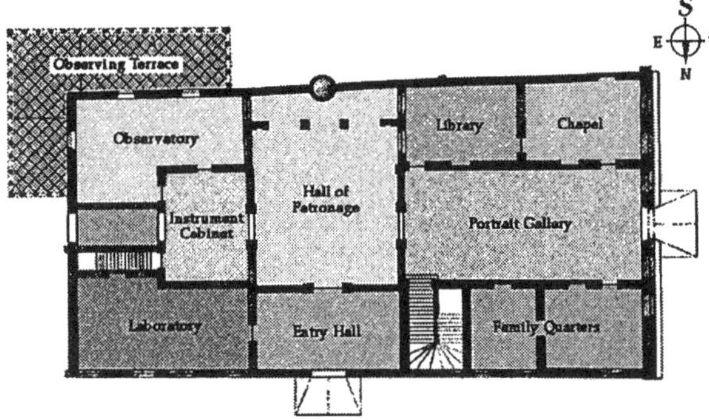

explosive growth in the use of electronic networks. The project's first year coincided with the World Wide Web's burst of popularity (courtesy of NCSA's Mosaic). Certainly, the Galileo Project is inconceivable without the integration of text and graphics, the ability to include animation and sound files, the ease of access to remote resources. The Galileo Project raises many of the same questions addressed by the other sessions in this conference. We have had to consider the ramifications of publishing a resource that exists exclusively online, the copyright of images, educational fair use in the networked environment, the commitment of university resources to training and support, among others.

While the Galileo Project raises many of the same issues faced by scholarly publishing projects that use electronic networks, three areas of particular significance to Galileo may be of general interest. The Galileo Project is distinguished from some of the other projects described and presented at the symposium by the participation of a librarian in the creation of an original work; a great deal of my work has been more similar to that of an editor or a researcher than to the work of public or technical services librarians. The Galileo Project has been a collaborative project from its inception; it is a work envisioned and led by a distinguished scholar, but which benefits from the participation of student developers. Other collaborations are planned for future development. Finally, the Galileo Project is envisioned as a lasting and developing resource; we have made a commitment to adapting to new technological environments as they present themselves.

The role of the librarian in the creation of online curricular resources was, as previously stated, the topic of the CLR grant. Fondren Library is committed to participating in the Electronic Studio; librarians are encouraged to work with electronic resources, to provide faculty with training and reference in the World Wide Web, and to create guides to subject-specific materials that faculty may use for their teaching and research. However, my role on the Galileo Project has gone beyond the boundaries commonly found in public services librarianship. I have worked closely with Dr. Van Helden on the creation of navigational aids for the project; these navigational aids are the primary strategies for reading and learning in the project. Unlike the types of finding aids associated with libraries, these aids are directly linked to the hypertext essays and serve as structures which provide the student with important contextual information. For example, the timeline of Galileo's life serves as a major organizational structure for the project; it is also a navigational aid, which provides the reader with links to longer essays, images, maps, and other timelines.

The primary difference between my work on the Galileo Project and traditional library work is my relationship to the information at hand. Rather than creating information about information, in the creation of catalog records, or helping the user find the information, in the provision of reference service, I am involved in the creation of the primary information. This shift is often noted by other librarians; some have questioned whether or not this is an appropriate function for librarians. My answer is an emphatic "yes." The Galileo Project is a new kind of work; it is not a book, a database, or a collection. It includes elements of all these things, combined to provide the reader with many choices about the information she will access and designed to be instructional.

The Galileo Project crosses a line from being a work by a single author to a reference collection where related articles and exhibits by other authors are immediately accessible. It is, in my opinion, a very small example of what we might hope to find in the digital libraries of the future which are the topic of much current discussion. The librarian's role is to make finding things in this ever-growing web of resources simple, to weed through and select items of quality, to work toward universal access and continued stability of mutable resources, and to serve users who might be overwhelmed if faced with the vast collection of resources available on the network. The Galileo Project is one approach to facing the new terrain of information resources which bears the unmistakable stamp of a librarian. (My personal insistence on a searchable bibliography and a direct link to our library catalog bears this out.)

Collaboration has been the central working method from the very start of the project. Dr. Van Helden has been the only of author of the essays thus far, but he is committed to encouraging experts in other areas of Galileo's life and work to make contributions to the project. The design of the navigational aids (the timelines, the maps, the villa, and the "book" resources) has been a team process. The future holds the promise of new collaborations. Rice University has formal ties with several Texas high schools; these schools are linked to Rice via a high-speed network. Science teachers will be invited to use the project and adapt it to their own pedagogical needs; it is hoped that their curricula will be made available over the network. Additionally, this year, Rice has joined the Houston Independent School District in opening the Rice School/La Escuela Rice--a laboratory K-8 school with an extensive array of information technology in each classroom. Two teachers from the Rice School are currently working on an integrated curriculum for middle school that will use the Galileo Project as its central source of information; they hope to make their curriculum available over the network as well.

Perhaps the most exciting direction for future collaboration is with the holders of the most important primary materials--the Instuto e Museo di Storia della Scienza and the Biblioteca Nazional in Florence. The museum is currently engaged in several major computer projects, including an online version of the Italian National Bibliography of the History of Science and a planned major exhibit that will include highly sophisticated computer models of the competing cosmological systems of Galileo's time. Perhaps the most exciting in relation to the Galileo Project is the multimedia catalog of the museum's collection, which includes a wealth of images and animations. These images and animations could provide students with information it would take years for those of us working on the Galileo Project to write. It is hoped that we will be able to work with the museum to include some of their work in the project. Furthermore, the museum is working with the national library and the Max Planck Institute in Berlin on the digitization of Codex 72 of Galileo's manuscripts, as well as other significant manuscript holdings related to Galileo. This project, which will begin in January 1995, holds the promise of greatly improved access to fragile primary sources. It is difficult to rein in one's imagination when the idea of access to the manuscripts is introduced. Certainly, when resources such as these are available either through CD-ROM or the network, the research applications of information technology will become clearer. It is easy to imagine a researcher's version of the Galileo Project, including digitized images of the manuscripts, images of the scientific instruments, reference works, and links to the major libraries with holdings in this area. And by linking these resources to the Galileo Project, the student can chose to use the researcher's tools and be introduced to the historian of science's craft.

The most daunting aspect of the Galileo Project is the thought that all of this work has gone into a project that is, by its very nature, going to be obsolete. Developments in information technology will continue at their remarkable rate. With any luck, the bandwidth problem will be resolved, and large animations and videos will become regular parts of networked multimedia projects. No doubt, the World Wide Web will be surpassed by something they're working on at Xerox PARC or CERN or someplace that isn't famous yet. Mosaic is already beginning to look somewhat creaky; the use of Netscape for presentations at this symposium makes me feel like a rare book librarian with my Mosaic screens, even though both are WWW browsers. And if I allow my wish list to flower, I can envision networked three dimensional models delivered from Italy where I can walk through museums, galleries, whole cities, and sense the space in which Galileo lived.

Our challenge is to stay fresh, to commit resources of time, people, and spirit to the continual renewal of the Galileo Project. It would be a tremendous shame to write off the work that has gone into this project as a mid-90s phenomenon, like all of those Hypercard stacks from 1990 that countless faculty made and then abandoned. As a project that is supported by a university and benefits from the preservationist tendencies of the librarians who work on it, the Galileo Project will attempt to remain current with technology, to use standard formats that will ease migrations, to grow and change when new developments make enhancements possible. It is our task to stay excited by change, to embrace the mutability that this format requires, rather than quit because we're no longer the new kids on the block with the neatest bells and whistles. And this task will require perseverance, support, and commitment.

This last point about the mutability and built-in obsolescence of electronic publications such as the Galileo Project leads me to some final comments on the metaphor introduced in the title. Obviously, if there are aftershocks, there must have been an earthquake. At this point, I think it is nearly impossible to identify any single earthquake that set this whole business of electronic publishing and the use of the network in motion. However, in the library community, there is a desire to understand and relate the present to the past in order to find one's bearings and plan for future development; this desire is probably widespread in the publishing field as well. When librarians look for models of the current state of publishing, information, and libraries, they often return to the invention of movable type and the history of printing. While studying this period of information technology history is fascinating and potentially significant (the continued increase in the creation of manuscript codices after the invention of printing is often cited when arguments against the withering away of the book are made), I think it can veer in potentially defeating directions.

Last fall, I heard Professor John Lienhard of the University of Houston make a compelling argument about the decreasing span of time between technological "revolutions." He was speaking to a group of art librarians, many of whom shared a sense of foreboding that the computer and the technologists were in the process of destroying the culture of the book and the institutions that preserved that culture. Dr. Lienhard suggested that each successive revolution crashed upon the existing order like a tsunami. The librarians appeared to be very responsive to this idea, and it would require only a day or two in any large library to find pockets of this sense of confusion and fear about the future of the library. Works such as the Galileo Project can add to that confusion, and librarians such as myself can trigger anxiety about the future of librarianship.

I would like to suggest another approach to the tsunami metaphor. First of all, it should be noted that what is a major earthquake to us is usually small potatoes to the earth. Be that as it may, we are living in the fault zone, and those of us in the library world are getting edgy. When I lived in southern California, I spent an inordinate amount of time worrying about earthquakes. And I learned that native Californians did not spend nearly the time I did thinking about them. They did not find themselves stopped under the Santa Monica Freeway hoping that the Big One didn't happen right then. They live with uncertainty, knowing that frightening and dangerous things will happen. And when they do, they pick up the pieces. And some of them take advantage of what the earthquakes cause--big, beautiful waves. They wait a couple of days and then they go surfing. I see the coming developments in information technology like aftershocks, knocking at the structure of the Galileo Project, prompting rebuilding with new materials, leading to what we hope will be an improved project. And I see myself and other librarians learning to surf, just the way the automation specialists in libraries have been adopting new systems over the past twenty fiveyears. I hope we can cultivate a sense of pleasure in some of the changes that will come with time and that our work in this emerging area can have moments of play and invention even when the windows are all broken and the chimney needs replacing. This is the time when we will have to go surfing, before we get back to work. And I suspect it will make everything we do better.

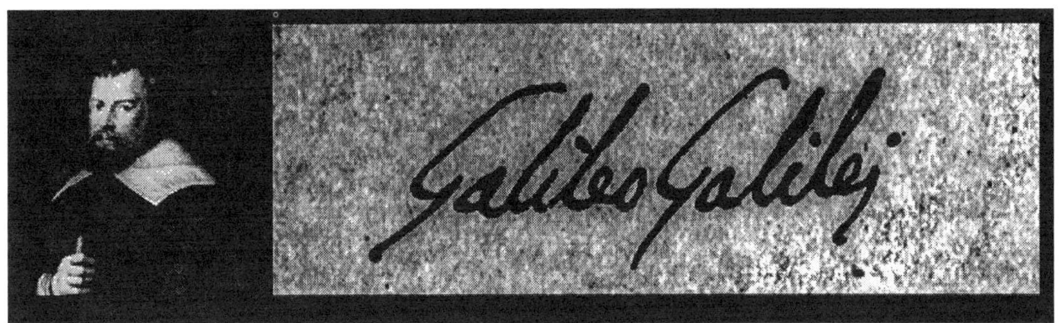

Elizabeth Burr
Electronic Text and Images Librarian
Fondren Library
Rice University
esb@rice.edu

Towards an e-*MED*: Converting the *Middle English Dictionary* into an Electronic Version

Henk Aertsen
Vrije Universiteit, Amsterdam

The compilation of a dictionary based on historical principles is a laborious and time-consuming task. The publication of the *Oxford English Dictionary*, we are told in the Introduction to this Dictionary, "extended over a period of forty-four years" [*OED*, Vol. 1, Historical Introduction]. Its first part was published in 1882 and its final part in 1927, but preparation for the dictionary had begun as early the 1850s. The comprehensive historical dictionary of the Dutch language, *Het Woordenboek der Nederlandse Taal*, had to publish supplementary volumes for the beginning of the alphabet at a time when the main dictionary still had to reach the end of the alphabet! The *Middle English Dictionary* (*MED*) is another historical dictionary with a long history of its own. Its first fascicle, treating the beginning of the letter E, came out in 1952. It was the result of a process of preparation which was begun in the 1930s but which was interrupted by World War II. After the war Hans Kurath took over the editorship, a fresh start was made and most of the material collected before the war was re-edited. This explains why the letter E was the first of the dictionary to be published. The fifth fascicle of the letter T is scheduled for publication at the end of this year, and the entire project is now expected to be finished by the end of 1999.

The long period of time that a historical dictionary is in the making inevitably leads to a kind of imbalance between the entries in the earlier and later parts. This imbalance, or lack of consistency or of uniformity, is to be explained as being due to changes in editorial staff and to subsequent changes in editorial policy and procedure over the years. In the case of the *MED* this imbalance between the earlier and later parts can, roughly speaking, be said to coincide with the parts that are not, or not yet, available in computer-readable format and those that are. In other words, the inconsistency is between the non-computerized part of the *MED* (the letters A - P) and the computerized part (the letters from Q on). In the non-computerized part there are basically three different types of formats, which result from different editorial principles concerning the organization of the lemmas, the definition of senses, the number of phrases defined, and the actual number of quotations quoted. Thus, the format used in E and F differs quite considerably from that used in G - P, while in A - D there is a kind of transition towards the more extensive coverage found in G - P. Even in G - P there is no uniformity of treatment, as a closer examination reveals that P is much more elaborate than G. For example, the letter E is characterized by short definitions and by few quotations, while in the letter T the definitions have become much more elaborate, the number of quotations is much larger, and the number of phrases listed as such is much larger as well.

In addition to the differences in format, there are differences that result from the advance of Middle English scholarship over the years: the publication of text editions of manuscripts previously unedited or available only in older editions, new insights into the datings of manuscripts and texts, and so on.

For a paper dictionary, these differences may not be very serious, but for an electronic dictionary they are. If, for instance, a new date for a text is adopted for quotations from that text in the dictionary, the result will be that for that particular text there are two datings in the dictionary, and since the quotations in a historical dictionary are arranged by their dates in chronological order, any change in the dating system of texts will have repercussions for electronic searches by date. Similarly, the fact that some of the texts that are frequently quoted in the later parts of the dictionary but are altogether absent from the earlier parts (often because the edition of the text became only available in the course of the compilation of the dictionary) is likely to produce unreliable search results.

An electronic version of the *MED* (e-*MED*) should try to redress this lack of balance and uniformity, and the harmonization of the various parts of the *MED* is essential for the electronic version to be a lexicographical and commercial success.

I will now give a detailed analysis of the problems I outlined above and will then show just how the updating and harmonization can be achieved electronically for those tasks that do not involve the editing of new lexicographical material or the re-editing of older parts, but even these admittedly time-consuming and therefore costly tasks can be less time-consuming if modern technological tools are used on a wider scale than they are at present.

In the organization of a traditional historical dictionary, the meaning of a lexical item is defined as one or more senses, which may be further subdivided into subsenses and/or subsidiary senses. Each sense, or subsense or subsidiary sense is then illustrated by examples, quotations from, in this case, Middle English sources. In the paper *MED*, these senses are given in chronological order, although the dating system underlying the chronological order is not immediately transparent. A brief explanation of this dating system is therefore in order. The *MED* distinguishes two kinds of dates, manuscript dates and composition dates. As is explained in the 1954 Plan and Bibliography of the *MED* (p.17), the composition date is added to the manuscript date if the composition date is believed to be at least 25 years earlier, but only the composition date is used and enclosed between parentheses when the date of composition is well established and less than 25 years earlier in the manuscript.

Figure 1 illustrates this practice:

Figure 1
Manuscript and composition dates in the MED

a1500 → manuscript date
(a1450) → composition date

(c1395) → composition date
(less than 25 years earlier than manuscript date)

Unless a precise date can be given to a manuscript, the *MED* assigns dates by quarter centuries, and these dates may be prefixed by *c* (for *circa*), *a* (for *ante*) or *?* (for 'doubtful'), which in combination with a date should be interpreted as follows:

c1350 = 1350, or up to a quarter century earlier or later
a1350 = before 1350, but probably not earlier than 1325
?a1350 = a1350, but less securely established (and possibly later than 1350)

In this type of dating system the manuscript date is given precedence over the composition date, and this is rather confusing, especially with known authors. For instance, if you are looking for a quotation from Chaucer among the various quotations under a particular sense, you may be tempted to look no further than the year 1400, the year Chaucer died, but you have to continue your search, because the chronology criterion applies to the manuscript date and not to the composition date. Table I illustrates the *MED* dating of some of Chaucer's works, and the manuscripts are usually from a much later date than the dates of composition.

Table I
MED dating of some of Chaucer's works

Texts	*MED* dating	
	manuscript date	(composition date)
The Book of the Duchess	c1450	(1369)
The Parlement of Foules	c1430	(c1380)
The House of Fame	c1450	(c1380)
Boethius	?a1425	(c1380)
Troilus and Criseyde	a1425	(c1385)

Now what, you might ask, is the significance of this kind of dating system for an electronic version? I must admit that at first sight it seems perfectly possible to use this system in an electronic version of the *MED*. There are, however, a few pitfalls. The first has to do with the sorting of quotations by date: since the manuscript date and/or composition date may be preceded by prefixes like *c* or *a* or by a question-mark, or by a combination of *c* or *a* with the question-mark, and since date and prefix can occur between brackets, the electronic version should provide a means by which sorting can be carried out by the user if he or she should wish to export a group of quotations from the dictionary to some other application and to merge them there with another group of quotations illustrating another sense of the same lexical item. In other words, the electronic version should provide the user with a sorting tool that will carry out the sorting by date of the group of quotations that results when the two groups of Table II are merged.

Table II
Dates of quotations under the first two senses of ME egge

sense 1a	sense 1b (a)
?c1200 *Orm.*	a1225(?a1200) *Trin.Hom.* ......
(c1325) *Recipe Painting(1)*	a1225(?a1200) Lay. *Brut* ......
c1390 *Disp.Virg. & Cross*	(c1384) *WBible(1)* ......
(a1398) **Trev. Barth.*	c1400(?c1380) *Cleanness* ......
a1425(a1382) *WBible(1)*	c1400(?c1390) *Gawain* ......
	(*MED*, s.v. **egge** n.(2))

Merging the two groups should ultimately produce the following list:

?c1200 *Orm.* ......
a1225(?a1200) *Trin.Hom.* ......
a1225(?a1200) Lay. *Brut* ......
(c1325) *Recipe Painting(1)* ......
(c1384) *WBible(1)* ......
c1390 *Disp.Virg. & Cross* ......
(a1398) **Trev. Barth.* ......
c1400(?c1380) *Cleanness* ......
c1400(?c1390) *Gawain* ......
a1425(a1382) *WBible(1)* ......

Such a sorting tool has now been developed by the *MED* staff for internal use but should be included in the software packet for the electronic *MED*. Another more serious problem arises when in the course of the dictionary the dating of a text is changed on the basis of new insights into the manuscript date and/or composition date. Changes in the dating of texts are introduced into the dictionary without notification and are not acknowledged until an update of the bibliography becomes available. Thus, the 1984 supplement to the original 1954 bibliography contains a fair number of these changes, but since 1984 there have been more re-datings, and the subscriber/user has no way of finding out when these re-datings were introduced into the dictionary. As I said before, all this may not be very serious for a paper dictionary, but for an electronic dictionary it is. In an electronic dictionary it simply will not do to have two dates for one and the same text: searches by date will become unreliable if, say, from the letter P on a given text is suddenly transferred to another period. And searches through the dictionary as a kind of database will be one of the main uses of an electronic dictionary. It is therefore essential that the dating of texts is harmonized and that there is one date for one and the same text. This is probably the simplest adjustment that will have to be made to the paper dictionary for the electronic version. It can be done electronically and almost automatically. A find and change command will do the trick, but it will have to be followed by a sorting command for every block of quotations in the dictionary. This second part of the operation is more troublesome and time-consuming but not impossible. Table III lists some of these re-datings, together with the place in the dictionary where the new dates were first used.

Table III
MED re-datings of texts

text	old dating	new dating	first used in
Harley Lyrics (the historical poems)	a1325	c1325	M
Destruction of Troy	c1450(?a1400)	c1540(?a1400)	Res-
Winner & Waster	c1450(c1353)	c1450(?a1370)	Str-
Layamon *Brut*	a1225(?a1200)	c1275(?a1200)	T-
Owl & Nightingale	c1250	c1275(?a1216)	T-

Taking the last example, we see that the Middle English poem *The Owl and the Nightingale* is re-dated "c1275(?a1216)" instead of "c1250", which means that the manuscript date is assigned to a later quarter century and that at the same time the probable date of composition (the year between brackets) is now believed to be different from the manuscript date and is believed to be a quarter century, but not more than a quarter century, earlier than 1216. Since texts are dated throughout the dictionary by quarter centuries, a change of this kind has far-reaching effects and should be harmonized throughout the electronic dictionary if this electronic dictionary is to be used as a database for searches.

More complicated is the updating of bibliographical references. The publication of text editions of manuscripts previously unedited or of new editions replacing older, often 19th-century, editions has led to changes in what in *MED* practice is called the preferred edition, i.e., the edition from which a particular text is quoted. Changes in preferred editions are frequent, and the 1984 Supplement to the 1954 Bibliography is full of them. A typical example is given below:

(1) 1954 Bibliography:

a1475 *Against Lollards* (Vsp) :: Political poems and songs, ed. T. Wright, RS 14.2 (1861). 243-7. [BR 1926]

(2) 1984 Supplement:

a1475 *Against Lollards* (Vsp) :: Historical poems of the XIVth and XVth centuries, ed. R.H. Robbins (1959). 152-7. [BR 1926]
[In A-G the stencil refers to Political poems and songs, ed. T. Wright, RS 14.2 (1861). 243-7.]

(3) Definitive bibliography:

a1475 *Against Lollards* (Vsp) :: Historical poems of the XIVth and XVth centuries, ed. R.H. Robbins (1959). 152-7. [BR 1926]

If in the final definitive bibliography the entries with double references of the 1984 Supplement are going to be simplified to a single reference as in (3) in the example above, it will be necessary to update all the quotations from the original preferred edition as well. For our example it means that in the letters A to G of the dictionary all quotations from Wright's edition of the poem *Against Lollards* must be replaced by those from the edition by Robbins. In this particular case it is unlikely that there will be major discrepancies between the two editions, but there are instances where the differences will be considerable, especially if the text in question was previously unedited and the *MED* relied for its quotations on photostat copies of the manuscript. This is true, for instance, of the twelfth-century manuscript of the *Ancrene Wisse* which was quoted from a photostat copy until the edition by J.R.R. Tolkien became available in 1962. Apart from adjusting the quotations to the readings of the new text editions, it will also be necessary to update the line references to those of the new edition, from folio and column of the manuscript to page and line of the edition. Similarly, quotations from the A-Text of *Piers Plowman* are no longer taken from Skeat's edition of 1867 but from the new edition by George Kane of 1960, and all the quotes from Skeat's edition in the letters A to F of the dictionary will have to be replaced by quotes from Kane's edition, since there may be changes in the actual wording of the quotes. This is clearly a much more complicated task, because it will be necessary to compare every quote from the manuscript or older text edition with the reading of the newer edition; it is, of course, possible to extract all the *Piers Plowman A* quotations from the dictionary electronically but all the adjustments will still have to be made by hand, unless the new text is available in electronic format as well.

Another consequence of new editions having become available since the publication of the first fascicles of the dictionary in 1952 is that there are no examples from these texts in the earlier parts of the dictionary. This is not a very serious problem, unless such a text is frequently quoted in the later parts. For the balance between the earlier and later parts it is essential that quotations from these frequently quoted texts are also introduced into the earlier parts, and this will require a special reading program, under which volunteers read the texts in question with strict instructions as to what words, uses and phrases to look out for. The availability of electronic editions of these texts will undoubtedly make this task much less burdensome and time-consuming, and fortunately more and more texts are being published as e-texts. I have drawn up a list of texts that qualify for such a reading program, but it is of little use to present that long list of titles here.

At the beginning of this paper I gave as one of the reasons for the imbalance between earlier and later parts the long period of time that takes to prepare a dictionary on historical principles. The first fascicles of the *MED* to be published were the letters E and F, and they are so different from the rest of the *MED* that a revision of E and F is absolutely necessary for an electronic version of the dictionary. Two more examples from the *MED* will help to define and illustrate the ways in which E and F are different. Consider again the entry for the verb *failen*. There are two uses in which E and F stand out from the rest of the *MED*. One is the use of so-called 'sense categories' or 'umbrella senses', which are denoted by Roman numerals; in the case of *failen*:

> **II.** To be unsuccessful, miss, avoid.

Under the umbrella sense **II,** several senses are grouped together: senses **4**, **5**, **6**, and **7**. It is remarkable that the use of this lexicographical device is restricted to the letters E and F. In none of the fascicles that came out after E and F is it to be found. Possible reasons why it was discarded in the later parts are in all probability the fact that the device of sense categories does not add anything to the semantic content of the entry, and the fact that the clarity of arrangement that this device aims at producing is not always sufficiently great to justify the additional dictionary space it requires. It would seem appropriate, therefore, in an attempt to harmonize the *MED* to drop all these sense categories from the dictionary. However, for an electronic dictionary, where the user is limited by the size of his monitor as to what and how much he can see at any one time, overviews of the meaning of a word and clarity in the arrangement of its senses are important if not essential. Therefore, it might be worthwhile to consider the possibility of introducing umbrella senses into the rest of the dictionary as well, especially in the longer entries, even though a decision on this may not be based on lexicographical factors alone, but is likely to depend on the financial resources available. Another striking phenomenon that *failen* illustrates is the use of subsenses: almost every sense is subdivided into subsenses, designated by a sense number followed by a letter: **3b**, **3c**, **4a**, **4b**, **4c**, **5a**, **5b**, and so on. Nowhere else in the dictionary is the device of the subsense used to the same extent as in E and F. Finally, *failen* shows that the sense definitions are very short and concise; in later parts, the definitions are much more elaborate and much longer.

E and F are also different from the rest of the *MED* with respect to the treatment of phrases. A good example of this is the entry for the noun *ende*. It shows that sense 24 is actually a phrase section for noun phrases, and six of them are grouped together, the first three of which appear below:

> **24.** Noun phrases:
> **(1) crop and ende**, everything from beginning to end. ......
> **(2) ord (ore, ordfrume) and ende**, beginning and end; -- a common epithet of the deity. ......
> **(3) ende and ord (word), ende of orde, ord (word) and ende, ord fram than ende**, beginning and end, everything, all; from start to finish. ......

In the same way, sense 23 lists six different prepositional phrases, and sense 25 ten verbal phrases. Also, each phrase is numbered separately with a number between round brackets: **(1)**, **(2)**, etc. This may be a solution to the problem of classifying a certain phrase under a given sense, but in most cases it is fairly simple to classify the phrases listed in these separate phrase sections under one of the senses of *ende*. Outside of E and F there are no phrase sections of the kind that we find under *ende* with separate sections for prepositional, noun and verb phrases, nor do we find outside E and F this particular kind of numbering. For the sake of clarity I would suggest transferring all these phrases to the senses where they semantically belong, as is done in the rest of the dictionary.

A revision, or a reorganization, of E and F, then, is an essential part of the overall harmonization of the paper dictionary and should be undertaken in order to produce a reliable and effective electronic dictionary. Ideally, A to D need to be harmonized as well, but the differences between A to D and the rest of the dictionary are less dramatic than those that exist between E and F and the rest of the dictionary. In A to D we find similar differences, though on a much smaller scale, in the definition and description of meanings, in the scope and range of illustrative quotations under a given sense, and in the treatment of senses. An updating of A to D is therefore less urgent at this moment but should eventually be undertaken when the appropriate funding becomes available.

So far in my paper I have only dealt with preliminary considerations for harmonizing the different formats of the paper dictionary for an electronic version. The technical aspects of the conversion I have not yet covered, partly because they are issues that are still under discussion, and partly because, some in the e-*MED* planning group say, these issues need not be resolved now, since the electronic dictionary cannot be realized until the last and final fascicle of the paper dictionary has appeared, which is now foreseen for the end of 1999. Another problem is that at this point we can only guess at what the state of technology will be like in 1999. Therefore, I can now only mention a few tentative solutions, which reflect my personal opinion and which are not necessarily shared by others in the e-*MED* planning group.

Tagging

First is the question of the kind of tagging that will be added to the text of the paper dictionary. Is it going to be SGML or HTML? Within the planning group there are proponents of either markup language, but it seems to me that a combination of the two is really needed. The encoding system of SGML is needed for marking up the dictionary entry proper (I will come back to this below) and the linking system that HTML allows is needed for linking support material to the dictionary entry. In HTML various kinds of links are possible, links to other texts, links to visual material, such as photographs and videos. For the electronic *MED* this could mean links to the source texts, from which quotations illustrating the meanings of a word are taken. In other words, these texts are going to be built into the dictionary, an enormous task but not altogether impossible as more and more texts are becoming available as e-texts.

The University of Michigan Library has revived its e-text program which is primarily intended for use within the University, the University of Michigan Press has launched its SEENET project for Early English and Norse electronic texts, and outside the University of Michigan environment, there is the ever growing Oxford Text Archive and the on-line archive of the University of Virginia's E-Text Center, to name just two of them. By making use of these texts in e-text format it will become possible to incorporate them into the dictionary, so that the wider context of a quotation can be made accessed on screen by simply highlighting, or selecting or just clicking on the word whose meaning the quotation is meant to illustrate.

The reverse should also be considered: when a Middle English scholar is working on or consulting a Middle English e-text, it should be possible for him, by highlighting or selecting a word in the text, to call up the entry for that particular word in the electronic *MED*, provided he has downloaded his own copy of e-*MED* or has access to one. Such a link can only be established if the existing e-texts are in a format that allows this kind of linking, and for new e-texts the matter is quite simple: choose the right format from the start.

Visual images could be linked to a dictionary entry, for example to a map showing the dialect distribution of a given word, such as the maps in the *Linguistic Atlas of Late Medieval English*, but also manuscript reproductions if a particular manuscript reading is doubtful or corrupt.

How Much Markup?

A problem related to that of the kind of markup language to be used is the question of the extent to which the text of the paper dictionary is going to be marked up. Related to this problem of the amount of tagging is the question of whether one is willing to cater for the need among scholars for an extensive Middle English database. Even now requests are coming in at the *MED* office for access to the *MED* database, which scholars assume already exists. But the truth of the matter is that there is no such database at the moment, and e-*MED* might be a first step towards one. But if so, it is essential that the proper encoding of the various elements in a dictionary entry be put in. Taking as our starting-point an entry such as *thank,* we might come up with the categories as in Figure 2:

Figure 2
Categories to be encoded in a dictionary entry

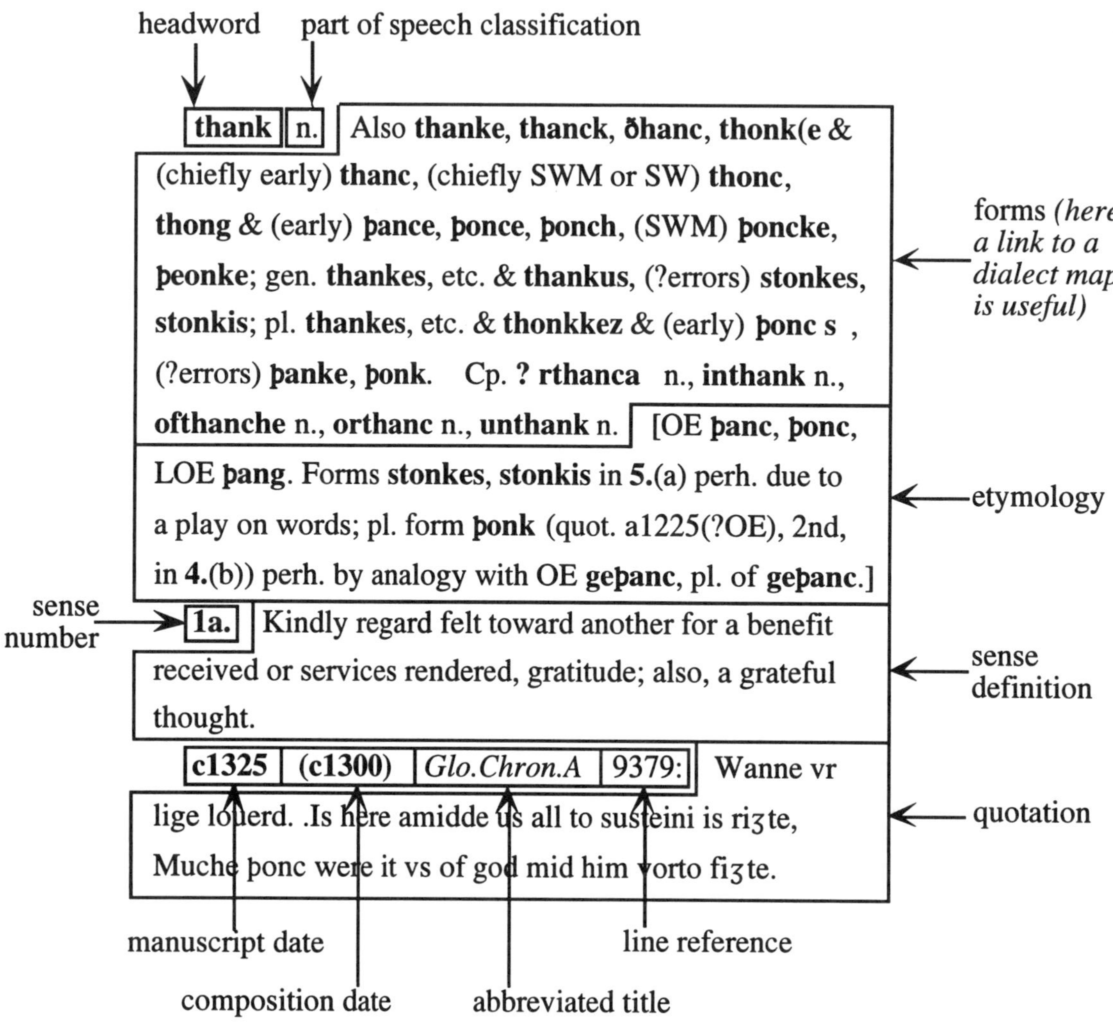

The section of the dictionary entry containing the various forms of the head-word should be encoded in such a way that a distinction is made between the uninflected forms, the forms of the genitive and those of the plural. Moreover, period labels ("early", "chiefly early"), dialect labels ("SWM", "SW", "chiefly ...") and labels for possible misspellings ("?errors") should be encoded as well. Similarly, the encoding of the etymology section should specify the language of the etymons, the etymons themselves, and other observations. The quotation itself should be encoded for part of speech information of the words making up the sentence but also for functional information, identifying the syntactic relations between the words of the sentence (subject, object, predicate, etc.). It is obvious that the extent to which quotation tagging is added will eventually determine the usefulness of e-*MED* as a database.

Finally a word or two on the question of the way in which e-*MED* will ultimately be available. I think we would have to decide on both a CD-ROM version and online availability: a CD-ROM version for libraries and heavy users, online for those who would only sporadically make use of e-*MED*. CD-ROM might also be the answer to the congestion that has been predicted for the Information Superhighway. Both formats allow the production of updates. The online version will be updated and extended continuously, and for the CD-ROM one can imagine yearly updates under a kind of subscription arrangement.

I have not mentioned possible spinoffs of the e-*MED* project, but one of the first things that come to mind is a Chaucer Dictionary.

A lot of work remains to be done before there will be an e-*MED*, work that has yet to start in a formal way, but of one thing I am now quite convinced (though at this time a year ago I was much more pessimistic): there will be an e-*MED* soon.

ACKNOWLEDGEMENT

From September 1993 to August 1994 I was granted a special leave of absence by my university, which enabled me to work on a research project in the offices of the *Middle English Dictionary* at the University of Michigan in Ann Arbor. In the course of that year I became involved in the preparations for an electronic version of the *MED*, and the present paper is a reflection of my involvement.

I wish to thank the *College van Bestuur* of the *Vrije Universiteit*, the Dean and Board of the Faculty of Arts and my colleagues in the English Department for making it possible for me to be away for a year, and the Editor-in-Chief and staff of the *Middle English Dictionary*, the Director of the University of Michigan Press and the Office of the Vice President for Research of the University of Michigan for making my stay in Ann Arbor so pleasant and fruitful.

Henk Aertsen
Department of English
Free University, The Netherlands
aertsenh@let.vu.nl

Scholarly Communications Project: Publishers and Libraries

Gail McMillan
Virginia Polytechnic Institute and State University

Foundations of the Scholarly Communications Project

That libraries seemingly are becoming publishers is, in part, an effort to improve library services. Libraries enhance services by producing and distributing information electronically not only to the local university community, students and faculty, researchers and scholars, but also to the expanding numbers of worldwide users who are anxious to find what they need quickly on the information highway.

Providing access to journals, articles, abstracts, photographic collections, bibliographies, newspapers, and more are among traditional library services. These services, of course, do not seem new or innovative--until one puts them in the context of the Internet and makes them electronically available at no charge to the university community and the electronic village. Then they take on a whole new meaning: electronic journals, timely distribution of current research, digital images (still and motion, with and without audio), references directly linked to their source articles--all available without leaving one's chair. Add to these current services even more electronic resources such as online reserve materials, theses and dissertations, and television news to get a glimpse of the current publishing and experimental activities of the Scholarly Communications Project at the University Libraries, Virginia Polytechnic Institute and State University. The increasing availability of this kind of information online, combined with the rapidly growing number of personal computers and the expanding use of world-wide computer networks, is contributing to the changing nature of library services and academic publishing.

When the Scholarly Communications Project was getting underway in 1989, the founding director, Lon Savage, envisioned a pioneering effort: exploration of new means of scholarly communications and ways to reduce costly distribution of print publications normally done through commercial publishers. Paul Gherman, University Librarian at Virginia Tech when the Project began, felt strongly that such a project belonged in the library; that it would be an opportunity for library staff to get involved in a new publishing medium that increasingly would be integral to the library's mission. Thus, the Project director, who often refers to himself as "an old newspaper man" and who is not a librarian, was very concerned about publishers' interests, while the librarian looked at electronic publishing as a way for libraries to use new technology to keep their services meeting the current information needs of their patrons.

Since the Scholarly Communications Project moved into the library in 1991, the founding director has retired, leaving a flourishing enterprise. The first electronic-only journal has been joined by four print-also journals, abstracts for two additional journals, two research databases, two experimental digital image collections, an experiment in providing access to television news, a regional newspaper, and the university faculty/staff newspaper. Thus, the activities of the Project have placed the library directly into the information provider's role, improving the level of services the library offers. Like the library, the Project provides its services free of charge to editors and publishers, to our university community, and to anyone else who can access our repository of information (ironically called a "server"). It is a collaborative venture that disseminates information--traditional library material--beyond the walls of the library and the academy.

Goals of the Scholarly Communications Project

1. Foster the mission of the university by disseminating the products of teaching, research, and public service
2. Promote the advantages of the electronic publishing
3. Make services available to the university community, and as a state institution, to local, regional, and statewide clientele
4. Be a resource for new editors on- and off-campus
5. Encourage new editors to take advantage of unique opportunities available with electronic publishing
6. Address the issues facing print publishers confronted with non-traditional, electronic publishing options
7. Address the strain on physical space available for the growing number of publications to be stored and accessed on-site and in off-site storage facilities, the rising shelving and binding costs, and the decreasing cost of online storage for libraries
8. Explore potential solutions to the increasing cost of information and its impact on the library's materials budget
9. Expand the range of library services

At the Scholarly Communications Project, we have amassed a considerable sum of information and knowledge gained from our experiences and we are very willing, in fact, anxious, to share it with others. We have had our success and our non-successes; we have experience doing things that work well, while we also are experiencing some less than ideal situations. We would like to save others from the pitfalls we have discovered.

Strategies for Achieving the Project's Goals

Strategies that have been implemented for achieving the Project's goals include offering editors a range of electronic publishing options. We do this by making plain text (ASCII) files available as well as by presenting via World Wide Web marked-up text with in- line graphics and links directly to references and citations. These two presentations have become our standard operating procedure since we began manually inserting HTML tags last year. When faced with providing access to a daily newspaper, the technical director immediately wrote the script that automatically inserts the tags. Recently, we have begun to receive already tagged materials; with these we take the opposite tack and strip the tags from a copy for ASCII presentations. This is not yet a trouble-free process which causes some concern for the Project staff. We want to make electronic publishing as easy as possible, especially for our busy faculty who usually serve as editors of scholarly journals while carrying full teaching loads. However, as the list of publications grows, our two person operation may need to require files in certain common or easily translatable formats. By working with our editors to get standardized files from them, and by doing as much automated processing as possible, we believe that we can keep the number of Project staff low, yet provide a high level of service for a large number of publications.

ASCII and marked up text are the most common but not the only display formats we offer. After one year of plain text, the editor of the weekly faculty/staff newspaper, *Virginia Tech Spectrum*, came back to us and asked, "What can you do to make the online version look more like the paper copy?" We prepared for him some bitmapped images (i.e., pictures of the pages) with hypertext links to the text of the articles. One of our other editors took a different approach. The editor of the *Journal of Technology Education* separates the graphics from the articles so that his readers with access to either low end or higher end equipment are all well served.

For both editors, the overwhelming constraint is that the bitmapped images and

PostScript files are not accessible to many of their readers. Also, bitmapped images are not word- searchable. To overcome this, we have linked the ASCII text to the online picture of the page, taking advantage of the best of both formats--content and visual layout.

When editors initially approach the Project, they are interested in giving their readers (usually their paid subscribers) the option of receiving hardcopy or electronic access. They see as quite peripheral exercising the benefits of electronic publishing, such as being able to reach a worldwide audience at all hours of every day, the lack of cost for distribution, the word indexing that facilitates searching and retrieval, permanent archiving, and the like. Many editors are still of the opinion that it will be a slow process to acquaint much of their traditional readership with the advantages of electronic publications. However, the Project's server logged an average of nearly 8000 file retrievals per month from all over the world during the 1993/94 fiscal year. The server was storing only 78Mb in January 1994, 146Mb in August 1994, and 479Mb October 1994 (largely due to the addition of a daily newspaper).

Another strategy for achieving the goals of the Scholarly Communications Project is an extension of our library-oriented perspective, to offer subscribers and any of our readers a broad range of electronic access options, thereby improving current library services. Our publications are viewable in many different formats, offered to meet the wide-ranging expertise and equipment of our readers. Text-only articles and files are available through FTP, Gopher, and WAIS for those with low-end equipment (like the 286 IBM-clone I use at home); for the more sophisticated users and those with higher-end equipment, we provide formats such as PostScript, Adobe Acrobat, and HTML through the World Wide Web. Offering a range of publishing options to our editors of course affects the end-user or reader of the publications. Usage statistics show very significant increases in Gopher and Web access to the Project's server. On the other hand, the number of people using FTP to get our publications has declined significantly.

Our third strategy focuses on timeliness and is also an extension of our role as a department within the University Libraries. As a librarian I see timely access to information as an excellent enhancement to the services libraries provide and as an obvious outcome of library-based electronic publishing.

There are several aspects of timeliness. With our small staff we attempt to give access to the most expedient version of an electronic journal first. This means that if it comes to us with hypertext tags, Web travelers will get access to it first. Gopher access will come later, after we've stripped the document down to ASCII. Sometimes there is not much difference in the time of availability, but we needed to establish some priorities mainly to address anticipated time pressures as our list of publications grows but our staff does not. We also feel compelled to respond first to the requests of our most immediate clientele, that is, other librarians and university faculty; uploading the file sent to me from out of state is more easily postponed. Humans, not machines, are usually the causes of delays.

The fourth strategy the Scholarly Communications Project has for achieving its goals is to maintain access to all of our electronic publications all day, every day, forever. We have not had a problem in this area, and we hope we never will for we consider a reduction in our access options to be the same as reducing the hours the library is open. In spite of all the University Libraries' difficulties in managing with a constantly shrinking budget, the library has not reduced its hours of operations and constantly is adding online storage capabilities.

It is also quite helpful in maintaining access that once a publication, a picture, or a database is residing on the server, it requires almost no human intervention to maintain open access for users. The result has been someone retrieving a file from the Project's server once every six or seven minutes of every hour of every day. The server, unlike like the library, did not shut down for a holiday or inclement weather.

Working within these goals and strategies, the Scholarly Communications Project staff has learned a lot about what works well and what has not worked well in our electronic publishing enterprise. What has not worked is persuading editors to take advantage of one of the real benefits of electronic publishing: there is no necessity to package together a group of articles as they must do for a printed publication. The editors tend to do all of their final file preparations at one time, rather than as each article finishes the review process. However, in the networked environment, where a publication does not have to fill a certain number of pages, each electronic article could be distributed to subscribers as soon as it is ready. Here is where the timeliness factor can have a major impact on the dissemination of scholarly research.

One option that our dual publication editors have found advantageous is putting back issues online. For example, even though we did not begin publishing the electronic *Journal of Technology Education* until 1991, the editor had saved all the previous issues on diskettes. It was relatively easy for Project personnel to load the back issues into the server and give access to the entire corpus of the *JTE* on the Internet. *Community Services Catalyst*, however, is more than twenty years old and back files are not available. With some financial support from the journal's sponsoring organization, students were hired to scan and OCR (optical character recognition) the two years prior to publication of the electronic version. Unfortunately, the funding ceased before the project was completed, and these back issues are not yet available online.

Collaborations with Traditional Publishers

An exciting upcoming project is *Technology, Science, Mathematics Connection Activities: A Teacher's Resource Binder*, from Glenco/McGraw Hill, a commercial publisher. The publisher's Director of Technical Education contacted me as a result of her conversations with the principal author, Dr. Mark Sanders (editor of the *JTE*), who presented her with the idea of electronically publishing these activities when he realized that the electronic version of his journal was reaching an audience far in excess of the printed version. The publisher's representative agreed because she saw the electronic publishing of this activity as a type of free advertising for the entire set. I saw it as an opportunity to collaborate with a commercial publisher, allowing us to gain some practical experience in and understanding of cooperative electronic publishing.

The problems: The software was not readily available nor familiar to the Project's technical director who at one time said, "If it's electronic, we can publish it." This is probably a true statement, but, practically speaking, we can most efficiently work with a limited number of familiar easily adaptable formats. Negotiating a mutually acceptable file format has become a more frequent topic of discussion between project staff and those to whom we offer our services.

Applying what we learned as journal publishers, I was able to offer some advice that also would apply to electronic books. For example, rather than receiving one big file, such as an entire journal or all 50 pages of this activity, we ask for each article or each component to be a separate file. There are several advantages in addition to the obvious ones of not slowing down transmissions or filling the reader's mailbox or disk with extremely large files. Readers should be able to get just the chapters or sections or articles they want to read, rather all the articles in an issue or every chapter in a book.

A cautionary note: when the files are separate, always put the name and date of the journal (e.g., fall 1994) or, in this case the name of the book and the chapter name and/or number in each file so that when it is separate from the terminal display and/or its source of information (e.g., a printout) so that it can be uniquely identified and reveals where it came from or what it belongs with. The same is true of the copyright statement; this should accompany each file, even if the statement is only a warning about fair use rather than a proprietary one.

Another collaborative experience is a radical departure from any of our previous publishing ventures. In July 1994, the listserv VPIEJ-L posted a proposal being explored by the Scholarly Communications Project called the VT Model. This is a co-publication plan that looks at a way for traditional commercial and/or academic publishers to collaborate with academic libraries to pool their resources to take advantage of what the information highway has to offer both. It is a way for traditional publishers to also publish electronically and to keep libraries as a source of current as well as historical electronic information. We contacted Birkhauser Boston about an announcement they made in the *Journal of Mathematical Systems, Estimation, and Control.* Combining the Birkhauser proposal with ideas from a discussion at an SCP Advisory Board meeting, we prepared the VT Model, a proposal, not the definitive answer to electronic publishing but an idea disseminated for academic discussion.

Our proposal is to co-publish electronic journals, sharing the work between a traditional publisher and a research library. Journal editorial boards would continue to function much as they do now, but papers accepted for publication would be processed in two parts. One part would be the full text subject to minimal copy editing but retaining all aspects of full peer review to retain high standards of scholarship. The full text would be electronically available at no charge through a research library. The other part would be a summary or extended abstract published by Birkhauser, either on paper or through a database with access charges. This would be carefully edited to efficiently communicate the content and significance of the full text.

As the information explosion progresses our system of publishing and distributing information must find ways to handle a much greater volume of new information. Libraries have the expertise to secure, organize, and indefinitely archive large quantities of information for public use. Publishers have expertise in the certification, sorting, and refinement of information. A much larger volume could be handled by both if we do not insist that everything pass through all parts of both systems. The VT Model proposes dividing the load between publishers and libraries to exploit the strengths of each.

How would the VT Model be beneficial to scholars? Scholars search for information in two modes: directed searches in which the objective is known, and browsing. Electronic networks offer wonderful tools for directed searching, especially when references embedded in an article link the reader directly to the referenced article. Electronic collections and tools like this are vastly expanding the directed search mode.

At the same time, browsing is not getting easier. The indexes and abstracts available for the huge spectrum of traditional journals is invaluable for more effective browsing and so far there is no real electronic substitute for the serendipity nourished by random browsing. Whether browsing paper or electronic files, high-quality abstracts or summaries can greatly improve the search results. We think that the vast majority of the people who "look at" an article are browsing, and read no further than the abstract. Therefore, it is not necessary to have the summary packaged with the full text; after information is discovered through a summary, getting the full text is a directed-search problem which can be handled efficiently.

The VT Model suggests a change in point of view about what a journal publisher's product should be. Currently the obvious product is full text. We suggest that the publisher's principle product could be summaries, and the full text would be regarded as an electronic supplement. The old mind-set was to deny access to non-subscribers. The new attitude would be that subscribers receive guides and aids to finding material which is in principle freely available, but in fact is buried in an avalanche of other electronic information.

Publishers Who Follow the VT Model Would:

1. Improve the availability of their electronic publications
2. Continue to manage the level of quality control through peer review process
3. Continue to be responsible for managing the distribution of scholarly information up to the costly points of printing and mailing
4. Save money by doing less printing--using less ink and less paper
5. Save money by not having to maintain, store, and mail back issues
6. Save money by not having to establish the electronic archives that would store, maintain, and distribute electronic issues
7. Save money by not editing for display purposes (unless markup is done here)
8. Save money by doing less content editing
9. Save money by not having to index a title

There is a "product" which is seemingly invisible but which is very important--quality control through editors and peer review. Traditional publishers currently have this track record and the VT Model offers a way to transfer this quality control to the network. Once the peer review process is completed, there should be little or no copy editing of the full-text file. Publishers cannot support copy editing of files for a free archive because editing is expensive and the costs cannot be recovered. Editing lies outside the expertise and mission of the library, so the library cannot support it either.

Editing here refers only to file and copy editing, and not content editing or refereeing; the full text should continue to meet the high standards of reliability, completeness, and scholarly integrity. Editors (and peer reviewers) should continue to request rewriting to improve usability and readability. A loss of aesthetics seems a reasonable price for the increase in efficiency, and, indeed, should not be too a great burden on the reader. If the vast majority of users read the summary and go no further, those who progress to the full text primarily will be specialists focussing on substance and content. This and readability can continue to be insured by the peer review process--perhaps with some enhancements. Finally, this argument applies to the preparation of electronic files as well as copy editing. It should be the responsibility of the author to provide a usable file. The extent of this kind of editing could be a part of the decision to publish (by the publisher and/or by the peer review board). If an author cannot write clearly, should the article be published?

Scholarly material should be available electronically. The innovation in the VT Model is that electronic files are maintained by a library rather than the publisher. Archives maintained by a commercial publisher would almost certainly have to generate revenue and would probably fare poorly in competition with free, non-commercial electronic journal archives. The segregation of information by publisher is also not practical for researchers and scholars. To be successful the archive should be free, and publishers, therefore, probably should not do it-- libraries should.

Why Libraries Rather than Publishers Should Maintain Electronic Archives

1. To maintain and enhance commitment to availability of information: improve services by always having issues available (never missing from shelves, never missing pages, never at the binder, never locking the doors)
2. Librarians know how to help people find the information they want
3. Librarians know how to respond to user access problems
4. Subject specialists have the expertise to know where to insert the "hot" links between cross references
5. Libraries provide equipment for patrons and clients to use to read and

print
6. Libraries are a known central source of information from all over the world

While librarians have experience creating and maintaining indexes; this function can now be given to machines to index every file and integrate the indexes of each file within a journal title.

Part of the mission of a research library is to archive material and provide access to information, especially the results of scholarly research. Supporting electronic journal archives would be a direct contribution to this mission, but it applies library resources in a non-traditional way. The net effect is that all users get better access to more information.

At the Scholarly Communications Project we still have a lot to learn about electronic publishing, whether the VT Model works or not. We want to know more about how our presentations and displays meet our readers needs or expectations. Are our links helpful? We also want to learn more about automating file transfers to the Project's server and automating document markup.

We are also about to get involved in some huge projects, including bringing our cooperative extension service publications, past and future, to the Internet. Another project will be providing Internet access to the library's reserve collection. So far, we have operated on the periphery of copyright issues; most of our materials are copyrighted by the authors, the editors, or the university. We have maintained our traditional library perspective and the latitude that fair use gives us.

The support for all of our activities comes from the library and the university, but we may have to seek supplemental funding. Our obvious initial choice is negotiating payments for our services with our commercial partners. It has been suggested that the services we provide to our university faculty could remain free, but we should charge off-campus collaborators for recovery of the cost for those services. I, of course, don't know what the future portends, but I would like to continue offering these improved library services without charging fees to the end users.

One of the remarkable things about the Scholarly Communications Project is that we are in a position to experiment, to make mistakes, and to not be overwhelmed or disappointed by the outcome. This wonderful opportunity has been supported for the last two years by our Interim University Librarian, Joanne Eustis, who has encouraged us to accept all the challenges of electronic information: "Just do it!" rather than devote too much time to investigating, studying, planning, testing, and analyzing. Electronic access to information is so new that over planning will not improve the chances of success; experimenting in brand new areas and learning from our experiences will.

This is why the Scholarly Communications Project is working with commercial publishers, with academic publishers, with editors and collection managers, with newspapers, and other produces of information. To date, none of our collaborators has seen anything but benefits from these electronic publishing endeavors. Paid subscribers have not been lost, and new, interested readers from throughout the world have been attracted to their publications. We will continue to build on our electronic publishing endeavors, learn from them, and continue to share them with you.

Appendix

Scholarly Communications Project Virginia Polytechnic Institute and State University

History and Purpose

To pioneer in electronic communication of scholarly materials was the primary goal of the Scholarly Communications Project when it was established in the fall of 1989 by then-Vice President for Information Systems, Dr. Robert Heterick. Lon Savage directed the project until his retirement in December 1993; Gail McMillan assumed that responsibility in January 1994. James Powell is the technical director.

The pioneering efforts of the Project have included publishing electronic journals, article abstracts, and raw research data. The Project has expanded its initial goal to include editors and publishers become involved in the electronic publishing process, resolve technical issues related to information presentation and its rapid dissemination, and assist subscribers, including libraries, to use the electronically available information. The Project's priorities are to provide free and open access as well as to experiment with new technology. However, resolving technical issues through experimentation sometimes means using various display formats that are not yet in common use by a journal's subscribers.

James Powell, shared by the SCP with the Libraries' Automation Department, is responsible for the technical wizardry behind the projects. Through his hard work and dedication to library services and electronic communications, the publications of the Scholarly Communications Project are viewable in many different formats, including ASCII (i.e., text-only), as well as marked-up texts (HTML) and PostScript graphics. These are available through FTP, Gopher, freeWAIS, and World Wide Web clients. Not every publication is available in every format; the Project is experimenting with finding the most useful retrieval and display formats for the subscribers, the university community, and the Internet community. The Scholarly Communications Project is committed to maintaining all issues of its publications online indefinitely. Additional disk storage is coming to ensure that the Project can continue to expand its activities, especially for digital images and newspaper access. Our October 1994 archive required 479Mb, up from 78Mb of storage we were using in January 1994.

Access the Project at:
http://scholar.lib.vt.edu/ and
gopher://scholar.lib.vt.edu:70/

Journal of the International Academy of Hospitality Research

JIAHR was the first electronic journal published by the Project (November 1990). Each article is published as it completes the peer-review and editing processes. All of its text-only issues have been distributed via the Internet, avoiding the costs of paper, printing, and postal charges. Its editors, originally Dr. Mahmood Kahn and now Dr. Eliza Tse, are on the faculty of Virginia Tech's Hotel, Restaurant, and Institutional Management Department.

Community Services Catalyst

Catalyst was one of the first print journals to be published both traditionally and electronically when the Project began publication via the Internet with the summer 1991 issue. Scanning and OCR (optical character recognition) technology have been used to extend the electronic archive of back issues to 1989. Founded in 1973, *Catalyst*, a journal for community college educators, is edited by Tech faculty member, Dr. Darrel Clowes.

Journal of Technology Education

Another print journal that is also published electronically by the Project is the *JTE*, edited Dr. Mark Sanders, Technology Education, Virginia Tech. Because he has been electronically preparing the journal for publication with standard word processing since its first issue in 1989, the Project easily made the entire run available online although actual electronic publishing began only in the spring of 1992. *JTE* is also unique because each issue contains graphics and that are part of the electronic publication. Readers with text-only capabilities have full access to the text of the journal, while readers with greater capabilities can also retrieve the graphic illustrations, either integrated into the article (as they are in traditional publications), or as separate PostScript files. Volume 6, no. 1 (fall 1994) was the first issue presented in HTML.

Journal of Industrial Teacher Education

The Project's newest electronic journal became available in November 1994 with the fall issue. *JITE* is our first publication to be edited by faculty at another institution; Dr. Scott Johnson is at the University of Illinois at Urbana-Champaign.

Journal of Veterinary Medical Education

In July 1994 the Project began publishing its most attractive electronic journal. *JVME* is our first scholarly journal with in-line color graphics and hypertext articles. Beginning with vol. 21, no. 1, it is available for World Wide Web clients; we use Mosaic. The editor was Dr. Richard Talbot, on the faculty of the Virginia-Maryland College of Veterinary Medicine.

Modal Analysis

The Project publishes the online abstracts of the print quarterly *Modal Analysis: The International Journal of Analytical and Experimental Modal Analysis*, a journal of the Society for Experimental Mechanics (SEM). The Project does not publish the articles because most subscribers cannot access and print Mosaic, PostScript, or Acrobat files, which are typically required to display the integrated text and "graphics" (i.e., non-ASCII characters such as mathematical symbols). In 1993 the print publication moved to SEM with the understanding that the Project would continue to publish the *Modal Analysis* abstracts as well as those of its *Experimental Mechanics*.

Journal of Fluids Engineering

Another challenge to electronic publication is the *JFE*, edited on campus by Dr. Demetri Telionis. The Project provides access to the raw research data used as the basis of papers disseminated in the print journal. A digital video of blade- vortex interaction experiments has been added to the Project's server. Future plans include establishing an interactive online discussion of *JFE* articles for fluids engineers.

Other Publications

Under this new heading on the Project's home page are: *The Report of the Scholarly Communications Task Force* (policies and procedures for making available electronic journal subscriptions through University Libraries Gopher) and *Scholarly Communications Project: Technology Summary* (a slide show about our current technology and some future plans). Also available are the FDA Approved *Animal Drug Data Base*, experimental work with electronic theses and dissertations, and in-house publications such as "Spinning the Web: Introduction to HTML (James Powell, Sept. 1994).

Spectrum

The text of our faculty/staff newspaper, the *Virginia Tech Spectrum*, has been available electronically through the Project's server since May 1993. While it is not mailed to a list of electronic subscribers, the complete text of each issue is available as a weekly publication and as an online, word-indexed, text archive. Towards developing an online publication that more fully replicates the design and layout of the original tabloid, two experimental issues are also available, one with hypertext and the front page photo, and one with a bitmapped image of the front page and links to the ASCII text.

VPIEJ-L

Available since June 1992, VPIEJ-L is a source of online discussions about all aspects of electronic publishing. Over 900 subscribers, including publishers, editors, technical staff, programmers, librarians, and others, have discussed such topics as what distribution methods work better than others; how end- users are accessing and using electronic publication; formats and mark-up languages; and software and hardware considerations for creation, storage, and access to electronic journals. Discussions have addressed the cost of electronic journal publishing as well as new ideas for collaboration between commercial publishers and libraries.

Digital Images

In the spring of 1994 images from the University Libraries' Special Collections Department were digitized by the university's PhotoGraphic Services through the Kodak CD processing. Two small collections (cadet uniforms worn by Virginia Agricultural and Mechanical College and Virginia Polytechnic Institute students, and Norfolk and Western railroad engines, bridges, and advertisements) are currently accessible on the World Wide Web. Project staff added brief text and appropriate hypertext links that connected, for example, N and W railroad pictures to the Virtual Railroad, and that linked an older style cadet jacket to its later version.

Digital Video--motion and sound

Through a donation from our local television station, CBS- affiliate WDBJ-7, the Project will have the opportunity to provide online access to WDBJ-7's news archives extending back to the 1950s. A small portion of the scripts, log books, and video clips from May 1977 is currently available for experimentation on the World Wide Web as we try to determine how best to make these materials available. The inclusion of hypertext links to move within this collection of local news would enhance its research value as would links between this local television archive and a local newspaper archive.

Virginia Pilot/Ledger Star

Through collaboration with Landmark Communications, the Project provides access for the Virginia Tech university community and the Blacksburg Electronic Village (BEV) to *VPLS*. Landmark also owns the *Roanoke Times* and *World News* which we hope to have online in the very near future. We are hoping to provide current, daily access. While a newspaper archive will be a useful by-product of this endeavor, same-day access is our goal but is not currently technically possible.

Experimentation and the Future

Electronic publishing of scholarly research will continue to be a priority as we continue to work with journal editors and publishers. The Project has agreed to publish nine new electronic journals fiscal year 1994/95; the abstracts of four more will result from collaborations with a British publisher and others. We are also working with other library units and the Virginia Tech Graduate School to publish electronic theses and dissertations of VT graduates. The current plans call for the Adobe Acrobat Reader for access to the full publication; the Project plans to provide open access to authors, titles, and abstracts in ASCII also. We hope that hypertext links eventually will provide easy access to related publications.

Gail McMillan
Director, Scholarly Communications Project
Virginia Polytechnic Institute and State University
gailmac@vt.edu
703-231-9252

Electronic Journals

- The Community Services CATALYST
- The Journal of Fluids Engineering DATABANK and related resources
- Journal of Industrial Teacher Education
- Journal of Mathematical Systems, Estimation, and Control
- Journal of Technology Education
- Journal of the International Academy of Hospitality Research
- Journal of Veterinary Medical Education
- Modal Analysis

Five Societies: One Journal Project

Keith L. Seitter
American Meteorological Society

Introduction

This paper describes the collaborative effort of five scientific societies to develop an interdisciplinary electronic journal. This journal is not yet in production but has been under development for over two years and is expected to go online during calendar-year 1995. The primary focus of this paper is the structure of the collaboration itself rather than the technical aspects of the electronic journal, but it includes some discussion of the proposed content of the journal and of the philosophy of the journal since these issues provide the foundation for the collaboration. The five collaborating societies are the American Meteorological Society (AMS), the American Geophysical Union (AGU), the Association of American Geographers (AAG), the Ecological Society of America (ESA), and The Oceanographic Society (TOS). These societies represent a broad range of size and available resources (**Table 1**). They also have had different electronic publishing experiences, and, as will be discussed here, are taking on differing levels of support for this project.

Initial discussions among representatives of AMS, AGU, ESA, and TOS began in late 1992, and AAG joined the collaboration in early 1994. From the start, discussions centered on the concept of an interdisciplinary journal focused on issues of what has been termed "earth system science." This area of increasing research effort includes the atmospheric, oceanic, hydrologic, and biological sciences and is largely focused on issues related to global change. There is a need for a scholarly journal in this rapidly growing research area and the extensive use of computer modeling and computer visualization by scientists working in earth system science makes it an attractive candidate for an all-electronic journal. No single society in the collaboration covers all disciplines in this area, but the collection covers the earth system sciences quite well. While each of the societies is carrying out some initiatives in the realm of electronic publishing, each felt that a collaborative effort on an electronic journal was an effective way to spread the financial risks while greatly improving the prospect of success.

NASA's "Mission to Planet Earth" program is expected to be an important source of observational data for future earth system science research. Since an electronic journal provides an innovative approach to the dissemination of research results stemming from the NASA program, it was felt that support might be obtained from NASA to cover some of the start-up costs of the journal. NASA was contacted early in the planning stages and was supportive of the idea, and a full proposal is currently under review at NASA headquarters.

Aspects of the Journal

A. *Basic philosophies*

Very early in the planning stages of the journal, several basic philosophies were agreed upon by the collaborating societies. The journal is to be peer reviewed at a high scholarly level so that it can stand on par with the best of the societies' print journals. This should allow it to attract high quality papers from excellent authors and should lead to it having a positive impact in promotion and tenure considerations. Articles will also undergo a full level of copy and technical editing to ensure a uniform style and a quality consistent with an archive journal. In addition, agreement was reached on two major issues that would drive the nature of the collaborative

Table 1

Comparison of Collaborating Societies

Name	Membership	Annual Budget
American Geophysical Union (AGU)	31,000	$16 M
American Meteorological Society (AMS)	11,000	$6 M
Ecological Society of America (ESA)	8,000	$2 M
Association of American Geographers (AAG)	7,000	$1 M
The Oceanographic Society (TOS)	2,000	$0.3 M

effort:

1. The journal should not seek to reproduce electronically what can be printed on the page but, instead, should strive to take the fullest advantage of the medium to go beyond the capabilities of the printed page.

Almost all scientists working in the atmospheric, oceanic, and related sciences are making extensive use of sophisticated computer graphics techniques in their research and are often faced with the dilemma of deciding how to present their results in a way that captures the essence of the visualization within the limitations of the printed page. Also, researchers would often like to be able to make available the extensive datasets supporting their published work in a way that allows others to validate and extend their results. Publication in an electronic form removes the restrictions of the flat, static, printed page for graphical presentation and allows data files to be attached (or at least pointed to) in a straightforward manner. All of the collaborating societies agree that the proposed journal must forge into the highest possible level of electronic sophistication in order to justify the need for an electronic journal over a paper one. Two years ago, it was not clear what standards would allow a journal of this type to be viable in a broad market encompassing a variety of computer platforms, but the staggering growth of World Wide Web documents as a result of the emergence of NCSA Mosaic over the past year has made it clear that the dissemination of graphical visualizations and animations will not pose a problem. The display of complicated mathematical expressions, which will also be important for the journal, is perhaps not a completely solved issue but probably will be very soon.

2. The journal must be structured in such a way to allow it to eventually be financially self-supporting (though outside funding will be sought for the start-up phase).

Most of the current electronic journals are offered free to subscribers (Okerson 1994) and are produced with some level of subsidized support. There has been a continuing debate on the economics of electronic journals compared to print ones (see, for example, Harnad 1994), with little apparent consensus on the issue. The collaborating societies in this project have determined, however, that the proposed journal will *not* be less expensive to produce than a comparable print one because of the high level of editorial quality that will be set as a goal and the expenses associated with structuring, formatting, and preparing the hypertextual links in the electronic files of the journal. The collaborating societies feel that their print journals should not subsidize the production of an electronic journal on a continuing basis, especially given the anticipated continued growth of electronic journals. It was therefore agreed that the proposed journal must be structured from the start in a way that would allow it to move toward economic self-sufficiency. The societies fully expect a major level of support to be required during the start-up and first few years of production and are seeking outside funds for a portion of that support.

A. Title and mission statement of the journal

The proposed title of the journal is *Earth Interactions*, and the overall scope of the journal is provided in its mission statement, which is currently proposed as:

> *Earth Interactions* publishes in the electronic medium original research in the earth system sciences with emphasis on interdisciplinary studies. Within this framework, the journal particularly encourages submissions that deal with interactions between the lithosphere, hydrosphere, atmosphere, and biosphere in the context of global issues or global change.
>
> Submissions introducing observational or modeled datasets that may be useful in the study of earth system science and that include both a description of the algorithms and/or processing techniques used and a brief, representative sample of the information in the dataset are also appropriate.
>
> The electronic medium in which the journal is published provides unique opportunities for data presentation, animation, and interaction. Authors should strive to take maximum advantage of the capabilities of the electronic medium, but any electronic manuscript that deals with the subject areas of the journal will be considered for publication.

C. Technical model for delivery of the journal

The journal is expected to be produced as a World Wide Web structured hypertext document amenable to delivery via NCSA Mosaic. It will probably be edited and archived as a more robust SGML document and converted to HTML for online delivery over the Internet. It is not clear yet whether other electronic delivery mechanisms such as CD-ROM will be used for the journal. Articles will be placed online as they are ready for dissemination (though they may be collected into "issues" for administration and archive purposes), and subscribers to the journal will be notified of new articles through e-mail.

D. A few aspects of the economic model

The economic model for the journal is quite similar to the model used for print journals. Revenue will be derived from both author charges and subscription fees. It is anticipated that author charges will fall into three categories:

1. A charge similar to page charges based on the size of the text portion of the article;

2. A charge based on the size of the files containing graphics and data supporting the article; and

3. A potential charge assessed to authors if their submitted files need more than the normal amount of work to be made ready for publication.

The concept of limiting access through the use of subscriptions is perhaps a bit controversial in the current climate of the Internet, but subscriptions provide an important component of the economics of print journals that allows the author charges to be kept reasonable. Subscription revenue also allows societies to publish work even when the author's institution does not have funds available to cover the author charges and the collaborating societies want to be able to continue that policy with the electronic journal. The subscription model being planned seeks to emulate the best features of the print model and address some of the concerns of both individual and institutional subscribers. The subscription will be a flat fee for a volume year of the journal, with a fee structure that provides for the lowest cost to members of the five societies in the collaboration, somewhat higher fees for individuals who are not members, and higher still fees for institutional subscribers. Since the subscription provides access to an electronic source, the subscriptions take on more of the character of individual and site (institutional) licenses under which the subscribers agree to adhere to the terms of their particular subscription type (including copyright restrictions).

The flat-fee subscription approach, as opposed to a pay-per-use one, is considered important because the flat-fee approach does not discourage users from browsing the contents on a frequent basis. Browsing is especially desirable for an interdisciplinary journal that hopes to foster linkages between scientists in different disciplines who are working on similar issues in the earth system sciences. An important component of the proposed subscription model is that the subscription fee for a given year will provide access to that volume year of the journal on a continuing basis. This addresses the concerns of both librarians and individuals who do not want to be in the position of having to download the contents of an electronic journal during the subscription year in order to have access to it at a later time. The intent would be to provide access on a continuing basis to the 1996 volume year of the journal, for example, to any individual or institution who subscribed in 1996, even if they drop their subscription for subsequent years. The details allowing implementation of this scheme have not been completed, but it is a driving philosophy behind the subscription model being developed.

During the initial start-up phase of the journal, author charges will be waived and some articles may be solicited by the editorial board to set the scope and character of the journal. In addition, while the concept of paid subscriptions will be in place at the start of the journal, subscribers will be able to redeem a freely available "coupon" for a year's subscription. While the coupons would initially cover the full subscription fee, they may provide only a reduction of the fee in subsequent years. This should allow the rapid development of a subscriber base with a gradual phase-in of subscription revenue. It clearly establishes the journal as *not* being free even though early subscribers will be able to receive it at no cost. An actual subscription fee will be set even for the first few years when coupons are in use, and this fee will be adjusted as the economics of the journal become clearer so that an appropriate and fair fee is in place as the coupons are phased out.

Aspects of the collaboration

A. Levels of activity in the collaboration

The five societies involved in this project vary greatly in their membership and available resources, and while each has something special to offer this project, they will not all contribute at the same level. Three of the societies are prepared to commit financial resources to the project and will be considered "co-publishers" of the journal: AMS, AGU, and AAG. The other two societies (ESA and TOS) are planning "in kind" support, which will include dissemination of information about the journal through their regular publications, help in identifying potential authors and reviewers in the fields covered by those societies, and a presence on governing boards for the journal.

The three societies serving as copublishers break into two additional categories. The AMS and AGU will be the lead societies in the publication providing support for the volunteer scientific editors who oversee the peer-review process and jointly carrying out all the production components necessary to take the accepted manuscript and carry it through to posting online. A AG will provide some of the financial support required by the volunteer scientific editors, as well as the sorts of in-kind support provided by the cooperating societies. There will be a fair amount of duplication of effort among the co-publishing societies, which could be viewed by some as an inefficient means of producing a journal. That duplication will, however, lead to the development in each of the societies of the capabilities to carry out similar electronic publishing initiatives on their own, an important byproduct of the collaboration.

B. *Intersociety committee structure*

There is a desire to have the journal operate in a manner similar to the journals produced by each society but it cannot be governed by the board of any one society, so an independent committee structure specifically for this journal is being established. This committee structure is intended to serve as the policy-setting governance for the journal and will include representation from all of the collaborating societies.

1. The Editorial Board will be made up of the volunteer scientific editors who oversee the peer-review process for the journal. It is anticipated that there will be four editors whose areas of expertise will allow broad representation of the disciplines making up the earth system sciences.

2. The Publications Policy Advisory Committee will be made up of approximately four individuals who are knowledgeable about publishing standards, policy, and practice. This committee will set the standards for the journal, refine the mission statement as needed, and establish the procedures governing the peer-review process. They will also monitor the scientific content of the journal to ensure its continued high quality.

3. The Technical Advisory Panel will be made up of about six volunteers from the collaborating societies plus a few staff members from the copublishing societies. This group will work out the technical details of the technical implementation of the journal including the production process and the specifications for the user interface and accounting procedures.

All these groups will work closely together, especially in the start-up phase of the project, to ensure that the policies, procedures, and standards implemented meet the needs of the scientific community being served and the need for the journal to be able to adapt to emerging and future technologies.

C. *Division of resources and revenues among the societies*

An important aspect of a collaboration of this sort is the fair and equitable division of resources and revenues among the partners. The copublishers have agreed to a fairly simple business arrangement based on the costs incurred by each. Each society will keep an accounting of direct expenditures made toward the journal project and will apply an indirect cost to all direct costs for which indirect charges are typically allowed (for consistency, each society will apply the AMS rate of 39% for the indirect costs). Those individual society expenditures will be used to calculate a percentage of the total for each society and the total revenue received from outside funding and journal revenue will be divided based on the expenditure percentages. Early in the project, even if outside funding is received at the levels desired, the journal will cost more than revenue intake, so revenue disbursement will only defray some of the costs. Later, as the journal becomes more nearly self-sufficient, this scheme should allow each society to recover the direct and indirect costs associated with the journal so that it does not require subsidization from other publications of the societies.

The collaborating societies view the costs incurred early in this project as an investment toward other electronic publishing initiatives. Changes in hardware and software and the development of new technical expertise among each society's publications staff that will be necessary to carry out this project will also be needed for other electronic publishing activities that each society carries on independently. This project allows a shared experience among the societies that should provide an opportunity for rapid development of high-level electronic publishing capabilities.

Conclusions

The project described in this paper seeks to create a new, peer-reviewed, high quality, scholarly electronic journal that takes advantage of the electronic medium to go beyond the limitations of the printed page for the presentation of scientific research results. It is important to note that despite the desire of the collaborating societies to use this project as a learning exercise, this journal is *not* considered an experiment. It is a full production journal of the collaborating societies that is intended to be an archive journal of important scientific results. It will test the market for an electronic journal of this type and will also test a specific cost-recovery model for electronic publication, but we will only be able to attract high-quality submissions if authors understand that the journal is intended to be a permanent, long-standing publication of the collaborating societies.

Publishing a journal in a collaborative effort is not as straightforward as publishing one as a single society. Coming to consensus on issues of policy and on business arrangements is difficult and can require several iterations of proposals before the societies' governing boards allow the project to move forward. The variety of experiences that can be brought to bear on the project from the various societies, however, makes up for any difficulties since this broad experience base leads to a more viable publication.

There has been talk of the rapid elimination of paper journals as soon as electronic journals of sufficient sophistication are available to replace them (see, for example, Quinn 1994). Some have also talked of a world in which the role of the scientific publisher is all but eliminated (see Harnad 1994). The project described here represents a group of scientific publishers working toward the development of precisely the type of high-quality, peer-reviewed journal that could conceivably replace a print publication in the same subject area. While we expect a transition from print to electronic publication over the coming years for many publications, the collaborating societies do not expect it to occur in our fields as quickly as some speculate it will in other fields, and we expect many of our publications continuing in print form for a substantial period. We are using this project to develop a model that will allow the transition form print to electronic to occur in an orderly fashion for the journals we publish and to develop an economic model that will allow our societies to continue serving as publisher while an ever-increasing portion of our publications move into the electronic medium. We believe quite strongly that the scientific community will require the services of a publisher to carry out the peer-review process and to add value both through consistent copy and technical editing and through the electronic composition process that allows the journal to live up to its potential.

References

Harnad, S., cited 1994: Full discussion archived in URL: ftp://ftp.princeton.edu/pub/harnad/Psycoloquy/Subversive.Proposal/

Okerson, A., ed., 1994: *Directory of Electronic Journals, Newsletters and Academic Discussion Lists*, 4th ed. Association of Research Libraries, Washington, DC, 575 pp.

Quinn, F., 1994: Consequences of Electronic Publication in Theoretical Physics. [Available from archive listed in Harnad 1994.]

Keith Seitter
Associate Executive Director
American Meteorological Society
seitter@aip.org

Naming the Namable: Names, Versions, and Document Identity in a Networked Environment

David M. Levy
Xerox Palo Alto Research Center

1. Introduction

A recent *Time* magazine reports that cyberspace is destabilizing the order of names. Under the heading "What's in a name?"[1] *Time* reports:

> The uncertainties of copyright law as it pertains to the Internet have created opportunities for sneaky entrepreneurs. Many companies, it seems, haven't laid claim in cyberspace to their most important assets: their names. Thus a few savvy Net surfers have adopted already famous trademarks for their own use. For instance, the address "mcdonalds.com" is owned by a writer from Long Island; "coke.com" is registered to a fellow in California.

As of press time, the article continues, the commercially significant names such as philipmorris.com, sunkist.com, and armani.com still hadn't been registered. Few of us are likely to be concerned over Philip Morris' loss, but we might do well to pay closer attention to naming practices in the digital domain if, as I will suggest, bigger issues are at stake than the rights to a group of hot commercial names.

In the preface to a book instructively titled The Order of Books[2], the historian Roger Chartier notes that an "immense effort motivated by anxiety" was undertaken "in Western Europe between the end of the Middle Ages and the eighteenth century [in the] attempt to master the enormously increased number of texts that first the manuscript book and then print put into circulation." Suggested in this work, and more forcefully argued elsewhere[3], is his belief that the order of books is being challenged by developments in digital technologies -- and that it will not hold. Are we then on the threshold of another immense effort?

Few of us need to be reminded that these are anxious times, least of all those of us in any way involved with libraries or publishing. Surely, the uncertainty of the times must have been one of the motives for the creation of the ARL/AAUP symposia, of which this is the fourth. And if Chartier is right, as I suspect he is, that we are in the early stages of determining how to organize and control new kinds of information artifacts, then we are engaged in a political enterprise of some considerable moment, with great consequences for all of us. For as the library theorist, Patrick Wilson[4], has put it: "Bibliographical control is a form of power, and if knowledge itself is a form of power . . . bibliographical control is in a certain sense power over power, power to obtain the knowledge recorded in written form."

2. An Unnatural Order

Chartier's reflections can be located in a growing body of literature, at the intersection of literary, legal and historical studies, which aims to uncover the political interventions, and the underlying principles and interests, which shaped the order of books. A recent work, *The Construction of Authorship* [5], contains a series of essays derived from a 1991 conference on "Intellectual Property and the Construction of Authorship." In the introduction, the editors observe that:

Taken as a whole these studies of writing practices from the Renaissance to the present suggest that the modern regime of authorship, far from being timeless and universal, is a relatively recent formation -- the result of a quite radical reconceptualization of the creative process that culminated less than 200 years ago in the heroic self-presentation of Romantic poets. As they saw it, genuine authorship is originary in the sense that it results not in a variation, an imitation, or an adaptation, and certainly not in a mere re-production . . . , but in an utterly new, unique -- in a word 'original' -- work which, accordingly, may be said to be the property of its creator and to merit the law's protection as such.

Another recent work tells a story of political intervention with suggestive parallels to the Internet. In Publishing and Cultural Politics in Revolutionary Paris, 1789-1910[6], Carla Hesse has reconstructed the history of publishing during the French Revolution. She describes how, under the banner of "freedom of the press," the new regime eliminated the previous system of royal patronage which had given a small group of Paris printers a monopoly on the book trade. The hope was that enlightened publications would flourish -- Rousseau on every street corner. Instead, Rousseau went out of print (because without protection, no one could make a profit publishing his works) and masses of anonymous pornographic and seditious literature poured off the presses. Within the first decade following the revolution, the government intervened, creating a new regulatory framework, the beginning of the modern French copyright system, which gave priority to books over more ephemeral materials, such as pamphlets, and made authors accountable for their works.

If, as these studies suggest, the order of books was created and modified through political intervention, it is also the case that it has been sustained through continual maintenance. The stability and invisibility of this order is an ongoing achievement;[7] that most of us can traffic in notions of text, work, edition, version, and author and never see the much messier reality, the much greater variability, that these abstractions hide, is a tribute to the ongoing work of the order-makers, among them the catalogers around the world who take "publications" and make them fit the descriptive categories the order has prescribed. Clearly, the current order is neither natural, necessary, nor inevitable, and its continued existence depends on its being maintained and reproduced.

3. Naming on the Net

Naming and categorizing are an essential part of this historically constituted, continually maintained order. And such activities -- both the work of developing an infrastructure of naming and of performing individual acts within that structure -- are acts of power and control, and squarely located in the political and social realm. Any attempts to modify this order are bound to have political (and, as the *Time* story suggests, economic) consequences.

It is not yet clear what revisions will be needed to accommodate digital documents, or how sweeping these changes will have to be. At the moment, there are a number of initiatives aimed at exploring the future of naming in light of ongoing developments in the digital domain -- some from within the library community, others from within the scholarly community, and still others initiated by the computer science community. One such effort is an outgrowth of the success of the World-Wide Web and browsing software such as Mosaic, which allows users to view and traverse an increasingly rich set of interlinked documents.

Currently, the principal naming mechanism on the Web is the URL, short for Uniform Resource Locator, which specifies, in a standardized notation, the "place" a document can be found. In Mosaic, one can type in a URL to view the document named by it (see figure 1); links from one document to another, indicated by underlining, also use URLs to indicate their destination.

Figure 1. Within Mosaic[8], a user types in a URL specifying the address of a document.

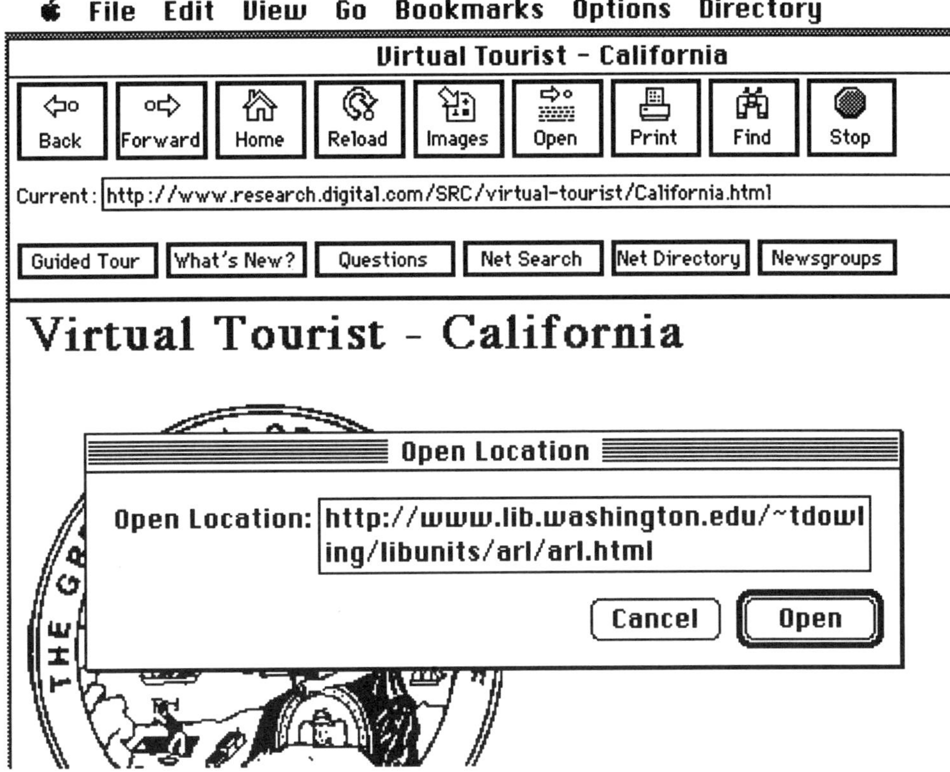

Figure 2. A note at the old location of the document indicates that it has moved.

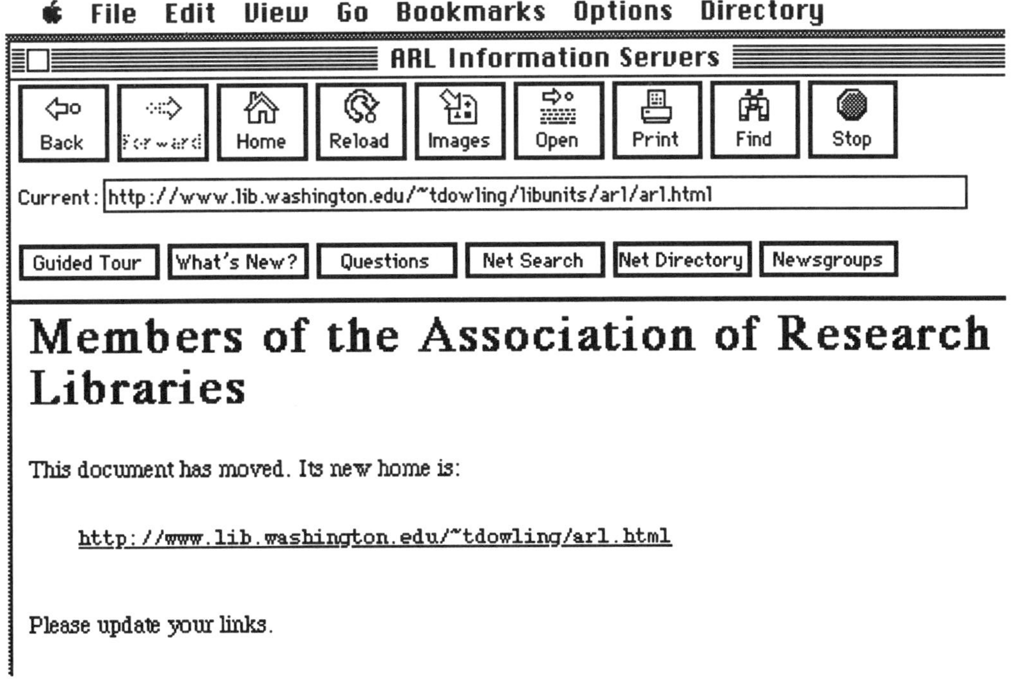

But what happens if the owner of a document moves it to a new location on the Web? The answer is that all URLs pointing to the old location are now invalid; there is no way to update them automatically. One solution now common is to signal a detour -- to place a note at the old location giving the new URL (see figure 2).

In response to this, as well as other perceived problems, the Working Group on Document Identifiers within the Internet Engineering Task Force (IETF) has been working to standardize two other types of identifiers: Uniform Resource Names (URNs) and Uniform Resource Characteristics (URCs)[9]. A URN is meant to provide a "location independent name" for a document on the Web; it is sometimes likened to ISBNs for books. URCs are viewed as analogous to catalog entries, and current thinking is that they would contain "meta-information" about documents, such as author and creation date, as well as URLs indicating where instances of the document can be found.

Two things are noteworthy about this effort. First, it is a conservative design -- literally, in the sense that it attempts to conserve and mirror aspects of the order of books, including unique identifiers for books, shelf locations, and catalog entries. Second, the designers have nothing to say about versions[10]. Or, to put this more precisely, they do have something to say about versions, namely that they have nothing to say about them (they've made no design decisions concerning them). Their design for URNs has two parts: a number uniquely identifying a "naming authority" (e.g. a publisher or library) and, relative to that naming authority, a number uniquely identifying the document. It is entirely up to a particular naming authority to decide what relationship one of its URNs bears to a particular document -- whether it names a particular version, the latest version, the work in general, a translation, or whatever.

To call this design conservative is not to criticize it. Considering how little is understood about digital documents, it makes a great deal of sense to mirror current structures and institutions. Moreover, it also makes sense to ignore versions and versioning, considering how little is understood about how to represent and deal with them. (Computer file systems are still quite poor at offering support for versions. Hypertext developers are at the early stages of theorizing about versioning. And in the library world, attempts to provide terminology and support for versions have thus far yielded little.)

4. The Variability of Digital Stuff

But it may turn out that issues underlying versions are actually so central to the digital order that they will, in the long run, contribute to the undoing of the order of books and naming schemes based on it. For versions are concerned with the management of variation and variability. Documents, of course, have always been subject to change[11], but it now seems likely that digital materials will manifest new forms of variability and some will undergo a faster rate of change.

One potential source of variability is the indeterminacy of the artifact. We know what the artifact is in the case of books: the physical volume. But when searching for the artifact amidst this digital material, this digital stuff, it's hard right now to find determinate things. For starters, digital documents are schizophrenic -- split between digital representations that reside on file servers and other storage media and the manifestations that appear on screens, paper, and in the airwaves[12]. Is it significant, or in what ways is it significant, that the digital representation is inherently invisible and can only be seen indirectly via the visible manifestations produced from it? Is it significant, or in what ways is it significant, that these visible manifestations may differ significantly in their information content from the digital source they purport to reveal? (That is, if the underlying representation is encoded with SGML, there may be substantial transformation of form and/or content in producing a perceptible image.) Under such circumstances, do we take the digital representation to be the artifact, or perhaps we take the digital representation plus its visible manifestations, or what?

The digital artifact is potentially indeterminate in another sense as well: it may not have clearly defined boundaries[13]. We see this now with documents on the Web. As I browse through material, traversing links, how do I know when I have crossed from one document to another? I may be able to determine that I have moved to a different server, or to material produced by a different author, but such information does not necessarily provide identity or boundary conditions. I can no longer use the boundedness of a physical artifact as a guide.

We are also likely to have a lot more documents than ever before, a lot more variants of previously existing material. Certainly, it is much easier to copy and modify digital documents, and to produce versions tailored to particular individuals or groups. Increasingly, we are able to assemble new documents from fragments (by which I mean, roughly, pieces that cannot stand on their own) either extracted from other documents or collected from databases of reusable components[14]. It seems likely that some notion of fragment will enter our shared ontology, thereby introducing stuff of much finer granularity. (Yes, we've always had finer grained elements in the book world, but never on such a scale as we may be about to see, and never so publicly available.)

New types of material in larger quantities may also come from self-publishing and the publication of special collections. Thus, publishing on the Web, freed from institutional gatekeeping, may give rise to new types (and possibly rapidly mutating types) of documents. And the trend toward making special collections available digitally, both by producing digital finding aids[15] and by digitizing the content of these collections, means that masses of private material -- rarely published and certainly not in such large numbers -- will become publicly available.

All this strongly suggests that we will have lots more stuff: more of it, more quickly changing. Of course, as noted earlier, the order of books had -- and still has -- much greater variability than most readers ever knew. But now, it seems, three things have changed. One, we have even greater variability and finer granularity than before. Two, we do not (yet) have categorizations of this new material -- partly because it's very much a moving target and partly because we haven't yet had enough experience with it -- which would help us neaten it up and simplify it. Three, we don't yet understand what kinds of surrogates (names, categories, descriptions, and so on) we will need for this new granularity, so for the time being we are reproducing the old order.

I see two possible futures. One is that we will find a way to sustain the old order, albeit somewhat amended. Through some combination of legislation and social practice, we will retain our ways of naming and categorizing, as well as a large number of the categories (editions, works, etc.). Indeed, if the IETF framework were to become a widely used standard, as the committee members hope, it might well be a factor in sustaining the old order. A second possibility is that we are headed for a much more radical transformation of the order, as Chartier believes. Increased variability and granularity, rather than hidden away, will be increasingly available, and we will have to confront a richer world of fragments and versions and to devise new schemes for naming and categorizing, and new kinds of surrogates.

But, it might be objected, in a much more fluid, variable cyberworld, a sea of information, we won't need names or other forms of surrogates. We will navigate this sea by following links, by searching and browsing, by sending forth "knowbots" to scout for us. In a world of links, why should we bother to name or categorize? The simple answer is: because we can't avoid it. The digital world is a highly mediated world; it verges on paradox, that the price we pay for immediacy of access is an intensely mediated infrastructure. By this I mean that we have achieved immediate access by creating digital representations that can be pulled from distant places and used to construct perceptible artifacts in the user's local environment. (Even in the new age, we still need to see what we read, which means it must be locally, immediately available.) To get these distant representations, we have to identify them, which we do with surrogates; there is no linking without naming and categorizing.

This being said, it may well be that the nature of our surrogates will change. If, as on the Web, documents can point "directly" to other documents, then we may no longer need to have a separate category of documents called bibliographies which act as surrogates for other documents. The primary surrogate might become the reference or link, which could be embedded in any document. But to say it one more time, this will not eliminate the need for mediation by surrogates; on the contrary, we are likely to see orders of magnitude more.

5. Naming the namable

There is a certain circularity in "naming the namable." It is obvious enough, a tautology, that we can only name that which is namable. But there is also a sense in which we create things in the world by naming them -- in which acts of naming create the things that are then by necessity namable.

Our dependence on naming in the digital world is clear. We cannot save material we haven't named. We cannot share it without divulging its name. And in more extreme cases -- such as the assembly of a new unity by issuing a query -- the act of naming will indeed bring into creation that which was so named. What this means is that frameworks we create for naming are hardly neutral schemes, for they will play a role in determining what exists, quite literally, and therefore how knowledge and understanding are to be represented and transmitted.

And thus we come back to questions of power and control. Naming is a necessary element in any system by which we gain and maintain, in Wilson's words, "power over power, power to obtain the knowledge recorded in written form." But how will we gain control over the new information artifacts? Who is "we"? What exactly will we have control over -- and toward what ends? It is my hope that the academic community will participate in answering these questions. Indeed, the academy seems uniquely qualified to bring a powerful combination of theory and practice to bear -- to help us understand and question the principles and world view on which the current order is based, and to participate in making the "technical" decisions that will no doubt play a role in determining the shape of a future order.

Acknowledgements

Thanks to Dan Brotsky, Larry Masinter, Ted Metcalfe, Fran Miksa, Susan Newman, Randy Trigg, and Brian Smith for their wise counsel during the preparation of this paper.

---

[1]"What's in a Name?" *Time*, October 17, 1994, p. 24.

[2]Chartier, R.,*The Order of Books*. Stanford, California: Stanford University Press, 1994.

[3]Chartier, R., *From Codex to Screen: Trajectories of the Written Word*, p. 2, 2, 160-171. Common Knowledge, 1993.

[4]Wilson, P., *Two Kinds of Power: An Essay on Bibliographical Control*. Berkeley: University of California Press, 1968.

[5]Woodmansee, M. and Jaszi, P. (eds.), *The Construction of Authorship: Textual*

Appropriation in Law and Literature. pp. 2-3. Durham: Duke University Press, 1994.

[6]Hesse, C., *Publishing and Cultural Politics in Revolutionary Paris, 1789-1910*. Berkeley: University of California Press, 1993.

[7]The idea that social order is an ongoing, and largely invisible achievement is developed in ethnomethodology. For a general introduction, see Heritage, J., *Garfinkel and Ethnomethodology*. Cambridge: Polity Press, 1984.

[8]The screen snapshot shows Mosaic Netscape 0.9, a public beta version produced by Mosaic Communications Corporation.

[9]The working group on document identifiers has produced working drafts on URLs, URNs, and URCs. These are available by anonymous FTP from the server ds.internic.net (East Coast) or ftp.isi.edu (West Coast) in the directory internet-drafts. The relevant drafts have the form draft-ietf-uri-....txt -- e.g. draft-ietf-uri-urn-req-01.txt.

[10]A cautionary note: As used here, and in the computer science community in general, the word "version" is used to mean "variant." It carries no assumptions about which properties of the document may vary -- form, content, or whatever.

[11]Levy, D. M., "Fixed or Fluid? Document Stability and New Media," in *European Conference on Hypertext Technology, 1994 Proceedings*. New York: Association for Computing Machinery, pp. 24-31.

[12]Levy, D. M., "What Do You See and What Do You Get? Document Identity and Electronic Media," in *Screening Words: User Interfaces for Text, Proceedings of the Eighth Annual Conference of the UV Centre for the New OED and Text Research*, pp. 109-117. Waterloo, Canada, 1992.

[13]Nunberg, G. 1993. "The Places of Books in the Age of Electronic Reproduction," *Representations* (1993) 42, pp. 13-37.

[14]Levy, D. M., "Document Reuse and Document Systems." *Electronic Publishing* (1993) 6, 4, pp. 339-348.

[15]Pitti, Daniel, "The Berkeley Finding Aid Project: Standards in Navigation." (This volume)

David Levy
Member, Research Staff
Xerox PARC
dlevy@parc.xerox.com

The Berkeley Finding Aid Project: Standards in Navigation

Daniel V. Pitti
University of California, Berkeley

Abstract

The archival community should develop and embrace an encoding standard for archive, museum, and library finding aids. Such a standard would ensure that Internet communication of finding aid data is effective, and that the data endures independently of the computer hardware and software used to create and use it. This is the underlying premise of the Berkeley Finding Aid Project. Some have attempted to encode finding aids in the MARC format, but with mixed results. Standard Generalized Markup Language (SGML) is recommended as a better vehicle, as it has the flexibility to handle the complex hierarchical structure of finding aids and to capture the individuality of unique collections. SGML can also facilitate access to digital surrogates of items in our collections. The availability on the Internet of fully functional collection information and item surrogates promises to dramatically alter access and preservation.

Introduction and Project Overview

The advent and rapid growth of the Internet is transforming scholarly communication worldwide. To take full advantage of the opportunities this development offers, the archive, museum, and library communities will need to develop and embrace standards to ensure that the communication is both useful and enduring. An encoding standard for finding aids is one such standard.

Finding aids are documents used to describe, control, and provide access to collections of related materials in library, archives, and museums. The materials in these collections are the natural by-products of the activities of individuals, families, and organizations. Many different kinds of materials are represented in these collections: manuscripts, correspondence, legal records and papers, photographs, tape recordings, video recordings, and more.

The Berkeley Finding Aid Project is a collaborative effort to test the feasibility and desirability of developing an encoding standard for archive, museum, and library finding aids. The Project is funded in part by a grant from the United States Department of Education Title IIA program. The Project began in October 1993, and will be completed in September 1995. The Project involves two interrelated activities. The first of these was creating a prototype encoding standard for finding aids. This prototype standard is in the form of a Standard Generalized Markup Language (ISO 8879) Document Type Definition (SGML DTD). Researchers at the University of California, Berkeley have developed the encoding standard in collaboration with leading experts in collection processing, collection cataloging, text encoding, system design, network communication, authority control, text retrieval, text navigation, and computer imaging. Project participants have analyzed the structure and function of representative finding aids. The basic elements occurring in finding aids have been isolated and their logical interrelationships defined. The DTD has been developed based on the results of this analysis.

Building a prototype database of finding aids is the second objective of the Project. Available hardware and software have been evaluated. We have selected ArborText's *AdeptEditor* as the SGML-based authoring and editing software, and Electronic Book Technologies' *DynaText* for providing networked access to the database.

Encoding the finding aids and building the database is providing the encoding scheme developers with computer application experience with which to refine and inform the DTD development process. The network accessible database will provide, in a later phase of the Project, a means for public and staff end users to evaluate the utility and desirability of encoded finding aids. The public and staff end users then will be able to provide new ideas and suggestions to the encoding standard developers.

The success of any standard depends upon broad participation in its development and, after it is developed, widespread recognition of its utility. Standards are the products of communities, not individuals working in splendid isolation. As the Project has unfolded, we have kept the community aware of its progress, and, in the near future, will solicit critical evaluations.

Before proceeding with a detailed description of the Berkeley Finding Aid Project, I would like to comment briefly on the archival community's interest in standards.

Finding Aid Standards and the Archive and Museum Communities.

For a variety of reasons the archive and museum communities have not been motivated to develop standards to govern the intellectual content and structure of finding aids. The economic benefits of sharing cataloging that motivated the catalogers of published materials are not available to the archive and museum community because items in their collections are mostly unique. Another possible motive for normalizing finding aid content and structure would be to make them more familiar and thus more immediately intelligible to the uninitiated. Charles Jewett, one of the earliest advocates of standardizing descriptive cataloging, addressed this issue of intelligibility in his Smithsonian Report of 1853. He said of cataloging rules:

> Now, even if the one [system] adopted were that of the worst of our catalogues, if it were strictly followed in all alike, their uniformity would render catalogues, thus made, far more useful than the present chaos of irregularities.[1]

Increasing mutual intelligibility, though, has not in itself been a sufficient impetus to overcome the countervailing tendency to fashion the content, structure, and aesthetics to fit the local institution and users, and the characteristics of the collection being described.

With the emergence of the Internet, we must confront the need for greater intelligibility of information that can be readily shared and interpreted by the world intellectual community. In this context, the importance of mutually comprehensible finding aids and the benefits to be derived from them take on new urgency. The Internet has the potential to provide immediate access to information about our collections and even to computer surrogates of items in those collections. And this access can be available anywhere at anytime. For those institutions choosing to take advantage of the power of the Internet, users will no longer be exclusively the familiar faces of the dedicated researchers. In order to provide the access described, the archive and museum communities must develop and/or embrace an array of standards. The means are there to communicate with one another, but to make this communication mutually understandable, we will need to work together.

In order for archivists and curators to communicate with users and one another in the network environment, our computers must be able to communicate with one another. We need to be able to move information freely from computer to computer over the network. An encoding standard will enable institutions to create finding aids that are independent of proprietary hardware and software. This will allow the data to be freely interchanged across platforms and applications, and still be instantly usable without time-consuming modification or adjustment. Such interoperability will support contemporaneous interchange of collection data, and it will ensure that our investment in the data will survive over time.

Finding aids created using proprietary word processing software such as WordPerfect and Microsoft Word, or database software such as dBase will remain usable only if they are reformatted each time the authoring software is updated. Of course, for this to work properly, software manufacturers must provide translation programs that provide 100% fidelity in the data migration process. This is not always the case, and so information can be lost or garbled. As finding aid collections grow, such reformatting through successive software versions will become more burdensome. Even if the institution can survive the ordeal of eternally updating software, another concern has to be the durability of the software firm itself, and the durability of its interest in the software. If the firm goes out of business, or if it no longer finds the product profitable, an archive can find itself with a database of finding aids stranded in time. If finding aids are encoded using a standard, then their survival is not contingent on a particular hardware and/or software configuration. An encoding standard would guarantee that the machine-readable finding aids created today would be usable tomorrow!

This and other benefits would result from making finding aids interchangeable through a standard encoding scheme. It would be feasible for users and institutions to have fully functional access to finding aids in real-time over the network. Remote access to finding aids would enable researchers to make direct use of collection information without the expensive mediation of reference staff, and mutual access to current collection information would have a major, positive impact on the management of archive and manuscript repositories. Direct access would give researchers more autonomy and control over their research, and it would facilitate inter-institutional cooperation in collection development and preservation where knowledge of the holdings of other institutions can help curators make difficult decisions about how to spend scarce dollars developing and preserving their own collections. The list of institutional benefits derived from the use of a standard, in fact, exceeds the simple but profound benefits that individual scholars would enjoy. It would also allow inter-institutional cooperation in the description of and access to dispersed collections and to independent but related collections. Perhaps even more important in the short-term, a standard would make it feasible for collection holding institutions, library oriented vendors, and supporting federal and state agencies to develop the human and material resources needed to convert existing paper finding aids into machine-readable form. Without a standard for finding aids, it is difficult to convince agencies to fund conversion because there is no benchmark by which they can evaluate how the money is spent.

MARC versus SGML

In order for an encoding standard to provide the infrastructure to support a full array of access, control, navigation, and print functions and uses, it must be well designed and constructed. It is the quality of the standard as an information infrastructure that will enable maximum exploitation of the encoded information.

In the early stage of developing this project, we considered using the MARC format as the basis for the standard. We did this because MARC was familiar, and because we had heard that many institutions were attempting to use it for encoding finding aids. We quickly decided that it was not the best available scheme. We had three principal reasons for making this decision.

First, we found MARC inadequate because records are limited to a maximum length of 100,000 characters. This represents approximately 30 8-1/2 X 11 pages of 10 pitch unformatted text stored in ASCII. Since many finding aids are longer than this, the size restriction is a prohibitive obstacle.

The second difficulty with MARC is its limited accommodation of hierarchically structured information. Since finding aids are hierarchically structured documents, the flat structure of MARC makes it unsatisfactory. As archivists are painfully aware, MARC was primarily designed to capture description and access information applying to a discrete bibliographic item. Describing and providing access to complex collections through descending levels of analysis quickly overburdens the MARC structure. At most, a second level of analysis can be accommodated, but the kind of information so supplied is limited. One possible way around this problem is to employ multiple, hierarchically interrelated and interlinked records at varying levels of analysis: collection-level, subunit, and item. The use of multiple records, though, introduces extremely difficult inter- and intra-system control problems that have never been adequately addressed in the format or by MARC based software developers. Even if the control issues were adequately addressed in the format, the control required to make multiple record expression of hierarchy succeed would entail prohibitive human maintenance.

The third reason for not using MARC for finding aids involves the marketplace. It is a gross understatement to say that libraries, archives, and museums are generally not resource-rich institutions. To put it into perspective, the price of one B-2 bomber would fund the Library of Congress for over three years. Lacking large amounts of capital, the MARC user community has been incapable of driving state-of-the-art hardware and software development.

Standard Generalized Markup Language or SGML is a promising framework or model for developing an encoding scheme for finding aids for a number of reasons. First, it has none of the problems associated with MARC mentioned above. SGML will accommodate hierarchically interrelated information at as many levels as needed. Furthermore, there are no inherent size restrictions on SGML based documents. SGML is an international standard embraced by an ever growing list of government, educational, research, and industrial institutions. Through the Computer-aided Acquisitions and Logistics Support or CALS initiative, the US Department of Defense has mandated that all contractors doing business with DOD must use four specific standards in communications. One of the four is SGML. Because the DOD budget is immense even if shrinking, this mandate has motivated intensive development of SGML oriented software. Besides not sharing the weaknesses of MARC, SGML has a host of other features recommending it to us.

SGML is not itself a text encoding standard, but a standard for uniformly developing standards for definable kinds or classes of documents. In SGML, a standard for a particular kind or class of document is called a Document Type Definition or DTD. Each community that uses and shares a particular type of document must assume responsibility for developing an encoding scheme specific to the type.

SGML is concerned with designating the logical elements that serve as the building blocks of documents and the interrelationships of these elements. The prototype SGML Document Type Definition for finding aids developed at Berkeley specifies what logical elements can be present, and, with varying degrees of specificity, how the elements interrelate. In this regard, it is similar to MARC and dissimilar to word processing applications. MARC captures description and access information. It does not specify how to index, display, or print the information. Markup that provides output specifications such as print or display formatting is called procedural markup. It is dedicated to a single end-use or application. Markup designating the elements constituting a kind of document is called descriptive markup. Both SGML and MARC are descriptive markup languages. Text encoded using descriptive markup is frequently called "structured text," while ASCII text is called "plain text."

Descriptive markup based on SGML enables maximum flexibility in the use of the text. Indexing, and display and print formatting can all be precisely controlled by the user of the text. SGML structured text facilitates sophisticated database and document indexing and searching such as document and document component specific keyword Boolean, word adjacency, word proximity, relevance ranking, and relevance feedback. Such "smart" indexing eases much of the inherent tension between recall and relevance that plague most large database searching systems. SGML structured text also supports advanced online text navigation. It is possible to juxtapose a dynamically generated table of contents and accompanying text to provide context to enhance reading comprehension and provide random, informed access to text. Structured SGML based text facilitates complete flexibility in automated production of printed finding aids and related print products essential to processing, control, curatorial functions, and donor relationships. The flexibility of SGML based structured text renders it unquestionably superior to hierarchically flat MARC structured text, plain text, and procedurally marked text.

The Information Future and Archives

While the Project is presently concerned only with finding aid text, it is looking to an imminent information future in which collection-level records lead to finding aids and finding aids lead to computer surrogates of primary source materials that exist in a variety of native formats: pictorial materials, graphics, three-dimensional objects, manuscripts, typescripts, printed text, sound recordings, motion pictures, and so on. The intersections between these various forms of information will be traversed by the click of a mouse or by entering a simple command. Information interlinked in this manner is called hypermedia.

It is critical, I believe, that we move toward providing network access to computer surrogates of items in our collections as we make information about our collection more accessible through network access to finding aids. Some believe that making MARC AMC records available increases requests for use of collections. Increasing the availability of the more detailed information in finding aids will perhaps have the same effect. Such increased demand and use will justifiably raise curatorial concerns. But by making surrogates of the most used portions of our collections available, we can simultaneously increase access and limit physical access to endangered collections. Access and preservation need not be in conflict.

The Berkeley Finding Aid Project envisions an information future in which serious scholars and the casually curious alike can easily find the cultural treasures they seek. In this future, information seekers follow clearly marked paths through catalogs to finding aids and from finding aids to a wealth of information in a multitude of computer and traditional formats ... and back. Developing a standard encoding scheme for finding aids is essential to the realization of this future.

By making primary source materials accessible anywhere, anytime, the Internet will challenge basic assumptions about the nature of archives, libraries, and museums. The Internet makes it possible to transcend the physical limits of our information environment. I would like to conclude by dwelling, for a brief moment, on the notions of physical "absence" and "presence."

In an information world dominated by physical media, the absence of the items has dictated that we create synoptic surrogates to represent them. These include both catalog records and finding aids. While each provides access mechanisms, it is the descriptive component that represents the absent item. Using the description, we are, in principle, able to identify the remote object, and decide whether it is what we want. The Internet, by rendering the absent present, will no doubt significantly alter the descriptive role of catalog records and finding aids.

Archives, museums, and libraries are situated in specific geographic locations, and generally serve the needs of the surrounding community. They are very present for the community in which they reside. The Bancroft Library at the University of California, for example, is located on the campus of the University, in the city of Berkeley, in the state of California in the Far West of the United States. The Bancroft Library, its collections, its staff, its mission, all reflect this presence in the community. But if the most sought after collections of The Bancroft Library are available on the Internet, anytime and anywhere, it becomes in a certain sense universally present, present in the World Community.

Universality requires effective communication and effective communication requires standards. Standardization necessarily creates tension with the particularity of individual collections and repositories. Developing a standard that enables effective communication and that also allows curators and collection managers to adequately represent the individuality of the collection and institution is the challenge before us.

For scholars, making the absent present over the Internet offers new possibilities of scholarly communication. Scholars inclined to make their interpretations of source materials available in a standards-based, machine-readable form on the Internet will be able to make both the source materials and their interpretations of it simultaneously available to their peers and students. And it will not matter where they or the materials physically reside. Furthermore, it will be feasible to link the finding aids that lead to the source materials directly to interpretations of them.

Over time, arrays of competing interpretations will accumulate around source materials, and provide alternative forms of access to and views of them. The prospect of bringing research materials to the scholar over the Internet in lieu of the scholar having to travel to them reveals yet another possibility. Agencies that fund research involving primary source materials should finance digitizing rather than traveling. A collection, once digitized, would be available to all scholars for all time.

About the author

Daniel V. Pitti is Librarian for Advanced Technologies Projects in The Library at the University of California, Berkeley. This paper was written at the beginning of a Department of Education Title IIA funded project in September 1993, and presented at the Meeting of the Society of American Archivists in New Orleans. It was revised a year later and presented at the Scholarly Publishing on the Electronic Networks symposium sponsored by the Association of Research Libraries and the Association of American University Presses in Washington, D.C. The author is grateful for the assistance of Tim Hoyer and Jack von Euw of The Bancroft Library, Berkeley, California, and Jackie Dooley of The Getty Center for the History of Art and the Humanities, Santa Monica, California.

dpitti@library.berkeley.edu

---

[1]Charles C. Jewett, *Smithsonian Report on the Construction of Catalogues of Libraries and Their Publication by Means of Separate, Stereotyped Titles.* Washington, D.C.: Smithsonian Institution, 1853, p. 9.

Research into the Reward System of Scholarship; Where Does Scholarly Electronic Publishing Get You?

H. Julene Butler
Brigham Young University

The research project described in this paper attempts to answer the broad question: Is the electronic journal a viable channel for formal scholarly communication? Two fundamental assumptions drive the research: (1) the electronic journal will serve as a viable channel for formal scholarly communication only as scholars are willing to publish in electronic channels; and, (2) scholars will demonstrate such willingness and submit manuscripts for electronic publication only when appropriate recognition and rewards are granted to those who publish in electronic journals.

These assumptions point toward the more precise focus of the research and suggest the specific question which the project addresses, namely: Does publication in electronic journals bring the author the expected rewards of research publication, including the desired recognition that comes through exposure to ideas within the research community?

Definition of Electronic Journal

Since the term "electronic journal" can be used to describe several different entities, it is important to clarify the definition of the electronic journal used in this study. Three elements are essential to this definition:

1. The electronic journal must publish original, scholarly research-based writings. It may also publish reviews, opinion columns, position announcements, and newsletter-type information, but is included in the study only if it publishes original research.

2. Submissions to the electronic journal must be reviewed by at least two readers in addition to the editor. This excludes most electronic lists, bulletin boards, and newletters.

3. The electronic journal must utilize electronic networks as the primary distribution channel. Publications which allow for supplementary distribution through paper, microfiche, or floppy disc are included in the definition. However, journals routinely distributed in both paper and electronic format are excluded.

Additionally, the scope of this research project limits the selection of electronic journals to publications from science and social science disciplines. The rationale for excluding journals from arts and humanities disciplines centers on the fact that within these disciplines the book is considered the primary channel for documenting scholarly contributions to knowledge and the journal takes a secondary role.

Figure 1 lists the journals included in the study. The list represents all electronic journals matching the above criteria which were known to be in active publication mode as of December 1993. One final factor for inclusion was willingness on the part of the journal editor to engage in dialogue regarding journal policies and practices.

The Sociology of Science

Sociologists of science, who address the manner in which new scientific knowledge is produced, are divided into two major schools of thought. The more traditional school, based largely on the ideas of Robert Merton, derived from the positivist philosophy of science. (Merton, 1973; Popper, 1959) Constructivists, the second school, emerged from the philosophy that

FIGURE 1: Electronic Journals Included in Study

Journal Title	Start Date
Education Policy Analysis Archives	1993
Electronic Journal of Communication	1990
Electronic Journal of Virtual Culture	1993
Flora Online	1987
Interpersonal Computing and Technology	1993
Journal of the International Academy of Hospitality Research	1990
MC Journal	1993
Online Journal of Current Clinical Trials	1992
Psycoloquy	1990
Public Access Computer Systems Review	1990

knowledge is socially constructed. (Knorr-Cetina, 1981) These groups differ dramatically in their conceptual foundations regarding knowledge generation and norms governing the institution of science. However, both agree that the ultimate end of doing science is the production of original knowledge and concur that such knowledge must be distributed to the scholarly community through formal publication channels.

Both sociological camps also agree that in return for contributions to the store of knowledge, scholars expect compensatory rewards, primarily in the form of peer recognition. Recognition comes to scholars in a variety of forms, categorized by Hagstrom (1965) as elementary and institutional recognition. Elementary recognition, largely unmeasurable, comes through informal exchanges at meetings, correspondence, or exchange of preprints. Formal institutional recognition involves more measurable activities, such as citation, published acknowledgement, invited lectureships, and bestowal of honorary awards. Formal recognition is also demonstrated through allocation of research funding, assignments to editorial positions, political appointments, consulting opportunities, and granting of tenure or promotion in the academic environment.

Criteria for Acceptable Scholarly Communication Channels

Scholarly contributions must be published in acceptable communication channels in order to qualify the author for receipt of recognition. The criteria of acceptability for these communication channels, which have evolved within the context of print journals over centuries of time, are inferred in the writings of the sociology of science. (Brown, 1977; Gaston, 1978; Merton, 1973; Zuckerman, 1977) It is assumed that recognition and receipt of formal scholarly rewards will be granted to those who publish in electronic channels only when the electronic journal meets the same criteria of acceptability traditionally required of formal scholarly print journals.

The criteria for acceptable scholarly communication channels include the following points.

1. An acceptable scholarly communication channel must convey knowledge certified through the peer review process.

2. Contents of an acceptable scholarly communication channel must be intellectually accessible to members of the scholarly community. Intellectual access to journal contents is typically provided through indexing and abstracting services, citations in other publications, browsing of tables of contents, and referrals from colleagues.

3. An acceptable scholarly communication channel must be retrievable by members of the scholarly community. Traditionally, retrievability has been assured through access to archival copies of journals housed in personal collections or libraries.

4. An acceptable scholarly communication channel must be known and respected by members of the scholarly community. The most highly respected journals are those which impose the most stringent review policies, those whose editorial board members have strong scholastic reputations, those with sponsorship by a well- respected institution, and those which receive positive post-publication reviews.

5. An acceptable scholarly communication channel must establish priority claims to new knowledge. The assumption is that research will be published in a timely manner sufficient to establish the author as the originator of new ideas.

6. An acceptable scholarly communication channel must contribute to further scholarly dialogue. The assumption is that communication of research, through formal publication as well as through less formal channels, will open further dialogue among members of the scholarly community and thereby enhance the process of knowledge production.

7. Finally, an acceptable scholarly communication channel must serve as the exclusive channel for initial dissemination of knowledge. It publishes only that research which has not been previously documented in other channels.

This study assumes that these criteria and the reward structures which sociology has observed in traditional knowledge production processes must be operational in any new scholarly communication channel if that channel is to be adopted by members of the scholarly community. The research project will attempt to determine whether individuals within the scholarly communities to which the electronic journals are addressed perceive these criteria and reward structures as operational within the context of formal electronic communication channels.

Research Methodology

In order to answer the research questions, data will be collected regarding the three domains outlined in Figure 2. First, data regarding the ten electronic journals selected for the study will be collected through interviews with editors and through examination of editorial discussion archives. Information regarding article submission patterns, review processes, indexing, readership, and archival practices will be of particular interest.

Secondly, data will be collected regarding the scholarly communities to whom the electronic journals are addressed. Contributors to the journals (including authors and members of editorial boards) will be queried regarding their personal and professional characteristics, their publication patterns, their satisfaction with the electronic channel, feedback, recognition and rewards they have received or failed to receive as a result of their involvement with the electronic journal. Users will be queried regarding their awareness of and attitude toward the electronic journal and their ability to retrieve material electronically.

Finally, data regarding citations to the contents of the journals will be collected. Standard indexing tools, citation indexes and subject bibliographies will be examined

FIGURE 2: Research Methodology

DATA REGARDING:	DATA SOURCES:	DATA COLLECTION TECHNIQUES:
Electronic Journals	Editors	Interviews Examine Editorial Discussion Archives
	E-Journals	Examine Journal Archives Examine Journal Policy Statements
Scholarly Communities	Contributors (Authors & Editorial Boards)	Survey
	Users (Actual & Potential)	Survey
Citations to E-Journals	Standard Indexes Citation Indexes Subject Bibliographies	Citation Analysis

to determine where and by whom articles in electronic journals are being cited. It is recognized that this data may be very sparse given the relative youth of the electronic journals being studied.

Contributors' Survey Results

The balance of this paper reports findings from the survey distributed to contributors to the ten electronic journals in the study. In the spring of 1994 the survey was distributed to 511 authors and members of editorial boards of these journals. 70% of the individuals received the survey electronically. The remaining 30% were contacted through surface mail. Thirty surveys were undeliverable, resulting in a total of 481 individuals who received the survey.

Response was gratifying, both in terms of speed of response and response rate. On day 1 (while surveys were still being distributed electronically) eight responses were received. By the end of day 2, response rate had reached 6%. Ultimately 199 responses were received, for an overall response rate of 41%.

Characteristics of Contributors

The vast majority of respondents (93%) were affiliated with an academic institution in some capacity. The types of institutions represented included universities, colleges, medical schools and secondary schools. Of those affiliated with an academic institution, most were involved in teaching and/or research. (See Figure 3) Also represented were librarians, administrators and students. Since the journals represented in the study were all peer-reviewed research-based publications, it was not surprising that the largest group of contributors were individuals involved in teaching and research.

The educational level of contributors was high, with nearly 80% of respondents holding degrees beyond the masters degree. (See Figure 4) Characteristics of electronic journal contributors have not been compared to characteristics of contributors to comparable print journals, though it would be of interest to make such comparisons at some point in the future. Of particular interest in the study were questions related to the tenure status and academic rank of contributors..

FIGURE 3: Academic Involvement of Contributors

Academic Involvement	Percent
Teaching & Research	59.02%
Teaching Only	5.46%
Research Only	7.65%
Librarian	12.57%
Administrator	2.73%
Student	8.20%
Other (primarily retirees)	4.37%
TOTAL	100.00%

FIGURE 4: Educational Level of Contributors

Educational Level	Percent
Post-Doctorate	18.27%
Doctorate	53.30%
"ABD" ("All But Dissertation")	8.12%
Masters	15.23%
Other	5.08%
TOTAL	100.00%

Note that slightly over half of the respondents (54%) were either already tenured or on a career track where tenure was not applicable. [54% represents a combination of the categories of tenured (26%) and not applicable (28%).] Similarly, a majority of respondents (59%) were in circumstances where movement upward in rank was not a matter of concern. [59% represents a combination of the categories of full professor (29%), other (6%), and not applicable (24%).]

One could surmise that for individuals who are not concerned with receipt of tenure or movement up in rank, electronic publication represents little or no risk to their career advancement. Since they have already achieved the highest levels of formal recognition within the academic system they place less on the line when they choose to publish in electronic journals than do their colleagues who must still move through the ranks and receive tenure. This detail may support the supposition that those concerned with the attitudes of tenure and promotion committees are less likely to utilize electronic channels. It could also represent a commentary on the fact that electronic journal editors are intentionally soliciting submissions from high profile authors in an effort to legitimize the journals in their infancy. Several editors acknowledged in interviews that they had intentionally adopted the strategy of seeking contributions from individuals already well-established in the field. (See Figures 5 & 6)

FIGURE 5: Tenure Status of Contributors

Tenure Status	Percent
Not Tenured	46.43%
Tenured	26.02%
Not Applicable	27.55%
TOTAL	100.00%

FIGURE 6: Academic Rank of Contributors

Academic Rank	Percent
Instructor	1.52%
Assistant Professor	22.34%
Associate Professor	17.77%
Professor	28.93%
Other	5.58%
Not Applicable	23.86%
TOTAL	100.00%

Perceived Benefits and Disadvantages of Electronic Journals

When contributors were asked to select the disadvantages of publication in electronic journals of greatest consequence to them, the results represented in Figure 7 emerged. Note that the two most frequently selected choices relate to the sociological questions central to this research project. 63% of all respondents were concerned with the fact that many of their colleagues perceive electronic publication as not "real." 54% were concerned that electronic journals were not as prestigious as other journals. Other disadvantages emerged dramatically lower on the scale than these two concerns, suggesting that technological and legal concerns are perceived as of less consequence than the sociological concerns central to the system of receipt of recognition and rewards. When asked to select benefits of publication in electronic journals of greatest importance, by far the strongest factor was the speed with which articles are accepted and published. Other benefits are detailed in Figure 8.

Receipt of Informal Recognition and Rewards

As mentioned earlier, the informal recognition which scholars hope to receive as a result of scholarly publication comes in the form of an extension of the scholarly communication process through informal channels. Receipt of feedback, establishment of contacts with people engaged in related research and of opportunities for ongoing exchange of ideas related to one's research represent examples of the informal recognition one hopes to receive as a result of publication. Contributors were asked whether they were receiving such informal recognition. Contributors were also asked to compare the feedback received for their electronic

FIGURE 7: Perceived Disadvantages of Electronic Publication

Disadvantage	* Percent
Perceived as Not "Real" Publication	63.24%
Less Prestigious	53.68%
Inadequate Graphics	38.24%
Inadequate Indexing	38.24%
Archival Instability	34.56%
Limited Audience	25.00%
Potential for Text Alteration	8.09%
Copyright Concerns	7.35%

** Represents % of all respondents selecting this option*

FIGURE 8: Perceived Benefits of Electronic Publication

Benefit	* Percent
Speed of Publication	71.32%
Reach Best Audience	55.15%
Enhance Scholarly Dialogue	47.79%
Low Cost to Readers	35.29%
Remote Geographic Access	33.09%
Publish Materials Unique to Electronic Formats	17.65%
Indexed Adequately	11.76%
Prestigious	5.15%
Hypertextual Linkages	3.68%

** Represents % of all respondents selecting this option*

publication with feedback they typically receive for print publication. Four categories of comparison were considered: amount, substance, channel and speed of feedback. These categories are represented in Figures 9 through 12.

One-third of respondents said they received more feedback for their electronic publication than they typically receive for print publications. But a slightly larger group (39%) said they received less feedback. (See Figure 9)

How substantive was that feedback? About half received substantive critique, the other half received mere congratulatory contact. For 37% this represented more substantive feedback than that which they typically receive for print publication and only 14% said it was less substantive. (See Figure 10)

Not surprisingly, electronic mail messages and listserv commentary served as the channel for the majority (55%) of the feedback. (See Figure 11) Notice that publication represented the feedback channel 6% of the time. Recall that the overall research design calls for citation analysis of references to contents of the electronic journals in the study. This dimension of the research has not yet been conducted, but will serve to amplify findings from the contributors' survey.

In terms of how rapidly feedback was received, 84% of respondents indicated they received feedback more quickly for their

FIGURE 9: Amount of Feedback

Amount (Compared to Print)	Percent
More	33.61%
Same	27.87%
Less	38.52%
TOTAL	100.00%

FIGURE 10: Substance of Feedback

How Substantive (Compared to Print)	Percent
More	37.18%
Same	48.72%
Less	14.10%
TOTAL	100.00%

FIGURE 11: Channel of Feedback

Channel	Percent
E-Mail/Listserv	54.55%
Face-to-Face	17.53%
Telephone	10.39%
Surface Mail	7.79%
Publication	5.84%
Other Channels	3.90%
TOTAL	100.00%

FIGURE 12: Speed of Feedback

How Quickly Received (Compared to Print)	Percent
Faster	83.55%
Same	13.92%
Slower	2.53%
TOTAL	100.00%

electronic publication than for print publication. (See Figure 12) This is not surprising given the fact that electronic channels represented the most frequently used channel for feedback.

Respondents were asked whether they had established new professional contacts as a result of their electronic publication. 36% indicated they had. When asked to explain the nature of those new contacts, most simply stated that their "network had expanded" or that they had engaged in further e-mail dialogue with people who shared research interests. In seven instances, however, the contact had led to publication opportunities and in six cases invitations to speak or to consult resulted from the publication. It appears then that electronic publication is serving to expand the informal contacts of some contributors.

Receipt of Formal Rewards and Recognition

Unfortunately, it has proven to be more difficult to determine whether contributors are receiving the more formal rewards and recognition one expects as a result of scholarly involvement. Rewards such as rank advancement, tenure, receipt of grants, fellowships, and other awards, honors and prizes are typically the result of the cumulative effect of scholarly achievements over time. It appears that it is too soon to determine whether electronic publication has played a role in the receipt of formal rewards. Some respondents refused to answer the section of the survey dealing with this category. Others commented that the receipt of a particular reward had little or nothing to do with their electronic publication. Either the electronic publication had been too minor to have an impact on decisions related to receipt of rewards or the publication had been too recent for any effect to have been noticed. There were, however, a few indicators and perceptions related to formal rewards that are worthy of mention.

Closely related to the question of receipt of formal rewards is the question of how those who control the receipt of those rewards view the phenomenon of electronic publication. Contributors were asked whether they believed their contribution to an electronic journal was viewed by those who evaluate their career performance as more or less important than their contributions to print publications. (See Figure 13) 43% believed that electronic publication was seen as less important than print publication. 21% believed it was seen as equal to print and only one individual (0.51%) believed it was seen as more important than print publication. The remainder did not know.

FIGURE 13: How Electronic Publication Is Seen By Evaluators

How Perceived (Compared to Print Publication)	Percent
More Important than Print	0.51%
Equal to Print	20.92%
Less Important than Print	43.37%
Don't Know	35.20%
TOTAL	100.00%

When asked what evidence they used to support this response, some interesting patterns emerged. Of those who believed their evaluators saw electronic publication as less important than print, over half based their response on anecdotal evidence only. In other words, it was simply a perception, no specific event or communication could be cited as firm evidence that electronic publication was less important. Only 17 contributors (9% of all respondents) based their response on the results of a formal evaluation or on actual feedback from members of a formal review board. The remainder of the responses were based on informal communication either with their administrative superiors or with colleagues.

Of those who believed their evaluators saw electronic publication as equal to print, about one-third of all respondents referred to formal evaluation feedback or to the fact that the electronic publication had been treated no differently than print publications. Another third based their views on informal communication with colleagues or administrators. The final third had anecdotal evidence only to support their response.

These findings suggest that in the formal evaluation and review process, electronic publication has been treated on an equal plane with print publication and that in only a few instances has there actually been negative response to electronic contributions. The findings also serve as further commentary on the perceptions (either existing or assumed) which people hold of electronic publication. It is interesting to contrast these perceptions (and the fears that surfaced in the question regarding disadvantages of electronic publication) with findings that relate to contributors' actual experience in relation to the status of electronic journals.

When contributors were asked: "Was your contribution to an electronic journal ever questioned as a viable scholarly activity by an advancement committee, promotion committee, or review board?" only 14% responded yes. (22% did not know.) A strong majority (64%) had never been questioned about the viability of the electronic channel for scholarly communication purposes.

When asked: "Have you ever supplied information to an advancement committee, promotion committee, or review board to help them better understand the nature of your contribution to an electronic journal?" only twenty-seven individuals (14%) answered yes. Of these, only nine supplied the information at the request of the committee. The other eighteen voluntarily included policy statements, author guidelines or statements from the editor in the packet provided to the committee.

Finally, when contributors were asked: "Since the time of your contribution to an electronic journal, have you failed to receive any rewards or recognition you felt you should have received?". Only twenty-four people (13% of respondents) answered yes. And of these, only four felt their electronic publication had been a factor in the failure to receive deserved recognition.

Summary

It seems safe to say that at this point in time very little negative response has been observed in the formal evaluation processes associated with academic life. One can conclude from the survey findings that electronic publication does not seem to have led to a failure to receive rewards. Additionally, very few contributors have been formally challenged regarding their electronic publication or asked to justify it in any way. Nonetheless, there are still a significant number of contributors who believe their colleagues and people in key positions perceive their involvement with electronic journals as less significant than their involvement with traditional print publications.

There are still many technical details which must improve in order to upgrade the opinion of many toward electronic communication. But the data from this survey suggest that the major barrier to acceptance of the electronic channel has little to do with such technicalities. The primary barrier seems to lie in peoples' fears and perceptions about what electronic publication is and what it can lead to.

Perhaps sharing the results of studies like this can help to allay some of the concerns regarding what electronic publication will or will not bring to the serious scholar. It is important that discussions focus on the differences between people's perceptions and fears of electronic publication and the actual experiences of contributors to electronic journals which suggest that electronic publication has been more positively received than is generally thought. Perhaps such discussions will lead to an adjustment in perceptions and to a greater willingness on the part of scholars to publish in electronic channels.

REFERENCES

Brown, H. I. (1977). *Perception, theory and commitment; The new philosophy of science.* Chicago: Precedent Publishing.

Gaston, J. (1978). *The Reward System in British and American Science.* New York: Wiley-Interscience.

Hagstrom, W. O. (1965). *The scientific Community.* New York: Basic Books.

Knorr-Cetina, K. (1981). *The Manufacture of Knowledge: An Essay on the Constructivist and Contextual Nature of Science.* New York: Pergamon Press.

Merton, R. K. (1973). *The Sociology of Science; Theoretical and Empirical Investigations.* Chicago: University of Chicago Press.

Popper, K. R. (1959). *The Logic of Scientific Discovery.* New York: Basic Books. (Original work published 1935).

Zuckerman, H. (1977). *Scientific Elite: Nobel Laureates in the United States.* New York: Free Press.

Julene Butler
Library Instruction Coordinator
Brigham Young University
hjb@hbll1.byu.edu

Scientific Scholarly Publishing: A Draft Proposal

David L. Rodgers
University of Michigan

The goal of this concept paper is to outline a solution strategy and implementation path for constructing a general purpose delivery system for scientific scholarly information that does not exclude participation by the social science and humanities disciplines. It makes the following assumptions:

- An outcome that creates an arbitrary array of vanity presses is extremely undesirable
- Few organizations have the resources or will, and fewer yet the in-house expertise, to implement viable general-purpose solutions
- An open architecture solution strategy is essential and use of off-the-shelf components in wide use is highly desirable
- Viable solutions must scale into the metaphor of the digital library, broadly defined

The University of Michigan is the recipient of one of six national awards under the NSF/DRDA/NASA Digital Library Initiative. It has entered into a cooperative agreement to develop a digital library (UMDL), broadly defined, with testbed collections in earth and space sciences. The UMDL:

- Is based on a general-purpose agent architecture designed for heterogeneous collections of document types and document representations (structured text, image, unstructured text)
- Will support SGML collections and develop enhanced retrieval capability based on structure
- Will support three retrieval engines (DIRECT, PAT, WAIS), one for which the University of Michigan owns intellectual property rights, one optimized for structured (SGML) text, and one public domain

Recently, a number of commercial organizations have signaled interest in, or announced that they will make important building blocks for information delivery systems FREELY available as part of their core business strategy:

- Adobe: Acrobat (Acrobat Viewer)

To support Adobe Capture, a product that creates PDF files from image data. Where possible, ASCII text is created; where not (e.g., mathematical expressions, tables, figures), the image representation is preserved.

- ArborText: ADEPTeditor (HTML browser/editor)

To support the ADEPTeditor product line, a collection of tools that support SGML-based publishing applications. Differentiating benefits are applications program interface (HTTP server and retrieval systems can be directly attached), arbitrary DTDs, equation editor, table editor, FOSI formatting, and a powerful imbedded command language. It is a power tool with a high degree of flexibility.

- MCC: NetScape Client (HTML browser)

To support server technology for industrial strength WWW applications that require validation and accounting capabilities. It is the class of the field in WWW browsers. A key question is MCC's interest in supporting FOSI/DSSSL formatting, a formatter neutral mechanism for specifying style sheets.

- SoftQuad: Panorama (SGML browser)

To support AuthorEditor, a general-purpose SGML editor. Differentiating benefits are a presentation grammar for layout, support for tables, compact and simple for simple documents, and arbitrary DTDs. (Product rollout is scheduled for November-December 1994.)

In each instance, the developer organization creates a NATURAL business opportunity for their products with their freely available version. Each is likely to view an association with the UMDL initiative as a benefit. Together, they provide a lattice of electronic publishing (capture, production, display and dissemination) options:

- Organizations could opt for PDF format and Adobe Capture as their retrospective conversion tool, selecting Adobe Acrobat as their viewer. They could adopt PDF as the derived format for prospective publications, leading to a seamless environment.

- Organizations could opt for SGML for prospective capture but deliver PDF format via the ArborText package, either to provide seamless environment with retrospective material, for compatibility with other collections, or because they preferred the Acrobat interface.

- Organizations could opt for SGML for capture, dissemination, and display, selecting SoftQuad or ArborText packages, depending on content or interface issues.

- Organizations could opt for SGML for capture, selecting NetScape or Panorama for display or dissemination, depending on requirements for interface, and accounting and authorization capabilities.

- Organizations could select HTML for capture, dissemination, and display, selecting NetScape for interface, enterprise-wide consistency, or accounting and authorization capabilities.

Clearly, the list of components and their application is intended to be representative of obvious possibilities, not exhaustive. It illustrates the richness of the options space.

Overall Solution Strategy

The University of Michigan was invited by the National Science Foundation to submit a proposal for an invited workshop on the status of scientific scholarly publishing. The workshop will be scheduled early in 1995 (tentatively February/March) and will:

- Build on a series of meetings in various scientific scholarly communities (e.g., astronomy, physics, mathematics) and tools (e.g., WWW, browsers) that have been held throughout the last half of 1994

- Benchmark initiatives now underway or planned by scholarly publishers

- Invite selected developers to discuss their product and marketing strategies

- Develop a framework solution for delivering scientific information

The overall solution strategy is to use the NSF Workshop to identify capabilities missing from FREELY available components that would allow them to aggregate into general-purpose solutions for delivering preprint and peer-reviewed scientific information. To get those holes plugged, contracted or cooperative development will be commissioned for work strategic partners will pre-commit to include in FREELY available components. Strategic partners have to agree to allow overall specifications, if not designs or implementation details, to be publicly discussed and documented. ***In***

this way, paths by which content providers can reliably attach to UMDL are created in parallel to development of the testbed collections.

These tools can then be used by a variety of scholarly societies, university presses, not-for-profit publishers, for-profit publishers, and information providers. Universities and libraries can join the fray. Organizations can either figure things out for themselves or contract the work, in whole or in part, to third parties experienced in such work, such as University of Michigan staff.

Business Strategy

I would estimate the cost of a complete working suite of components to be about $500,000, namely about 5 FTEs for a year. Maintenance might incur costs of $100,000 per year. A more specific estimate of costs is will be made in conjunction with the NSF Workshop.

The University of Michigan will raise 20% of the total, or $100,000, as part of a foundation proposal (e.g., NSF, Mellon, Kellogg) for the difference ($400,000). Grant funds will be used to negotiate required contracted/cooperative development with strategic partners. The benefit to strategic partners is that they will be positioned to sell their products to scientific publishers and information providers. The benefit to participating organizations is that they will have an opportunity to shape the outcome and would be positioned for early deployment. The benefit to the University of Michigan is that there are some organizations invested in a good design/implementation that it can also deploy. The benefit to the scientific scholarly community is a general-purpose delivery system for scientific information.

David Rodgers
Research Associate
School of Library & Information Studies
University of Michigan
drodgers@sils.umich.edu

Multimedia Patent and Copyright Issues: The Need for Lawmakers to be Multimedia Literate

Fred T. Hofstetter
University of Delaware

"The fair use doctrine does have applicability to the products of the new technologies no matter whether groups, individuals, or copyright proprietors attempt to mislead by the publication of official-sounding documents to the contrary." Nancy H. Marshall (1992 p. 243).

Multimedia is one of the fastest growing markets in the world today. According to the Information Workstation Group (1993), the number of multimedia PCs will increase fivefold to 13.3 million by 1996, and the size of the multimedia production and services markets will grow more than tenfold to $30 billion by 1998. In an information society, multimedia is a strategic industry. Nations that do not succeed in multimedia will be unable to compete in the new global economy in which citizens who cannot use multimedia computers for videoconferencing, education, just-in-time training, home shopping, and on-line financial services will become disenfranchised.

Multimedia is putting new pressures on the legal system, which has been slow to learn about new media. Embarrassing mistakes have been made in the patent office, and misunderstandings about copyrights are preventing fair use in multimedia. Law makers and enforcers need to become multimedia literate so they can bolster the use of new media on the Information Superhighway instead of retard its progress through lack of understanding.

This paper will demonstrate how fortune seekers have tried to profit from the legal system's lack of experience by patenting basic multimedia technologies that were already widely used. It will explain how the time and energy devoted to the furor this caused would have been better spent improving existing products and inventing new ones. On a related issue, this paper will proceed to cite four provisos in faculty copyright guidelines that deny the teacher's right to Fair Use of multimedia. After demonstrating how these provisos deny fair use, this paper will conclude by calling upon campus copyright officials to get organized, take the lead, and revise their faculty copyright guidelines to permit these fair uses of multimedia.

Patents

Recently the Patent Office granted two multimedia patents so broad in scope that the awardees blatantly announced all other vendors owed them royalties on all past, present, and future products. This created an industry-wide protest so severe that one of the vendors withdrew its claim, while the Patent Office overturned the other. In both cases there was so much prior art that for people in the industry these claims were likened to trying to patent sunlight (Wall Street Journal 3/25/94 B2).

The Optical Data Patent

The first case involved a patent awarded to Optical Data for the instructional methodology used in their Windows on Science program. Their syllabus-based curriculum outlining method is so basic to the teaching process that practically all other products already used it. Kinnaman (1993) tells how Videodiscovery filed a lawsuit seeking a declaratory judgment finding the patent invalid because of prior art and the obviousness of the claims. The Interactive Multimedia Association (IMA) supported the Videodiscovery complaint; as IMA president Philip Dodds politely stated: "Patents such as these, which require nearly every company involved in interactive multimedia and education to license an idea and application that have a long history and are widely known, are not in the best interest of the industry or educators." (Kinnaman 1993)

To stop the flow of negative publicity stemming from the patent, Optical Data Corporation dedicated the patent permanently to the public. According to Optical Data chair William Clark, "It was never our intent to use this patent to inhibit the development of multimedia based interactive teaching methods. A tremendous amount of concern--including a lawsuit by one of our competitors--arose from this patent award. We hope that by voluntarily dedicating this patent to the public, we will end any unfounded fears that Optical Data, or any other company, might try to limit the diversity of interactive, multimedia programs available to educators." (Kinnaman 1994)

But Foremski (1993) tells how there was another company attempting just that. Compton's caused an uproar by claiming at Fall Comdex 1993 that they had been awarded a patent that would require all multimedia developers to pay them royalties. As Compton's CEO Stanley Frank said: "We helped kick start this industry. We now ask to be compensated for our investments. We will do whatever it takes to defend our patent."

The Compton's Patent

The Compton's patent is very broad. It covers any type of computer-controlled database system that allows a user to search for mixed media that includes text with graphics, sound, or animation. Compton's did not limit their claims to CD-ROM products; they also claimed rights to any type of database involving interactive TV or the Information Superhighway.

The title of the Compton's patent is *Multimedia search system using a plurality of entry path means which indicate interrelatedness of information.*

The Compton's patent claims:

A computer search system for retrieving information, comprising:

- means for storing interrelated textual information and graphical information;
- means for interrelating said textual and graphical information;
- a plurality of entry path means for searching said stored interrelated textual and graphical information, said entry path means comprising:
- textual search entry path means for searching said textual information and for retrieving interrelated graphical nformation to said searched text;
- graphics entry path means for searching said graphical information and for retrieving interrelated textual information to said searched graphical information;
- selecting means for providing a menu of said plurality of entry path means for selection;
- processing means for executing inquiries provided by a user in order to search said textual and graphical information through said selected entry path means;
- indicating means for indicating a pathway that accesses information related in one of said entry path means to information accessible in another one of said entry path means;
- accessing means for providing access to said related information in said another entry path means; and
- output means for receiving search results from said processing means and said related information from said accessing means and for providing said search results and received information to such user.

Compton's presented all multimedia developers with four patent royalty payment options. Kinnaman (1994) explains how they included "... entering into a joint venture with Compton's; distributing products through the company's *Affiliated*

Label Program; licensing Compton's *SmarTrieve* technology; or paying royalties." Compton's had the audacity to require back royalties of 1% of net receipts from sales before June 30, 1994, and 3% thereafter.

To say the least, developers reacted negatively to Compton's demands. Some suggested that users should burn all Compton's CD-ROMs and refuse to purchase future titles from any company that would try to force such a Machiavellian proviso on the multimedia industry. As a result of public hearings held by the U.S. Patent and Trademark Office to review its handling of software patents, the Compton's patent was rescinded.

Hopefully the furor caused by the Optical Data and Compton's patents will cause the Patent Office to review more carefully such broad claims in the future. In fairness to the government, industry leaders like Optical Data and Compton's who know better should stop trying to profit from patenting prior art; instead, they should concentrate on improving their products and moving the industry forward.

Meanwhile, the U.S. Patent and Trademark Office has pledged to rework the software patent system. Reforms include publicizing patent applications, hiring seven software specialists as examiners, revamping the examiner bonus program so it does not encourage superficial review, and requiring more information about patent applications before decisions get made (*Wall Street Journal* 4/11/94 B6).

Copyright

All of the audiovisual elements used in a multimedia application--including illustrations, text, movies, video clips, documentaries, music, and software--are protected by copyright. Whenever you plan to publish a multimedia work, whether on a CD-ROM, diskettes, or the Information Superhighway, you must make sure you have the right to use every object in it.

The National Music Publishers Association is suing Compuserve for allegedly distributing the song "Unchained Melody" without permission. They claim the ballad has been infringed at least 690 times by subscribers who download the song onto their multimedia PCs (*Wall Street Journal* 12/16/93 B1). The Software Publishers Association took action in 1993 against 577 organizations for pirating commercial software, resulting in $3.6 million in fines (*Atlanta Journal-Constitution* 2/3/94 C2).

Even if you do not plan to publish the material, but just wish to present it, you may still have to seek permission. For example, Wertz (1993) tells how a University of South Carolina student preparing for a juried media festival called MediaFest included a song by *The Doors* without obtaining copyright permission to use it. South Carolina's attorneys ruled that the university's agreements with ASCAP, BMI, and SESAC do not cover dramatic uses of musical works, nor synchronization rights; moreover, they ruled that the MediaFest, which is open to the public, probably violated fair use. So the student sought permission. After a copyright search led the student to the copyright holder, it turned out to be a company that would not allow use of the song without a significant fee. As Wertz reported, "It mattered not to the company that the user was a student."

Fair Use

Fair Use is a section of the US Copyright Law that allows the use of copyrighted works in reporting news, conducting research, and teaching. The fair use law is only half a page long, followed by seven pages of historical notes and twelve pages of case law decisions. The law states:

Notwithstanding the provisions of section 106, the fair use of a copyrighted work, including such use by reproduction in copies or phonorecords or by any other means specified by that section, for purposes such as criticism, comment, news reporting, teaching (including multiple copies for classroom use), scholarship, or research, is not an infringement of copyright. In determining whether the use made of a work in any particular case is a fair use, the factors to be considered shall include:

(1) the purpose and character of the use, including whether such use is of a commercial nature or is for nonprofit educational purposes;

(2) the nature of the copyrighted work;

(3) the amount and substantiality of the portion used in relation to the copyrighted work as a whole; and

(4) the effect of the use upon the potential market for or value of the copyrighted work.

Interpreting Fair Use for Teachers

To summarize the fair use law for teachers, one may paraphrase its first paragraph as follows: "... the fair use of a copyrighted work for ... teaching (including multiple copies for classroom use) ... is not an infringement of copyright." The difficulty arises from interpreting the four tests, which are intentionally left vague, as the law goes on to state that "Although the courts have considered and ruled upon the fair use doctrine over and over again, no real definition of the concept has ever emerged. Indeed, since the doctrine is an equitable rule of reason, no generally applicable definition is possible, and each case raising the question must be decided on its own facts."

The vagueness of the law and the fear of lawsuits has led school administrators to publish guidelines that are much more restrictive than the spirit of the law intends. Some of these guidelines are especially detrimental to the classroom use of multimedia, and it is important for lawmakers to provide leadership in changing them.

For example, consider the following provisos in the Howard Community College *Faculty Copyright Manual;* problems for multimedia appear in bold print.

New Medium Proviso

An educator **may not convert** one media format into another (e.g., film to video, filmstrip to slide, etc.) without permission.

Using multimedia computers to present slides, pictures, videos, texts, and audio recordings requires that they be digitized, which changes the medium of the work. Declaring that it is not a fair use for teachers to change the medium of a work prevents their using multimedia computers to create classroom presentations and networked cooperative learning projects.

Frequency of Use Proviso

Recorded commercial television programs may be retained for forty-five calendar days from date of recording. **After forty-five days they must be erased** or permission must be obtained for continued retention and use. Programs may be shown to a class once, **and repeated once for reinforcement,** during the first ten "teaching days" following a broadcast.

It takes a lot of time and effort to digitize a video clip. If its repeated showing in a class does not deprive the commercial television station of profit, which it rarely would, why require teachers to pursue the difficult permissions process or erase their digital video clips after forty-five days? Moreover, the limit of repeating the clip only once negates one of the most important educational principles of hypermedia, which permits access to a clip as often as needed to accomplish the instructional goal. Less able students may need to view it more than twice.

Electronic Editing Proviso

Programs need not be used in their entirety but **may not be edited or electronically altered or combined**.

One of the most effective multimedia techniques is to cut, copy, and paste video clips, rearranging the material to juxtapose video sequences for teaching purposes. For example, consider the use of the Memorex commercial in the videodisc The Puzzle of the Tacoma Narrows Bridge Collapse. To help students understand the sympathetic vibration caused by the wind striking the bridge, a video clip of Ella Fitzgerald breaking a champagne glass by singing has been cut into the clip of the bridge collapse. Surely the fair use law never meant to prevent teachers from creating effective teaching materials like this.

Transmission of Audiovisual Works Proviso

Cable "transmission" of copyrighted works is limited to non-dramatic literary works. Because audiovisual works are excluded from the definition of literary works, **audiovisual works may not be transmitted without a license.**

One of the most effective uses of multimedia technology is to provide students access to the material via networks that permit review and study from computer labs, dorm rooms, and homes. Is it the intent of Fair Use to prevent students from reviewing the material presented in class? And what about classes conducted solely over networks; are they thereby denied fair use? Since networks can deny access to users who are not registered for a course, should not networked students have the same fair use as classroom students?

Fair Use for Multimedia

By including references to photocopiers and phonograph records in the fair use law, its authors clearly intended to permit the fair use of technology. Since the law has not been revised since 1976, it omits the personal computer revolution that has occurred since then.

Multimedia computers clearly require a fresh interpretation of fair use. It must be fair for teachers to change the medium of a work, electronically combine it with other works for didactic purposes, use it as frequently as needed for students to master the learning objective, and provide students registered in the class with access from computer labs, dorm rooms, and homes over the Information Superhighway. The author believes that all of these uses are within the spirit of the law and the four tests of infringement. Campus copyright officials need to take the lead and revise their faculty copyright guidelines to permit these fair uses of multimedia.

To quote Dr. Kenneth Crews (1992 p. 17), Professor of Business Law at San Jose State University: "The objective of an institutional copyright policy should be not merely to achieve compliance with the latest standards, but also to identify maximum opportunities for the institution to lawfully pursue its informational and academic objectives. Many standard form policies, particularly the Classroom Guidelines, are questionable responses to a flexible law that should address diverse circumstances."

In the words of American Library Association council member Nancy H. Marshall (1992 p. 243), "The fair use doctrine does have applicability to the products of the new technologies no matter whether groups, individuals, or copyright proprietors attempt to mislead by the publication of official-sounding documents to the contrary."

References

Crews, Kenneth D., "Copyright Law, Libraries, and Universities: Overview, Recent Developments, and Future Issues. Working paper." Presented to the Association of Research Libraries, October 1992.

Foremski, Tom, "Straight Outta Compton's: A Patent Play," *Morph's Outpost* (January 1994), Volume 1 Number 5, 1 / 16-17.

Information Workstation Group, *Multimedia Opportunities*. 1993. Alexandria: Information Workstation Group. Phone (703) 548-4320 to order this 600-page five-year forecast. $1,890 for the first copy, $200 for additional copies ordered at the same time.

Kinnaman, Daniel E., "Videodiscovery Files Complaint Against Optical Data," *Technology & Learning* (November-December

1993), Volume 14 Number 3, 9.

Kinnaman, Daniel E., "Comptons Re-ignites Patent Wars," *Technology & Learning* (February 1994), Volume 14 Number 5, 14.

Marshall, Nancy H., "Copyright and the Scholarly Community: The Library's Responsibility to Guarantee Users' Rights," In: *Japan -U..S. Collaboration in Enhancing International Access to Scholarly Communication: Looking Toward the 21st Century.* Tokyo University Academy Press, 1992.

Wertz, Sandra, "Using Copyrighted Music in Public Performances." *Tech Trends* (October 1993) Volume 38 Number 5, 11-12.

 This paper is from the Regulatory Issues section of Dr. Hofstetter's new textbook *Multimedia Literacy* (New York: McGraw-Hill, 1995). ISBN 0-07-911956-5.

Fred Hofstetter
Director, Instructional Technology Center
University of Delaware
fth@brahms.udel.edu

The U.S. Government's Interest in Copyright and Fair Use

Terri Southwick
Attorney Advisor
U.S. Patent and Trademark Office

Ms. Southwick presented an informal talk about the NII Intellectual Property Task Force's draft report (released in July 1994) on Intellectual Property Rights. She described the group's working process and the national process through which the IP issues are being discussed, debated, and taken into consideration by the Task Force. She answered an array of questions from the Symposium audience. The final report (White Paper) is due in Spring 1995.

Below is the Executive Summary of the National Information Infrastructure Task Force draft report on intellectual property rights. The complete report is available on the IITF Bulletin Board, accessible through the Internet by pointing the Gopher Client to iitf.doc.gov or by telnet to iitf.doc.gov (log in as gopher).
For a paper copy, call (703) 305-9300 or write NII, USPTO, Box 4, Washington, D.C. 20231- 0001.
To access on the World Wide Web URL: http://www.uspto.gov/niiip.html

INTELLECTUAL PROPERTY AND THE NATIONAL INFORMATION INFRASTRUCTURE; A Preliminary Draft of the Report of the Working Group on Intellectual Property Rights.

Executive Summary

INTRODUCTION

The Working Group on Intellectual Property Rights, chaired by Assistant Secretary of Commerce and Commissioner of Patents and Trademarks Bruce A. Lehman, was established as part of the White House Information Infrastructure Task Force. The Task Force, chaired by Secretary of Commerce Ronald H. Brown, was created to articulate and implement the Administration's vision for the National Information Infrastructure (NII). The Task Force is working with the private sector, public interest groups, Congress and State and local governments to develop comprehensive telecommunications and information policies and programs that best meet the country's needs.

The Preliminary Draft of the *Report of the Working Group on Intellectual Property Rights* represents the Working Group's examination and analysis to date of the intellectual property implications of the NII. While it addresses each of the major areas of intellectual property law, it focuses primarily on copyright law and its application and effectiveness in the context of the NII. The Working Group is issuing the *Preliminary Draft* to solicit public comment prior to issuing a Final Report. The Working Group will also hold public hearings on the Draft.

BACKGROUND

The NII has great potential to increase access to information and entertainment resources that will be delivered quickly and economically anywhere in the country in the blink of an eye. For instance, hundreds of channels of "television" programming, thousands of musical recordings, and literally millions of "magazines" and "books" can be made available to homes and businesses across the United States and, eventually, the world. It can improve the nation's education and health care systems. It can enhance the ability of U.S. firms to compete and succeed in the global economy, generating more jobs for Americans. New job opportunities can also be created in the processing, organizing, packaging and dissemination of the information and entertainment products flowing through the NII.

The NII is much more than computers, telephones, fax machines, scanners, cameras, keyboards, televisions, monitors, printers, switches, routers, wires, cables, networks and satellites. What will drive the success of the NII is the ***content*** moving through it. Therefore, the potential of the NII will not be realized if the content is not protected effectively. Owners of intellectual property rights will not be willing to put their interests at risk if appropriate systems -- both in the U.S. and internationally -- are not in place to permit them to set and enforce the terms and conditions under which their works are made available in the NII environment. Likewise, the public will not use the services available on the NII and generate the market necessary for its success unless access to a wide variety of works is provided under equitable and reasonable terms and conditions, and the integrity of those works is assured.

FINDINGS AND RECOMMENDATIONS

A. LAW

The *Draft Report* analyzes current copyright law and its application in the NII environment. The Working Group concludes that, with the following limited amendments and clarifications, the Copyright Act will provide the necessary protection of rights in copyrighted works -- and appropriate limitations on those rights.

1. DISTRIBUTION BY TRANSMISSION

a. THE DISTRIBUTION RIGHT

The Copyright Act gives a copyright owner the exclusive right "to distribute ***copies or phonorecords*** of the copyrighted work" to the public. A copy or phonorecord is a material object in which a copyrighted work is fixed, such as a compact disc, a videocassette or a paperback book. It is not clear that a transmission can constitute a distribution of copies of the work under the current law.

Yet, in the world of high-speed, communications systems, it is possible to transmit a copy of a work from one location to another. This may be the case, for instance, when a computer program is transmitted from one computer to ten other computers. When the transmission is complete, the original copy remains in the transmitting computer and a copy resides in the memory of, or in a storage device associated with, each of the other computers. Therefore, this transmission results essentially in the distribution of ten copies of the work.

The Working Group recommends that Section 106 of the Copyright Act be amended to reflect the fact that copies of works can be distributed to the public by transmission, and that such transmissions fall within the exclusive distribution right of the copyright owner. The Working Group also recommends that the definition of "transmit" in Section 101 of the Copyright Act be amended to delineate between those transmissions that are communications of performances or displays and those that are distributions of reproductions. When a transmission may constitute both a communication of a performance or display and a distribution of a reproduction (such as when a phonorecord of a sound recording is distributed and the recipient may listen to it while it is being downloaded), the Working Group recommends that such a transmission be considered a distribution of a reproduction if the ***primary purpose or effect*** of the transmission is to distribute a ***copy or phonorecord*** of the work to the recipient of the transmission.

The Working Group also recommends that the prohibitions on importation be amended to reflect the fact that copies or phonorecords of copyrighted works can be imported into the United States by transmission. Although the Working Group recognizes that the U.S. Customs Service cannot, for all practical purposes, enforce a prohibition on importation by transmission, given the global dimensions of the information infrastructure of the future, it is important that copyright owners have the other remedies for infringements of this type available to them.

b. PUBLICATION

The legislative history to the Copyright Act makes clear that any form of dissemination of a work in which a ***material object*** does not change hands is not a "publication" of the work, no matter how many people are exposed to it. Thus, a transmission of a performance or display via the NII would not constitute publication, since a material object does not change hands. However, in the case of a transmission of a reproduction, the recipient of the transmission ends up with a copy of the work. Therefore, the Working Group recommends that the definition of "publication" in Section 101 of the Copyright Act be amended to include the concept of distribution by transmission.

c. FIRST SALE DOCTRINE

The first sale doctrine allows the owner of a particular, lawfully-made copy of a work to dispose of it in any manner, with certain exceptions, without infringing the copyright owner's exclusive right of distribution. In the case of transmissions, a copy of the work remains with the first owner (and the recipient of the transmission receives a reproduction of the work); the owner does not dispose of his or her copy. Therefore, the Working Group recommends that Section 109 of the Copyright Act be amended to make clear that the first sale doctrine does not apply to transmissions.

2. TECHNOLOGICAL PROTECTION

The ease of infringement and the difficulty of detection and enforcement will cause copyright owners to look to technology, as well as the law, for protection of their works. Technology can be used to help protect copyrighted works against unauthorized access, reproduction, manipulation, distribution, performance or display. It can also be useful in the authentication of the integrity of copyrighted works and in the management and licensing of the rights in such works. However, it is clear that technology can also be used to defeat any protection that technology provides.

Therefore, the Working Group recommends that the Copyright Act be amended to prohibit the importation, manufacture and distribution of devices (or any component or circuitry incorporated into any device or product), or the offering or performance of any service, the primary purpose or effect of which is to avoid, bypass, remove, deactivate, or otherwise circumvent, without authority of the copyright owner or the law, any process, treatment, mechanism or system which prevents or inhibits the exercise of any of the exclusive rights under Section 106. The Working Group also recommends other related amendments to provide civil causes of action and remedies for violations of the proposed prohibition.

3. COPYRIGHT MANAGEMENT INFORMATION

In the future, the copyright management information associated with a work -- such as the name of the copyright owner, and the terms and conditions for uses of the work -- may be critical to the efficient operation and success of the NII. The public should be protected from fraud in the creation or alteration of such information. Therefore, the Working Group recommends that Section 506 of the Copyright Act be amended to prohibit fraudulent copyright management information and fraudulent removal or alteration of copyright management information.

4. PUBLIC PERFORMANCE RIGHT

Sound recordings are the only copyrighted works that are capable of being performed that are not granted a public performance right. The Working Group believes that it is time to rectify this inequity. The Working Group notes that the Administration supports two bills introduced in Congress that would grant a limited performance right to sound recordings. The bills, H.R. 2576 and S. 1421, would add to the exclusive rights of a copyright owner in a sound recording the right to perform or authorize the performance of the sound recording by "digital transmission." The right granted in the bill is not the full performance right granted to other copyrighted works. For instance, the legislation would not change the law with respect to live public performances. It would also not touch analog transmissions -- the transmissions currently received over the radio. It would only grant a right with respect to transmissions in a digital format -- those that pose the greatest threat to the copyright owners of sound recordings.

5. FAIR USE

The Working Group has significant concerns regarding the ability of the limitations on copyright owners' exclusive rights -- particularly those limitations found in Sections 107 (fair use), 108 (library exemptions) and 110 (1) and (2) (educational uses) -- to provide the public with adequate access to copyrighted works transmitted via the NII. As more and more works are available primarily or exclusively on-line, it is critical that researchers, students and other members of the public have opportunities *on-line* equivalent to their current opportunities *off-line* to browse through copyrighted works in their school and public library. Public libraries and schools historically have been safeguards against the United States becoming a nation of information "haves" and "have nots." We must ensure that they continue to be able to assume that role.

Guidelines for library and educational use of printed matter and music were voluntarily adopted by diverse parties and set out in the House and Conference reports accompanying the 1976 revisions to the Copyright Act. While the principles should still be applicable, it is difficult and, perhaps, inappropriate, to apply the specific language of some of those guidelines in the context of digital works and on-line services. Therefore, the Working Group will sponsor a conference this summer to bring together copyright owner and user interests to develop guidelines for fair uses of copyrighted works by and in public libraries and schools. While participation in the conference will be by invitation, the public may attend.

6. LICENSING

With limited exceptions, intellectual property law leaves the licensing of rights to the marketplace. In certain circumstances, particularly where transaction costs are believed to dwarf per-transaction royalties, Congress has found it necessary to provide for compulsory licenses. The Working Group finds that under current conditions, additional compulsory licensing of intellectual property rights is neither necessary nor desirable. The marketplace should be allowed to develop whatever licensing systems may be appropriate for the NII.

7. INTERNATIONAL

There must be adequate and effective protection for entertainment and information products delivered via the global information infrastructure (GII). This protection should be granted on the basis of national treatment -- without regard to the origin of the transmission or the nationality of the author. An appropriate intellectual property rights regime to protect the content transmitted over the GII is an essential condition precedent if the full benefits of the GII are to be enjoyed.

To attain the needed level of protection internationally, we must also find ways to span the differences between the continental *droit d'auteur* and neighboring rights systems and the Anglo-American copyright systems. An essential element of this effort will be to harmonize levels of protection.

B. TECHNOLOGY

Interoperability and interconnectivity of networks, systems, services and products operating within the NII will enhance its development and success. Standardization of copyright management (standardized header information and format, for instance) as well as technological protection methods (such as encryption) may also be useful. However, intellectual property rights should not be diminished in the standard-setting process, unless agreed to by the owners of such rights.

C. EDUCATION

Effective education of the public about intellectual property rights is crucial to the successful development of the NII. Therefore, the principles of intellectual property law must be taught in our schools and libraries. Educational efforts to increase the public's awareness of their own intellectual property rights, as well as those of others, will increase respect for those rights. Clearer guidelines with respect to the exclusive rights of copyright and other intellectual property rights holders, as well as the limitations on those rights, will make compliance with the law easier.

Following its conference on fair use, the Working Group will sponsor a second conference on intellectual property education. The purpose of that conference will be to develop curricula that may be used in schools and libraries. Additional means of education, particularly those that use the NII itself, will also be explored and developed. Participation in the conference will be by invitation, but all proceedings will be open to the public.

The Working Group solicited public comment on the Preliminary Draft. The public submitted well over 1,000 pages of written comments to the Commissioner of Patents and Trademarks in the summer/fall of 1994.

The Working Group also held public hearings on the *Preliminary Draft* in Washington, D.C., Chicago and Los Angeles and began a standing, informal "conference on fair use" in Washington, DC in the fall. As of this writing (1/95) the discussants are in early days of describing the fair use issues involved in electronic creation and dissemination of information.

Will We Need Fair Use In The Twenty-First Century?[1]

Georgia Harper
University of Texas System

1. Introduction

Over the last two years I have observed numerous developments, listened to many conversations and queries, and reviewed countless licenses that, individually, usually evoked the same response from me: "But that's fair use!" or "What about fair use?" or some variation on that response. Collectively, however, these events and developments caused me to begin to question my assumptions about the role of and need for fair use in the electronic environment.

For example, two summers ago when I first read the *Texaco*[2] case, which I will discuss in more detail later, I was very critical of the holding because it seemed to use circular reasoning and was results-oriented. The court found that if there were reasonable mechanisms in place for Texaco to pay for copies, then it should not have fair use available as a defense to an infringement claim. The Second Circuit's opinion affirms the lower court's holding.[3] Both opinions sharply threaten the non-profit research community's use of fair use even though the Second Circuit tried to limit its holding to the specific facts of the case before it. The court severely restricted its definition of research purposes, a definition which other courts may well adopt, and it created a tremendous incentive for publishers to establish a fully functional market for reprints.

I was similarly alarmed as I read database license agreements that contained no acknowledgment of the fair use rights of users but appeared to assume that all uses are "chargeable events."

The Green Paper,[4] which I will also discuss in more detail later, implicitly and explicitly assumes that fair use will not be necessary in the electronic environment. Much of the Green Paper's controversial stance makes sense if in fact the Working Group is correct about this assumption; otherwise, the proposals may sharply increase the cost of access to copyright material without necessarily increasing the production of knowledge.

It was the accumulation of events seeming to indicate an improvement in the market's ability to respond to the needs of users and a suggestion I had begun to hear from publishers, that fair use might be the cause of some market inefficiencies such as high journal prices, instead of the other way around, that caused me to begin to wonder: Could fair use be both the effect of market failure *and* the cause of it? Could the difference between the print and electronic environments be sufficient to justify these new assumptions and the events predicated upon them and at the same time offer a glimpse of a way out the fair use maze? Will we need fair use in the 21st Century?

As you may guess, the answer to that question is not a simple yes or no. What I found was this:

- Fair use covers basically different activities; some are greatly affected by electronic creation, communication and distribution; some are hardly affected at all.
- Fair use frees users from different obligations, some of which are dramatically affected by electronic creation, communication, and distribution; some are only indirectly affected, if at all.
- The pace of change in the electronic

world makes any prediction of the future somewhat foolish.

Still, I concluded that electronic creation, communication, and distribution, which I will refer to for convenience as the electronic environment, makes a sufficient difference to justify efforts to differentiate the components of fair use. Under some circumstances we are likely to need fair use despite the medium; under other circumstances the medium may substantially undercut the need for fair use, making it possible to begin to shift the focus away from the fair use debate and towards a more cooperative exploration of the many ways that creators, publisher's and users of information may mutually exploit and benefit from the electronic environment.[5]

So, this paper is first, an exploration of the meaning of fair use so that we may focus attention on those parts of its function that are most affected by the electronic environment; second, an examination of that effect; and third, an evaluation of the supposed benefits of fair use and alternative ways to achieve those benefits given the impact of the electronic environment on fair use.

2. History and Evolution of Fair Use, Particularly the Effect of Technology Development on the Balance Between the Rights of Users and Owners of Copyright Material

Fair use has come to be widely understood as a balancing point between the rights of authors to exclusive control over their works and the rights of users to have free access to the ideas contained in those works. We began trying to strike this balance in the mid-eighteen hundreds as it became evident that some limitations would have to be placed upon the "exclusive" rights of the copyright owner, in order for the law to truly further the purpose for which it was established.[6] It became clear that some exercises of an author's exclusive rights could *stifle* creativity by withholding from the public the raw materials of new creations. In effect, we began to identify activities that furthered the goals of copyright even though they may have treaded upon the copyright owner's exclusive domain.

At its inception, copyright only concerned itself with the protection of printing, reprinting, publishing, and vending, and only for a short period of fourteen years. When copyright had such a narrow scope, there was little need of fair use.[7] It was only as copyright expanded to cover substantially longer periods of time (currently, life of the author plus 50 years, with discussion of extending the term to life of the author plus 70 years); to embrace the exclusive rights to make and distribute copies; to display and perform works; to protect not only literature, but music, sculpture, architecture, photographs, and computer programs; and to include as infringement the taking of non-literal elements (for example, structure, sequence and organization), that it became necessary to balance such expansion with correspondingly expanded exemptions from liability for infringement, including rights of fair use.[8]

In some ways, our Copyright Law today would be unrecognizable to those who first set it out 200 years ago. This is in large part the result of technological changes and the law's continual need to accommodate those changes. Balances between the rights of copyright holders and users of copyright material achieved under one set of circumstances only hold up for awhile and invariably need revision as the facts of our lives change. In this century, the photocopying machine and now the computer have drastically altered the balances achieved in earlier eras. It is quite remarkable that the law has accommodated as much growth and change as it has. This is, no doubt, a tribute to its flexibility and our system of interpreting the law in the light of change. Nevertheless, this course of events has brought us undeniably to the point where we are today, where I have yet to find among those who must use and understand the law of copyright and fair use, *excluding in particular those lawyers, judges and academics who are paid to try to understand it*, very many who are satisfied with the precarious balance we have today as we stand inelegantly poised to enter the 21st century and the electronic age.[9]

3. The Actual Role of Fair Use Today; How it Functions; What it Does for the Research Community and What it Does Not Do; What it Really Costs

A. *Fair Use Comprises Many Different Activities*

Fair use subsumes a number of very different kinds of activities and it consists of several different elements. Since the impact of the electronic environment varies over the range of these activities, I want to take a moment to explain these distinctions.

The statute includes an illustrative list of activities that may qualify for fair use, depending upon whether the activity "passes" the weighing and balancing test described in the statute.[10] The activities listed include criticism, comment, news reporting, teaching (including multiple copies for classroom use), scholarship, and research. Other activities that are not included have been found to be a fair use, for example, home taping of television programs for personal use; and it must be understood that some comment, news reporting, etc. is not a fair use because it goes beyond the parameters defined by the factors enumerated in the statute's weighing and balancing test. Nevertheless, these listed activities can reasonably be considered "favored" in the eyes of the law.

Parody, criticism, news reporting and comment are examples of activities that a copyright owner might not be inclined to permit at any price, given complete control over his work.[11] Our public policies, however, favor such activities. Thus, the courts carved out exemptions from the requirement to obtain permission and pay fees for the use of portions of an author's work for those purposes. These uses typically involve the second author's using short quotations from the protected work in the creation of a new work, although parody usually involves borrowing more from the protected work than other uses in this category. Many times the critical elements in deciding whether the use is fair are how much was taken and whether the new work competes with the original.

Teaching, scholarship and research have also been recognized as socially valuable activities that we can not unduly burden. Until recently, the high costs associated with the requirement to obtain permission and to negotiate a price for use of protected works would have discouraged these very valuable activities. So, again, the courts carved out an exception for these uses of copyrighted materials. This second category of uses usually involves photocopying articles from periodicals, chapters or other parts of books or charts, graphs, or illustrations and in most cases does not directly contemplate the same kinds of uses described above.[12] The purpose of this copying is most often to make access to the ideas contained in the works more convenient. The critical elements in this analysis appear to be whether the use is for non-profit purposes and what impact the use will have on the market for the original.[13]

B. *Ownership's Twin Restraints Upon Use*

All uses of a protected work require, first, permission from the author, and second, the payment of whatever price the author might ask for permission. Thus, fair use frees the user from two constraints: the obligation to ask permission and the obligation to pay a fee for the use. The costs involved in determining who the owner is, making contact with him, negotiating the amount of the fee and arranging for payment are called "transaction costs" and are distinct from the actual amount of the fee. In many cases, the obligation to ask permission costs the user more than the actual fee.

Either of these obligations may act as a total bar to a desired use: users may be unable to locate the copyright owner at all;

the owner may refuse permission; transaction costs may be too high to justify the effort; or the fee required may be more than the user wants to pay. Thus, arrangements that equate the elimination or substantial reduction of transaction costs with elimination of the need for fair use, as the Green Paper, *Texaco,* and *Texaco II* have done, may be taking only part of the function of fair use into account.

C. *The Impact of the Electronic Medium*

The impact of the electronic environment will vary over the range of these activities and obligations. It will affect iterative copying to a significant extent, but copying that involves the incorporation of parts of one work into another will most likely become easier and more common and accounting for such uses of others' works will require analyses similar to those undertaken herein.

Similarly, the electronic environment will have significantly more impact on copying for which permission itself is not an issue (iterative uses for research, scholarship and education where publishers seem quite willing to make works available). Where permission itself remains the primary obstacle, the effect of the electronic environment will be negligible.[14]

Thus, the electronic environment has its greatest immediate impact on transaction costs associated with the requirement to seek permission to copy books and periodicals for scholarly, academic and research purposes;[15] as transaction costs become less of an obstacle, the primary obstacle to access and use will become the price charged by the copyright owner. It does not appear though that the electronic environment has any *direct* effect upon the price. This may be the biggest impediment to the user community's willingness to let go of fair use. So, the broad inquiry, "Will we need fair use in the 21st Century?" becomes more pointedly, "Will we need fair use to derive a fair price for access to information for scholarly, research and educational purposes?" Within that context, let us turn to an examination of the purpose or function of fair use, what it is supposed to do for us and what it really does.

D. *The Source of the Fair Use Debate*

The law of fair use is admittedly one of the most difficult to understand. The extent of fair use is unclear even in the print environment where the body of law is more than 150 years old. Defining fair use in the electronic environment will not be simple either. At the heart of the difficulty is the fact that fair use is not and has never been exact. What is fair changes with every set of facts. For example, if a user sets out all the facts about a proposed use of another's works (the character of the proposed use, the nature of the work and amount to be copied, the effect on the market for the original) undertakes the fair use analysis as best she can and arrives at a conclusion, her conclusion is only good for that particular set of facts. If one of the facts changes, the result of the analysis could be incorrect for the new circumstance. Further, the analysis itself is very subjective and open to considerable disagreement as to how each of the four factors should be weighed in each particular circumstance. Two lawyers each undertaking the same analysis of the exact same facts could come to completely opposing conclusions and support them with citations to the same or different cases! One's result is, therefore, not necessarily predictive of what a court would really do given the same set of facts. It is very hard to know for sure that a proposed use is or is not a fair use.

This difficulty stems at least in part from the fact that we have many different theories about the justification for fair use. For example, fair use has been "[t]raditionally conceived as based on authors' implied consent to reasonable uses of their works;"[16] as integrally a part of the constitutional grant of rights and not subject to the ordinary rights of individuals to contract;[17] as mandated by the market's failure to provide reasonable access, and to the extent markets can provide such access, as irrelevant.[18] These different explanations for the existence of fair use lead to disparate conclusions about whether a particular use might be fair.[19] Some describe fair use in much more general terms, as protecting critical access needs of the public to expression or insuring that "the reach of the exclusive rights provisions of copyright law do not defeat the ultimate purpose of copyright law which is to promote `science' (knowledge)."[20] For these observers, fair use might have a role to play regardless of changes in specific economic circumstances, for example, changes in custom or tradition, reductions in transaction costs or even the advent of a compulsory license scheme.[21]

The market failure justification for fair use underlies the result in the *Texaco* and *Texaco II* decisions.[22] Both Judge Leval (district court) and Chief Judge Newman (appellate court) agreed that to the extent the Copyright Clearance Center had made asking for permission and paying publishers easy, the scope of fair use had correspondingly diminished.[23] Thus, those who believed that *Texaco* constituted a ringing endorsement of the Copyright Clearance Center and sounded the death knell for fair use in the research community beyond the walls of academia have the further support of the Second Circuit for their predictions.[24] Unreasonably high transaction costs are certainly part of the basis for the existence of fair use under many theories; however, as noted above, the price for the copy may still be a distinct impediment to use. The Copyright Clearance Center may have done much to reduce transaction costs, but thus far it has not affected permission prices. Thus, even with the Copyright Clearance Center, there may still be a perceived need for a right of fair use because research and education may be impeded by high permission fees just as much as by high transaction costs.[25]

In summary then, there is considerable argument about the basis for fair use, its scope, and whether it can be effectively bargained away by contract. Against this background of debate over fair use in the print environment, we now take up the argument over how to value fair use in the electronic environment.[26] *Not whether*, but how to take it into account and incorporate a value for it into the technical computerized systems we will be devising to make access easier, cheaper, faster, and more efficient. But if different lawyers cannot agree on what is and is not fair use, how easy will it be to come to agreement on a computer program's formula for fair use?[27]

E. *The Economic Benefit of Fair Use*

It seems obvious, given the response to the Green Paper, that this dialog will continue into the electronic future; nevertheless, we owe it to ourselves to examine some of the premises underlying our attachment to our positions in the print environment, especially since the balance we have supposedly achieved may in truth be more like a stalemate. The escalation in journal prices illustrates this point: users believe publishers charge a price that reflects what publishers think they are losing because users make fair use (and interlibrary loan) copies; users cancel subscriptions and make more copies because they cannot afford the journals and then publishers charge more because they perceive that fair use and interlibrary loan copies are further displacing subscriptions.[28]

This example suggests that fair use may not really be doing what everyone thinks it is, at least in the context of scholarly access to information. Perhaps our attempts to determine its extent, to figure it into the electronic equation, and, in effect, carry its ambiguity into the 21st Century will only perpetuate a system that frustrates all the parties at its very best. We think fair use means free use; we think fair use protects us from price escalations; we think it balances the rights of users and owners by providing us free access to the ideas contained in protected works. I would suggest that examining each of these assumptions will show that fair use falls far short of the claims made for it. In truth, access is getting more expensive; our libraries are spending more money on fewer titles.[29] It seems quite likely that increasing reliance upon fair use and interlibrary loan is directly related to these statistics.

First, let us look at what fair use costs. Fair use does not mean free use. There is an enormous cost associated with fair use if one considers inflated prices for books and journal subscriptions and adds to that the actual costs of making a copy.[30] Think through a typical copying activity, for example, obtaining a copy of a journal article from the library. If you include *all* the costs, the time away from other work (lost productivity), transportation costs, the money going into the copy machine, the paper, the people the library has to hire to tend to all the consumables associated with copying, and then imagine the millions of copies made every day, you may begin to appreciate the enormity of the resources that go into making "free" copies. Within the framework of what users are already paying for fair use, it should be possible to substitute other valuable services that could be provided by electronic publishers and authors willing to make their works available in a manner that more effectively meets users' needs. Electronic substitutes for these transactions do not have to be *free* to be considerably more attractive than fair use. This may be a very important point to remember as we look for ways to explore electronic alternatives: their costs may not have to be entirely *in addition to* what users are already spending; they may be, in many cases, *in lieu of* what users are already spending.[31]

Second, let us examine the assumption that fair use helps to contain costs because as library budgets continue to shrink and the price of information continues to escalate, there will remain an urgent need to contain costs in any manner possible. So long as fair use is believed to save money, users will not be willing to consider alternatives that do not take fair use into account.

Cost savings are presumed to flow from the exercise of fair use rights as counterpoint to the exclusive rights holder's dominion, a sort of shield against the effects of unreasonable escalations in the price of access to information. After all, if the early court cases determined that an exclusive rights scheme without fair use would invite abuse, fair use must be about curbing abuse.[32] I began to question this assumption at least partly as a result of presentations made at last year's Symposium by Janet Fisher, Peter Givler, Colin Day, Michael Jensen and Isabella Hinds.[33] These speakers suggested that price escalations may in fact be *caused by users' reliance upon fair use* rather than the other way around, but most importantly, they convinced me that regardless of which came first, the two are inextricably linked and both publishers and users may go down together if we cling to them.

At last year's Symposium I heard *publishers* say that they understood that price escalations do not achieve the purpose for which they are theoretically designed; that the benefit from the right to charge ever higher prices for books and periodicals is somewhat illusory since there is only so much money in the university community and the more that goes to high-priced journals, the less goes to books and the more a book costs, the fewer are purchased. It seems logical to suggest that fair use may not be achieving the purpose for which it is theoretically designed either.

I conclude that if both publishers and users may be mistaken regarding the extent to which their rights in this context are meaningful and provide them some power to control events, we should be willing to try alternative approaches. The most handy and flexible alternative is negotiating new deals in the new environment. This is not the only alternative, and I will address others later, but first I want to make note of an important aspect of alternatives generally.

4. Alternative Approaches: The Implications of Copyright Without Fair Use

Any copyright system, including our own, is

essentially a proxy for a deal that induces creation and makes ideas accessible to the public. Alternative systems can accomplish the goals of copyright too. Our first instinct, however, is to compare alternatives to our current system, rather than to evaluate them with reference to the underlying goals of copyright. When compared to our current system, most alternatives would appear to have shocking implications.

For example, when I first encountered them, I balked at license arrangements that seemed to contemplate that every use required a payment since this clearly did not take fair use into consideration.[34] Actually, in this period of transition, I believe there are many examples of bad outcomes for users who "give up" fair use; I have frequent occasions to review such licenses and I note that others are experiencing similar shock and disbelief over some of the deals they are being offered.[35] Thus, one of the implications of contracting without reference to fair use is that users may not get as good a deal as the deal they get under Copyright Law. But in order to compare two deals, users have to know the value of each. As I have suggested, I am not sure we really know what we have with fair use.

Blanket license proposals offer another example. Many proposals do not take into account that some works or parts of works may not be protected at all, or that some uses of a work are not an infringement.[36] "Fair use," "ideas," "works in the public domain," and "facts," to name but a few, are descriptions of either unprotected material or uses that are by law not an infringement. The idea of eliminating any or all of these distinctions between what is protected and what is not is extremely controversial; it cuts at the heart of our system. In fact, agreeing to give up fair use in private contracts could effectively begin undermining our current system because, as the argument goes, if users agree to pay authors for what they could otherwise have "for free" the parties are ignoring an important distinction the law makes.[37] The next question might be whether users shouldn't be willing to ignore other distinctions as well; shouldn't they, for example, agree to pay for reading others' works despite the fact that they have the right to look at a work for free right now; and shouldn't they be willing to pay for facts even though our system does not protect facts?

The Green Paper assumes it is already an infringement to look at a digital work since in the electronic environment looking at a work entails making a copy of it.[38] Indeed, the singular idea of a copy as the basis for accounting logically results in payments for almost any conceivable interaction with digital information; in the electronic environment, access = copy.[39] But if this were the law, it would represent the greatest expansion in the coverage of copyright ever conceived; it would obliterate the distinction between what we see now as unprotected and protected works, and between infringement and fair use. One implication of such a massive shift might be that in keeping with the way our law has changed historically, such a monumental expansion of copyright would logically require an equally monumental expansion of fair use.[40] On the other hand, another implication might be the ultimate collapse of our system of copyright protection. It is almost impossible to say whether that would be good or bad without knowing what system would replace it.

As I indicated earlier, implications derived from comparing alternatives to our current system of copyright can be shocking, but that is not the only comparison we can or should make. It may be more productive to evaluate alternatives with reference to the underlying purposes of copyright law: If an alternative has some reasonable potential for success, it should merit serious consideration, even if it is based upon principles that are substantially different from those with which we are more familiar.[41] In particular, if an alternative can achieve affordable and easy access, low transaction costs associated with getting permission, no or few restrictions on use, and payments to authors and publishers that are sufficient to induce creation, theoretically, we should be willing at least to consider it. The alternative of contracting can potentially achieve these ends and can do so without the necessity of prior change to our current system.

5. Impediments to Changing Relationships

There must be many factors that prevent publishers and users from developing new models of how to create, disseminate and exchange information in the electronic environment; I do not pretend to understand them all, or even very many of them, or to suggest that this should be easy. I do understand that so long as either party to negotiations focuses on nonnegotiable demands and reserves the right to be unreasonable, the other party will not be willing to give up its similar nonnegotiable demands or its right to be unreasonable, regardless of whether the two understand the untenable nature of such a bargaining process.

Nevertheless, I have heard it expressed by others and have myself thought for some time that if university presses, libraries and faculty collaborated, we would be able to go beyond the stalemate, beyond arguments about fair use. But there is (at least) one serious problem with this belief: there are many publishers who are not a part of the university community. The problem is that the statute gives authors, and by virtue of our traditions, their publishers, a monopoly, so they will always have the *right* to raise prices and there is nothing users seem to be able to do in response, except cancel subscriptions and make copies, etc., even though fair use and interlibrary loan may not be the solution they appear to be.

The ability of publishers to charge users whatever price publishers desire will probably insure a future for fair use in the next century: further (endless) escalation in prices will be met by more extensive reliance upon fair use and other legal exceptions; spiraling technological controls to prevent access and use will be met by equally sophisticated countermeasures by users; and each action by users will be met by increasing intimidation when pricing and controls fail to make buyers out of users. This is not an exciting prospect.

So long as users and publishers each exercise what appears in the other's eyes as the right to be unreasonable, that is the right to demand to use for free on the one hand and the right to charge whatever they so desire on the other, and without much publisher competition in certain fields of study relevant to this discussion, there is no reason to expect anyone to be willing to give up anything.

6. Breaking the Cycle

Users and publishers are not locked into this relationship. They have market options and legal options. Although no option is particularly easy or attractive because all involve rather fundamental changes in our perspectives on the problems, the electronic environment does offer us an opportunity to break through considerable entrenchment.

A. *The Market Option*

Perhaps part of the problem, at least with respect to scholarly publishing, is that university users and authors believe their publishing options are very limited. In fact, in the print environment, they are right. But, again, the electronic environment offers a unique opportunity to change the dynamic. The university community may have new power to create publishing alternatives, to transact business with more user friendly publishers, and to offer the fruits of its labors in fields dominated by the most problematic, over-priced publications to publishers who are a part of our community or who are in any event willing to deal with users in a reasonable manner.[42] Authors could work together with university presses to create alternative channels for publication for subject matter that has become or becomes unaffordable. Competition is a much more powerful tool to bring down prices than cancelling subscriptions and making copies could ever be.[43] We must recognize the strength that we have naturally because we are all part of the same enterprise.[44]

B. *Legal Options for Change*

When a legal structure functions suboptimally, there are typically a range of possible responses: we live with it for a certain period of time; we talk of changing the law either through legislation or the development of caselaw (sue or be sued); sometimes we ignore the law and contract for more favorable arrangements to the extent that doing so is permitted (copyright law generally permits this).

(1) **Living with it.** We care too much to do nothing, especially because inaction at this time could have severe repercussions for access to information. Those who stand to profit the most from *restricting* access are not sitting back. We cannot afford to sit back either.

(2) **Changing the law: Caselaw development.** *Most cases raise more questions than they answer. Texaco II*, for example, will undoubtably raise many, many questions in the minds of copyright attorneys (and their clients), even though the court explicitly tried to limit its holding to the facts of the case and states that no broad issues of fair use in the research community were before the court.[45] Attorneys will not read the case and comfortably say to themselves, "Well, I'm glad that's settled." Instead they will pose question after question about the potential application of each and every sentence in the opinion to whatever prospective strategic battles they might believe are in their clients' best interests in the fair use war. Further, the cost/benefit analysis of this method of change does not make it a good choice, especially given the short effective life of caselaw in this field.

(3) **Changing the law: Legislation.** Many facets of information creation, distribution, and exchange do not work in the electronic environment the way they worked in the print environment. These dysfunctions come at a time when access to information is becoming more and more critical to our international competitiveness. For example, a 50 to 100 year monopoly over access may be too costly a right to carry into the future. The constitutional guarantee to authors of the exclusive rights to their works for a limited period of time was intended to further the important goal of increasing knowledge and information. If it no longer furthers that goal but actually frustrates it by making it prohibitively expensive to attain,[46] perhaps we need to change the details of the grant of rights.

Copies are another example: they are a meaningful unit in the print medium; they are not an equally meaningful unit in the digital medium; yet our natural inclination is to treat them the same. For example, controlling copies has become immensely harder, and I would argue, useless and counter-productive, in the electronic environment, yet most suggestions for protecting intellectual property still revolve around this mechanism.[47] It is time to look for new economic controls besides counting copies.[48]

The words "electronic publishing" are an oxymoron. The definition of publishing does not have application to the electronic medium.[49] I have seen many very fine discussions on the Internet that illustrate the difficulty of treating the two environments as though they were the same and reasoning by analogy to determine how the old law applies in new situations: Is the placement of a file into an ftp archive a performance or display on the part of the archive owner? In general, or when someone retrieves the file? When it's put there as an archival file or for "real time viewing?" Which state's or nation's laws would apply to acts of infringement committed on borders or in seemingly more than one place at a time, as would happen if infringement were accomplished through an international electronic network like the Internet? Such an analysis is complicated and confusing even under a print scenario but it is absolutely dizzying under a digital scenario.

Sometimes the attempt to understand the new realities in the context of the old laws may not be very helpful, though it certainly is good mental exercise. But, is it really the best way to decide how to structure relationships to take best advantage of the new medium?

I have little hope that we will achieve changes in our statutes that fully address in a direct, thoughtful and forward-looking manner the complex issues of electronic information creation, distribution and exchange. Further, if such changes could be achieved, I doubt that the new law would be as responsive to the needs of the university community as it would be to, say, the cable, telephone and entertainment giants. And finally, if the university community were able to have a significant effect upon such theoretically insightful legal changes, it probably would not be long before the law would be hopelessly hobbled again by some new, unanticipated techno-reality. The times they are a changin' too fast for law to keep up.

Nevertheless, the drama of legislative change is beginning to unfold right before our eyes: the Green Paper and the comments to it presage a long and arduous *battle*; the parties appear to be assembled, *not for a reasoned discussion of how best to utilize this medium for the public good,* but for a land grab the likes of which we have not seen since the Government opened up the Northwest Territory for settlement. Thus, the legislative process will proceed, but it may not be a pretty sight.

Ironically, I see in the Green Paper's suggestions some continuity between the Working Group's vision of the future and what I am suggesting might be the end result of discussion and negotiation among the parties, that is, shifting the focus away from fair use, broadening the base of paying users, and focusing on access at a reasonable price. The Working Group, however, seems to be going about it in a very divisive manner, though that may simply be a function of the nature of the legislative process. If this were a transportation study and the Working Group were considering how to transition to driving on the left side of the road as they do in England, their recommendations would be the equivalent of "We'll start with ***trucks first.*** " Some things should not be changed one side at a time; changing copyright law will require symmetry, give and take on both sides. It just will not work to permit copyright owners to have it both ways, able to charge for every conceivable use of their works and able to charge whatever price they so desire.[50]

Many commentators called upon the Working Group to establish another CONTU (The Commission of the New Technological Uses of Copyrighted Works) to consider changes to the law on a grander scale, but the Working Group rejected this idea. I think the idea has tremendous appeal, even though it might lengthen the process considerably. In fact, lengthening the process will give us all a chance to use the medium; laws that evolve out of actual experience will be far superior to those based upon theory. In any event, we do not need to *wait* for the law to develop to proceed on our own with private negotiations. Such negotiations may offer a flexible way to derive the benefits of fair use without the divisiveness of fair use.

(4) **Contracting**. Contracting does, of course, have its flaws just as the other methods do. It would require immense cooperation between parties who have historically viewed each other as enemies; it would require that we each give up something we may think we can not do without, and it would involve *ab initio* premises that may undermine the entire structure of Copyright Law eventually... But, frankly, I believe many premises of Copyright Law have already been unalterably undermined by the electronic medium itself.

a. Working with Publishers. First to go would have to be the premise that publishers and users are and will continue to be adversaries. The real hope for change, at least for the research community, may lie in our recognition that publishers and users are not adversaries, or at a minimum that *we do not need to be adversaries* -- that we are in fact different pieces in the same puzzle. We are the different elements in an equation. We are all necessary and important to any solution. We can work together in ways that enlarge the return to all of us, not just financially, but in terms of the creation of knowledge, prestige, power, and recognition. We can recognize that our powers should not be used to bludgeon each other, but to support and encourage each other. We can verify right now where being adversarial has lead; and because we can reasonably predict that, carried into the electronic environment, it will lead to the same place again, but at a new and more costly level of expenditure, with new and more extravagant waste of resources, that is, the power of the electronic medium, we could decide instead not to be adversaries.

b. Mutual compromise. Neither side can be expected to unilaterally give up its leverage; trucks cannot go first; users will not be willing to give up fair use so long as they believe that publishers can demand nonnegotiable charges (and vice versa); but we could both agree to restrain ourselves (at least as an experiment) and in effect, walk away from the problems associated with fair use.[51] What would be the *quid pro quo* for giving up fair use? It is no more than a fair price. That is my answer to the question, "Will we need fair use to derive a fair price..." The electronic environment in and of itself will not obviate the need for fair use; it only gives us a window, an opportunity, an impetus to structure a different deal. If we can achieve the benefits of fair use without fair use, then we do not need fair use.

Georgia Harper
Office of General Counsel
University of Texas System
gharper@utsystem.edu

---

1 Thank you to John Garrett who provided encouragement and comment.

2 *American Geophysical Union v. Texaco Inc.*, 802 F. Supp. 1 (S.D.N.Y. 1992) (hereafter, "*Texaco*").

3 *American Geophysical Union v. Texaco Inc.*, No. 92-9341, 1994 WL 590563 (2nd Cir. Oct. 28, 1994) (hereinafter, "*Texaco II*").

4 In July, 1994, the Working Group on Intellectual Property Rights (the "Working Group"), a subcommittee of the Information Policy Committee of President Clinton's Information Infrastructure Task Force, released for comment a preliminary draft of its report, "Intellectual Property and the National Information Infrastructure" (the "Green Paper"). The Green Paper, responsive comments, testimony from the public hearings and other related documents have been made available by Professor Mary Brandt Jensen at the University of South Dakota's Gopher site (sunbird.usd.edu) under Academic Divisions/School of Law/NII Working Group on Intellectual Property. These papers should also be available through many university Gophers under Government Information directories. The government's Information Infrastructure Task Force bulletin board (iitf.doc.gov) also maintains copies of some of these documents.

5 I have come to better understand the Copyright Clearance Center's role since undertaking this exploration. As Joseph S. Alen states, "Successful, large-scale copyright licensing can be accomplished without `bright line' definitions of fair use. ... So long as the parties stay focussed on the objective of fairness, our experience suggests that the fair use doctrine stated in general terms without `bright-line' definitions need not pose an insuperable obstacle to successful licensing arrangements." Statement of Issues for the Fair Use Conference held by the Working Group, presented by the Copyright Clearance Center, Inc., Joseph S. Alen, President.

6 "The Congress shall have Power ... to promote the Progress of Science and useful Arts, by Securing for Limited Times to Authors and Inventors the exclusive Right to their

respective Writings and Discoveries." 1 U.S.C. Const. Art. I, Section 8, Clause 8; *Folsom v. Marsh*, 2 F.Cas. 342 (C.C.D. Mass. 1841) (No. 4901).

7 Edward Samuels, *The Public Domain in Copyright Law*. 41 J. Copr. Soc'y, 137, 145 (1993).

8 *Id.*

9 Perhaps it was acceptable to have an esoteric balancing act for determining fair use when only a few lawyers and judges needed to use it once every 30-40 years or so. Today, with the ubiquitous nature of trade in information, and with the future promising an increase in such trade on an order of magnitude, everyone (even elementary school children!) will need to know about this balancing test and be able to use it on a daily basis. The Green Paper recommends that education must be more widely undertaken as a means of protecting intellectual property rights (Green Paper at 126-127). Educating university faculty and staff about the subtleties of fair use is a daunting task; it is difficult to imagine teaching the concepts of fair use to children in a manner that will satisfy both users and publishers.

10 Section 107. Limitations on Exclusive Rights: Fair Use

> Notwithstanding the provisions of section 106, the fair use of a copyrighted work, including such use by reproduction in copies or phonorecords or by any other means specified by that section, for purposes such as criticism, comment, news reporting, teaching (including multiple copies for classroom use), scholarship, or research, is not an infringement of copyright. In determining whether the use made of a work in any particular case is a fair use the factors to be considered shall include
>
> (1) the purpose and character of the use, including whether such use is of a commercial nature or is for nonprofit educational purposes;
>
> (2) the nature of the copyrighted work;
>
> (3) the amount and substantiality of the portion used in relation to the copyrighted work as a whole; and
>
> (4) the effect of the use upon the potential market for or value of the copyrighted work.
>
> The fact that a work is unpublished shall not itself bar a finding of fair use if such finding is made upon consideration of all the above factors.

11 The recent case, *Campbell v. Acuff-Rose Music, Inc.*, 114 S. Ct. 1164, 1174 (1994), involved such a refusal: Campbell (2 Live Crew) asked for permission but Acuff-Rose refused to allow Campbell to create and market a rap parody of "Oh Pretty Woman." The Court found that the parody might well be a fair use (the Court remanded the case to the district court for further proceedings) and further indicated that Campbell's asking for permission and being denied could not be held against Campbell in the fair use analysis.

12 The Second Circuit noted before it undertook its analysis of fair use in *Texaco II* that the body of fair use law had principally concerned the copying described above (parody, criticism, etc.), and offered the opinion that the traditional analysis was of questionable applicability to mechanical (iterative) copying (the kind of copying described in this paragraph and at issue in *Texaco*). *Texaco II*, 1994 WL 590563 at 3-4.

13 The Second Circuit addressed the issue of the changing "market" that is the subject of the fourth factor analysis in *Texaco II*, 1994 WL 590563, at 18. It held that the recent creation and growth of a viable market for licensing photocopies now makes it appropriate to consider the loss of potential licensing revenues in evaluating the fourth factor. *Id.* Thus, to the extent the Copyright Clearance Center, for example, provides a relevant market, lost revenues from photocopying will weigh against the user in the fair use analysis.

Jacobs, J., dissenting, refutes the idea that the fourth factor should favor publishers: he notes that the Copyright Clearance Center has only modest coverage, passes through sometimes unreasonable fees and that publishers already charge enough to cover copies in initial institutional subscription prices. *Texaco II*, 1994 WL 590563, Jacobs, J., dissenting at 18. In essence Jacobs asserts that the system works fine as it is (ie., leave it alone); the majority asserts that it will also work fine without fair use. The success or failure of the majority's proposition may depend upon how quickly the elimination of fair use is followed by other steps that bring balance to the equation.

14 Note, however, the possibility that we are moving towards a "remuneration-only" model that reserves for the author the right to require a fee for the use of her work, but denies the author the right to withhold permission. Marci A. Hamilton describes the evidence of this trend in Marci A. Hamilton, *Artists May Have to Settle for Remuneration Alone*, The National Law Journal, Monday, October 31, 1994, pp. C29-C30 (hereafter, "Hamilton").

15 For example, authorship, ownership, terms upon which a work will be licensed, including range of uses and fees, and payment mechanisms may all be incorporated into an envelope that surrounds and accompanies electronic works. Collective rights organizations should be able to facilitate the transfer of rights in works that are not "equipped" with their own rights information.

16 *Texaco II*, 1994 WL 590563, at 3, citing *Harper & Row, Publishers, Inc. v. Nation Enterprises*, 471 U.S. 539, 549-50 (1985).

17 Robert L. (Bob) Oakley, *Re: Haworth Press Journals*, via email on the cni-copyright listserv, 4:18 pm, April 8, 1994; Don Berman, *Re: Haworth Press Journals*, via email on the cni-copyright listserv, 5:33 pm, April 11, 1994 (with additional comments regarding the relationship between fair use and the First Amendment); Mary Brandt Jensen, *Re: Copyright & Fair Use*, via email on the cni-copyright listserv, 3:26 pm, April 13, 1994; Buford Terrell, *Re: Copyright & Fair Use*, via email on the cni-copyright listserv, 4:07 pm, April 21, 1994.

18 Green Paper, p. 45 (an observation at the end of discussion of fair use that technology may obviate its necessity); *Texaco*, 802 F. Supp. at 23 - 25 and *Texaco II*, 1994 WL 590563 (the reach of fair use is commensurate with high transaction costs associated with asking for permission; as such costs decline, so should the scope of fair use); *See generally* Wendy J. Gordon, *Fair Use as Market Failure: A Structural and Economic Analysis of the Betamax Case and Its Predecessors*, 31 J. Copyright Soc'y 601 (1984).

19 *Texaco II's* majority and dissenting opinions are an excellent example of this phenomenon. The majority opinion essentially embraces the market failure theory as a justification for fair use: fair use only exists to meet the need that the market cannot efficiently provide, in this case socially beneficial research related access to copyright works. To the extent the market can efficiently provide such access, fair use should no longer be necessary.

The dissent states flatly, "I do not agree at all that a reasonable and customary use becomes unfair when the copyright holder develops a way to exact an additional price for the same product." Texaco, Jacobs, J. dissenting at 6-7. The dissent rejects the market failure theory as justification for fair use. What appears to the dissent as circular reasoning (illogic) is the core logic behind the market failure theory of the majority. These two points of view do not appear reconcilable.

20 Pamela Samuelson, quoted in Trotter Hardy, *Re: Constitution & Copyright*, via email on the cni-copyright listserv, 5:15 pm, October 15, 1993.

21 Compulsory licensing schemes could play some role with respect to works that are otherwise inaccessible, for example, where the copyright owner cannot be located. See Comments of Professor Mary Brandt Jensen on the Green Paper; John Garrett, *Re: Canadian System for Unlocatable Copyright Owners*, via email on the cni-copyright listserv, 4:42 pm,

October 3, 1994; John Garrett, *Re: Compulsory License*, via email on the cni-copyright listserv, 3:32 pm, October 4, 1994; Mary Brandt Jensen, *Re: Compulsory License*, via email on the cni-copyright listserv, 10:25 pm, October 5, 1994.

The Second Circuit suggested that if the parties in *Texaco II* are unable to resolve their dispute, the case may be "an appropriate case for exploration of the possibility of a court-imposed compulsory license." *Texaco II*, 1994 WL 590563 at fn 19. Also, *see generally* Hamilton.

22 *Texaco*, 802 F. Supp. 1; *Texaco II*, 1994 WL 590563. Numerous publishers and publishing associations sued Texaco alleging that its research library made infringing copies of articles from the plaintiffs' publications. Texaco circulated issues of plaintiffs' journals among Texaco's scientists who would request copies of those articles they wished to retain. Texaco defended, *inter alia*, on the basis that the copies were a fair use. By stipulation of the parties, the court considered only the fair use defense since the outcome on this issue could be dispositive of other issues in the case. The district court found that Texaco's copying was not a fair use and the appellate court affirmed "[t]hough not for precisely the same reasons," *Texaco II*, at 1.

23 But see Judge Jacob's strong dissent.

24 The reasoning of *Texaco* could not have been logically limited to the for-profit corporate environment because of the way the court reached its conclusion. Texaco lost the case largely on the basis of two facts: its *research* was done for profit and the court equated this fact with Texaco's *copying* being done for profit under the first fair use factor; and Texaco's unauthorized copying denied the plaintiffs revenues they would have received if Texaco had asked for permission to copy, thus tipping the fourth fair use factor in favor of the publishers. For a fuller discussion of the implications of this case for nonprofit research, see Georgia Harper, *Professional Fair Use After Texaco: Second Circuit Affirms Lower Court's Decision*, a publication of the Office of General Counsel, University of Texas System, available electronically at: http://gold.utsystem.edu/OGC/Intellectual_Property/cprtindx.htm (hereafter, "Harper").

The Second Circuit greatly clarified the relationship between for-profit status and commercial or non-commercial purposes under the first factor but it took a very narrow view of what constitutes research purposes. Overall the court's discussion of the first factor does little to alleviate the concerns of nonprofit research entities that the holding will be generalized to them. The court's discussion of the fourth factor provides an even stronger basis for extending the holding of *Texaco II* beyond its context, despite the court's insistence that the holding is limited to the specific facts of Texaco's copying: it strongly endorses the Copyright Clearance Center and the role it has played in the development of a viable market for permission to photocopy.

When the weight of the third factor is additionally against the user (articles being considered entire works), it remains to be seen whether courts following *Texaco II* will consider typical nonprofit research copying "an otherwise fair use," and give it special consideration under the fourth factor analysis. See *Williams & Wilkins v. United States*, 487 F.2d 1345 (Ct. Cl. 1973), *aff'd by an equally divided Court*, 420 U.S. 376 (1975); *Texaco*, 803 F. Supp. 1.

25 Additionally, as noted earlier, other aspects of fair use that are more critically affected by the requirement to obtain permission (parody, comment, criticism, news reporting) may not be affected at all by reduced transaction costs.

26 It is very easy to predict a healthy future for the fair use debate. The Working Group prescribed changes in Copyright Law described as "no more than minor clarification and amendment" (Green Paper at p. 8) to address issues raised by electronic media. Respondents, however, have characterized the Working Group's proposals as "dramatic expansion" of the rights of copyright owners (Comments of Professor Pamela Samuelson); enhancement of

the copyright owner's exclusive rights by adding "the exclusive right to control reading, viewing or listening to any work in digital form" (Comments of Professor Jessica Litman); and "[giving] the copyright holder truly monopolistic control over access to copyrighted work in the electronic environment" far beyond that necessary to encourage owners to make their works available electronically (Comments of Professor Mary Brandt Jensen). Many commentators took issue with the Working Group's assumption that fair use might have little future prospect in the electronic environment.

27 And in those situations still handled personally, how easy will it be for a teacher, a librarian, a doctor, a high school or elementary school student, an author or anyone else to determine what is fair use?

28 The Working Group noted that legitimate users of copyrighted works pay higher prices to cover infringing uses (Green Paper at p. 115). To the extent that fair use and interlibrary loan copies are perceived as infringing, this principle applies here as well; *Texaco II*, Jacobs, J., dissenting, notes as well that serials prices for institutional subscriptions are twice those for individuals. *Texaco II*, 1994 WL 590563, Jacobs, J. dissenting at 18. The "fuzzy" boundaries of fair use and interlibrary loan contribute to the perception of infringement: indeed, fuzzy boundaries give those on each side much reason to believe that the other side's activities near the boundary are actually "over" the boundary.

29 Nicola Daval, *Rising Prices Continue to Plague ARL Libraries*, ARL Newsletter, May, 1994, pp. 1-2. Serials purchased in ARL libraries over the period 1986-1993 were down 5% while expenditures were up 92%; monographs purchased were down 23% while expenditures for same were up 16%. *Id.* at 1.

30 Compare the similar costs of making "free" interlibrary loan copies. G. Jaia Barrett, *The Cost of Interlibrary Loan*, ARL Newsletter, January, 1993, pp. 1-2. "Extrapolating the results of the cost survey to these figures suggests that in 1991-92 all ARL libraries spent well over $71 million on interlibrary loan operations: $26 million on operations to borrow materials for local users and $45 million to loan materials to other libraries." *Id.* at 1.

31 If the amount users are already spending incorporates a charge for copies publishers believe are infringing, it is easy to understand why users mistrust publishers' motives and intentions: by demanding permission fees in addition to inflating subscription prices, they are insisting they have the right to charge *twice*, not just once, for fair use copies.

There is, nonetheless, room in the equation for charges for services that are above and beyond those provided in the print environment. For example, in many instances the speed and convenience of express document delivery services that pay copyright fees for electronic access (in the case of libraries, in accordance with Section 108 and/or the CONTU guidelines) is well worth the extra expense.

32 In all honesty, the early court cases were dealing with uses other than the kind we are considering here: they did not concern themselves with noncommercial iterative copying for research and educational purposes. If they had, they likely would have found such uses completely outside the scope of matters with which copyright concerned itself; they would not have even reached the issue of fair use. But technology has changed that theoretical result.

33 Their presentations appear in *Gateways, Gatekeepers and Roles in the Information Omniverse; Proceedings from the Third Symposium*, November 1993.

34 Indeed, in earlier publications I have commented that this premise was unacceptable since users should not be charged for copying that they have the right to do for free. See Georgia Harper, *Professionals' Fair Use of Journal Articles for Scholarship, Reference and Research*, a publication of the Office of General Counsel, University of Texas System, available electronically at:
http://gold.utsystem.edu/OGC/Intellectual_Property/cprtindx.htm

35 One contract required the library to include the following notice on each printed copy of an image from the database: "copying is prohibited." Since copying is not legally prohibited, what can be the purpose of such a statement other than an attempt by the database proprietor to affect the fair use rights of third parties, the library's patrons, using the library as its agent against them.

Arguably, a library may contract away its own right of fair use, but it can not contract away a third party's right of fair use; yet such provisions have the appearance of attempting to accomplish just that. (The contract discussed herein was the subject of a post by Jennifer Paustenbaugh, *Re: Meaning of Copyright Notice/Warning*, via email on the cni-copyright listserv, 6:48 pm, May 6, 1994.)

36 Indeed, trying to take such things into account may be fruitless in any event if it only means that the negotiations would have as a central feature the same dispute over the extent of fair use though posed as "what percentage discount should fair use equal?" Wouldn't publishers feel they had to charge more initially (or next time) to counter the inevitable fair use discount?

37 Pamela Samuelson and Bob Glushko make this point in their critique of Ted Nelson's proposal for a kind of national database called Xanadu. Pamela Samuelson and Bob Glushko, *Intellectual Property Rights for Digital Library and Hypertext Publishing Systems*, 6 Harv. J. L. & Tech. 237 (hereafter, "Samuelson").

38 The Green Paper at pp. 29-30. The Green Paper does not question this assumption as it might apply to ordinary reading of digital works and appears to presume that such use would not be a fair use.

39 Francis Dummer Fisher, *The Electronic Lumberyard and Builders' Rights*, Change, pp. 13-21, at 21, May/June 1989 (hereafter, "Fisher").

40 This is precisely what many of the comments to the Green Paper have suggested; without a corresponding expansion of fair use, the proposed changes will drastically alter the balance of rights between owners and users of copyright. For example, if the Working Group's suggestions for amending Copyright Law are enacted, free browsing and lending of electronically stored works will be eliminated, resulting in a tremendous burden upon Sections 107 and 108 for users' rights of access. These sections, however, are just too limited under even the most generous interpretations to accommodate the increased burden without clear, unambiguous, and substantial expansion. But rather than proposing an expanded role for fair use, the Green Paper evidences very little regard for the role of fair use in the future (Green Paper at p. 45).

On the other hand, the relentless nature of escalation makes it possible to see where this is going and to consider other ways to interact in the electronic environment. The idea of an exclusive rights regime moderated by an esoteric balancing act in favor of *some* public uses to *some* generally unknowable extent may have gone about as far as it can go.

41 The Internet itself is an example of a copyright culture of sorts that diverges in some important ways from our statutory regime. Those who participate seem to value their copyrights quite differently from those who do not. It is not true that participants "check their copyrights at the door," but they evidence little concern for who might be making copies of or displaying their posts. They probably would protest commercial exploitation of their contributions, but for the most part they appear to value discussion, sharing and the development of ideas, activities that clearly further progress of science and the arts, without reference to the incentive the law offers in exclusivity.

Similarly, negotiated agreements that side-step fair use can produce satisfying results as the steady growth of licensed databases acquired by our libraries indicates. I have, however, had at least one occasion to advise a department to refuse to license a database of images on terms that failed to meet even minimal needs of the user community.

42 There is an undeniable irony in the cries of the university community that science, technical and medical journals are overpriced: it is by many accounts the university system of faculty rewards and incentives that has helped to put certain publishers in control. The Report of the Association of American Universities' Task Force on Intellectual Property Rights in an Electronic Environment (April, 1994) (hereafter, "AAU/IP Report") recommends that the university community begin to take advantage of the opportunity the electronic environment offers it, take some control over its copyrights and better manage the process of scholarly publication.

43 The AAU/IP Report suggests that an alternative scholarly works database shared by university faculty, libraries and presses would assure the community access to precisely the kinds of materials threatened by spiraling prices. One member of the Task Force suggested that "[w]here scholars are writing primarily for other scholars, the process will arguably be managed directly by faculty involved and conducted outside the "money economy" of conventional publishing." Whether alternative distribution systems develop by conscious design or simply naturally evolve from practical use of the medium, it seems clear that there could be multiple "tiers" of scholarly publication, and with respect to the greater body of copyright works, multiple tiers of publication generally.

44 *See generally*, Colin Day, *The Economics of Electronic Publishing: Some Preliminary Thoughts*, from Gateways, Gatekeepers and Roles in the Information Omniverse; Proceedings from the Third Symposium, November 1993; AAU/IP Report.

Jean-Claude Guedon, in remarks before the 4th Symposium on Scholarly Publishing on the Electronic Networks (November 1994) suggested that since the public funds most research at one end of the research activity continuum and subsidizes libraries to purchase the results at the other end, scholarly publication and library functions could theoretically merge and eliminate the transaction that seems to interfere with the unity of an essentially public undertaking.

45 *Texaco II*, 1994 WL 590563 at 2.

46 Fisher, p. 18. "Charges for the right to re-use bits and pieces of expressions in new and unanticipated combinations may not only be unnecessary to promote the original creation, but may also dampen re-creations" because of disagreements over the value of the contribution. In one case, the author of the original piece may price the new use based on his idea of what the original was worth by itself; in another, he may price the new use based upon what the new work is worth instead of what was necessary to induce the creation of the original. In neither case are the original copyright owner and the new user likely to agree on the price. See also discussion of library preservation issues associated with long copyright terms: Mary Brandt Jensen, *Re: Term and Purpose of Copyright*, via email on the cni-copyright listserv, 12:04 pm, October 20, 1993; Mary Brandt Jensen, Trotter Hardy, Don Berman, *Re: Copyright & the Constitution*, via email on the cni-copyright listserv, October 26, 1993.

47 John Perry Barlow, *The Economy of Ideas: A Framework for Rethinking Patents and Copyrights in the Digital Age*, Wired, March 1994 (hereafter, "Barlow"). Barlow describes the fundamental problems we are encountering as we attempt to make our intellectual property laws stretch to apply to technologies that are likely to alter the calculus of human interaction more profoundly than any technology ever has and he concludes that the laws cannot be made to fit: "we simply don't know how to assure reliable payment for mental works ... [unfortunately] at a time when the human mind is replacing sunlight and mineral deposits as the principal source of new wealth." *Id.* at 86. He predicts that the increasing difficulty of enforcing our existing copyright laws in the electronic environment will eventually imperil the free exchange of ideas. *Id.*

48 Barlow, p. 128-129. Barlow describes a number of possible economic controls based on *relationship* rather than on *possession* (control over copies); the value of real-time performance, provision of service and support, mediating among users, and providing opportunities for direct interaction with authors.

49 The Green Paper recommends changing the law to make electronic distribution the equivalent of publication. This recommendation, like all the others the report has made thus far, favors the rights of copyright owners.

50 Similarly, *Texaco* and *Texaco II* seem to knock the legs out from under users with little consideration for the untenable position this will put them in with copyright owners able to charge for more uses *and* whatever price they demand. If the second step in this process were that subscription prices and permission fees began to drop as the volume of requests increased, the result would be encouraging, but the second step appears instead to be that users are reacting quickly to reestablish the lost balance, thus assuring a long and heated dispute over any move to a market-driven mechanism instead of fair use. Perhaps publishers are missing an opportunity here in the "off-balance" period. Perhaps, as well, this same opportunity is what the *Texaco II* court had in mind with its suggestion in footnote 19 that if the parties were unable to resolve their dispute, the case was appropriate for the imposition of a court-ordered compulsory license. *Texaco II*, 1994 WL 590563 at fn 19.

51 As Paul Robinson's automatic fortune cookie once opined, "No problem is so formidable that you can't just walk away from it." Via email on the cni-copyright listserv.

Access to Digital Objects: A Communications Law Perspective

Patrice A. Lyons, Esq.
Law Offices of Patrice Lyons

When developing systems for the management of copyright, patent, trade secret, mask work and other rights and interests in the national information infrastructure (NII), an important consideration is how to provide a legal environment that will maximally encourage the development of new products and services. While the so-called "intellectual property" aspects of digital communications have been discussed in various fora, and, in particular, the copyright law implications of access to computer formatted works, there has been little attention paid to the role and impact of communications law. Perhaps this is due to the recent struggles in Congress to pass communications legislation. However, from a business perspective, it is vital that a coherent legal approach to regulation of the communications marketplace be available, or put in place, or developed.

From the perspective of public interest in the development of information resources and ease of access to such information or material, it is useful to consider the application of the concept of fair use from a communications law vantage point. In light of current experience, it is evident that a different set of constructs than those currently understood under copyright may be relevant. This is the case today in the areas of broadcasting and cable television. For example, a subscriber to a cable service usually pays on a monthly basis for access to certain program offerings. A subscriber would usually not inform a cable system that he/she has determined that the system made a "fair use" of certain information content, and, therefore, does not intend to pay all of the monthly fee. The public interest in this situation might be represented through local franchise requirements that apply to the communications services provided by the cable system. There are also limits placed on the cable system by the regulations of the Federal Communications Commission, as well as rules governing provision of public access channels.

I am not suggesting that any or all of the current cable restrictions should be carried forward to all programming on the evolving NII; however, before deciding on the details of a fair use analysis for the NII, it is important to consider what the infrastructure will look like from a communications law perspective. This will most likely govern the decisions reached concerning permissible fair uses of any content. It may emerge that public access under communications law is a more appropriate way to frame the issue of accommodating the public interest rather than fair use of the underlying content. Therefore, my talk today will focus on what I view as fundamental issues in approaching the regulation of information flows from a communications law perspective. Once agreement is reached at this level, we will then be in a better position to consider how to accommodate the public interest in access to information resources.

Attempts have been made to pigeonhole new communications services into dated concepts such as "electronic publishing" or "video programming." Although these approaches were tried in the communications bills that Congress considered this year, I believe they were inadequate. Efforts were also made to adapt existing concepts of broadcasting, cable television, cable satellite programming, libraries and publishing to the world of digital communications. These are fragmentary approaches to a complex area. Exciting possibilities may be available commercially in the coming years which do not easily fit into the current communications law scheme. It is necessary to begin now the dialogue required to accommodate the dynamic new services that are under development. It would be especially helpful before introducing or reintroducing communications legislation in the next Congress for the Federal Communications Commission to undertake a careful evaluation of experiments underway on new capabilities.

There really is an issue when moving into a new regime about what the legal environment should be. These have been well developed for entities like cable systems, satellite carriers, telephone companies and broadcast stations; however, none of them map very well into the requirements for information service providers over global computer networks. A basic issue is separating out the various rights under copyright, patent, trade secret, trademark and other laws relating to content, from rights under communications law. Without a clear framework, these rights may overlap in ways that are confusing at best and obstructive at worst. In any event, the lack of clarity may delay entry of new business into the developing information infrastructure.

A useful model would be one in which an information service provider acts much like a bank today. While a bank provides certain financial services, there is generally limited liability with respect to the underlying transactions. For example, when you pay a bill with a check, and a bank pays the amount noted on the face of the check to the account of the organization designated, the bank is not usually required to go behind the information on the face of the check to verify its accuracy. At the other extreme, there may be instances where an information service provider will want to operate much like a broadcaster. In that case, the provider may assume certain responsibilities with respect to content.

A model of an information service provider that is currently being developed on an experimental basis is that of a repository containing digital objects. The repository may include computer programs which are used to access other digital objects, or it could provide access to them directly. We assume browsing and indexing services are available which may include more intelligent network capabilities. From a business perspective, a digital object as a "package" incorporating information in the form of a sequence of bits appears to be a useful concept to develop.

For commercial enterprise to take full advantage of the NII, it is helpful to separate out the need for clearance of copyrights and other rights and interests that may be claimed in connection with a given digital communication from the task of delivering packaged objects independent of their contents. For example, in the broadcast industry, retransmission consent is viewed as a separate, albeit connected level of authorization. There are similar provisions relating to cable programming under section 705 of the communications law. Various package delivery companies like UPS or Federal Express need not obtain permission from a copyright owner or other owners of rights in the content in order to move a physical package from one place to another. However, this is not the same as communication to the public, where there is a dual level of authorization required, one covered by the communications law applying to the program-carrying signal (this has come up recently in the context of NAFTA), and one applying to the public performance and/or display of any underlying works that may be subject to copyright.

An example where this dual level of authorization would be helpful arises in connection with the concept of access to repositories of information (which I assume contain digital objects). While there has been some reference to "information object" as an entity in a digital communication network, the notion of a digital object which incorporates the information in the form of a sequence of bits is a basic entity in the system. With proper authorization, one can always unwrap objects to obtain the information entities they contain. By analogy, one can talk about performance of an episode of an audiovisual work like MASH as an information object and the transmission program MASH as the package which contains the performance of the work. Television broadcasters, cable systems and other information service providers all have similar needs to deal with packages of information rather then the underlying works. Apart from the licensing of any rights and interests in the content under copyright or other bodies of law, digital objects, and the legal framework under communications law that governs access to such objects, should be addressed in this context.

There has been work going forward on the development of a frame of reference for locating and/or invoking digital communications services and objects on a computer network. In this context, a digital object is simply a set of sequences of bits, plus a unique identifier for the object called a "handle." Formally, a handle is just a unique string that identifies the object. A digital object may incorporate information or material in which copyright or other rights or interests are claimed, although this need not always be the case. There may also be rights associated with the digital object itself (and some digital objects may be considered as computer programs or computer databases).

Digital objects may be placed and retained for possible subsequent retrieval in a "repository." These may be operated in a variety of ways spanning the range from storage depot to bulletin boards to broadcast stations on the net. The digital storage system or repository may contain other related information and management systems, and provide users access to stored objects under some set of policies. The digital object has co-located with it in the repository an associated "properties record" which is a table or set of database entries that describe basic properties of the digital object. The properties record may contain entries such as the handle for that object, the originator of the object, the name of the object (if any), a description of any work or other information or material incorporated in the object, time and date of deposit, format information, and stated terms and conditions for access and usage of the object.

From a copyright perspective, it is important to stress that a handle identifies a fixation of a work in some digital format and not the work itself. For a given work, there may be several handles or unique identifiers assigned depending on the different versions, e.g., a work may be given a handle for Postscript, a second handle for the word perfect version, and a third handle for Group IV facsimile. There is also a concept of a "meta" handle or indirect handle. When a user supplies a meta handle to a repository, the digital object it gets back may contain all the handles for a given work rather than a particular fixation of the work. The repository itself has no deep knowledge of what the work is or even what the object contains; it treats all digital objects alike. In the case of a meta handle, it just happens that the object's contents can be interpreted as handles.

To take an example, if you put a computer program into a repository that knows about other digital objects, e.g., the program is based on or incorporates thousands of photographs of rocks landing on the planet Jupiter, the program may contain separate handles for each of the photographs that are only used internally. The information about each separate handle may be made available to anyone outside; however, the program may or may not let a user interact with the photographs in this way. The program as a whole would be invoked in the repository as a digital object using its own handle.

In dealing with a repository, there are at least three different modes of access that may be anticipated, although a given repository may provide several different types of service either separately or on an integrated basis:

(1) Here the repository assumes that the user knows what he/she wants and has already obtained a handle to get started. The user may supply the handle for a

particular word perfect version of Hamlet and get it back directly.

(2) The repository has some knowledge about content and is often able to retrieve specific elements stored. Generally, the repository operates like the first example, plus some mechanism for indexing or browsing, e.g., a user may want a particular version of Hamlet, but not know its handle; an index service could provide the handle information.

(3) A more complex repository may be viewed as an "expert system," a "knowledge-based system," or a computer program.

Whatever the actual label attached to the data, expertise, and mathematical equations in the repository, and, apart from the possible copyright, patent, or other legal claims in particular units of data or programs that may be embedded in the system, it is an operational system, consisting of various algorithms and pieces of data, that processes input and produces output. Generally, in such a repository, the output is not measured simply with reference to the information stored in the system, e.g., where one or more computer programs are stored in a repository, the rules or heuristics may be used to form inferences on a particular topic. It is possible that a repository may contain digital objects that fall into each of the three categories, particularly if the repository is of a distributed character.

Let us now get back to the legal underpinnings for a business strategy that might be developed. Conventional communications law focuses primarily on the unauthorized interception and further communication of a program-carrying signal or service. For example, section 325(a) of the Communications Act of 1934 states in part: ". . .nor shall any broadcasting station rebroadcast the program or any part thereof of another broadcasting station without the express authority of the originating station." The Federal Communications Commission has construed section 325(a) as requiring consent of the station whose signal is rebroadcast even in those cases where property rights in the program material may rest elsewhere.

The latest chapter in communications policy granting rights to broadcasters is the new section 325(b) of the 1992 Cable Act, which for the first time grants broadcast stations the right to withhold consent from carriage of their signals by cable systems. This is not a copyright right, but rather a communications right which is separate from any copyright claims in underlying works. As suggested in the legislative history of the 1992 Act: "Congress created a new communications right in the broadcaster's signal, completely separate from the programming contained in the signal. Congress made clear that copyright applies to the programming and is thus distinct from signal retransmission rights." In other words, there is a right at the "package" or program-carrying signal level.

Perhaps the most important section of the communications law that cuts across all delivery media (except broadcasting) is section 705. Section 705 precludes the interception and divulgence of radio and wire communications not generally available to the public. Section 705 was called into play in the on-line computer world in Telerate Systems, Inc. v. Caro, 689 F. Supp. 221 (S.D.N.Y 1988). Telerate, a provider of financial market data available through a dial-up service, sought a preliminary injunction against a company which had developed a computer hardware/software interface which allowed authorized Telerate subscribers to manipulate the Telerate data in an enhanced fashion. The court granted Telerate's preliminary injunction request on a variety of grounds, including breach of contract, copyright infringement, and theft of trade secrets.

In addition, the court, again in the context of a preliminary injunction motion, found that Telerate had demonstrated a high degree of likelihood of prevailing on the merits of its section 705 claim. The court found that there had been an interception of a transmission not intended for the public, and that there had been a "publication" of such transmission. In so finding, however, the court acknowledged that it had to create several legal fictions to reach its conclusion.

The problem with the Telerate case, however, is that, in fact, the subscribers had paid for the transmission of the data, but Telerate, through contract, was attempting to limit their use and manipulation of such data by limiting the hardware/software which could be utilized to massage the data. The court had to resort to "legal fictions" in order to bring within its jurisdiction the unauthorized use and manipulation of data after its transmission.

The acts of rebroadcast, or interception and divulgence, that are currently regulated for the broadcast and cable industries, fit uneasily as a basis for developing any business which relies on the digital communications arena. The provision and facilitation of access to repositories of computer programs or computer databases, or some combination thereof, will be a fundamental element in future business plans. There is a need to consider developing the communications law basis for access and use of digital objects that may be stored in repositories, whether the repositories are maintained by what are now labelled as publishers, libraries, broadcasters, cable systems, telephone companies, or others. Repositories may also be made available by corporations in the manufacturing sector; and the implications for flexible production practices hold great promise because of the need to share designs and other manufacturing information. It should even be possible for an individual to allow access to a personal repository of information under agreed terms and conditions, including free of charge if they wish.

The notion of access to perform stated operations on a sequence of bits is a potentially important new addition to the provision of communications services which appears to fit comfortably in the context of communications law. The rules governing such access should be articulated within the framework of communications law. Where computer programs are used not just at the point of reception to interpret bits and manifest whatever information or material may be incorporated therein, but at the point of origination as well as at various points in the communications path, there may be multiple actions that require authorization. Such authorization may often be provided in situations where there is no knowledge of the underlying content.

We are at an early stage of a convergence between computers and communications that portends a fundamental change in the way industry approaches the regulation of communications. Where computers and computer programs play an active role in the provision of communications services, these elements should be viewed as an integral part of the communications service as such for purposes of regulation under the communications law. For example, the service may consist in the provision of access on an interactive basis to repositories of digital objects that, when unwrapped, may be programs in themselves such as video game computer programs. The service may also include the transport of performances of such video game programs in the form of sets of sequences of bits. Programs used in the context of a communications service as such should fall within the ambit of the communications law, while any performance of a computer program embodied in a given communication would be subject to licensing under the copyright law, and, perhaps, other bodies of law.

Patrice Lyons
Law Offices of Patrice Lyons
Washington, DC
0003432266@mcimail.com

Virtual Publication and the Fair Use Concept

John Lawrence
Morningside College

I speak to you today--not as a theorist, or advocate of a particular interpretation of copyright--but as a fair use administrator. I represent a large, non-profit electronic communication enterprise that calls itself H-Net. I am providing an overview of what we do about copyright. In keeping with the "filling the pipeline and paying the piper" theme of the conference, I will also convey a sense of our economics. Finally, I point to some tensions we feel with the law. We hope, of course, to see them resolved amiably as we make the transition to a more fully electronic era in publication and scholarship, but we are also prepared to squabble our way to the future.

I. Profile of H-Net

H-Net is a group of moderated, academic discussion lists served by host computers at the Universities of Illinois-Chicago and at Michigan State.[1] In the world of list publication, most lists stand alone. H-Net differs in adopting a corporate model with executive officers, boards of directors, and uniform policies that serve a large number of lists simultaneously. There are advantages to this model in training, policy formation, relationships with book publishers, and in grant seeking.[2] There may be a long term advantage in our ability to generate revenue. Of that I say more later.

I am a list editor (or moderator) and the Chair of our copyright policy committee. My handout, "H-Net: A Brief Profile, October 1994" (Appendix I) mirrors us at this moment. Not evident in this static snapshot is the surging growth both of the lists and of subscriber numbers during our short history. In October of 1992 we did not exist at all. In October of 1993, we had twenty-one lists, three policy making officers, and 5000 subscribers. One year later we have twice as many lists and three times as many members. We now have more than a dozen elected executive officers, appointed policy makers like myself, and trainers who assist our moderators and run training workshops on electronic communication and list management.

Almost every activity of our organization is virtual. A majority of the officers, policy makers and list moderators have never seen each other; we only know one another's electronic personnae. Yet this has not prevented intensive communication and debates about the needs for a member ratified charter, for a set of officers and directors, for netwide copyright policies, etc. Given the infectious enthusiasm within our virtual organization, we can reasonably extrapolate total subscribers of at least twenty to twenty five thousand by this time next year.

II. The Stakes of H-Net in Fair Use

H-Net has a dual stake in developing and maintaining electronic fair use. We are obviously publishers (or at least virtual publishers) of more than one million messages per month. These messages range from conference announcements, to extended book reviews, bibliographies, course syllabi, detailed plans for or chapters from dissertations, calls for contributors, etc. We maintain searchable back files for our subscribers, a gopher for the whole world to come to, and are now beginning to develop a home page for the World Wide Web. From the copyright owner standpoint, we want users who read/download our material to be fair both with our list contributors and with the orientation and policy material that we create for our network. At this time,

EVERYTHING that we offer to our subscribers, including the gateway to our material, is free. Fair use to us as producer/publishers means that our users acknowledge the creators of materials that they take, do not alter them in ways that change their identity or quality, and do not attempt to independently or commercially exploit the material of H-Net or its contributors.

We also reproduce in limited degree the publications of others. Quotable, comment-worthy material comes to us increasingly from electronic sources. In the spirit of critically free, documented inquiry, we want to carry forward the fair use traditions of the print world--quoting without fear. We find the four use factors of Section 107 (quantity, purpose and nature of the use, the nature of the copyrighted work, and effect on markets) a reasonable way to think about what we do.

Our operational principles, worked out through months of online discussion, are reflected in "Working Policy: Copyright and Fair Use at H-Net." (Appendix II) First of all, we have tried to dispel some common mistakes we found in thinking about electronic property. Among pioneers of the lists, we found the belief that electronic publication in and of itself constituted a gift to the public domain. One of our lists even attempted to formalize this understanding by telling its subscribers that any message posted on the list immediately acquired a public domain copyright status. Those of us who had envisioned H-Net as a pre-print medium were alarmed. We wanted subscribers with ideas that they would generously share, but we hardly expected them to give them away on the spot! Another occasional practice in the early days of H-Net was the posting of full texts from articles by leading news sources such as the *New York Times*, *Washington Post*, *New Republic*. These articles had originally appeared at electronic news stands on the Internet or they had been keyboarded for e-publication by diligent list members. The few people who had actually read Section 107 of the Copyright Act of 1976 paid careful attention to "the effect on the market" criterion and reasonably concluded that, for example, posting a *NY Times* obituary on a figure important for a field, was a contribution to scholarly discussion that could hardly displace or even affect the *NY Times*' market for its news. As the issue matured in debate among ourselves, we reached consensus that the copyright holders, well equipped with attorneys for litigation, would not want to make that contribution to scholarship. Consequently, we scaled down the permissibility of fair use limits in line with "10. Posting from other Sources." (Appendix II) Even if right philosophically, we were not confident that we could mount the needed legal protection in the face of corporate hostility.

Summarizing where we stand, one can say that our views and policy statements are cautiously mainstream. But that hardly protects us from problems. We live in a world where others, even in the academic world, do not share or respect our understandings. And the conditions under which we publish material make it difficult for us to achieve uniform compliance with our own principles. I will illustrate with some examples and problem areas.

Listnapping

A central principle in our policy statement is the retention of author and network rights. (See the Charter provisions and Section I, "Author Rights" in Appendix II.) Through friendly informants, we recently discovered that some of our lists were being echoed in the gopher of a university where we had individual subscribers. No acknowledgment was made within the gopher that an H-Net list was the source of the material. This behavior persisted after we complained about it. We felt that we had to discontinue all list subscriptions at that university until the matter was resolved. But why does mirroring our list within someone else's gopher matter--particularly if we are currently giving our product away? Obviously there is the academic credit issue addressed in "1. AUTHOR RIGHTS." (Appendix II) There are also the long range economic implications. If we decide that we must charge for individual subscriptions to our network, it will be important to retain the principle of individual subscribership. That we will need more money than we have now will become clear when I describe our financial resources.

List subscription economics

How do we manage to meet the costs of operating our lists? Several dozen lists translates into a lot of training in both the technical and in the editorial side of a moderated list. Millions of messages per month to subscribers represent a lot of computer power and error messages. Subscription maintenance and merely reading error reports on misdirected or rejected messages is a significant task for each list. Where is the money to pay for the most drudgery filled tasks? Policy making is time consuming, particularly when debates are keystroked. Our main economic strategy to date has been what I call carpal tunnel equity--we do the work ourselves, and then we don't pay ourselves.

Such funds as we currently have for salaries come to us principally through grants. NEH has been our best benefactor to date. Much smaller contributions have been made by some scholarly associations that have developed an affinity for our lists. Their funds and grants have provided minimal, hourly pay for persons who supervise moderator training or offer technical support in working with list maintenance, gophers, file servers. They have also provided modest stipends for persons who conduct summer training institutes for NEH Seminar participants. Outside financial support has also permitted some gatherings of H-net staff members.

Grant support does not cover any salaries for executive management or editorial work on the lists. Fortunately some universities have donated time from employees for H-net work by by formally recognizing our tasks in their job descriptions. The capital portion of our enterprise has come to us from the universities who have provided the listservers. They have rightly anticipated that electronics is the future of scholarly communication. Such dependencies are always a fragile base on which to build the future.

Advertising is something that we have often discussed as a potential source of revenue, but that topic is cloudy from a legal standpoint and unusually contentious on the Internet, particularly for a non-profit organization. When we talk about individual list subscribership charges, we are also warned that we might violate the spirit of the Internet. (The spirit of Stewart Brand's "Information wants to be free" often expresses itself.) We are also reminded that many of our subscribers are graduate students and that a $35 to $50 fee would mean losing many of them. Older scholars who could afford to pay are less facile with the technology, less inclined to be interested in electronic communication. So, a dilemma. Those who can pay are not so interested and capable of participating in an electronic network; and those more interested and capable do not have the will or means to pay.

Another source of income could be the professional associations. We can and already are performing important functions in helping some of them form conference programs, posting announcements, publishing book reviews. But so many of their members are averse to or ignorant of the Internet that they cannot yet take the gamble of shifting their paper functions (now accomplished by expensive mailings and document printing) to an electronic organization.

The university or college as a source of income is similarly unpromising at this time. Those potential sources seem preoccupied with the costs of providing internet service within their own institutions. After paying their annual fee to the Internet and their leased line charges for telecommunications to a hub site, they do not believe that they have additional resources left to pay an outside organization for access to scholarly discussion--especially if there is not a faction of mature scholars within their institution who insist that electronic communication is the future.

The upshot of this is that even though we have many of the producer-owner perspectives on fair use issues, we do not have a product that we can market at this time except by giving it away. Can we pay other producers of material for material that we might relay to our subscribers? We would like to, but we must first make the passage to better times by developing steady revenues.

I have paid detailed attention to our economic profile to give you a sense of the mindset with which we approach the user side of the fair use equation. Since we give away what we have and are provably non-profit, our feelings about the fair use privilege are probably more assertive than the prudent, print based policy that we have adopted.

III. Some Problems with the Administration of Fair Use in the Online Environment

Administrative Slippage

Electronic lists and electronic journals have created a new environment for copyright that I will call "distributed gatekeeping." In the past, scholarly publication has remained close to presses that worked at a slow pace and employed print professionals. Production times of several years are still not unusual in the print world. Copyright decisions can be made in a leisurely way by consulting legal counsel to the press. Academic presses tend toward caution and have maintained a good record of avoiding conflicts with copyright owners. In fact, since they are owners and employees themselves with some tangible assets to protect, their conservatism is very understandable.

The new electronic environment moves at a much faster pace and employs many list moderators (e.g., editors) who know, prior to their training by us, little to nothing about copyright. Many of our list moderators are graduate students. They do not have assets to protect. The net is not a place with physical equipment; it is not a paying job. The "owners" (universities with listservers) may be thousands of miles distant from the moderators. The time between submission and publication is sometimes a few minutes. Legal counsel is a remote possibility for most list moderators.

Although we seek to train and supervise our list moderators, it is not unusual to see a copyright/fair use mistake. By that, I mean incidents such as the following, which occurred either within our group of lists or in others that I occasionally browse in:

- Posting material obtained from other e-publications without permission or acknowledgement;
- Publishing in its entirety copyrighted pieces obtained from electronic newsstands;
- Publishing bibliographies derived from metered use services like Dialog;
- Publishing substantial segments of material translated from freshly published foreign books--without permission of the copyright holder.

Within our group of lists, such variations are ephemeral because we are conscientious about reigning them in and clarifying policy for moderators as quickly as someone spots it. That in turn means that moderators will be more cautious and ask first if they are faced with a future copyright decision. So, while we can't be perfect, we can maintain a pattern that we are comfortable with.

Some Tensions with the Law and With Our Own Policies

Many critical commentators on the *Green Paper* of the NII have referred to the excessive desire for control. It appears that some copyright owner lobbies would like to bypass the traditional fair use criteria and flatly equate any reproduction at all with harmful infringement. At the same time, the moderators that I work with cannot understand why we cannot have a more liberal interpretation of the fair use reproduction right in the electronic environment. They cannot see how the publication of ephemeral material can adversely affect the interests of those who produce. I have taken an attitude survey that demonstrates this conclusively. The message is, "Hey, get people who make laws to loosen up on us! We're not hurting anyone." This, of course, is an easy argument to use if you don't know how copyright legislation is actually made.

But I cannot give a philosophically convincing answer when someone wants to reproduce a brief article that they fetched from an electronic newsstand. Neither is the single instance of unauthorized reproduction harmful nor is a pattern of occasional reproductions, providing that they are integrated into the context of discipline-related commentary on the subject of the article. I am reduced to saying, in these arguments, that those companies have lawyers who would be opposed to the reproduction of their material without their permission--and they do not give permission in a timely manner that fits the objectives of contemporaneous discussion of an event. So ultimately the argument is that it's more important to avoid the threat of litigation than it is to be right about an issue in free speech.

I think that this is an important area for negotiation, perhaps for some licenses related to certain kinds of electronic publication and duplication. This in turn will require that we have some means to pay, if it comes to that.

I look forward to those debates as we try to help our electronic media mature and hope that we will find plenty of allies who believe, as we do, that documented electronic discussion is one of the important ways to advance the arts and sciences of our republic.

---

[1] See ARL's *Directory of...Academic Discussion Lists*, May 1994. At that time, 1785 lists were identified.

[2] The conception of H-Net is largely that of its energetic current president, Professor Richard Jensen of the History Department at the University of Illinois-Chicago.

Appendix I **H-Net: A Brief profile, October, 1994**

[adapted from "H-Net: Humanities Online, October 24, 1994"]

GOALS. The goals of H-NET lists are to enable scholars to easily communicate current research and teaching interests; to discuss new approaches, methods and tools of analysis; to share information on electronic databases; and to test new ideas and share comments on current historiography. Each list is especially interested in methods of teaching in diverse settings. The lists feature dialogues in the discipline. They publish book reviews, job announcements, syllabi, course outlines, class handouts, bibliographies, listings of new sources, guides to online library catalogs and archives, and reports on new software, datasets and cd-roms. Subscribers write in with questions, comments, and reports, and sometimes with mini-essays of a page or two. Currently our lists have over 16,000 subscribers in 54 countries. All lists are moderated, some with as many as four or five moderators. Each message passes through the hands of at least one moderator before being posted to the list. Lists post, on average, 15-60 messages per week. This translates into thousands of editorial decisions during a month's time. Dozens--if not hundreds--of those decisions will involve discretion with regard to a copyright issue.--John Lawrence, Co-Moderator of H-PCAACA & Chair of H-Copy

H-Net Lists in Operation:

1. H-Albion British and Irish history
2. H-AmStdy American Studies
3. H-AntiS Antisemitism
4. H-Asia Asian history
5. H-CivWar US Civil War history
6. H-Demog demographic history
7. H-Diplo diplomatic, international affairs
8. H-Ethnic ethnic & immigration history
9. H-Film scholarly studies & uses of media
10. H-German German history
11. H-Grad for graduate students only
12. H-Ideas intellectual history
13. H-Italy Italian history and culture
14. H-Judaic Judaica, Jewish History
15. H-Labor labor history
16. H-LatAm Latin American history
17. H-Law legal and constitutional history
18. H-Pol US political history
19. H-PCAACA Popular Culture & American Culture Assoc
20. H-Rhetor history of rhetoric & communications
21. H-Rural rural and agricultural history
22. H-Russia Russian history
23. H-SHGAPE US Gilded Age & Progressive Era
24. H-South US South
25. H-State welfare state
26. H-Teach teaching college history
27. H-Urban urban history
28. H-West US West, frontiers
29. H-Women women's history
30. HOLOCAUS Holocaust studies
31. IEAHCnet colonial; 17-18 century Americas
32. H-Business business history
33. DATABASES design & management of historical

34. EconHist economic history
35. ECONHIST.TEACH teaching economic history
36. EconHist.Macro macroeconomic history, business cycles
37. H-High-S teaching high school history/social studies
38. H-Mac Macintosh users
39. H-MMedia high tech teaching; multimedia; cd-rom
40. H-Survey teaching US Survey
41. H-W-Civ teaching Western Civ
42. H-World World History & world survey texts
43. HABSBURG@purccvm Austro-Hungarian Empire (Planning stage for fall 1994)
44. H-Africa African History
45. H-Canada Canadian studies
46. H-CLC comparative literature & computing
47. H-France French History
48. H-Japan Japanese history & culture
49. H-Local state and local history & museums
50. H-NZ-OZ New Zealand & Australian history
51. H-T-Amst teaching American Studies
52. H-War military history

H-Net Gophers:
try the H-NET gopher at U of Illinois-Chicago
look under "researcher"/ "history" / "H-Net"

Appendix II: Working Policy: Copyright and Fair Use at H-Net

[The following text is a working document that is used in orientation of list members and moderators to copyright practices. It is also used as a point of reference in issues that come up with particular cases.]

H-NET STATEMENT ON AUTHORS RIGHTS/FAIR USE
[This material is for circulation among list editors and subscribers.]

Welcome to H-Net. You have become part of a significant electronic publishing enterprise. As a contributor to your list, you are an author and your list moderator is an editor. H-Net wants to respect the rights of participants by operating within a framework that is consistent with norms of fairness in scholarship and with laws defining intellectual property rights. The Charter of H-Net, ratified in 1994, contains two important provisions that you should be aware of. We quote from Sections G and H.

> G. H-Net respects the copyrights of authors whose material is posted on its lists and/or stored in its logs, fileservers, and gopher. Authors who post items to H-Net lists convey to H-Net only the right to electronically reproduce their work on H-Net lists and in H-Net files.
>
> H. H-Net owns the name of each subject-area list, its roster of subscribers, its on-line files, and its gopher and related files. All funds raised by advertisements and fees charged by the subject-area lists belong to H-Net and are under the control of the treasurer. H-Net's assertion of ownership is meant only to protect the rights of H-Net and shall not infringe on the copyrights of authors regarding any files or documents they may have made available to H-Net.

Stated in slightly different language, we emphasize the following:

1. AUTHOR RIGHTS. Scholars are usually much more concerned about author's rights than with copyright. Authorial rights are the credits the academic community pays to the originator or developer of an idea. These credits are bestowed through citations, notes and bibliographies. The stock of a person's academic credit comprises a major component of the curriculum vitae on which academic jobs, promotions, fellowships, etc. depend. It is a very grave offense against the academic community to unfairly appropriate another person's authorship rights. It is plagiarism. H-NET is committed to protecting the authorial rights of its contributors.

2. PLAGIARISM. H-NET will not tolerate any infringement of your authorial rights. No plagiarism. Citations are just as essential to posting with us as they are in journals or books.

3. RETENTION OF COPYRIGHT. Contributors do not lose copyright rights by publishing at H-Net. H-NET does not ask for the power to authorize a third party to distribute an item. And you may, if you choose, also publish your work elsewhere.

We regard H-Net as a "virtual print medium" that can carry the intellectual authority and status of any other scholarly publishing medium. Under the U.S. copyright law, your writings in electronic space enjoy copyright status, even if not registered--and even if they contain no copyright notice. To preserve your identity as an author, we urge you to clearly identify yourself and your affiliation when you make a submission. It is common practice on the net to provide this full identification at the end of a contribution.

4. YOU BECOME A PART OF OUR HISTORY. When you submit a comment on a posting or a message to your list, it then becomes a part of our log--the recorded transactions of the list for calendar periods. The logs can be searched by index commands and individual contributions can be retrieved by that means. In some cases, where a particular contribution is repeatedly sought by subscribers, it will be placed on the file server or at our gopher site <gopher.uic.edu>, where it can be retrieved by individual file name. If an individual wishes to have a file deleted from the file- or gopher server, we will honor that request. The original posting will remain embedded in the historical log of transactions for the list.

5. PUBLIC DOMAIN. An item in the public domain has no copyright. That means, anyone can reprint it without permission or fee or attribution. However, you should take note of the fact that very little of what is on the electronic networks is really in the public domain. Copyrighted items frequently reappear with their copyright notice stripped off. The lack of a copyright notice in a list posting or a file's presence in a gopher or in an anonymous ftp server does NOT mean that the text is in the public domain. Nor does the presence of a permission statement allowing further copying and redistribution nullify the author's copyright in the text.

6. QUOTING, REPOSTING, AND FAIR USE ON H-NET. The principle of fair use permits a scholar to reproduce portions of a copyrighted text, WITHOUT PERMISSION OF THE COPYRIGHT OWNER--for the purpose of criticism, scholarship and comment.

Mere convenience or saving the reader the cost of purchasing the original book or article is not sanctioned by fair use. And fair use does not permit H-NET to reprint textbook or encyclopedia materials except for the discussion purposes mentioned above.

Copyright law contains no statutory definition of how much use or reproduction is permissible. There is no pertinent case law for the electronic scholarly environment and no lawsuits at the moment of this writing. Litigation and case law for print materials provide only limited guidance in this area. The Congress and the courts have not addressed the question of fair use in the electronic world. They can be expected to develop new legislation or regulatory guidelines that will affect what we do.

How then proceed? We make these assumptions and recommendations.

7. MATERIALS WITH COMMERCIAL POTENTIAL. Authors who post their material on H-NET are typically not concerned about financial losses from the piracy of their work. Given the ease with which your work can be reproduced by others, we recommend that if you plan to sell an essay to a popular magazine, do not publish it here. But in saying this, H-NET is NOT asking that you assign any of your rights to it. We ask only for a very limited right of publication and storage.

8. H-NET created materials. H-NET is creating its own guides to on-line sources and techniques. These may be freely reused by scholars in an academic setting, provided credit is given to H-NET for authoring them.

9. BEING QUOTED. Assume that you will be quoted and reposted during the discussion of your ideas.

10. QUOTING. In order to maintain authorial rights, items on on H-NET should be cited properly, just as you would in writing for a print medium. When doing so, acknowledge your sources within parentheses. Keep your quoting within limits. We recommend that the citation give the name of the author, the name of the list, the subject line, and the date.

10. POSTING FROM OTHER SOURCES. Entire articles bearing copyright notices are now floating at numerous locations in electronic space. They are easy to trap and transfer to another location such as your list at H-Net. Please do NOT reprint an entire newspaper or magazine story. You may quote extensively from such a story if the main purpose of your quoting is to add new commentary or criticism.

FINAL THOUGHTS

Copyright law and fair use are notoriously discretionary. If you have followed the cases in court, they are often decided at Appelate or Supreme Court levels by one-vote margins. The decisions are probably more like art criticism than auditing. We ask you to be patient with these uncertainties and help to maintain a demeanor that does not invite hostile attention from scholars or publishing enterprises who feel that we have abused their rights.

John Lawrence, Chair of H-Copy at H-Net, Professor of Philosophy, Morningside College, Sioux City, IA 51106-6400, ac712-274-5310 <JSL1@chief.morningside.edu>

Project SCAN

Sandra Whisler
University of California Press

University of California Partners Seek Trailblazers for the Electronic Frontier

Would you like to help shape the electronic future of humanities scholarship? You can do so the next time you sit at your keyboard, by exploring SCAN--Scholarship from CAlifornia on the Net. SCAN is a pilot project to facilitate broad scholarly access to humanities journals and monographs by publication on the Internet. This project is a collaboration among the University of California Press, the University Libraries at Berkeley, Irvine, and Los Angeles, and the Division of Library Automation of the Office of the President. It draws together the resources of the University of California community to harness electronic technologies in support of new methods of scholarly communication in teaching, learning, and research. Because the goal of SCAN is to create a viable electronic publishing and research model, the SCAN partners are encouraging librarians, faculty, researchers, and students to help test and enhance the pilot project.

In its pilot phase, SCAN represents an early experiment to develop an economically viable publishing model for humanities scholarship that integrates electronic publishing, library access, and scholarly use. Initially, the SCAN partners have created a prototype electronic edition of an existing print journal, *Nineteenth-Century Literature*, to test networked access from remote and local workstations, ease of use, searching tools, and cost recovery mechanisms. To encourage widespread use and feedback, the current and recent back issues of *Nineteenth-Century Literature - Electronic Edition (NCL-E)* are available free of charge on the gopher server of the Library at the University of California at Berkeley.

The *NCL-E* files can be reached by the following gopher path: at the prompt, use gopher to connect to infolib.lib.berkeley.edu (make sure your settings indicate port 70 and gopher+ [Gopher Plus] server.) Once you have reached infolib through gopherspace, select menu items: Electronic Journals, Books, Indexes and Other Sources; Journals; Nineteenth-Century Literature.

Nineteenth-Century Literature - Electronic Edition features full texts of the current year and the past three years of the journal, including tables of contents, all articles, books reviews, notes, and descriptive lists of contributors. New issues will be added as they are released. To facilitate the broadest possible use, the articles are formatted in two different ways: text-only version (ASCII), and Rich Text Format (Microsoft RTF). The text-only versions of the articles are included in a WAIS index to facilitate limited on-line browsing. A simple command from the *NCL-E* gopher menu allows you to use keywords, such as an author's name or a particular term, to search across the entire on-line collection, providing paragraph-by-paragraph views of the search hits. These hits can be used to locate the abstract of the article, which can then be read on-screen to confirm interest in the selection.

In order to view the full, formatted text, you will need to download or print the file. The downloaded files can be manipulated using a variety of standard word-processing programs, including all versions of Microsoft Word, newer versions of WordPerfect, and the Write application of Windows.

A brief set of instructions is included below. In addition to complete instructions for using the search and formatting features, the *NCL-E* gopher menu contains a questionnaire soliciting feedback and suggestions for how the electronic journal prototype can be further developed to meet the needs of scholars. We encourage you to fill out and return this questionnaire.

The University of California partners are currently seeking funding to expand the pilot project to include additional journals, monographs, and primary source materials in literary studies, classics, and history. They envision SCAN as a base of scholarship enhanced with authoring and document-preparation tools and sophisticated electronic-navigation tools that will enable scholars working at individual workstations to access a database from which pieces can be combined and repackaged to meet a variety of specialized research, teaching, and learning needs.

With SCAN, the University of California partners are beginning the development of a sustainable model for the creation, dissemination, and utilization of humanities scholarship that both offers an economically viable transition to electronic communication and also supports the University's mission of providing widespread public access to the research results achieved by its scholars.

Nineteenth-Century Literature
ELECTRONIC EDITION

A. Overview

This document provides instructions for *Nineteenth-Century Literature Electronic Edition (NCL-E)*. Because there are many different versions of gopher client and server software, the descriptions contained here cannot address all the needs of all users. Instead, we offer helpful guidelines for using this electronic product.

B. NCL Menu Structure and File Locations

1. *NCL-E* currently includes files for Volumes 46-49:2
2. To access ASCII files
   a. Go to *NCL-E* gopher menu
   b. The top menu item will let you search all the files (see below)
      • text-only (ASCII) versions of the articles are included
      • the full ASCII files are not available separately
3. To access Rich Text Format (Microsoft RTF) files
   a. Look for them by volume and issue number
   b. Download the file (see below)
   c. On your computer, open your word processor FIRST open the RTF file from inside your word processor

C. Searching *NCL-E*

1. If you know the volume and issues you want
   a. Select it from the top-level *NCL-E* gopher menu
2. If you want to conduct a keyword search
   a. Go to NCL-E menu
   b. Choose "Search Index to *Nineteenth-Century Literature*"

c. Dialog box will appear asking for words for which to search.

Keep the following in mind:

- You may enter more than one word at a time, but independent searches will be done
- Search command is NOT case-sensitive
- You cannot use boolean search qualifiers such as AND or OR to limit searches

D. Downloading Articles

1. Use hits information to identify the RTF files you want
2. To download articles from the gopher server
   a. Select from menu
   b. Enter file name
   c. File will be placed in home account under filename
   d. You may need to move the file from a server to your own computer. (If more details are needed, consult your local system administrator or technical support staff.)

E. Questions and Suggestions

NCL-E and this document are currently in development. We encourage you to complete the on-line user questionnaire that is available from the main *NCL-E* menu. We welcome feedback to the following addresses:

via e-mail: journal@garnet.berkeley.edu
via post: University of California Press
Journals Division
2120 Berkeley Way
Berkeley, CA 94720

ELECTRONIC SURVEY

Press: American Psychiatric Press, Inc.

Project Title: ***Project I:*** American Psychiatric Electronic Library
Project II: Electronic DSM-IV

Project Description: ***Project I:*** It includes the major English language psychiatric journals and textbooks. The program features a Hypertext edition of the Diagnostic and Statistical Manual of Mental Disorders, Fourth Edition, with the library. From any word, phrase, code, or reference, users can go electronically to the related material in any of the books or journals selected.

Project II: This project contains every word from the DSM-IV. The Electronic DSM-IV is a fully searchable disk format. A traditional search window allows you to search on a single word, and/or words, and phrases or symptoms. It allows you to bring up the table of contents in three ways, alphabetical, numerical, and an outline of the classification.

Project Format: ***Project I:*** CD-ROM
Project II: Floppy disk

Technical Specifications: ***Project I:*** American Psychiatric Electronic Library is available in both IBM-PC Windows 3.1 and Apple Macintosh.

Project II: Designed to be installed in hard drives of both desktop and laptop computers. The computer system should have 640K and about 6MG of hard disk space available. The DOS version will run with DOS 2.1 or later.

Contact Person: Mark Bloom

Phone Number: 202-682-6213

Press: The University of California Press

Project Title: Project SCAN (Scholarship from California on the Net)

Project Description: Project SCAN offers an electronic version of first humanities journals and then monographs over the Internet, working in cooperation with the UCBerkeley Library. The first journals will be *Nineteenth Century Literature* and *Classical Antiquity*. The project will concentrate on the development of SGML coding and on cost-recovery experiments and mechanisms.

Project Format: On-Line access

Technical Specifications: It will be providing both ASCII (for searching) and formatted files. Will be available by FTP-access with passwords required.

Contact Person: Sandra M. Whisler, Director, Journals Division

Phone Number: 510-642-4247

E-Mail Address: smw@garnet.berkeley.edu

Press: The University of Chicago Press

Project Title: *The Electronic Word: Democracy, Technology, and the Arts* by Richard A. Lanham, A Chicago Expanded Book

Project Description: The personal computer has revolutionized the structure of communication, concealing beneath its astonishing versatility and consumer appeal a bold transition to electronic, postmodern culture. Unchecked by the inherent limitations of conventional print, digitized text has introduced a radically new medium of expression. Interactive, volatile, mixing word and image, the electronic word challenges all our assumptions about artistic, educational, and political discourse.

The Electronic Word, Richard Lanham's collection of witty, provocative, and engaging essays, explores this challenge. With hope and enthusiasm, Lanham surveys the effects of electronic text on the arts and letters and how they might be taught in a newly democratized society.

This hypertext edition allows readers to move freely through the text, marking "pages," annotating passages, searching for words, and immediately accessing annotations, which have been enhanced for this edition. In a special prefatory essay, Lanham introduces the features of this electronic edition and gives a vividly applied critique of this dynamic new medium.

Project Format: Shipped on two 1.4MB floppy disks for installation on a local hard drive.

Technical Specifications: Any Macintosh computer with at least 2MB of RAM and a hard disk drive (4MB of RAM are recommended). System software 6.0.7, and HyperCard 2.1 or HyperCard Player 2.1 (or later versions) are required.

Contact Person: Bruce Barton

Phone Number: 312-702-7651

E-Mail Address: bbarton@press.uchicago.edu

Press: University Press of Colorado

Project Title: No title

Project Description: The University Press of Colorado publishes eight journals, with subscriptions ranging from as low as 250 to a high of 2,500. Our project goal is to make all our journals available on the Internet. The journals will be available to subscribers via a server located in the University of Colorado Library system.

Project Format: At first, the journals will be offered concurrently in print and in electronic formats, but our plan calls for the eventual discontinuance of the print format.

Technical Specifications: Not yet determined

Contact Person: Luther Wilson, Director

Phone Number: 303-530-5337

E-Mail: lwilson@spot.colorado.edu

Press: Columbia University Press

Project Title: Full-Text, Networked, Reference Collections

Project Description: Since 1991, Columbia University Press, in cooperation with Columbia University Academic Information Systems, has delivered reference materials over the campus network to the Columbia community. Texts available either currently or in the near term include the Concise Columbia Electronic Encyclopedia (updated monthly), The Columbia Grangers World of Poetry, The Columbia Electronic Encyclopedia, The Columbia Dictionary of Quotations, The Columbia Guide to Standard American English and The Columbia Chronicles of American Life.

Project Format: On-line.

Technical Specifications: Servers are on distributed Unix platforms. Clients currently include the ColumbiaNet campus information system and HTML browsers (Mosaic, Lynx, etc). Network transport is standard Internet (TCP/IP) with either a "Kerberos"-style or address-screening security layer. Search and presentation software and data formats have ranged from locally-developed, to informal Internet standards (WAIS, HTML), to high-performance commercial engines (OpenText PAT).

Contact Persons: David Millman, Coordinator of Research & Development, Academic Info Systems
Hal Dalby, Director of Marketing for Columbia University Press

Phone Number: Millman's phone number is: 212-854-4284
Bollini's phone number is: 212-666-1000, ext. 7128

E-Mail Address: Millman's e-mail address is: dsm@columbia.edu
Bollini's e-mail address is: ub2@columbia.edu

Press: Georgetown University Press

Project Title: The Knowledge/Power Project

Project Description: The Project aims at creating on the Internet a database of research on public policy issues. Starting with foundation support, the database expects to offer information on a subscription basis and thereby to become self-sustaining within four years. The Brookings Institution and Rand are expected to take part in the project.

Project Format: The project expects its social-scientific studies to be accessed via Internet. It is possible that ancillary products (perhaps compact discs) will be spun off from Knowledge/Power.

Technical Specifications: A selection of search-engine software is currently underway.

Contact Person: John Samples, Director

Phone Number: 202-687-5912

E-Mail Address: samplesj@guvax.acc.georgetown.edu

Press: Georgia State University Business Press

Project Title: Directory of Foreign Manufacturers in the US, 5th ed.

Project Description: A compilation of data and indexes on U.S. subsidiaries of foreign and international manufacturing firms and their products; also contains analysis of global patterns of manufacturing and distribution demographics.

Project Format: floppy disk

Technical Specifications: R-Base 5000

Contact Person: Gerald Garrett or Cary Bynum

Phone Number: 404-651-4253

E-Mail Address: bpurcb@gsusgi2.gsu.edu

Press: Indiana University Press

Project Title: MOTIF-INDEX OF FOLK-LITERATURE
by Stith Thompson

Project Description: The project is a classification of Narrative elements in folk tales, ballads, myths, fables, mediaeval romances, exampla, fabliaux, jest-books, and local legends in six volumes. Stith Thompson's *Motif-Index* remains the single most essential reference work in the field of folklore worldwide. Users will be able to instantly search all six volumes.

Project Format: CD-ROM

Technical Specifications: The *Motif-Index* is bundled with the powerful search-and-retrieval software Folio-Views. Each cross-reference in the *Motif-Index* is linked to the main entry for the item using Views Hypertext Links. One may search for a word or words, immediately find all entries and associated cross-references containing the search terms, and follow links to windows containing the main entry for each cross-reference of interest.

Contact Person: John Gallman, Director

Phone Number: 812-855-4773

E-Mail Address: jgallman@ucs.indiana.edu

Press: The John Hopkins University Press

Project Title: Project Muse

Project Description: The current issues now available via a freely accessible prototype are *Configurations, Modern Language Notes,* and *English Literary History.* A short-range goal of Project

Muse is the creation of an easy-to-use electronic journal environment. Their long term goals are to offer electronic journals and works of scholarship at reasonable prices and make these widely available to university libraries and the university community.

Project Format: On-Line

Technical Specifications: The prototype is accessed through a networked information retrieval system which runs optimally under the Mosaic reader. Mosaic readers are available via most operating systems such as Mac, Unix and Windows machines.

Contact Person: Susan Lewis, Journals Administrative Manager

Phone Number: 410-516-6980

E-Mail Address: ejournal@jhunix.hcf.jhu.edu

Press: University of Minnesota Press

Project Title: Untitled.

Project Description: The Press in conjunction with Computer and Information Systems (CIS) and the University of Minnesota Libraries proposes to convert out-of-print scholarly books to electronic form, format the electronic text (e-text) using a reader-friendly model, and provide easy access to the e-text both through electronic networks and physical media. The intent of the project is not simply to make out-of-print books available again, but to develop a process whereby future books never fall out of print and/or are available in both print and electronic forms.

Project Format: On-Line and Docutech.

Technical Specifications: Combination of bitmapped images of typeset pages and ASCII files (created with OCR software) with hypertext links. No decision regarding software has been made. "Books" would also be available on demand via Docutech.

Contact Person: Lisa Freeman, Director

Phone Number: 612-624-0356

E-Mail Address: defron@cs.umn.edu

Press: The MIT Press

Project Title: Chicago Journal of Theoretical Computer Science

Project Description: The project is a peer-reviewed electronic journal whose scope will include articles describing significant research results in all areas of theoretical computer science. The journal will also include articles on Structural Complexity, Computational Geometry and Applications of Logic to Computer Science. In addition there will be a feature called "Forward Pointers" in which every paper will have an associated file of forward pointers referring to subsequent papers, results, improvements, etc., that are relevant to it. Every paper will also have a file of associated comments which will be unrefereed, unmoderated, and easily accessible from the article. Authors will be allowed to rewrite accepted papers, to incorporate new results, to allow better exposition, etc., and rewritten papers will be peer-reviewed again.

Project Format: On-Line.

Technical Specifications: The journal will be published on an article-by-article basis and will be made available to subscribers in either LaTeX source file or Postscript form.When an article is ready, subscribers will receive notification of article title, author, and the abstract, and directions on how to retrieve the article from the Press's WAIS server via FTP or Gopher.

Contact Person: Janet Fisher, Associate Director for Journals Publishing

Phone Number: 617-253-2864

E-Mail Address: fisher@mitvma.mit.edu

Press: Modern Language Association of America

Project Title: Current publications: MLA International Bibliography

Project Description: Bibliographic database with subject indexing for scholarship in literature, language, linguistics, folklore, popular culture, performance studies, and numerous other humanities topics. National literatures ranging from American to Zambian are covered, as are genres from autobiography to romance novels. The database contains over 1,000,000 records covering scholarship from 1963 to the present, and approximately 40,000 new records are added annually. Coverage is international, and is derived from a wide range of document formats, including journal articles, dissertations, book chapters, and conference proceedings.

Project Format: Online, CD-ROM, and magnetic tape

Technical Specifications:

Contact Person: Daniel Uchitelle
Director, Center for Information Services

Phone Number: 212-614-6350

E-Mail Address: daniel@mla.org

....

Project Title: Forthcoming publications:

1. Wing Short Title Catalogue
2. Directory of Periodicals/Directory of Scholarly Presses

Project Description:

1. Bibliographic database of all extant English books, pamphlets, and broadsides printed between 1641 and 1700. Approximately 120, 000 records.

2. Directory database listing over 3,200 journals and series, and `over 300 scholarly presses in the humanities. Provides detailed information on editorial scope, submission requirements, and other information.

Projects Format: CD-ROM

Technical Specifications:

Contact Person: Daniel Uchitelle
Director, Center for Information Services

Phone Number: 212-614-6350

E-Mail Address: daniel@mla.org

Press: University of Nebraska Press

Project Title: Library of the Open Frontier

Project Description: A 400 public-domain titles, 3,000 images all pertaining to the History of the American West. The press will also develop new publication forums with teachers, scholars and experts in the field using the Library of the Open Frontier. They are working with the Libraries, the Computer Science/Engineering Departments and the Computing Resource Center.

Project Format: On-line via Internet. National Science Foundation Grant pending on this project.

Technical Specifications: Using Mosaic as a primary interface, the press plans to tailor it to the needs of the system. Will be using SyBase in conjunction with Mosaic and WAYS. Will be using a log-in server, for which purpose is to test billing systems and cost-recovery methodologies.

Contact Person: Michael Jensen, Electronic Media Manager

Phone Number: 402-472-3541

E-Mail Address: jensen@unlinfo.unl.edu

Press: University of North Carolina Press

Project Title: "UNC Press Online"

Project Description: Internet users will be able to browse through a bibliographic listing of the more than 950 UNC Press titles that are in print. Separate modules include brief descriptions of recently published books and "subject catalogs" of books in particular fields, such as gardening and classics. UNC Press Online also includes information about the press's history, a staff directory, and information on the press's editorial procedures. These features will provide academics with valuable information about submitting a manuscript for consideration at the Press. There is also be a section called "What's New at UNC Press," a bimonthly electronic newsletter that includes information about UNC Press books and authors that are in the news--or ought to be.

Project Format: UNC Press Online is now available on the Internet.

Technical Specifications: Users can access UNC Press Online via the University of North Carolina Sunsite from the Internet using the gopher program by typing "gopher sunsite.unc.edu" and choosing menu item 10, UNC -Gopherspace then menu item 9, UNC Press Online.

Contact Person: Marjorie Fowler or Joseph Carroll

Phone Number: 919-962-4199

E-Mail Address: fowler@unc.edu
carroll@gibbs.oit.unc.edu

Press: Oxford University Press

Project Title: The Oxford American Writer's Shelf

Project Description: The Oxford American Writer's Shelf contains four of OUP's most popular dictionaries. This easy-to-use, pop-up utility gives you instant access to Oxford references within your word processing package. All your questions on grammar, spelling, usage, punctuation, quotations, and more will be answered in seconds. Whether you are writing for business or pleasure, the Oxford American Writer's Shelf will be an invaluable addition to your PC or Macintosh computer.

Technical Specifications: Hard Disk Space Requirements: Macintosh - 8Mb; Windows - 8Mb - Price: $75.00

Contact Person: Amy Roberts

Phone Number: 212-679-7300, extension 7342

E-Mail Address: abr@oup-usa.org

....

Project Title: The Oxford Companion to the English Language, Electronic Edition

Project Description: Presented here, for the first time in electronic format, are 4,000 article by some 100 specialist contributors from around the world. Subjects covered include the history of English; teaching and learning English; the language of literature; names and jargon; usage, grammar, and style; English in the media, and language and technology - available at the immediate touch of a button.

Technical Specifications: Hard Disk Space Requirements: Macintosh - System 6.07 or higher - 5.5Mb; System 7 .x - 35Mb; Windows - 4Mb - Price: $75.00

Contact Person: Amy Roberts

Phone Number: 212-679-7300, extension 7342

E-Mail Address: abr@oup-usa.org

....

Project Title: The Oxford Companion to English Literature, Electronic Edition

Project Description: Anyone with a computer and a love for literature will want to own the electronic edition of Oxford's best selling reference work on English Literature. The electronic edition offers easy and rapid access to this indispensable reference brimming full of useful plot summaries, entries on important fictional characters, and countless biographies of authors and other important figures in the world of letters.

Technical Specifications: Hard Disk Space Requirements: Macintosh - System 6.07 or higher - 5.5Mb; System 7 .x - 3.5Mb; Windows - 4Mb - Price: $75.00

Contact Person: Amy Roberts

Phone Number: 212-679-7300, extension 7342

E-Mail Address: abr@oup-usa.org

....

Project Title: The Oxford Dictionary of Quotations and Modern Quotations, Electronic Edition

Project Description: Quotations are used to convince in practically all disciplines. If you want to make a point more persuasively and imaginatively then this is the package for you. Now you can access Oxford's best-selling quotations dictionaries in seconds, either as a stand-alone program, or as a fast-access utility from your wordprocessing package. With over 20,000 quotations at your fingertips, you will be able to find a quote for every occasion. Anyone who uses quotations in their work or anyone who simply has a love of quotations will find this package invaluable.

Technical Specifications: Hard Disk Space Requirements: Macintosh - System 6.07 or higher - 5.5Mb; System 7 .x - 4.5Mb; Windows - 5Mb - Price: $75.00

Contact Person: Amy Roberts

Phone Number: 212-679-7300, extension 7342

E-Mail Address: abr@oup-usa.org

....

Project Title: The Oxford English Dictionary on CD-ROM, Second Edition

Project Description: The Oxford English Dictionary has always had universal appeal, and the general user will find that the OED2CD is not only easy to use but also provides the ideal means to explore the Dictionary at a depth which does full justice to its encyclopedic potential. Powerful search-and-retrieval facilities will satisfy both scholar and browser with infinite opportunities for entertainment and instruction using the Dictionary in its electronic form. All 20 volumes of the OED2 are available on a single compact disc at one-third the price of the printed edition. This is not an abridgement. Nothing is missing. What's more, the OED2CD takes up less than one-twentieth the space of the printed editions. The Windows and MacIntosh versions on screen are near mirror images; they are identical in features, functionality, and screen layout.

Technical Specifications: MAC Version: 68030 processor; Mac System 6.07 or higher; CD Drive; 4Mb free RAM (recommended); Windows Version: IBM PC (or full compatible); 80386 processor; DOS 3.0 or higher; 4Mb RAM (recommended; CD drive; Microsoft CD-ROM extension software version 2.0 or higher; Windows 3.0 or higher; EGA/VGA monitor.

Contact Person: Ursula Bollini

Phone Number: 212-679-7300, extension 7120

....

Project Title: The Oxford Language Shelf

Project Description: Four of Oxford's popular bilingual minidictionaries will be available in electronic format, with the publication of the Oxford Language Shelf. Covering the essential vocabulary of everyday life, these minidictionaries are especially designed to meet the needs of tourists, students, and business people alike. The minidictionaries provide full guidance on meaning and use, up-to-date information on colloquial and technical words, and verb tables.

The Oxford French Minidictionary: This new edition has been revised, updated, and expanded to include over 48,000 words and phrases and 70,000 translations.

The Oxford German Minidictionary: This is a completely new reference work for modern German and English containing over 50,000 words and phrases and 70,000 translations.

The Oxford Spanish Minidictionary: Another completely new minidictionary containing over 45,000 words and phrases and 70,000 translations.

The Oxford Italian Minidictionary: This well-established reference book contains over 40,000 words and phrases and 45,000 translations.

Technical Specifications: Hard Disk Space Requirements: Macintosh - 4Mb; Windows - 4Mb - Price: $75.00

Contact Person: Amy Roberts

Phone Number: 212-679-7300, extension 7342

E-Mail Address: abr@oup-usa.org

....

Project Title: The Oxford Science Shelf

Project Description: The Oxford Science Shelf is the ultimate resource for instant access to the latest advances in science, medicine, technology, and computing. Now, without leaving your chair, or even your screen, you can check preferred spelling, definitions of terms, correct abbreviations and acronyms, and even make sure your writing is consistent with the guidelines recommend by such international scientific bodies and IUPAC and IUPAP. Whether you're editing a scientific report, reading an article on the latest breakthroughs in genetic engineering, or simply need to quickly consult a chart of mathematical symbols or geological timescales, The Oxford Science Shelf - an easy-to-use, poputility - is the one tool you'll need.

Technical Specifications: Hard Disk Space Requirements: Macintosh - xMb; Windows - xMb - Price: $75.00

Contact Person: Amy Roberts

Phone Number: 212-679-7300, extension 7342

E-Mail Address: abr@oup-usa.org

Press: University of Pennsylvania

Project Title: *Project 1:* Multimedia editions of major texts from the Penn Reading Project
Project 2: Reengineering the Textbook

Project Description: ***Project 1.*** In the Penn Reading Project, before their arrival all incoming undergraduates receive a common text, to be discussed during orientation week in small groups led by faculty from different disciplines across the University, and featured in subsequent events throughout the school year. The first edition in the planned series will focus on the 1993-94 academic year selection, Mary Shelley's "Frankenstein." It will include all major text variants, critical analyses, treatments of "Frankenstein" in the cinema and other media, and other study resources.

Project 2. A novel case study approach to Introductory Materials Science is the basis for a new engineering textbook to be published by the University of Pennsylvania Press. In conjunction with its publication, a continuing series of multimedia modules are being developed with animation, simulation, and three-dimensional graphical representations that cannot be provided in the print version. While the modules can be produced on magnetic or CD-ROM media, distribution on a licensing basis via the Internet will be explored.

Project Format: Regarding which format to use, a decision has not yet been made for both projects, although CD-ROM and network distribution are currently under consideration.

Technical Specifications: Decisions have not been made regarding the choice of development tools and target platforms, although the latter will be Macintosh and/or Windows.

Contact Person: Michael F. Eleey, Associate Vice Provost, Information Systems and Computing

Phone Number: 215-898-5304

E-Mail Address: eleey@crc.upenn.edu

Press: Penn State Press

Project Title: Electronic Monograph Publishing in Latin American Studies.

Project Description: Same as above

Project Format: Documents are accessed via Docutech and On-Line.

Technical Specifications: The intention is to use SGML coding.

Contact Person: Sanford G. Thatcher, Director

Phone Number: 814-865-1327

E-Mail Address: sgt3@psuvm.psu.edu

Press: Rutgers University Press

Project Title: The REBECCA Project (tm) by Lauren Rabinovitz & Greg Easley

Project Description: In 1939, Alfred Hitchcock came to the United States to film Daphne du Maurier's bestselling novel REBECCA for David O. Selznick. REBECCA (1940) garnered critical acclaim and Hitchcock's only Academy Award for Best Picture. REBECCA has been continuously popular for over 50 years as a beloved novel and as a favorite film. Now it has been made easier to study through this multimedia CD-ROM containing film clips, hypertext critical essays, and rarely seen documents. This electronic encyclopedia is designed for interactive, flexible use by anyone interested in film, women's studies, or American cultural history.

Technical Specifications: Plays on all color-capable MacIntosh computers with either external or internal CD-ROM drive.

Contact Person: Leslie Mitchner (editor-in-chief)

Phone Number: 908-932-7782

E-Mail: harrie@zodiac.rutgers.edu

Press: Southern Illinois University Press/Library Affairs, Information Technology

Project Title: Freedom of the Press Online

Project Description: The Southern Illinois University project involves making available on the Internet *Freedom of the Press;* an Annotated Bibliography, published by the Southern Illinois University Press and authored by Ralph McCoy, the Emeritus Dean of Library Affairs and former Executive Director of the Association of Research Libraries. As an added feature, the online version will indicate which items described in the bibliography are held in the SIUC Library Special Collections' extensive and eminent Freedom of the Press Collection. The final element of the project will be a link between the abstracts and an image of the item described by the abstract, if it is held by the library and has no copyright, or if the library has obtained permission to reproduce it.

Project Format: Documents are accessed via Online.

Technical Specifications: McCoy's work has three volumes published over the last 26 years. This project will involve the first volume which was published in 1968. Since the text is not in machine readable form, the first step of the project involved scanning sample pages and using OCR software to create text files. That test has been successful. The second phase is a test of the feasibility of using Mosaic as a vehicle for the project. Staff from the Library and Information Technology are currently evaluating this potential.

Contact Person: Jay Starratt

Phone Number: 618-453-2681

E-Mail Address: starratt@siucvmb.siu.edu

Press: University Libraries, The University of Tennessee, Knoxville

Project Title: A Southern History Sampler

Project Description: A Southern History Sampler will integrate text, hypertext, and images in the maiden electronic publication of the University of Tennessee Press. The Sampler will consist of excerpts from at least ten titles in southern history, a primary focus of the UT Press. The digital collection will include a table of contents, several lists of illustrations, and a representative chapter or some excerpts. Each title will be accompanied by a scanned image of the book's jacket art or related art work or photographs taken from the work.

Project Format: The Sampler will be offered as a free, networked resource available over the Internet. The files will reside on a file server and be distributed On-Line.

Technical Specifications: Files with embedded word processing or SGML tags will be mapped to hypertext mark-up language (HTML) for On-line presentation. The files will be mounted on the University Libraries' World Wide Web server running on a NeXT using UNIX and NCSA mosaic.

Contact Person: Tamara Miller, Associate Professor

Phone Number: 615-974-4304

E-Mail Address: miller@utklib.lib.utk.edu

Press: University of Texas Press

Project Title: Thrinaxodon: Digital Atlas of the Skull

Project Description: *Thrinaxodon liorhinus* is an extinct, distant relative of mammals that is known from 225-million-year-old fossils found in Africa, Antarctica, and China. Though not itself a mammal, it has played a central role in understanding the early history of mammals because it records many anatomical details of the primitive structure from which mammals ultimately descended. The information in this project presents a complete digital analysis of the skull and reveals all of the minute anatomical details of this rare and remarkable fossil--the first such analysis ever published. It includes 800 images of the cross-sectional anatomy of the skull, anatomical labels for the imagery, and animation depicting the three-dimensional structure.

Project Format: The *Digital Atlas* is the first work to exploit the extraordinary power of the newest high-resolution computed axial tomographic (CAT) scanning technology for interpreting fossils. All presented by disc there are articles that introduce the disc, describe how to use it, and discuss the importance of *Thrinaxodon*. Also included are digitally reprinted studies on *Thrinaxodon*, which provide a library of the major technical work on its anatomy and importance.

Technical Specifications: PC computer (386 or higher recommended) with DOS 3.2 or higher, CD-ROM player, color monitor with super VGA graphics adapter.

Contact Person: Sherry Solomon

Phone Number: 512-471-7233

Press: University Press of Virginia

Project Title: *Afro-American Sources in Virginia: A Guide To Manuscripts*

Project Description: An illustrated, updated hypertext version, (to be published on-line in February 1995) of a print directory prepared by Michael Plunkett, Director of Special Collections, University of Virginia Library, and published by the press in 1990. Through this greatly updated electronic version, the 26 principal collections in Virginia can be accessed by subject, by individual, by historical period, and by geographic location. Eighteen images -- photographs and manuscript pages -- give a hint of the visual records to be found.

Project Format: On-line access

Technical Specifications: To be made available on the university server, accessible in February 1995 from the press's home page --http://www.virginia.edu/~press/ -- to internet users of any World Wide Web program such as Mosaic.

Contact person: Nancy Essig

Phone Number: (804) 924-3131

E-mail address: nce6x@virginia.edu

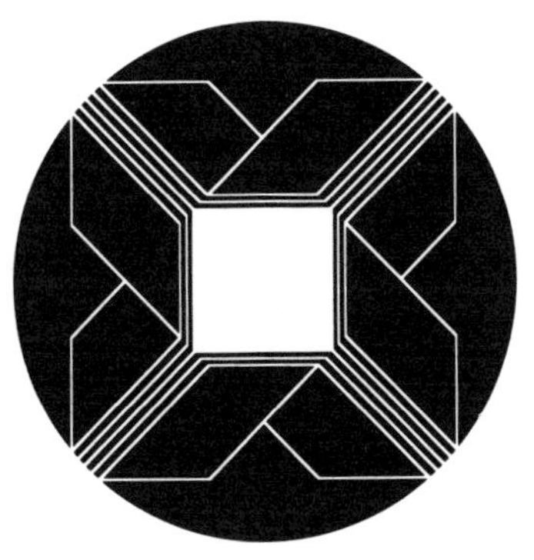

Association of Research Libraries
Association of American University Presses

In Collaboration With:

The University of Virginia Library
The Johns Hopkins University Press
The American Physical Society

Scholarly Publishing on the Electronic Networks

Filling the Pipeline and Paying the Piper

Demonstration Projects
Cost Recovery
Electronic Fair Use

November 5-7, 1994
The Washington Vista Hotel
Washington, DC

November 8, 1994
University of Virginia Library
Charlottesville, VA

The Johns Hopkins University Press
Baltimore, MD

Scholarly Publishing on the Electronic Networks: Filling the Pipeline and Paying the Piper

This three-day symposium, the fourth in a series sponsored by the AAUP and ARL, with a great deal of help from our many friends, is specifically aimed at university presses, learned and professional society publishers, librarians, and academic faculty and researchers interested in beginning electronic publications, particularly for distribution via electronic networks. The Symposium's objective is to promote information-sharing and discussion among people interested in developing the potential of the networks, particularly for formal publishing, with particular emphasis on not-for-profit models. Anyone interested in this topic is eagerly welcomed to join us. Presenters will discuss some of the latest research and development from the not-for-profit sector, including faculty, societies, presses, and libraries.

The Symposium has established itself as a place where not-for-profit participants and supporters talk to each other about their work and confront vexing issues together. This year, in particular, we have focused on the controversial areas of cost recovery in an electronic environment and electronic fair use. The program committee, encouraged by registrants' comments, hopes that symposiasts can help to build understanding and progress in these topics, which are critical to a robust, organized future for scholarly communications.

e-mail address for inquiries of general interest: symposium@e-math.ams.org
e-mail for individual questions or registration inquiries: Lisabeth King (lisabeth@cni.org)

Program Committee:

Ann Okerson, Association of Research Libraries (ann@cni.org)
Lisa Freeman, University of Minnesota Press (lfreeman@staff.tc.umn.edu)
Robert Kelly, American Physical Society (rakelly@aps.org)
Susan Lewis, The Johns Hopkins University Press (suelewis@jhuvm.hcf.jhu.edu)
Karen Marshall, University of Virginia Library (kkm7m@poe.acc.virginia.edu)
David Rodgers, University of Michigan (drodgers@sils.umich.edu)

Daily Schedule of Events

Day One
Saturday, November 5th

4:00 - 6:00 OPENING SESSION

Opening Remarks and Welcome
Ann Okerson, Office of Scientific and Academic Publishing, Association of Research Libraries, Washington, DC

"Frankenstein Redux: Organization and Cultivation of Electronic Scholarship," A Multimedia Event by Michael Eleey, Associate Vice Provost, University of Pennsylvania

Keynote: Over the Horizon
[To Be Announced]

6:00 - 7:00 OPENING RECEPTION

Day Two
Sunday, November 6th

8:45 - 12:00 MORNING SESSION

"Labyrinth, One-Stop Shopping for Medieval Publications," A Multimedia Event by Deborah Everhart, Georgetown University

PANEL: Cost Recovery in an Electronic Publishing Environment: Issues and Perspectives

Sandra Braman, Institute of Communications Research, University of Illinois
Colin Day, University of Michigan Press
Andrea Keyhani, Electronic Publishing, OCLC
Jean-Claude Guedon, Department of Comparative Literature, Universite de Montreal
Hal Varian, Department of Economics, University of Michigan

12:00 - 1:30 Lunch Buffet Provided

A Conversation with Pamela Samuelson Faculty of Law, University of Pittsburgh

AFTERNOON MINI-SESSIONS

1:45 - 3:15

Session 1: Using Technical Standards to Accomplish Projects:

"The Combined AAUP Online Catalog/Bookstore Project," Chuck Creesy, Princeton University Press and Bruce Barton, University of Chicago Press
"Campus Publishing With TEI and HTML," David Seaman, University of Virginia Library

Session 2: Publishing Your Entire Journals List Electronically:

"Project Muse: Tackling 42 Journals," Susan Lewis, Johns Hopkins University Press and Todd Kelley, Eisenhower Library, JHU
"Publishing e-prints, Preprints, and Journals in the Sciences," Robert Kelly, American Physical Society

3:45 - 5:15

Session 3: In the Scholarly Pipeline

"Riding the Aftershocks: The Galileo Project," Elizabeth Burr, Rice University
"Towards an Electronic Medieval English Dictionary," Henk Aertsen, Free University, The Netherlands

Session 4: Collaborations That Work -- and How They Do It

"Scholarly Communications Project: Publishers and Librarians," Gail McMillan, Virginia Polytechnic Institute and State University
"Five Societies: One Journal Project," Keith Seitter, American Meteorological Society"
(Dinner on your own.)

Day Three

Monday, November 7th

8:45 - 10:15 MORNING MINI-SESSIONS

Session 5: Finding and Navigating Networked Scholarly Works

"Naming the Namable: Document and Version Identity," David Levy, Xerox PARC
"The Berkeley Finding Aid Project: Standards in Navigation," Daniel Pitti, University of California, Berkeley

Session 6: Reporting Out

"Research into the Reward System of Scholarship; Where Does Scholarly Electronic Publishing Get you?" Julene Butler, School of Communication, Information and Library Studies, Rutgers University
"A Workshop Report and Invitation," David Rodgers, University of Michigan, reports on a recent NSF journals-publishing workshop and followup planned

10:45- 12:15 MORNING PLENARY SESSION

"Creating Multimedia: Intersections Between Teaching, Scholarship, and the Copyright Law," A Multimedia Event by Fred T. Hofstetter, University of Delaware

PANEL: Perspectives on Electronic Fair Use

Terri Southwick, U.S. Patent and Trade Office and staff to the NII Task Force on Intellectual Property

12:30 - 1:30 Lunch Buffet Provided

A Conversation with John McChesney, Technology Correspondent, National Public Radio

2:00 - 4:00 Panel Perspectives on Electronic Fair Use, Continued

Georgia Harper, Office of the Counsel, University of Texas System
Patrice Lyons, Law Offices of Patrice Lyons
John Lawrence, H-Net and Morningside College
Response and Wrap up

Day Four

A DAY AT THE PRESS
Johns Hopkins University
The Eisenhower Library

Monday, November 7th

Overnight in Washington, DC

Tuesday, November 8th

10:00 am: Buses arrive at The Johns Hopkins University from Washington, DC

10:00 - 11:30: Access *Muse* and other Mosaic experiments

11:00 - 12:30: Tour A Baltimore Museum

12:30 - 1:30: Lunch in the JHU environs

1:30 - 1:45: Walk to the University Press

1:45 - 3:30: Greetings from Jack Goellner, Director, The Johns Hopkins University Press. Break up into small groups and tour departments.

3:30 - 4:45: Bus to Press's distribution facility, an operation of special interest to librarians and small publishers.

4:45: Bus departs for Washington, DC

A DAY IN THE ACADEMICAL VILLAGE
University of Virginia Library

Monday, November 7th

4:00 pm: Bus departs for Charlottesville, Check in at Cavalier Inn Best Western.

7:00 - 9:00: Dinner, welcome from University Librarian, overview, and distinguished keynote.

Tuesday, November 8th

8:30 - 12:15: Four concurrent sessions, groups of ten participants

(1) E-text center
(2) Digital image center
(3) Social science data center and GIS lab
(4) Electronic classroom

Box Lunch Provided

1:30 - 2:15: Choose one out of four options

(1) Institute for Advanced Technology in the Humanities
(2) Cataloging and organization of electronic materials
(3) Multimedia Center
(4) Free time/Lawn tour

2:30 - 3:15: Choose one out of four options

(1) Institute for Advanced Technology in the Humanities
(2) Special Collections and Music Centers
(3) Electronic Centers Roundtable
(4) Free time/Lawn tour

3:30: Bus departs for Washington, DC

REGISTRANT LIST

Scholarly Publishing on the Electronic Networks, 1994

John Ackerman
Director
Cornell University Press
Sage House
512 E. State St.
Ithaca, NY 14850
607-277-2338 x227

Jimmy Adair
Manager of Information Technology Services
Scholars Press
P.O. Box 15399
Atlanta, GA 30333-0399
404-727-2320
jadair@unix.cc.emory.edu

Henk Aertsen
Department of English
Free University, The Netherlands
De Boelelann 1105
1081 HV Amsterdam, The Netherlands
011-31-20-4446447
aertsenh@let.vu.nl

Helen Aguera
Division of Education Programs
National Endowment for the Humanities
1100 Pennsylvania Avenue, N.W.
Washington, DC 20506

Philip Alperson
Editor, Journal of Aesthetics & Art Criticism
University of Louisville
Department of Philosophy
Louisville, KY 40292
502-852-0458
paalpe01@ulkyvm.louisville.edu

Bruce Antelman
President
Information Express
3250 Ash St.
Palo Alto, CA 94306
415-494-4787
bruce@express.com

Bruce Barton
MIS Manager
University of Chicago Press
5801 S. Ellis Ave.
Chicago, IL 60302
312-702-7651
bbarton@press.uchicago.edu

James Beach
Museum Informatics Specialist
University of California, Berkeley
2111 Bancroft Ave, Suite 501
Berkeley, CA 94720-6200
501-642-0246
beach@violet.berkeley.edu

Dinah Berland
Publications Coordinator
J. Paul Getty Trust
4503 Glencoe Ave
Marina del Rey, CA 90292-7913
310-822-2299
dberland@getty.edu

Jean Black
Science Editor
Yale University Press
P.O. Box 902040
New Haven, CT 06820
203-432-7534
jblack@yalevm.cis.yale.edu

Dean Blobaum
Marketing
University of Chicago Press
5801 South Ellis
Chicago, IL 60637
312-702-7706
dblobaum@press.uchicago.edu

Michael Boudreau
Electronic Publishing Specialist
University of Illinois Press
1325 S. Oak Street
Champaign, IL 61820
217-244-7177
m-boudreau@uiuc.edu

Sandra Braman
Institute of Communications Research
University of Illinois
222B Armory, 505 E. Armory Avenue
Champaign, IL 61820
217-244-1419
braman@vmd.cso.uiuc.edu

Catherine Brieger
New Technology & Innovations Advisor
Industry Canada
235 Queen Street, O2W
Ottawa, Ontario K1A OHS CANADA
613-997-3896

Paul Buchanan
Director of Computing & Telecommunications
Washington University Libraries
Campus Box 1061, One Brookings Dr.
St. Louis, MO 63130
314-935-5400
buchanan@library.wustl.edu

Elizabeth Burr
Electronic Text and Images Librarian
Rice University
Fondren Library
6100 South Main St
Houston, TX 77005-1892
713-527-8101 x3634
esb@rice.edu

Julene Butler
Library Instruction Coordinator
Brigham Young University
2404 Lee Library-BYU
Provo, UT 84602
801-378-2813
hjb@hbll1.byu.edu

Carole Cable
Deputy Asst Director for Library Development
University of Texas at Austin
General Libraries
Austin, TX 78713
512-495-4382
carole.cable@mail.utexas.edu

Elizabeth Caskey
Head, David Lam Management Research Library
University of British Columbia
2033 Main Mall
Vancouver, BC V6T 1Z2 CANADA
604-822-9392
ecaskey@unixg.ubc.ca

Curtis Clark
Associate Director/Marketing Director
Southern Illinois University Press
Box 3697
Carbondale, IL 62902-3697
618-453-6623

Hilde Colenbrander
Coordinator of Electronic Information Svcs
University of British Columbia Library
1956 Main Mall
Vancouver, BC V6T 121 CANADA
604-822-6742
hilde@datalib.ubc.ca

M. Joan Comstock
Head, Books Dept.
American Chemical Society
1155 16th St, NW
Washington, DC 20036
202-872-4563
mjc96@acs.org

John Cook
Academic Marketing Representative
The Douglas Stewart Company
2402 Advance Road
Madison, WI 53704
800-279-2003
73324.1105@compuserve.com

Stephen Cox
Director
University of Arizona Press
1230 N. Park Avenue, Suite 102
Tucson, AZ 85719-4140
602-621-1441
sfcox@ccit.arizona.edu

Chuck Creesy
Director of Computing & Publishing Techs.
Princeton University Press
41 William Street
Princeton, NJ 08540-5237
609-258-5745
creesy@pupress.princeton.edu

John Curley
Network Systems Advisor
National Research Council of Canada
Montreal Road Bldg. M-55
Ottawa, Ontario K1A OS2 CANADA
613-998-6913
john.curley@nrc.ca

Melissa Dadant
Special Assistant, Examining Division
U.S. Copyright Office
Library of Congress Dept. 17
Washington, DC 20540
202-707-8211
dadant@mail.loc.gov

Heather Dalterio
Director of Publishing
American Astronomical Society
2000 Florida Avenue NW
Washington, DC 20009
202-328-2010
dalterio@aas.org

Jinnie Davis
Assistant Director for Planning & Research
North Carolina State University Libraries
Campus Box 7111
Raleigh, NC 27695-7111
919-515-2843
jinnie_davis@ncsu.edu

Colin Day
Director
University of Michigan Press
839 Greene Street
Ann Arbor, MI 48106-1104
313-764-4388
colinday@umich.edu

Kurt De Belder
Asst Curator, Western European Lit & Lang
New York University
70 Washington Square South
New York, NY 10012
212-998-2515
debelder@is.nyu.edu

Patricia Denault
Associate Editor, Business History Review
Harvard Business School Publishing
Soldiers Field
Boston, MA 02163
617-495-6954
pdenault@cchbspub.harvard.edu

Elizabeth Diefendorf
Chief Librarian, General Research Division
New York Public Library
Fifth Ave & 42nd St. Rm 315
New York, NY 10018
212-930-0770
beth@nyplgate.nypl.org

Rich Dodenhoff
Journals Manager
American Statistical Association
1429 Duke Street
Alexandria, VA 22314-3402
703-684-1221 x141
rich@asa.mhs.compuserve.com

Sharon Eckert
Technical Services Coordinator, Library
University of New England
PO Box 1099
Kennebunkport, ME 04046-1099
207-283-0171 x364
seckert@mailbox.une.edu

Michael Eleey
Associate Vice Provost, Info Systems & Comp
University of Pennsylvania
1202 Blockley Hall
Philadelphia, PA 19104-6021
215-898-5304
eleey@crc.upenn.edu

Deborah Everhart
Coordinator of the Labyrinth
Georgetown University
238 Reiss Hall
Washington, DC 20057
202-687-6096
labyrinth@gusun.georgetown.edu

Robert Faherty
Director of Publications
The Brookings Institution
1775 Massachusetts Avenue, NW
Washington, DC 20036
202-797-6250
rfaherty@brook.edu

Laine Farley
Coordinator of Bibliographic Policy and User Services
University of California
300 Lakeside Dr., 8th floor
Oakland, CA 94612-3550
510-987-0552
laine.farley@ucop.edu

Carol Fleishauer
Associate Director for Collection Services
MIT Libraries
145-312
Cambridge, MA 02139
617-253-5962
fleish@mit.edu

William Fontaine
Social Sci & Humanities Ref. Bibliographer
Dartmouth College Library
Hanover, NH 03755
603-646-2669
william.fontaine@dartmouth.edu

Marjorie Fowler
Composition Mgr/Electronic Projects Crdr
University of North Carolina Press
116 Boundary Street
Chapel Hill, NC 27515-2288
919-966-3561
Marjorie_Fowler@unc.edu

Ralph Franklin
AUL-Research Collections
Yale University
P.O. Box 208240
New Haven, CT 06520-8240
203-432-1763
rwfrank@yalevm.cis.yale.edu

Lisa Freeman
Director
University of Minnesota Press
111 Third Avenue South, Suite 290
Minneapolis, MN 55401
612-627-1971
lfreeman@maroon.tc.umn.edu

Catherine Fry
Associate Director
Louisiana State University Press
P.O. Box 25053
Baton Rouge, LA 70894-5053
504-388-6666
cfry@lsuvm.sncc.lsu.edu

Lorrin Garson
Head, Advanced Technology Department
American Chemical Society
1155 16th Street, N.W.
Washington, DC 20036
202-872-4541
lrg96@acs.org

Marilyn Geller
Internet Product Specialist
Readmore, Inc.
436 School Street
Belmont, MA 02178
617-484-7379
mgeller@readmore.com

Peter Givler
Director
Ohio State University Press
1070 Carmack Rd
Columbus, OH 43210
614-292-6930
pgivler@magnus.acs.ohio-state.edu

James Graber
Technology Assessment Manager
Library of Congress
101 Independence Ave. S.E.
Washington, DC 20540-9304
202-707-9628
jgra@loc.gov

Hope Greenberg
Humanities Computing Specialist
University of Vermont
Academic Computing
238 Waterman
Burlington, VT 05405
802-656-1176
hope.greenberg@uvm.edu

Peter Grenquist
Executive Director
American Association of University Presses
584 Broadway
New York, NY 10012
212-941-6610
aaupco@netcom.com

Frances Groen
Associate Director of Libraries
McGill University
3459 McTavish St
Montreal, Quebec H3A 1Y1 CANADA
514-398-4722
groen@lib1.lan.mcgill.ca

Jean-Claude Guedon
Professor, Dept. of Comparative Literature
University of Montreal
C.P. 6128, Succursale A
Montreal, Quebec H3C 3J7 CANADA
514-343-6208
guedon@ere.umontreal.ca

Mary Guitar
Journals Production Manager
University of California Press
2120 Berkeley Way
Berkeley, CA 94720
510-642-6221
mary.guitar@ucop.edu

Michael L. Hall
Assistant Director for Seminars
National Endowment for the Humanities
1100 Pennsylvania Avenue, N.W. Room 316
Washington, DC 20506
202-606-8463
mlhall@netcom.com

Nancy Hammerman
Vice President and Director
Sage Publications Press
2455 Teller Road
Thousand Oaks, CA 91320
805-499-0721
nancy_hammerman@sagepub.com

Georgia K. Harper
Office of General Counsel
University of Texas System
201 W. 7th
Austin, TX 78701
512-499-4462
gharper@utsystem.edu

Sherre Harrington
Assistant Director for Public Services
Vanderbilt University Libraries
Central and Science Libraries
419 21st Avenue South
Nashville, TN 37240
615-343-6043
harrington@library.vanderbilt.edu

Lillian Hastie
Projects Director
Oxford University Press
200 Madison Avenue
New York, NY 10016
212-679-7300
lmh@am.oup-usa.org

Fred Heath
Dean, Sterling C. Evans Library
Texas A&M University
Evans Library-Administration
College Station, TX 77843-5000
409-845-8111
fheath@tamu.edu

Stuart Hehn, Jr.
CASIAS Project Leader
EBSCO
5724 Highway 240 East
Birmingham, AL 35240
205-980-2791
stuart@vax.ebsco.com

Jim Heilik
University of Alberta Library
4-40 Cameron Library
University of Alberta
Edmonton, Alberta TST 0LS Canada
403-492-5282
jheilik@vm.ucs.ualberta.ca

Colleen Heinkel
Associate Director; Mgr, Placement Test Div.
University of Wisconsin Press
114 N. Murray St.
Madison, WI 53715
608-262-4928
cheinkel@facstaff.wisc.edu

Gail Hixenbaugh
Chief, Publications Production
National Institute of Standards and Technology
Building 416, Room 122
Gaithersburg, MD 20899-001
301-975-2777
gailh@micf.nist.gov

Fred Hofstetter
Director, Instructional Technology Center
University of Delaware
Willard 305
Newark, DE 19716
fth@brahms.udel.edu

Frank Immler
Head, Coll.Dev., Humanities/Social Sciences
University of Minnesota
309 19th Ave. So.
Minneapolis, MN 55455
612-625-0156
f-imml@vm1.spcs.umn.edu

John Inglis
Director
Cold Spring Harbor Press
1 Bungtown Rd
Cold Spring Harbor, NY 11724
516-367-8823
inglis@cshl.org

Martin Irvine
Associate Professor, Dept. of English
Georgetown University
306 New North Building
Washington, DC 20057
labyrinth@gusun.georgetown.edu

David James
Manager, Electronic Publications
Royal Society of Chemistry
Thomas Graham House, Science Park
Cambridge, CB4 4WF United Kingdom
44 (0) 223 420066
jamesd@rsc.org

Ewa Jankowska
Librarian
New York Public Library
Fifth Avenue and 42nd Street, Room 315
New York, NY 10018
212-930-0826
ewa@nyplgate.nypl.org

Robert Janz
University of Groningen
P.O. Box 800
Groningen, 9700 AV The Netherlands
31 50 633402
r.e.janz@rc.rug.nl

Dick Kaas
University of Utrecht
P.O. Box 80011
Utrecht, 3508 TA The Netherlands
31 30 531450
kaas@cc.ruu.nl

Todd Kelley
Co-Manager, Project Muse
Johns Hopkins University Library
MSEL, 3400 N. Charles Street
Baltimore, MD 21218
410-516-4930
kelley@milton.mse.jhu.edu

Robert Kelly
American Physical Society
500 Sunnyside Blvd.
Woodbury, NY 11797-2999
516-576-2365
rakelly@aps.org

Andrea Keyhani
Manager, Electronic Publishing
OCLC
6565 Frantz Road
Dublin, OH 43017-0702
Andrea_Keyhani@oclc.org

Douglas Kincade
Publisher, Electronic Products
Princeton University Press
41 William Street
Princeton, NJ 08540-5237
609-258-2167
doug@pupress.princeton.edu

Lisabeth King
Research Assistant
Association of Research Libraries
21 Dupont Circle
Washington, DC 20036
202-296-2296

Bruce Kingma
Assistant Professor, Economics
SUNY, Albany
School of Information Science and Policy
Department of Economics
Albany, NY 12222
518-442-5123
b.kingma@albany.edu

Cees Klapwyk
University of Leiden
Witte Singel 27
Leiden, 2311 BG The Netherlands
31 71 232834
klapwyk@rulu82.leidenuniv.nl

David Koch
Director, Special Collections & Development
Southern Illinois University
Library Affairs, Mail Code 6632
Carbondale, IL 62901-6632
618-453-2516
dvkoch@siucvmb.siu.edu

Betsy Kulamer
Editorial Consultant
Resources for the Future
1616 P Street, NW
Washington, DC 20036
202-328-5026
kulamer@rff.org

Ian Lancashire
Director, Ctr for Computing in the Humanities
University of Toronto
78 Strath Ave
Etobicoke, Ontario M8X 1R5 CANADA
416-231-2659
ian@epas.utoronto.ca

Rebecca Lasher
Head Librarian and Bibliographer
Stanford University
Mathematical and Comp. Sciences Library
Stanford, CA 94305
415-723-0864
rlasher@forsythe.stanford.edu

John Lawrence
Professor of Philosophy
Morningside College, H-Net
Sioux City, IA 51106-6400
712-274-5310
JSL001@chief.morningside.edu

Maria Lebron
Associate Publisher
American Physical Society
One Physics Ellipse
College Park, MD 20740
301-209-3202
lebron@aps.org

Shirley Leung
AUL, Research & Instructional Services
University of California, Irvine
P.O. Box 19556
Irvine, CA 92713-9556
714-856-4295; 714-725-3702
syleung@orion.oac.uci.edu

Mary Berghaus Levering
Associate Register for National Copyright Programs
U.S. Copyright Office
Library of Congress Dept. 17
Washington, DC 20540
202-707-8350
levering@mail.loc.gov

David Levy
Member, Research Staff
Xerox PARC
3333 Coyote Hill Road
Palo Alto, CA 94304
415-812-4376
dlevy@parc.xerox.com

Susan Lewis
Online Projects Manager
Johns Hopkins University Press
2715 N. Charles Street
Baltimore, MD 21218
410-516-3875
suelewis@jhuvm.hcf.jhu.edu

Jane-Ellen Long
Electronic Publishing Manager
University of California Press
2120 Berkeley Way
Berkeley, CA 94720
510-642-6522
andy2@violet.berkeley.edu

Ann Lowry
Journals Manager
University of Illinois Press
1325 S. Oak St.
Champaign, IL 61821
217-244-6856
alowry@uiuc.edu

Alan Lupack
Curator, Robbins Library
University of Rochester
Rush Rhees Library, 416
Rochester, NY 14627
716-275-0110
alpk@dbl.cc.rochester.edu

Patrice Lyons
Law offices of Patrice Lyons
1401 Sixteenth Street, NW
Washington, DC 20036
202-939-9666
0003432266@mcimail.com

Bonnie MacEwan
Collection Development Coordinator
Pennsylvania State University
E 308 H Pattee Library
University Park, PA 16803
814-863-8158

Stephen Maikowski
Acting Director
Rutgers University Press
109 Church Street
New Brunswick, NJ 08901
908-932-7761
maikowski@zodiac.rutgers.edu

Marybeth Manning
Dir. Communications & Information Services
SPIE
International Society for Optical Engineering
P.O. Box 10
Bellingham, WA 98225
206-676-3290
marybeth@spie.org

Wayne Marr
First Union Professor of Banking
Clemson University
307 Monaco Circle
Clemson, SC 29631
803-653-5516
marrm@clemson.edu

Robert Martin
Associate Dean for Special Collections
Louisiana State University Libraries
Louisiana State University
Hill Memorial Library
Baton Rouge, LA 70803
504-388-6551
notrsm@lsuvm.sncc.lsu.edu

Nancy Matthews
Publications Officer
Smithsonian Institution Libraries
NHB 26A, MRC 154
Washington, DC 20560

John McChesney
Technology Correspondent
National Public Radio
2601 Mariposa St.
San Francisco, CA 94110
jmcchesney@aol.com

Thomas McFadden
AUL
Northern Arizona University
P.O. Box 6022
Flagstaff, AZ 86011-6022
602-523-9036
+gm1@a1.ucc.nau.edu

Robert McHenry
Editor in Chief
Encyclopedia Britannica
310 S. Michigan Ave.
Chicago, IL 60604
312-347-7450
bmchenry@eb.com

Gail McMillan
Director, Scholarly Communications Project
Virginia Polytechnic Institute
University Libraries
Blacksburg, VA 24061
703-231-9252
gailmac@vt.edu

Ross McPhedran
Professor
University of Sydney
Department of Theoretical Physics
Sydney, NSW 2006 AUSTRALIA
ross@physics.su.oz.au

Sian Meikle
Librarian
University of Toronto Library
130 St. George St.
Toronto, Ontario M5S 1A5 CANADA
416-978-7687
meikle@library.utoronto.ca

Lee Miller
Editor-in-Chief and Managing Editor
Ecological Society of America
328 E. State
Ithaca, NY 14850
607-255-3221
lnm2@cornell.edu

Dru Mogge
Electronic Services Coordinator
Association of Research Libraries
21 Dupont Circle
Washington, DC 20036
202-296-2296

John Moore
President and Director
Columbia University Press
562 West 113th Street
New York, NY 10025
212-666-1000
jm235@columbia.edu

Andrew Mytelka
Assistant Director, Electronic Services
The Chronicle of Higher Education
1255 23rd St, NW, Suite 700
Washington, DC 20037
202-466-1000 x4089
andrew.mytelka@chronicle.page1.com

Caroline Newman
Director, New Media
Smithsonian Institution Press
470 L'Enfant Plaza, S. 7100
Washington, DC 20560
202-287-3738 x352

Kees Nijsen
University of Utrecht
P.O. Box 16007
Utrecht, 3500 DA The Netherlands
3130 536514
c.nysen@ubu.ruu.nl

Jim O'Donnell
Professor of Classical Studies
University of Pennsylvania
840 Montgomery Avenue #901
Bryn Mawr, PA 19010
215-527-2102
jod@ccat.sas.upenn.edu

Ann Okerson
Director, Office of Scientific and Academic Publishing
Association of Research Libraries
21 Dupont Circle
Washington, DC 20036
202-296-2296

Isabella Owen
Heldref Publications
Washington, DC

Eric Pepper
Director of Publications
SPIE
International Society for Optical Engineering
P.O. Box 10
Bellingham, WA 98225
206-676-3290
eric@spie.org

Lewis Perelman
Keynote speaker

Washington, DC

D. E. Perushek
Associate Dean for Collection Services
The University of Tennessee
611 John C. Hodges Library
1015 Volunteer Blvd.
Knoxville, TN 37996-1000
615-974-6640
perushek@utklib.lib.utk.edu

Ronnie Pitman
Librarian
North Carolina State University Libraries
Box 7111
Raleigh, NC 27695-7111
919-515-7556
ronnie_pitman@ncsu.edu

Daniel Pitti
Head, Authorities Section, Catalog Dept.
University of California, Berkeley
The Library
Berkeley, CA 94720
510-643-6602
dpitti@library.berkeley.edu

Sam Pointer
PC Programming Mgr
EBSCO
P.O. Box 1943
Birmingham, AL 35201
205-980-3856
pointer@ebsco.com

Dana Pratt
Chadwyck-Healey Inc.
7514 Old Chester Road
Bethesda, MD
301-320-2538

Christopher Quinlan
Manager
Cornell University Press Services
Sage House
512 E. State St
Ithaca, NY 14850
607-277-2969

Enayet Rahim
Librarian
National Endowment for the Humanities
1100 Pennsylvania Avenue, N.W.
Washington, DC 20506

Vicky Reich
Information Access Analyst
Stanford University Libraries
Green Library
Stanford, CA 94305-6004
415-725-1134
vicky.reich@forsythe.stanford.edu

Stephen Roberts
Associate Director of Libraries
SUNY, Buffalo
433 Capen Hall
Buffalo, NY 14260
716-645-2966
uldsmr@ubvm.cc.buffalo.edu

David Rodgers
Research Associate
University of Michigan
School of Library & Information Studies/304
Ann Arbor, MI 48103-1092
313-761-2372
drodgers@sils.umich.edu

Julia Rudy
Director of Publications and Editor
CAUSE
4840 Pearl East Circle
Boulder, CO 80301
303-939-0308
jrudy@cause.colorado.edu

Amy Rule
Archivist
Center for Creative Photography
University of Arizona
Tucson, AZ 85721
602-621-7968
amy@ccp.arizona.edu

Pamela Samuelson
School of Law
University of Pittsburgh
3900 Forbes Avenue
Pittsburgh, PA
PSA2@vms.cis.pitt.edu

Patricia Scarry
Associate Journals Manager
University of Chicago Press
5720 S. Woodlawn Ave.
Chicago, IL 60637
312-702-7359
pscarry@journals.uchicago.edu

Ann Schaffner
Asst Director, Science Library
Brandeis University
South St
Waltham, MA 02173
617-736-4720
schaffner@logos.cc.brandeis.edu

David Seaman
Coordinator, Electronic Text Center
University of Virginia
Alderman Library
Charlottesville, VA 22903
804-924-3230
etext@virginia.edu

Keith Seitter
Associate Executive Director
American Meteorological Society
45 Beacon Street
Boston, MA 02108-3693
617-227-2426 (x220)
seitter@aip.org

George Shipman
University Librarian
University of Oregon
1299 University of Oregon
Eugene, OR 97403-1299
503-346-3056
univlib@oregon.uoregon.edu

Jennifer Siler
Director
University of Tennessee Press
293 Communications Bldg
Knoxville, TN 37996-0325
615-974-3321
siler@utkvx.utk.edu

Rebecca Simon
Journals Manager
University of California Press
2120 Berkeley Way
Berkeley, CA 94720
510-642-5536
rrs@violet.berkeley.edu

William P. Sisler
Director
Harvard University Press
79 Garden St.
Cambridge, MA 02138
617-495-2601
wsisler@harvarda.harvard.edu

Audrey Smith
Director, Design/Production
Columbia University Press
562 W. 113 Street
New York, NY 10025
212-666-1000 x7105

Carol Sosnin
Data Processing Manager
EBSCO
801 Fifth Avenue South
Birmingham, AL 35233
205-226-8480

Terri Southwick
Attorney Advisor
U.S. Department of Commerce
Patent and Trademark Office
Box 4
Washington, DC 20231
703-305-9300
southwic@uspto.gov

Christine Steiner
Assistant General Counsel
Smithsonian Institution
1000 Jefferson Dr., S.W.
Washington, DC 20560
202-357-2583
ogcem004@sivm.si.edu

Peter Sutherland
Systems Specialist
Brookhaven National Laboratory
Technical Information Division - Bldg. 477B
Upton, NY 11973-5000
516-282-5159
suther@suntid.bnl.gov

Annette Theuring
Associate Editor
Journal of Democracy
1105 Fifteenth St. NW, Suite 802
Washington, DC 20005
202-293-0300

Robert Townsend
Managing Editor
American Historical Association
400 A St. SE
Washington, DC 20003
202-544-2422
rbthisted@aol.com

Pamela Upton
Asst. Mnging Editor/Electronic Ms. Specialist
University of North Carolina Press
P.O. Box 2288
Chapel Hill, NC 27515-2288
919-966-3561
pam_upton@unc.edu

Hal Varian
University of Michigan
Department of Economics
Ann Arbor, MI 48109-1220
313-764-2364
Hal.Varian@umich.edu

Duane Webster
Executive Director
Association of Research Libraries
21 Dupont Circle, NW
Washington, DC 20036
202-296-2296
duane@cni.org

Sandra Whisler
Assistant Director, Electronic Publ. & Journals
University of California Press
2120 Berkeley Way
Berkeley, CA 94720
510-642-7485
smw@garnet.berkeley.edu

Luther Wilson
Director
University Press of Colorado
P.O. Box 849
Niwot, CO 80544
303-530-5337
luther.wilson@colorado.edu

Flo Wilson
Associate Director
Vanderbilt University Library
419 21st Avenue South
Nashville, TN 37240
615-322-7374
wilson@library.vanderbilt.edu

Lynne Withey
Associate Director
University of California Press
2120 Berkeley Way
Berkeley, CA 94720
510-642-5393
lynnew@violet.berkeley.edu

Kate Wittenberg
Editor-in-Chief
Columbia University Press
562 W. 113th Street
New York, NY 10027
212-666-0000 x7119

Emily Young
Associate Director & Marketing Manager
Duke University Press
905 W. Main St. Suite 18B
Durham, NC 27701-0660
919-687-3654
eyoung@acpub.duke.edu

Ralph Youngen
Asst. Dir., Electronic Products and Services
American Mathematical Society
201 Charles St.
Providence, RI 02904
401-455-4061
rey@math.ams.org